NASA AERONAUTICS BOOK SERIES

Flying Beyond the Stall

The X-31 and the Advent of Supermaneuverability

Douglas A. Joyce

Library of Congress Cataloging-in-Publication Data

Joyce, Douglas A.
  Flying beyond the stall : the X-31 and the advent of supermaneuverability /
by Douglas A. Joyce.
     pages cm
  Includes bibliographical references and index.
  1. Stability of airplanes--Research--United States. 2. X-31 (Jet fighter plane)
  3. Research aircraft--United States. 4. Stalling (Aerodynamics) I. Title.
  TL574.S7J69 2014
  629.132'360724--dc23

                          2014022571

During the production of this book, the Dryden facility was renamed the Armstrong Flight Research Center. All references to the Dryden facility have been preserved for historical accuracy.

ISBN 978-1-62683-019-6

9 781626 830196   90000 >

This publication is available as a free download at
http://www.nasa.gov/ebooks.

Table of Contents

Author Dedication

To Phyllis Joyce

*The wind under my wings in life
And the thrust vector for this book.*

X-31 Initial test pilots at Plant 42: (left to right) Fred Knox, Dietrich Seeck, Ken Dyson, and Karl Lang. (Rockwell)

The World's First International X-Airplane

On Wednesday, October 11, 1990, a small blue-and-white jet took to the air from Air Force Plant 42 at Palmdale, CA. For the next 38 minutes, it cruised at 10,000 feet over California's Antelope Valley, reaching a top speed of 340 miles per hour (mph) before Rockwell International test pilot Norman K. "Ken" Dyson returned it gently to Earth.

By the standards of the Antelope Valley—known to locals as "Aerospace Valley" (AV)—it was a seemingly innocuous flight. Over the four previous decades, AV had witnessed the birth of supersonic flight. Palmdale, one of its two major communities, was the roost of the Mach 3+ SR-71 Blackbird and its subsonic stablemate, the U-2. Edwards, less than 25 miles away, was home to both the Air Force Flight Test Center and the National Aeronautics and Space Administration (NASA) Ames-Dryden Flight Research Facility (now the NASA Armstrong Flight Research Center), where exotic high-performance military and research aircraft routinely flew over its vast, baked dry lakes—Rosamond and Rogers. In 1977, the Space Shuttle was first flown freely through its skies, and in 1981, the Shuttle Columbia returned from orbit to land at Edwards, heralding the era of the reusable, refurbishable spacecraft.

To those unfamiliar with aircraft, at first glance, the little airplane looked like any other fighter overflying the Mojave Desert. But appearances were deceiving, for this was the X-31, then the latest of the U.S. X-planes, the legendary research tools of the supersonic era that had pushed back the frontiers of flight beginning with the Bell XS-1. Each of the X-planes had their own uniqueness and X-31 was no different in that regard—in fact, it was unique in many ways. Perhaps the most distinguishing characteristic of the X-31 program was that it was the only multinational program of the X series of research vehicles. It was the product of German-American interest. The X-31 was intended to fulfill four goals: demonstrate controlled flight and high agility beyond the stall, using thrust vectoring that was integrated with electronic flight controls; investigate the benefits of enhanced maneuverability for future military aircraft via close-in air combat maneuvering tests; develop design requirements and a database for future aircraft applications; and validate low-cost international prototyping. To fulfill those purposes, Rockwell and German manufacturer Messerschmitt-Bölkow-Blohm (MBB) designed, developed, and built two of the shapely X-31 aircraft using a variety of new and off-the-shelf components blended with creative and insightful engineering and design.

Over the next 14 years, through its final Vectoring ESTOL (extreme short takeoff and landings) Control Tailless Operation Research (VECTOR) flight (on April 29, 2004), the X-31 accomplished all this and more. As the program drew to a close, it received several major awards, notably the American Institute of Aeronautics and Astronautics (AIAA) Aircraft Design Award (September 1994). In July 1995, with the program then thought to be concluded, the Smithsonian Institution presented the X-31 International Test Organization with the prestigious National Air and Space Museum Trophy for Current Achievement, an honor established to recognize extraordinary service in air and space science and technology. In making the award, Smithsonian Provost Robert S. Hoffmann stated the following:

> The X-31 International Test Organization is being awarded the 1995 Trophy for Current Achievement for an unprecedented record of engineering and flight exploration accomplishments in the past year. You have culminated a highly successful experimental program with a series of momentous "firsts" in aviation history, demonstrating the significant value of post-stall agility in close-in air combat, developing and demonstrating revolutionary helmet-mounted visual and aural pilot aids for situational awareness under WVR [within visual range] combat conditions, and conducting an epoch-making series of flights in which the X-31 employed its thrust vectoring to demonstrate the feasibility of tailless flight at supersonic speeds.[1]

It should also be noted that, consistent with its heritage, it was awarded the 1995 German Society for Aeronautics and Astronautics (DGLR) Willy Messerschmitt Award for collaboration in international aeronautical research and development (R&D).

But the X-31 was far from done, and though "retired," it returned to the air nearly 6 years later, in February 2001—itself a remarkable and unprecedented milestone. When it did so, it was in skies far removed from the harsh, hot bleakness of the Mojave. Flying from verdant Patuxent River Naval Air Station, on the shores of Maryland's picturesque Chesapeake Bay, it served as an R&D asset to test new naval operational concepts enabled by thrust vectoring. There, it simulated extreme short takeoff and landings for operations on aircraft carriers, approaching to land at hitherto unachievable angles of attack (reduced speed and energy) with precise control to flare and touchdown. Altogether, the two X-31 aircraft (the first of which had crashed in January 1995; fortunately, the pilot ejected successfully, though he did sustain relatively serious injuries on landing in his parachute) completed over 660 flights, making the program extraordinarily productive for the amount of money and effort the United States and Germany had invested in it. More than this, as previously stated, the X-31 represented a unique international flight-testing and flight-research partnership; it was the first—and, to this time, only—X-series airplane with such international involvement. It served, in the words of one summary report, "as a benchmark for future international cooperation and achievement" in aeronautics.[2] Recognizing its significance, the International Council of the Aeronautical Sciences (ICAS) awarded the American and German X-31 teams its Theodore von Kármán Award for international cooperation in aeronautics, hailing their "over 20 years of successful trans-Atlantic R&D [research and development] teamwork producing the first-ever international X-plane and significant breakthroughs in thrust-vectoring control."[3]

This book is the story of the X-31 program, ranging from the visionary Wolfgang Herbst, a remarkable pioneer of extreme maneuverability who tragically died before his concept realized its fullest potential, to the realities and discoveries of flight research in the skies over NASA Dryden and Patuxent River. It is to the men and women of the X-31 International Test Organization, and all those on both sides of the Atlantic—in the multitude of contractors, research centers, and governmental departments—who conceived, designed, supported, funded, maintained, flew, and employed the X-31 for its various research purposes, that the author dedicates this book with the greatest respect and admiration.

Endnotes

1. Robert S. Hoffmann, letter to Col. Michael S. Francis, July 12, 1995, M.S. Francis personal collection. I thank Colonel Francis for making this letter available to me.

2. Peter Huber, *X-31 Enhanced Fighter Maneuverability Final Report* (Manching, Germany: Daimler-Benz Aerospace, December 22, 1995), p. 32, copy in Dryden Flight Research Center (DFRC) Archives, hereafter Dryden archives. The Bell X-5, the world's first inflight-variable-sweep-wing airplane, was inspired by the abortive Messerschmitt P.1101 research airplane program, which was exploited by Allied technical intelligence at the end of the Second World War. However, there was no subsequent participatory role by Messerschmitt personnel once the X-5 was placed in development; nor did, of course, the postwar German government play any role in overseeing and supporting the X-5 research aircraft. Thus, the X-31 claim to be the first international X-plane is valid. There have been, of course, many multinational military and commercial aircraft development programs, but these are quite different endeavors than the X-series development efforts.

3. Jay Levine, "X-31A team captures von Kármán Award," *The X-Press* 45, no. 6 (August 29, 2003), p. 1.

The Participants

This is the story of a unique research airplane—unique because the airplane and the programs that supported it did things that have never been done before or since. The major purpose of this book is to tell the story of NASA's role in the X-31 program. In order to do this, though, it is necessary to put NASA's participation in perspective with the other phases of the program, namely the genesis of the concept, the design and fabrication of the aircraft, the initial flight testing done without NASA participation, the flight testing done with NASA participation, and the subsequent Navy X-31 Vectoring ESTOL (extreme short takeoff and landings) Control Operation Research (VECTOR) program.

The book is written from the perspective of a tester. This is done for three reasons. First, the airplane is a research tool. Its whole reason for being was to conduct research through flight testing and to get answers to critical questions. Second, when studying the available material documenting a program, the greatest amount of documentation is from test reports on *each flight* and the final reports that summarize the test programs. Taken in total, these read like a diary of the airplane while it was flying. Lastly, the author is a career tester, so the perspective of the program from a tester's viewpoint is most easily interpreted.

The X-31 was the flight-verification tool for obtaining answers to support the goals of the Enhanced Fighter Maneuverability (EFM) program. The following were the goals of the EFM program:

- Rapidly demonstrate high-agility maneuvering concepts.
- Investigate the benefits of Enhanced Fighter Maneuverability technologies.
- Develop design requirements and a database for future applications.
- Validate a low-cost international prototyping concept.

Additionally, while the program had very focused goals, certain other experiments were conducted either because EFM research results indicated a need or because it was realized that an airplane with unique EFM technologies offered additional high-payoff opportunities for assessing other concepts that needed validation.

Following a significant hiatus, the airplane was returned to flight from storage to support the Navy's VECTOR program. The VECTOR program had the following goals:

- Demonstrate that the ESTOL concept was workable and had significant payoff, especially for carrier operations.
- Show that an operational-type air data system was achievable in the Advanced Air Data System (AADS).
- Prove that a simple Global Positioning System (GPS)–based location system was a potential precision geolocation system for operational application for both ESTOL and conventional takeoffs and landings.

The X-31 program was the first international X-plane program. The participants were the United States and Germany. Therefore, the "players"—the contractors who designed and built the airplanes and supported its flight test as well as the government agencies tasked with managing the program—were twice as many as would be seen in a typical U.S.-only program.

Rockwell International, the American contractor partner on the X-31 program, had a distinguished legacy and a history of convoluted evolution. The aviation portion of Rockwell International came from North American Aviation, which itself was rooted in the early Fokker company. Under legends such as James "Dutch" Kindleberger, Edgar Schmued, and Lee Atwood, it had produced great aircraft such as the prewar T-6/SNJ trainer, the P-51 Mustang fighter and B-25 Mitchell bomber of World War II, and the MiG-killing F-86 Sabre from the Korean War. In the 1950s, North American produced America's first supersonic jet fighter, the F-100 Super Sabre; the world's first hypersonic airplane, the Mach 6+ X-15, which took winged flight across the transatmosphere into space; and the XB-70, a Mach 3 bomber prototype, which was the largest, fastest, and most ambitious supersonic airplane ever flown. The Apollo spacecraft, B-1 Lancer bomber, and the Space Shuttle were also among North American's great aerospace vehicles. Through several mergers and acquisitions, North American evolved into North American Rockwell in 1967. This resulted from a merger with Rockwell Standard to form a true industrial conglomerate (a strong trend of the times) to balance industrial and defense business cycles. Then, in 1973, the company was renamed Rockwell International, adding consumer electronics and aircraft avionics to producing aircraft and spacecraft.

In 1996, Rockwell International sold its defense and aerospace business—including North American Aviation—to Boeing, and 2 years later Boeing also bought McDonnell-Douglas. At that time, Boeing was divided into two major operating units—Commercial Airplanes and Integrated Defense Systems. A third unit, called Phantom Works, was designated as the center for R&D.

Phantom Works was originally headquartered in Seattle, WA, before moving to southern California and finally to St. Louis, MO. It was Boeing, through its St. Louis–based Phantom Works, that was responsible for the VECTOR program.[1]

The German partner on the X-31 was the Messerschmitt-Bölkow-Blohm (MBB) company, which coalesced out of many company mergers and acquisitions between 1968 and 1981. Many of these companies were familiar names from aviation history, with Messerschmitt being the best known. A merger with Bölkow and the aviation division of Blohm und Voss (the latter a traditional shipworks and heavy industries manufacturer) resulted in Messerschmitt-Bölkow-Blohm. The 1981 acquisition of Vereinigte Flugtechnische Werke (VFW), which itself arose from a merger of Focke-Wulf, Focke-Achgelis, and Weserflug, enfolded other "legacy" firms into the MBB consortium.

In 1989, during the construction and airframe-assembly phase of the X-31 program, MBB was acquired by Deutsche Aerospace AG (DASA).[2] DASA was subsequently reorganized as Daimler-Benz Aerospace in 1995, coincident with the X-31's stellar performance at the Paris Air Show.[3] When Daimler-Benz and Chrysler Corporation merged in 1998, their aerospace division was renamed DaimlerChrysler Aerospace AG. This was the name of the former MBB at the start of the VECTOR program. In 2000, just as the X-31 returned to Patuxent River for refurbishment, a consolidation of the European defense industry led to DASA being merged with Aerospatiale-Matra of France and Construcciones Aeronauticas SA (CASA) of Spain to form the European Aeronautic Defense and Space Company (EADS). Since that time, the military aircraft division of EADS (where X-31 was conducted) has been renamed Cassidian, but it is still an integral part of EADS.

The U.S. Government's top-level management of the X-31 program resided within the Defense Advanced Research Projects Agency (DARPA), an organization within the Department of Defense that is responsible for the development of new military technology. DARPA generally manages relatively high-risk, military-oriented programs with the assistance of a military service that takes day-to-day management responsibility by acting as its agent for program management, technical expertise, contracting, and administrative services.[4]

DARPA had approached the U.S. Air Force to act as its agent for X-31, but the service was too involved in various force-restricting issues to participate at the level of involvement that would have been required to oversee the program. Chief among Air Force involvements was the stealth Advanced Tactical Fighter, which became the Lockheed-Martin F-22A Raptor stealth fighter.[5] A so-called "Fifth Generation" jet fighter, it featured stealth, supercruise (i.e., supersonic cruise using "military power" engine throttle settings rather than fuel-consuming afterburning), sensor fusion via advanced avionics, and beyond visual range (BVR) missiles to showcase "first look, first shot, first kill" capabilities.

Thus, the Air Force had little interest in any program that might distract it from acquiring the F-22.

As a result, DARPA selected the U.S. Navy as their military agent for X-31. In the case of the X-31, this was the Navy through Naval Air Systems Command (NAVAIR), which oversees all naval aircraft research, development, test, evaluation, and acquisition. In the middle of the X-31 program, on February 22, 1993, President William J. Clinton briefly changed the name of DARPA back to ARPA, its original name at its founding in 1958, reflecting his desire that ARPA support technology programs other than defense.[6] But such a shift in focus did not occur (though much of the agency's work does influence technology more broadly than simply defense) and, slightly over 2 years later (following the performance of the X-31 at the Paris Air Show and the end of the Enhanced Fighter Maneuverability program in July 1995), the agency's name changed back to DARPA.[7]

The Navy has five Navy systems commands (SYSCOMS) that manage research, development, and acquisition of systems and facilities for the Navy:

- Naval Air Systems Command (NAVAIR)
- Naval Sea Systems Command (NAVSEA)
- Space and Naval Warfare Systems Command (SPAWAR)
- Naval Facilities Engineering Command (NAVFAC)
- Naval Supply Systems Command (NAVSUP)

Since the X-31 was an aircraft research effort, it was natural that the Navy would appoint Naval Air Systems Command to be the program manager for the X-31. NAVAIR's mission is to provide full life-cycle support of naval aviation aircraft, weapons, and systems operated by sailors and marines. This support includes research, design, development, and systems engineering; acquisition; test and evaluation; training facilities and equipment; repair and modification; and in-service engineering and logistics support.[8] While the lion's share of effort at NAVAIR is in support of weapons system development, having a pure research effort under the management umbrella of NAVAIR was not unprecedented.

NASA had two major organizations that supported the X-31 program. The Langley Research Center supported the X-31 program in a major way through wind tunnel testing and the flight of a replica subscale drop model. The Langley Research Center is the oldest of NASA's field centers. It was established in 1917 by the National Advisory Committee for Aeronautics (NACA), the administrative predecessor of the present-day NASA. The Center devotes approximately two-thirds of its programmatic efforts to aeronautics and the remaining third to space flight. Researchers at the Center use more than 40 wind tunnels to advance aircraft and spacecraft safety, performance, and efficiency.[9]

NASA's Ames-Dryden Flight Research Facility (later the Dryden Flight Research Center) also supported the X-31 flight-test effort through most of the EFM program. Dryden's history dates to the summer of 1946, when the first NASA personnel arrived at Muroc, CA. In the summer of 1947, the NASA contingent was established as the Muroc Flight Test Unit, an adjunct of the NACA's Langley Aeronautical Laboratory (now NASA's Langley Research Center) that was created specifically to support flight testing of the Bell XS-1 (later X-1) supersonic research airplane.[10] The Muroc Flight Test Unit became the NACA High-Speed Flight Research Station on November 14, 1949, and then became an autonomous unit called the NACA High-Speed Flight Station on March 17, 1954.[11] In 1959, it became the NASA Flight Research Center, and then in April 1976 it was renamed for Hugh Dryden, one of the most prominent of early pioneers in aeronautical research. In 1981, the Center was merged with the Ames Research Center at Moffett Field, CA, to become the Ames-Dryden Flight Research Facility. It remained an Ames adjunct for the next 13 years, until common sense prevailed and the Agency restored it to the independence it so richly deserved. Thus, in January 1994, during the last year of X-31 EFM testing, it was again granted autonomy and renamed the Dryden Flight Research Center.[12] (In 2014, the Dryden facility was renamed the Armstrong Flight Research Center (AFRC). In this book, all subsequent references to Dryden or DFRC have been preserved.)

The U.S. military's flight-testing activity within the X-31 program was supported by the Naval Air Test Center (NATC) at Naval Air Station (NAS) Patuxent River and the Air Force Flight Test Center (AFFTC) at Edwards Air Force Base (AFB).

Within Germany, ultimate government responsibility for program oversight resided with the Federal Ministry of Defence (Bundesministerium der Verteidigung [BMV]), a cabinet-level agency that is headed by the Federal Minister of Defence and is roughly equivalent to the American Department of Defense. The BMV signed a Memorandum of Agreement with DARPA in May 1986 expressing the intent to develop, manufacture, and flight-test two experimental Enhanced Fighter Maneuverability aircraft, leading to the X-31.[13] Within the BMV, the Federal Office of Defence Technology and Procurement (Bundesamt für Wehrtechnik und Beschaffung [BWB]) oversees national and international defense projects, and within the BWB there are several Defence Technical Centers (Wehrtechnische Dienststelle [WTD]) that are responsible for the management of different key technologies. There are seven WTD centers, which include the following:

- WTD 41—Automotive and Armored Vehicles
- WTD 51—Engineering and Field Technologies
- WTD 52—Protective and Specialist Technologies

- WTD 61—Flight Test and Airworthiness
- WTD 71—Naval Platforms and Weapons
- WTD 81—Information Technology and Electronics
- WTD 91—Weaponry and Ammunition

These technical facilities are operated primarily for the benefit of the German Armed Forces; however, they are also used for supporting Germany's allies, other foreign governments, and international defense companies.[14] The BWB is roughly equivalent to the U.S. Navy's NAVAIR or the Air Force's Air Force Materiel Command. WTD 61, established initially at Oberpfaffenhofen in 1957 and moved to Manching less than a decade later, can similarly be thought of as equivalent to the Air Force Flight Test Center at Edwards AFB or the Naval Air Test Center at NAS Patuxent River. Therefore, it was natural that the BMV would delegate program responsibility for X-31 to the BMB and also that WTD 61 would be delegated responsibility for overseeing flight-testing aspects of the program. For example, Karl-Heinz Lang, one of the X-31 pilots, was a test pilot for WTD 61.

The genesis of the X-31 EFM program was in the early 1970s when Dr. Wolfgang Herbst, a German engineer working for MBB on a fighter design that would eventually become the Eurofighter Typhoon, became convinced that the best way to gain a tactical advantage in the era of increasingly capable short-range missiles was to have the ability to perform well in the post-stall region of flight up to a 70° angle of attack. Early professional collaboration with Michael Robinson of Rockwell led to the creation of the EFM program. Tragically, on October 19, 1991, just as the X-31 was starting to explore maneuvering in the post-stall regime, Dr. Herbst was killed while flying a subscale replica of a Second World War–era Focke-Wulf Fw 190 fighter. Dr. Herbst thus did not live to see his dream of a fighter-like research aircraft achieving true post-stall maneuverability come true, a personal tragedy that engendered much sadness among his colleagues and those who knew of his great dedication to aeronautical science and the equally great personal enthusiasm and satisfaction that he took in all aspects of flight.

The X-31 programs (EFM and VECTOR) were successes far beyond their specific goals. They demonstrated that fully collaborative international programs can work and be very cost effective. The airplanes flew more flights than any other X-plane and supported two different programs separated by nearly a decade. As the only X-plane to perform to date at any Paris Air Show, the X-31 showed the world that supermaneuverability was real.

What follows is the fascinating story of this amazing airplane.

Endnotes

1. Throughout this book, "Rockwell" is used to refer to this contractor's participation in the EFM program, and "Boeing" has been used to refer to its participation in the VECTOR program.
2. Deutsche Aerospace, *Roll-out to Tactical Evaluation—A German View* (Munich: Deutsche Aerospace AG, 1990), p. 12.
3. Daimler-Benz Aerospace AG, "Paris Air show X-31 Maneuvers," *Daimler-Benz Aerospace AG Military Aircraft Brochure* (1995).
4. Defense Advanced Research Projects Agency, *http://www.darpa.mil*, accessed November 1, 2011.
5. For F-22 (which at one point was redesignated the F/A-22), see Jay Miller, *Lockheed Martin F/A-22 Raptor Stealth Fighter* (Hinckley, UK: Midland Publishing Co., 2005. See also Lane E. Wallace, *Nose Up: High Angle-of-Attack and Thrust-vectoring Research at NASA Dryden 1979–2001*, Number 34 in the *Monographs in Aerospace History* series (Washington: NASA SP-2006-4534, 2006), p. 35.
6. Gerard Keijsper, *Joint Strike Fighter* (Barnesley, UK: Pen & Sword Aviation, 2007), p. 16.
7. Ibid., p. 28.
8. U.S. Navy, "Naval Air Systems Command," *http://www.navair.navy.mil*, accessed November 1, 2011.
9. NASA, "Langley Research Center," *http://www.nasa.gov/centers/langley*, accessed November 1, 2011.
10. Richard P. Hallion and Michael H. Gorn, *On the Frontier—Experimental Flight at NASA Dryden* (Washington, DC: Smithsonian Books, 2003), pp. 7 and 21.
11. Ibid., pp. 31 and 41.
12. NASA, "Dryden Flight Research Center," *http://spinoff.nasa.gov/spinoff1998/ard3.htm*, accessed November 1, 2011.
13. Deutsche Aerospace, *Roll-out—A German View*, p. 15.
14. AMDS Support Services, "BWB—Bundesamt für Wehrtechnik und Beschaffung," *Need a Test Range*, *http://www.needatestrange.net/range_bwb.html*, accessed November 1, 2011.

The X-31 at high angle of attack, 1994. (NASA)

CHAPTER 1

Origins, Design, and Development

When one conjures up a vision of a research airplane—many of which have received an X-series designation—vehicles that have "pushed the envelope" in one way or another most often come to mind. In many cases, one thinks in terms of "higher and faster," which in the cases of the Bell X-1 family, Bell X-2, Douglas X-3, North American X-15, Boeing X-20, and Rockwell X-30 was certainly true. X-planes explored other areas of the envelope as well, including vertical flight with the Ryan X-13, Bell X-14, Hiller X-18, Curtiss-Wright X-19, and Bell Aerospace Textron X-22. Some X-planes explored unique and different configurations, such as the Northrop X-4 tailless test bed, which had no horizontal empennage surfaces; the Bell X-5, which had variable-sweep wings; the Martin X-23 and X-24 lifting bodies; and the Grumman X-29, a forward-swept wing (FSW) demonstrator. Some X-planes were actually prototypes for intended production aircraft, including the Bell X-9 systems test bed for the Rascal cruise missile; the North American X-10 test bed for the Navajo cruise missile; Convair's X-11 and X-12, which influenced the Convair SM-65 Atlas intercontinental ballistic missile (ICBM); the Bell X-16, a proposed high-altitude reconnaissance aircraft like the U-2; and the Lockheed X-27, a proposed lightweight fighter prototype. While some aircraft that received an X-plane moniker, such as the X-16 and X-27, were arguably not true research aircraft but were instead actual prototypes—which can be considered a misuse of the X designation—most X-planes represented attempts to expand the flight envelope, thus increasing the arena in which flight was possible.[1]

The following is a notional "flight envelope" for a supersonic airplane. It can readily be seen that while expanding the envelope to the upper right ("higher and faster") requires more thrust and less drag, the limit on the left side of the envelope is aerodynamic stall, which is defined as flight beyond the maximum coefficient of lift. Flight at angles of attack beyond that for maximum coefficient of lift not only results in coefficients of lift less than the maximum, but often also produces unwanted and uncontrolled excursions in pitch, roll, and/or yaw.

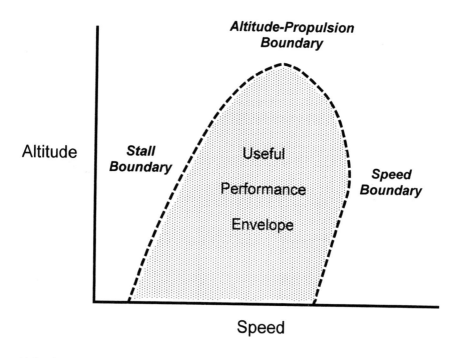

Notional envelope of a typical high-performance airplane. (R.P. Hallion)

So why, tactically, would one want to fly on the far left of the flight envelope beyond the maximum coefficient of lift? Historically, it has been thought in fighter tactics that the best approach is to use radar missiles to shoot from beyond visual range at the enemy and then execute some sort of escape maneuver. This was one of the reasons that, in the late 1950s and early 1960s, fighter aircraft were designed without a gun. However, the Vietnam conflict changed all that; the rules of engagement required closure to within visual range for positive visual identification of the enemy, meaning that many encounters swiftly changed into close-combat "furballs" (swirling hard-maneuvering close-in dogfights between opposing airplanes), typically very high-risk and highly lethal "win-lose" encounters. The following is an interesting note that Bob Hoover quoted from his vast experiences: after enlisting in the Royal Air Force in World War II, he was taught that the fighter tactic was to do a point intercept, shoot down the enemy, and return to base. After missing that point intercept shot and getting shot down himself, however, he learned that you had to outmaneuver your enemy when locked in a furball. According to Hoover, in every conflict since then (i.e., Korea and Vietnam), similar tactics were taught initially before pilots learned the same lesson in combat, when they inevitably ended up in a furball.

So guns were put back on fighters, most notably the F-4E. Additionally, evolutionary improvements in sensors, guidance, and flight control of infrared air-to-air missiles (IRAAMs) made it possible to employ these weapons by just pointing at the enemy. There was no longer the need to obtain a rear-aspect or tail-chase position in order to employ infrared air-to-air missiles, as was illustrated when British Sea Harriers in the Falkland Wars shot down Argentine fighters and strike aircraft using the all-aspect AIM-9L Sidewinder.

In the Beginning…: The Quest for "Supermaneuverability"

After Vietnam, there was interest in increasing the maneuverability of U.S. fighters but to do so without the high–angle of attack (AOA) loss of control that was so prevalent in fighters of the 1960–1970 period. Over 100 F-4 fighters were lost in the Vietnam War era due to loss of control in high-AOA situations while their pilots were trying to maneuver during close-in engagements. Even in peacetime, the U.S. Air Force (USAF) lost 147 aircraft (of all types) to stall/spin and departure accidents in the 1966–1970 timeframe. This prompted a conference in December 1971 known as the "Stall/Post-Stall/Spin Symposium" that was held to highlight the Air Force's concern over losses of this type. The conference was held at Wright-Patterson AFB and was sponsored by Air Force Systems Command's Air Force Flight Dynamics Laboratory and Aeronautical Systems Division. The output of this conference was a series of proposals that the next generation of fighters meet requirements for better maneuverability and more controllability at high angles of attack.[2]

This was easier said than done. There was, for example, the matter of the maximum coefficient of lift boundary on the flight envelope. The advent of fly-by-wire (FBW) flight control computers would allow the use of unstable aircraft configurations that would maximize an aircraft's agility close to the stall boundary. British Aerospace's (BAe) Active Control Technologies (ACT) Jaguar test bed (a modified Jaguar strike fighter) and Rockwell International's Highly Maneuverable Aircraft Technology (HiMAT, a subscale remotely piloted research vehicle) demonstrated the advantage of using inherently unstable airframes controlled by advanced fly-by-wire control systems. The production General Dynamics (later Lockheed Martin) F-16 was also an unstable airframe that used an advanced fly-by-wire control system. But for safety reasons, the F-16 was physically prevented from entering the area beyond maximum coefficient of lift by an AOA limiter.

If an aircraft *could* fly to the left of the flight envelope, beyond the maximum coefficient of lift, then that airplane would be able to generate very high turn rates with very low turn radii. This would give the pilot a distinct advantage in a dogfight situation, especially if the opponent did not have this capability. This very slow-speed dogfight regime is sometimes referred to in the fighter pilot community as "a knife fight in a phone booth." As stated previously, however, the major problem in this arena is the departure from controlled flight that follows a stall, in which a pilot is effectively helpless. So the key is to be able to maintain complete control in this so-called "post-stall area of the envelope." Any aircraft that could do so could be said to have not merely good but superb maneuverability—hence advocates dubbed this quality "supermaneuverability."

Russian designers of the Sukhoi design bureau had focused on aerodynamic improvements to allow their Su-27/30 Flanker aircraft to briefly point their noses well off-axis and then rapidly recover to the non-post-stall conventional flight arena. These maneuvers, in which the angle of attack is briefly increased beyond 90 degrees to the flightpath angle, are known as the "Cobra" and the "Hook" (which is essentially a horizontal Cobra). They have more than airshow crowd–pleasing value; in air combat, such a maneuver would allow a quick snap shot of a heat-seeking missile or a very rapid deceleration to destroy an enemy's tracking solution. The downside is that these are very transient maneuvers with minimal missile-firing opportunities, while the airspeed bleed-off (and thus energy loss) is great. If the fighter did not destroy its opponent with a snap shot, it would likely be destroyed itself as its pilot tried to regain the energy lost in the maneuver.

Far better would be to be able to maintain full control in the post-stall regime and be in a position to rapidly reacquire energy following the foray into this arena.[3] In 1977, Wolfgang Herbst and Karl Knauer at Messerschmitt-Bölkow-Blohm spearheaded research into post-stall supermaneuverability. The Industrieanlagen-Betriebsgesellschaft-GmbH (IABG) at Ottobrunn—an aerospace and defense analysis and testing organization founded in 1961—undertook piloted fighter aircraft combat simulations using a "generic" fighter aircraft that possessed post-stall maneuver capability in one-versus-one ("1-v-1" in fighter pilot shorthand) engagements.[4] In 1978, similar studies were conducted at McDonnell-Douglas's simulation facilities in St. Louis. At the completion of these studies, about 15 operational pilots from the USAF and the Luftwaffe (the German Air Force) had the opportunity to experience post-stall maneuvering capability and, in the process, they generated statistical data about its effectiveness.[5] The results of these simulations were impressive, indicating that combat effectiveness in 1-v-1 engagements was improved by a factor of at least two.

Supermaneuverability thus provided a fair chance to survive against two opponents of similar conventional performance. Somewhat counter intuitively, the benefits of supermaneuverability tended to increase in outnumbered situations! But would supermaneuverability pay off in actual flight? Aviation history is littered with ideas that seemed excellent in the laboratory or on a computer but proved wanting in the cold reality of atmospheric flight tests. Simulation, while extremely useful, is not the same as really flying because it cannot, in most cases, replicate the actual dynamics of aircraft behavior, the interaction of aerodynamic and propulsion control systems, or the human-machine interface with the fidelity needed by aircraft designers and operators.

At about the same time, a group of USAF researchers from what is now the Air Force Research Laboratory (AFRL) and the Air Force Academy, headed by the academy's Maj. Jim Allburn, were studying the dynamics of flight at angles of attack above stall and how to safely capitalize on it operationally. They recognized that, when flying in this very slow post-stall regime, the effectiveness of pure aerodynamic controls is limited, but that it was possible to minimize the adverse aerodynamics to ameliorate the issue. But they also realized that additional control would be needed. One possible solution was to employ thrust vectoring of the engine exhaust to provide sufficient forces and moments to control the aircraft. This can be accomplished by either a rotatable nozzle (as in the current F-22 and some Flankers, and in the older British Harrier vertical/short takeoff and landing [V/STOL] strike fighter) or by inserting moveable surfaces directly into the exhaust stream that, like rudders, deflect flow and thereby "point" the thrust in a particular direction to achieve the desired orientation and attitude. Since both aerodynamic controls and thrust vectoring are to be employed, the plane's fly-by-wire flight control system must be able to seamlessly control both the aircraft's aerodynamic control surfaces and the thrust vectoring together—a major challenge.

What was needed was an actual flight-test research airplane to prove the usefulness of a thrust-vectored aircraft in the post-stall regime. Herbst did not necessarily want a research airplane; in fact, he was quite frustrated that others did not yet fully subscribe to the implementation of supermaneuverability. Mike Robinson and several others from both the United States and Germany worked to convince him that a flying demonstrator was needed if there was to be any chance of acceptance of the concept.

Defining a Supermaneuverable Airplane: The Path to EFM

Before exploring the evolution of the X-31 from concept to design, it is instructive to review where the various parties who would ultimately become participating partners were in their corporate planning. Messerschmitt-Bölkow-Blohm

(MBB)—whose Herbst had initiated the concept and the initial simulations of supermaneuverability or post-stall maneuverability (PST)—had been involved in studies for a new fighter. Germany had been exploring potential replacements for its Lockheed F-104G Starfighter fleet as early as the late 1960s under a program called Neue Kampfflugzeug (NKF, or "New Warplane"). By the late 1970s, European fighters such as the F-104, Northrop F-5, Dassault Mirage III/V/F-1, and Jaguar were becoming outdated in comparison with newer models, including American fourth-generation fighter aircraft such as the F-15, F-16, and F/A-18, and Soviet fighter designs such as the MiG-29 Fulcrum and Su-27 Flanker. Britain, Germany, and France had been pursuing new fighter studies for some time—Germany for a replacement for the aforementioned F-104, and Britain and France for a replacement for their Jaguar fighter-bombers. Britain was insistent that the new aircraft have significant air-to-air capability, so from the start, the new fighter had to be a multirole airplane. In response, Germany evolved a series of designs into what became the Luftwaffe's Taktisches Kampfflugzeug 1990 (Tactical Combat Aircraft 90), or TKF-90.

Germany, France, and Britain had many discussions about collaborating on a new fighter, but when it finally became evident that the French had a different timeline (and agenda), Germany and Britain held separate bilateral discussions. These discussions also failed, however, and the collaboration was cancelled. While this ended the TKF-90, BAe realized that eventually Britain (and Europe) would need a new fighter and so continued their efforts in-house. They resurrected the Anglo-German-Italian "Panavia" consortium (which had built the Tornado) to collaborate on a new machine, the Agile Combat Aircraft (ACA). The ACA program eventually led to the Experimental Airplane Program (EAP), resulting in two prototypes. The EAP had the cranked delta wing (i.e., the inner portions of the delta wing were swept at a higher angle than the outer portions of the wing), with longer coupled canards as well as an underfuselage intake reminiscent of the TKF-90. Gone, however, was the twin-tailed design of the TKF-90, replaced by a single-tail configuration.[6]

It had been intended that Britain and Germany would each fund one of the EAP prototypes; however, barely into the start of the program, MBB withdrew in response to pressure from the German government, which had decided not to fund the German EAP vehicle. Even without a formal Royal Air Force Air Staff Requirement, BAe pressed ahead with its prototype demonstration program while MBB maintained its own interest in a low-key fashion. The resulting EAP demonstrator first flew on August 8, 1986, and it would complete 259 flights before its retirement on May 1, 1991. The EAP resulted in the development of a European staff requirement for an aircraft known as the European Fighter Aircraft (EFA, or "Eurofighter"), which became the EF-2000

A Eurofighter Typhoon FGR 4 fighter of Britain's Royal Air Force. (U.S. Air Force photo by SrA Kayla Newman)

Typhoon that is now in service with the air forces of Britain, Germany, Italy, Spain, and Austria.[7]

This background is important to the X-31 story because the TKF-90/EAP wing planform and wing-canard relationship were what MBB used on its development of the post-stall maneuvering studies. As the X-31 developed, MBB and Rockwell mutually decided that it would avail itself of these characteristics because high-alpha characteristics tend to be planform-driven. This decision saved significant time, money, and risk.

Meanwhile in the United States, Rockwell International, the manufacturer of the B-1B strategic bomber, was interested in expanding the company's posture for future fighter programs (its heritage was fighters as well as bombers—P-51, F-86, F-100) as a hedge against program cancellations and to keep design teams in place and up to date.[8] In a similar vein, Rockwell had explored the possibility of producing a highly maneuverable piloted flight demonstrator with forward swept wings, the so-called Rockwell Sabrebat, but lost out to Grumman, who won the award for production and flight test of their rival X-29. As noted previously, Rockwell had begun working on enhanced transonic maneuverability with the J85-powered HiMAT remotely piloted research vehicle (RPRV) test bed, air-launched by a Boeing NB-52B Stratofortress mother ship. This vehicle explored high-acceleration (g) maneuvering at transonic speeds with an inherently unstable airframe using advanced digital fly-by-wire controls. This demonstrator completed its first flight in 1979 and flew through 1983.

Rockwell HiMAT RPRV in flight. (NASA DFRC)

Rockwell briefly considered using HiMAT for post-stall maneuvering demonstrations, but the benefits of doing this with an unpiloted platform were considered marginal because the human-machine interface for PST operation that would be a key factor had yet to be demonstrated. But the wing's aerodynamic and composite structural designs represented the state of the art and were the most appropriate for any fighter-like PST demonstrator—another source that would eventually offer the X-31 program experience and databases that saved money, risk, and time.

At this time, Rockwell and MBB were both supporting the Swedish (Saab) JAS-39 Gripen development program. Rockwell was assisting in the overall configuration design and wing aerodynamic and structural design (based in HiMAT), and MBB was assisting with the flight control system design. Meanwhile, Saab was conducting related flight demonstrations using a modified JA-37 Viggen test aircraft to demonstrate Roll-Coupled Fuselage Aiming (RCFAM), or flightpath decoupling.[9] This technology would allow the aircraft's fuselage to be "pointed" away from the flightpath to allow head-on gun attacks without intersecting with the opponent aircraft's flightpath, thus minimizing the chance of collision. It was at Saab and at international meetings of the American Institute of Aeronautics and Astronautics that Rockwell's Mike Robinson and MBB's Herbst met. Herbst still desperately wanted to gain acceptance of his post-stall maneuvering technology concepts.

In conversations with Robinson, he found that Rockwell saw potential merit in PST and felt that a joint demonstration could form the basis of a valuable joint venture. Moreover, Robinson felt that he could get U.S. Department of Defense (DOD) sponsorship through the Defense Advanced Research Projects Agency (DARPA). He knew that Jim Allburn, who was now a lieutenant colonel at DARPA's Tactical Technology Office (TTO), would be interested based on Allburn's earlier high-alpha work. Both parties agreed that it was crucial to get the military involved to ensure buy-in of the demonstrated concept. Herbst felt that if the DOD got involved, then the German Ministry of Defense would also join the program. Thus, the MBB-Rockwell collaboration on what became the X-31 was born, and thereafter the two companies and their engineering staffs worked closely together.[10]

Robinson outlined a program consistent with earlier (e.g., X-29) DARPA demonstrations, and a small Rockwell-MBB team set about developing a presentation to define the program and its goals, objectives, and challenges. They dubbed the proposed program the Super-Normal Attitude Kinetic Enhancement (SNAKE). The demonstrator aircraft that the program would use would incorporate vectored thrust, integrated flight and propulsion control, and improved protection for the pilot against linear and lateral accelerations.[11]

On February 11, 1983, Mike Robinson, Wolfgang Herbst, and a team composed of both Rockwell and MBB specialists presented a briefing to Allburn and a team of Government experts that Allburn drew from the earlier high-alpha work USAF had done while Allburn was at the Air Force Academy. The SNAKE team suggested a multiphase research program to include a Feasibility Study (Phase I), Preliminary Design (Phase II), Detail Design and Fabrication (Phase III), and Flight Test (Phase IV) of a custom-built, dedicated research aircraft. The object was to demonstrate the tactical utility of post-stall maneuvering, and the program had four goals:

- To quickly provide a demonstration of high-agility maneuvering concepts,
- To investigate the tactical benefits of Enhanced Fighter Maneuverability (EFM) technologies,
- To validate a low-cost international prototyping concept, and
- To develop the design requirements and database to support future applications.[12]

Allburn and his team were very receptive to the scheme, for DARPA had a long involvement in supporting advanced piloted and unpiloted military aircraft development programs, most notably the crucial first two "low observable" (i.e., "stealth") reduced radar signature test beds: the Lockheed XST Have Blue (which led to the F-117A stealth fighter) and the Northrop Tacit Blue test bed (which influenced the design of the B-2 stealth bomber). Though not a stealth program per se, SNAKE fit right in because it promised to potentially revolutionize fighter agility. Accordingly, Rockwell formally proposed and Allburn arranged funding for the program's feasibility study. Abroad, as Herbst had predicted, the BMV also supported this feasibility study, which marked the onset of Phase I of the X-31 development effort. The following were the Phase I Feasibility Study's conclusions:

- Close-in combat would probably continue to be necessary in future air-combat scenarios, and supermaneuverability does have the potential for a significant enhancement of air-to-air effectiveness by maintaining significant exchange ratio advantages;
- A new dedicated research vehicle should be developed rather than modifying an existing aircraft; and
- Such a vehicle should be configured to be representative of a potential operational fighter.[13]

Earlier piloted combat simulations at the German IABG and at McDonnell-Douglas helped to empirically develop several technical features intended for the SNAKE (which DARPA named the Enhanced Fighter Maneuverability program) while illuminating some substantial technical challenges. These included the following:

- Mechanization of lateral stick input (to roll the aircraft around the flightpath at zero sideslip angle, rather than around the aircraft body axis);
- Angle of attack and n_z (vertical acceleration, with respect to the aircraft) demand with proper blend-over;
- PST-entry mechanization by the flight control system;
- Gravity and gyroscopic moment compensation;
- Consideration of inertial coupling;
- Scheduling of control surfaces and thrust-vectoring blending; and
- Response characteristics and maximum deflection of the thrust-vectoring system in pitch and yaw, and the criteria for body-axis roll.

Since it was desired that test-flight results would be transferable to a potential operational fighter aircraft, a "fighter-like" design evolved. Fighter-like supermaneuverability required the following aircraft characteristics:

- a thrust-to-weight (T/W) ratio of at least 1.0;
- an electronic flight control system;
- an intake configuration to allow full-power engine operation up to 70° angle of attack;
- a low wing loading and high leading-edge sweep;
- certain aerodynamic characteristics to allow smooth transition into the post-stall regime;

- a horizontal control surface that moves into the wind at increasing angle of attack as a "pitch down" safety device;
- a configuration layout that is preferably unstable in pitch at subsonic speeds for better supersonic performance; and
- resistance to enter a spin and an easy recovery from a spin once entered, necessary to avoid the thrust-vectoring system from becoming a safety-critical item.

With the Phase I Feasibility Study complete and no "show stoppers" identified, the task was now to find funding for the next phase, Preliminary Design (Phase II). In April 1986, the Packard Commission on U.S. defense management had strongly advocated prototyping and proof-of-concept demonstrations by DARPA as a means of reducing risk in the early part of developmental programs. A special acquisition task force formed by the committee and chaired by William J. Perry (one of the pioneers of stealth) made the following recommendations:

> DARPA should have the additional mission of stimulating a greater emphasis on prototyping in defense systems. It should do this by actually conducting prototype projects that embody technology that might be incorporated in joint programs, or in selected Service programs. On request, it also should assist the Services in their own prototyping programs. The common objective of all of these prototyping programs should be to determine to what extent a given new technology can improve military capability, and to provide a basis for making realistic cost estimates prior to a decision on full-scale development. In short, the prototype programs should allow us to fly—and know how much it will cost—before we buy.[14]

Simultaneously, Senator Samuel Nunn, then the chairman of the Senate Armed Services Committee, jointly with Congressman Dan Quayle, of the House Armed Services Committee, proposed legislation that would permit the Pentagon and the North American Treaty Organization (NATO) to jointly fund research and development programs, thus reducing the cost burden on each nation. The so-called Nunn-Quayle NATO cooperative research and development amendment was passed into law by the U.S. Congress in 1986 and subsequently furnished an average of $112 million per year from fiscal year (FY) 1987 through FY 1991.[15] Following its passage, John Retelle, DARPA program manager for the EFM program, immediately set out to acquire Nunn-Quayle funding with which to start Phase II, Preliminary Design. In May 1986, a Memorandum of Agreement (MOA) was signed by the German Ministry of Defense and DARPA. This MOA established a joint German-American research effort designated the Enhanced Fighter Maneuverability program, which would result in the design, construction, and flight test of two research aircraft to study the supermaneuverability concept in the air. The program made history even before its first flight, for what was to become the X-31 would thus be the first *international* X-plane. The goal of the program was to have first flight by 1989.[16]

Phase II commenced in September 1986 with the following objectives:

- Quantify additional tactical benefits of supermaneuverability.
- Quantify abilities of enabling technologies.
- Verify pilot-vehicle compatibility.
- Accomplish preliminary design and definition of the aircraft.

At this juncture, as is common with DARPA programs, DARPA sought an executive agent within the military to manage the program. DARPA initially approached the Air Force, which had actively participated as an informal DARPA agent during the Phase I program and had previously been the managing agent for the X-29 program. But, in DARPA's view, the concept of supermaneuverability (involving close-in, slow-speed maneuvering in a lethal furball dogfight) ran counter to the Air Force's then-current concept of using stealth, high speed (supersonic cruise), and beyond-visual-range missiles, as exemplified by studies for its next-generation fighter, the Advanced Tactical Fighter (which eventually spawned the F-22). Moreover, the Navy's flight-test center at Patuxent River, MD, under the leadership of Rear Adm. Edward J. "Ned" Hogan, was aggressively pursuing business outside the traditional role of certifying new and modified systems for entry into the fleet. Thus, in essence, DARPA ran a competition between USAF and USN for the agent position. The USAF, having just come off the X-29 program, could not accept the aggressive cost goals that the EFM team had set. They felt that the X-29 model was the proper cost model. By contrast, the Navy said the goals were extremely aggressive and perhaps not achievable, but they agreed to work to achieve the cost goal (or as close to it as possible). So, instead of the Air Force, DARPA selected the Navy as the managing agent for EFM, with the service's Naval Air Systems Command (commonly abbreviated "NAVAIR") chosen to be the implementing command. In Germany, the Bundesamt für Wehrtechnik und Beschaffung (the Federal Office for Defence Technology and Procurement) managed the program for the Ministry of Defense.[17]

Rockwell had responsibility for the aircraft's configuration and aerodynamics, as well as vehicle construction, simulation, redundancy management, and flight control software (FCS) hardware development. MBB, which was continuing its post-stall studies, was assigned the task of developing the aircraft's advanced fly-by-wire flight and propulsion control laws, analyzing flight data on the combat advantage of PST, developing the thrust-vectoring system, and fabricating the wings. Additionally General Electric was brought on board to ensure that the propulsion system was consistent with their F404 engine.[18]

Design and Development of the X-31

Initially, Rockwell and MBB engineers explored modifying an existing aircraft for the demonstration program. There were several precedents, both successful and not; for example, Martin had modified its stubby X-24A lifting body into the X-24B, a slender delta. Ling-Temco-Vought (LTV) modified a TF-8C Crusader into a supercritical wing (SCW) test bed. Rockwell cobbled together an unsuccessful V/STOL prototype, the XFV-12A, using components from various aircraft. Much more successfully, Grumman had modified a Northrop F-5A into the X-29 FSW demonstrator. Rockwell and MBB considered the Douglas A-4C Skyhawk, the Northrop F-5E Tiger II, the General Dynamics F-16A Fighting Falcon, the McDonnell-Douglas F-15C Eagle, the McDonnell-Douglas F/A-18A Hornet, the Northrop F-20A Tigershark, the North American T-2C Buckeye, the Grumman X-29, the Rockwell HiMAT RPRV, and even the Korean War–vintage North American F-86H Sabre for such modification.[19]

Of all these, the Sabre—the most elegant and evocative of all early jet-age airplanes—had the greatest appeal. Old ex–Air National Guard F-86H aircraft were available from the Navy at Naval Air Station (NAS) China Lake, where they were being converted into target drones. The figure

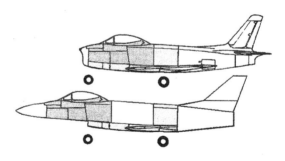

From F-86H to EFM. (Dan Raymer, Michael Robinson)

to the right shows how an F-86H might have been converted into the EFM. Making this an attractive proposition was that the entire tail of the F-86 comes off for engine removal, meaning that a new tail section could easily be fabricated to use the same attachment points. The portions of the F-86 that the EFM would use are indicated in the figure as the shaded areas of the forward fuselage and the wing box. The cockpit is moved forward from the midsection and the "hole" behind the cockpit is filled in with a "flat-wrapped" skin over a new internal structure.[20] A chin inlet, nose cone, and canard are added, and then the F-86 wing leading and trailing edges are removed and replaced with a delta wing around the old F-86 structural wing box. Further increasing the idea's attractiveness is that many parts and components from the original F-86H could be reused, including the wing box and carry-through structure, tricycle landing gear, cockpit and canopy, large portions of the fuselage, engine mounts, fuel system, and many subsystems. Rockwell's Dan Raymer built a foam-board model to show how it would be done. Though the F-86 was an understandable choice for the EFM project, concerns over the likely fatigue life of an elderly airframe that was at least 30 years old, as well as its relatively heavy fuselage weight, led to dropping the Sabre from contention.[21] Indeed, the two companies concluded that the costs of modifying and retrofitting any existing aircraft were actually higher than simply starting from scratch and designing an entirely new demonstrator aircraft, for which they also could tailor the design to optimally meet the program's goals.[22] This did not, however, preclude using components from other aircraft to keep costs and fabrication time to a minimum, and as ultimately built, the X-31 used components from the F/A-18, the F-16, the F-20, and the Cessna Citation business jet.[23]

Even though Mike Robinson was located at the Rockwell Los Angeles (LA) division, he had Rockwell's Columbus, OH, division conduct the initial portions of the program. This was because the Los Angeles division was very busy with the recently restarted B-1 program, and there were insufficient engineers for a full design effort. The Columbus division produced a configuration that was somewhat like HiMAT to allow both Rockwell and Government participants to get firsthand experience in extremely-high-AOA flight in a fighter-type configuration. It was selected because both Rockwell and NASA had significant recent databases and wind tunnel models of the general configuration. They flew a model in powered free-flight wind tunnel tests, where it flew at almost 90° angle of attack. Shortly thereafter, Rockwell's Columbus division was refocused toward solving B-1 manufacturing problems, with a cutback of engineering personnel assigned to the EFM. Thus, the program was moved back to the Los Angeles division with significant support from the Columbus team to ensure a smooth transition. As work commenced in LA, the cost goal and the philosophy previously discussed, whereby the program would avail itself of the German TKF planform database and the HiMAT aerostructures database, were both considered.[24] Dan Raymer, one of the EFM's designers, recalled, "We started over, blank sheet of paper, when the project moved to Los Angeles. The Columbus configuration concept was simply to allow a rapid Phase I study to be conducted and served as the basis to develop low cost concepts—it was never considered as a final demonstration aircraft configuration. The plane that flew was basically the LA design, with the overall planform and inlet placement based on the previous German work."[25] Mike Robinson, then

F-8 digital fly-by-wire test bed, 1972. (NASA DFRC)

Rockwell's EFM program manager, recalled that while the planform for the design originated with MBB and TKF-90 concepts, its wing design (with factors such as twist, camber, and composite structures) originated at Rockwell.[26]

Since one of the objectives of Phase II was to "quantify abilities of enabling technologies," it is instructive to consider some of the "enabling technologies" that were useful—and in many cases required—for the design of EFM to progress. On the German side, the flight testing of a Control Configured Vehicle (CCV) F-104G that incorporated an all-digital, modern-control-theory, fly-by-wire control system was certainly a contributor to the available technology, particularly to MBB.[27] In parallel and on the U.S. side, the NASA Dryden F-8 Digital Fly-by-Wire (F-8 DFBW) program, which was first flown on May 25, 1972, and continued to be flight-tested for the next 13 years, certainly proved the concept of digital flight controls.[28] Additionally, the NASA Dryden Integrated Propulsion Control System (IPCS) that was flown on an F-111E from 1973 to 1976 to demonstrate digital engine control showed that the digital aerodynamics and propulsion control technologies necessary for EFM were sufficiently technologically mature to be applied to the new plane.[29]

Initially, the goal of Phase II was to perform design studies for a demonstrator aircraft; however, the two companies had actually been working on potential designs even before the MOA was signed. The blended U.S.-German concept that is described above was the chosen baseline. Another key configuration driver was engine selection, which was done before many other configuration features had been determined. The chosen engine was the General Electric F404-GE-400, which produced 12,000 pounds of thrust in military power and 16,000 pounds in maximum afterburner. It was selected because it had the attractive feature of being able to tolerate disrupted airflow—a useful attribute for any aircraft expected to fly at very high angles of attack. This turned out to be fortuitous because the F404 was used on the Navy's McDonnell-Douglas F/A-18A through D Hornets, thus ensuring that the program would have readily available spares through the Navy, which later became DARPA's managing agent for the EFM program, as noted earlier.

By late 1987, the configuration of the EFM concept was rapidly taking on the appearance of the definitive X-31. In line with one of the conclusions of the Phase I Feasibility Study—namely, that such a vehicle should be configured to be representative of a potential operational fighter—the airplane evolved to have a cranked delta planform with a chin-mounted inlet (an excellent position for high-AOA propulsion operation because it would not be blanked by the aircraft's pitch or yaw motion), which had an articulating lower lip that would droop at high angles of attack to improve airflow. The plane's canards were incorporated primarily as a pitch recovery control but also coordinated with the trailing-edge flaps for secondary pitch control. The canards were designed to remain unloaded during angle of attack changes; however, a power approach mode could be selected in which the canards produced lift with the elevons deflected down, which reduced approach speeds by approximately 15 knots.[30]

As a side note, the X-31's cranked delta planform was already a flight-proven configuration that had appeared previously on several other aircraft, including the 1950s Saab J-35 Draken and the 1980s General Dynamics F-16XL (an elegant if unsuccessful competitor for the production contract won by McDonnell-Douglas with their longer-legged, higher-payload F-15E Strike Eagle). For the EFM, it promised low supersonic drag, maximum lift at corner speed, minimum induced drag at the design maneuver points, and a balance between relaxed stability at low angles of attack (for minimum drag) and sufficient pitch-down recovery moment availability at high angles of attack.[31]

Wind tunnel testing was conducted at Rockwell tunnels in the Los Angeles division and at the NASA Langley Research Center (LRC) at Hampton, VA.[32] Langley's influence on the evolution of the EFM and the subsequent development and flight testing of the X-31 was profound.[33] Langley had worked with Rockwell on the HiMAT effort, and in 1984, it began evaluating the initial Rockwell Columbus SNAKE concept, used as a feasibility study surrogate, under lead engineer Mark A. Croom. This surrogate SNAKE configuration had twin vertical fins located at midwing position (similar to HiMAT) and, oddly, ventral vertical endplate fins on its wingtips. Testing in the famed Langley 30- by 60-foot Full Scale Tunnel (FST) promptly revealed that the SNAKE configuration had serious stability and control issues and was, in fact, unstable about all three axes. Assisted by Langley engineer Joseph L. Johnson, Croom recommended a series of configuration changes to Rockwell that included abandoning the end-plate ventral fins. LRC did great work on this wind tunnel effort, but it must be remembered that the effort was done as a learning exercise using tools that NASA and Rockwell had readily available (i.e., databases and wind tunnel models). The actual configuration that was tested was never intended to be the EFM aircraft.

The SNAKE model was later modified to incorporate research by NASA engineer Bobby L. Berrier on multiaxis thrust vectoring (a follow-on to earlier NASA Langley studies on a Grumman F-14A Tomcat test bed modified with yaw-vectoring panels), and it subsequently demonstrated fully controlled flight at extreme angles of attack approaching 90° during FST testing in 1985. The paddles were used as a wind tunnel test device to enable thrust vectoring but were not considered as airplane configuration items at the time. MBB still held out for a thrust-vectoring nozzle for the demonstration airplane. Langley's support was invaluable in helping both the DOD sponsors and industry understand the phenomenology of PST, so in 1986, DARPA requested that Langley partner in the program.[34] From 1987 to 1989, Langley's testing of the EFM configuration moved into high gear.

Rockwell and MBB worked together so closely that both contractors had personnel assigned to the other partner's facilities to ensure the closest and most efficient coordination and cooperation possible, and by now the two had come into congruence on merging the best of the HiMAT and the TKF-90 into a single configuration. Langley evaluated the initial X-31 demonstrator configuration in its 14- by 22-foot High-Speed Tunnel (HST), did rotary balance tests in its 20-foot Vertical Spin Tunnel (VST), and performed more tests in the FST. Langley researchers flew a 0.27-scale, 540-pound drop-test model of the EFM, and as discussed in a later section, these tests proved critically important. Early wind tunnel evaluations had been done at Rockwell's North American Aviation laboratories' 11- by 14-foot low-speed wind tunnel using a simple model, while all high-speed testing, up to Mach 2, was done at Rockwell's 7-foot transonic wind tunnel in El Segundo, CA, using a 10-percent model. Many of the tests were done with "two entries," of which the first testing was with an F-16 forebody because the Air Force was still expected to be DARPA's executive agent. The testing was repeated with an F/A-18 forebody when the Navy was chosen as the executive agent. The change of cockpit forebody was important because forebody shape is critical to high-AOA aerodynamics. Flow visualization was done in Rockwell's small water tunnel and in the water tunnel at Dryden. Damping derivatives were measured using a relatively large 19-percent model in the Tracor Hydronautics water basin/tow tank near Laurel, MD.[35] Configurations of the evolving design were also tested in wind tunnels in Emmen, Switzerland. In parallel, MBB was proceeding with control system design at their Ottobrunn facility, which was no easy task given the magnitude of the forces and moments the aircraft would experience as it transitioned, particularly with its vectored-thrust propulsion system.[36]

Since one of the four goals of the program was validating the concept of a low-cost international prototype, the companies were very motivated to develop a cost-effective design even though the airplane itself was to be a custom-built new aircraft. This led to the approach of using existing flight-qualified components from other aircraft in the design. The cockpit, the canopy (manufactured by Swedlow), and much of the cockpit controls and flight instruments came from the F/A-18. This allowed the F/A-18 ejection seat to be used, and it could be qualified "by similarity" because the cockpit and canopy were similar, thus further reducing development time and avoiding the need for a separate ejection-seat test effort.[37] F/A-18 electrical generators, an airframe-mounted accessory gearbox, leading-edge actuators, and control stick and throttle were also used. The landing gear (manufactured by Menasco) and fuel pump (manufactured by Argo-Tech) came from the F-16, as did the rudder pedals, nosewheel tires, and emergency power unit. The experimental cranked arrow wing F-16XL donated its leading-edge flap drives. The flight control computers (manufactured by Honeywell/Sperry) were adopted from those used on the Air Force's Lockheed C-130 Hercules High Technology Test Bed (HTTB), another technology demonstrator airplane. Control surface actuators and trailing-edge control modules (manufactured by Allied-Signal) came from the Bell-Boeing V-22 tilt-rotor, then under development, and the wheels and brakes (manufactured by B.F. Goodrich) came from the Cessna Citation business jet. The F-20's low-cost, hydrazine-fueled, emergency air-start system was selected, but it subsequently proved difficult to use and maintain. Other parts also did not perform well when applied to the X-31. The control surface actuators did not live up to expectations and so the design team ended up designing entirely new ones. The original generator (which was relatively inexpensive) also did not perform well in the X-31's environment and had to be replaced with a more expensive one.[38]

The magic of the EFM concept was in its thrust vectoring. The physical vectoring of the thrust can be accomplished by designing a sophisticated axi-symmetric gimballing exhaust nozzle to vector the engine's exhaust in both pitch and yaw simultaneously. This system has been mechanized in more recent thrust-vectoring applications, such as the USAF's F-16 Multi-Axis Thrust-Vectoring (MATV) program and the joint NASA-USAF F-15 Advanced Control Technology for Integrated Vehicles (ACTIVE) program. However, for the EFM, a much lower-cost and simpler approach was desired.

One approach would be to use exhaust vanes located in the exhaust flow to vector thrust. This method had first been used in the mid-1940s with the German V-2 ballistic missile, which used graphite exhaust vanes to stabilize the missile at lift-off and climb-out until its aerodynamic control surfaces could gain effectiveness. A variation of this placed paddle-like vanes outside of the exhaust nozzle that could be pivoted into the flow by actuators, thus deflecting it. The use of paddles to deflect exhaust flow by using large actuators to push the paddles into the flow had been developed for the Navy by Rockwell's Columbus division to support a flight-test program called the F-14 Yaw Vane Technology Demonstration Program, which used a modified Grumman F-14A Tomcat to address that airplane's notorious flat-spin problem (as immortalized in the movie *Top Gun*). This program, begun in 1985, was flown from 1986 to 1987 at the Naval Air Test Center in Patuxent River. The plane had two paddle-like exhaust vanes installed, one on each side of its speed brake housing between the afterburners of its two Pratt & Whitney TF30 engines. These could be operated differentially to change the exhaust flow's path vector from straight aft to the side. Flight testing successfully defined the vane (i.e., paddle) operating environment, determined vane performance, and confirmed engine performance during thrust vectoring.[39]

This Rockwell-developed paddle concept was selected by the team as a sufficient and low-cost approach to achieve the required vectoring at a fraction of the cost of a multiaxis vectoring nozzle. Moreover, the paddles were downstream of the engine nozzle so the program did not have to address the issue of "back-pressuring" the engine. Here again, NASA Langley played a key role in the X-31's development. Aggressive testing continued into 1989, including evaluation of nearly 500 paddle and nozzle configurations for the F404 engine.

The thrust-vectoring paddles used on the F-14 experiment—as well as the paddles that were eventually designed for the F/A-18 High Alpha Research Vehicle (HARV), another NASA high-AOA research vehicle—were made of Inconel, a very heavy, high-temperature-resistant, nickel-based alloy. As a structural element, Inconel first came to prominence with the development of the hypersonic North American X-15, which employed Inconel as its primary structural material. But Inconel was inappropriate for the EFM, which demanded the lightest possible paddles due to their location far aft of the airplane's center of gravity. Their use would have mandated that significant weight be added to the nose in an already weight-critical design. Something lighter was needed, and for this, Rockwell and MBB decided to manufacture the thrust-vectoring paddles out of carbon-carbon composite material. This material had been tested in high-temperature environments and had been used in space applications (most notably on the leading edges of the Space Shuttle). Carbon-carbon was very brittle—a property that, alas, would play a key role in the loss of the Space Shuttle Columbia during its reentry from orbit in 2003—so this approach was considered risky. The carbon-carbon paddles proved up to the task, however. MBB had responsibility for paddle development and saw the opportunity to gain experience with this new technology. Initially, engineers planned to have four paddles (two for pitch, two for yaw) located around the exhaust in a cruciform pattern. However, integrating four panels into the design and its flight control system proved so difficult that, instead, they chose to use three panels arranged axisymmetrically, 120° apart.

In initial configuration iterations, the fuselage had an area-rule (i.e., Coke-bottle) shape that would have required complex "compound bend" skin forming and necessitated that each major fuselage frame be unique. However, designers discovered that there was no significant wave drag penalty associated with using a non-area-ruled shape when combined with the cranked double-delta wing. This allowed the fuselage to have simple flat-wrapped skins. Moreover, several of the midfuselage frames could be identical, which allowed for significant cost savings. Another cost reduction (and design simplification) was to store all of the fuel in a single fuselage tank centered about the center of gravity.[40] Rockwell and MBB held a concept review on December 3–4, 1986, at which the baseline concept was affirmed. The aircraft was officially designated the X-31A on February 23, 1987. By late 1987, preliminary design was complete and the aircraft configuration was the one recognized today as the X-31. However, funding was not in place yet to commit to the vehicle's detail design and fabrication, so the first of many variations in program "phaseology" emerged to allow progress until commitment could be made. While they were never formalized, these variations took the nomenclature of Phase IIa–d. In addition, because of variations in the U.S. and German funding cycles, at times Rockwell was working under one phase while MBB was working under another. That said, the industry and government teams made it work with little disruption.

Fabrication to Eve of First Flight

In August 1988, funding was received for the construction of two prototype X-31 aircraft. This represented a compromise because, initially, the X-31 project team had wished to build three airplanes. However, sufficient funding for a third could not be procured. The two aircraft were to be built in 22 months for $47.3 million through a fabrication program that constituted Phase III.[41]

Phase III program activities involved drawing preparation, tooling up, fabrication, assembly, and proof testing. The aircraft were to be assembled at Rockwell's Palmdale, CA, facility with MBB providing a number of major components and subassemblies, most notably the wings and thrust-vectoring paddles. MBB was also responsible for the integrated flight and propulsion control laws, including control integration for the thrust-vectoring paddles,

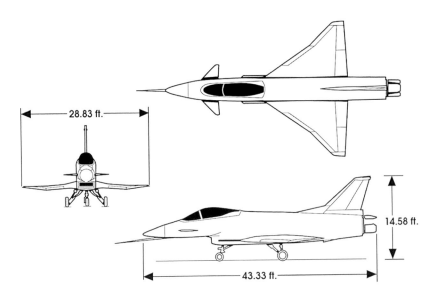

The X-31A configuration. (Rockwell)

and for the cockpit symbology display that allowed the pilots to monitor post-stall maneuvering.[42]

At this time, the DARPA program manager was Col. John "Tack" Nix. His experience was mainly in so-called "black" programs, particularly Lockheed's XST and F-117, and so he subscribed to the philosophy that Lockheed's legendary Clarence "Kelly" Johnson espoused of very small design and manufacturing teams colocated to maximize productive efficiency. With the X-31, this would be difficult because the program obviously would have personnel thousands of miles apart in Germany and in Palmdale. This was solved by having personnel from each contractor at the other's location. Since the teams were small, this also mitigated another potential problem; Rockwell, at the time, had a number of classified or otherwise proprietary programs in the Palmdale facility, but since the X-31 team was small, they could be housed in a small area of their own with no need to interface with other Rockwell programs and possibly compromise them. Oddly, having teams in both Germany and Palmdale worked to the benefit of the program. If one team had issues that needed to be coordinated with the other team, information requests were sent to that team. The time difference allowed the receiving team to work the problem and have an answer back to the sending team when they arrived for work the next morning.[43] This was before the days of massive e-mail (or other file transfer) systems, but General Electric (GE) had developed a messaging system that had a portal in Belgium. The X-31 program was able to lease time on this GE system and that, plus huge faxes, became the modus operandi.

The work share was divided between the two countries not on the basis of money but on a work package split, with a rough target of 75 percent in the United States and 25 percent in Germany. Each country was responsible for funding its own industry: the United States, from DARPA via the Navy, disbursed their money to Rockwell; Germany, via the BWB, disbursed their money to MBB. Thus, there was no transfer of funds between the companies unless specifically agreed to under special circumstances. This was a unique approach, but it saved money that, if passed between governments, would have required funding an infrastructure to manage. This approach was actually derived from the Germans, who had worked many multilateral government-to-government efforts. Their experience was that at least an additional 25 to 30 percent of funding was required to manage such a joint infrastructure. Finally this program approach had another benefit in that because the program was dependent on both nations, cancellation of the program by a single government would risk a potentially ugly international spat.[44]

As the construction contract started, uncertainty continued over the number of aircraft to build. The team wanted to build three but lacked sufficient funding for more than two, and they even considered building only one. In the end, two aircraft were built, allowing the team to have a backup airplane that allowed the program to accomplish more test flights in a shorter period of time. The team also considered having one X-31 "fight" the other in the combat maneuvering phase of the flight-test program, with one airplane using thrust-vectoring and the other not. Since both aircraft were otherwise identical, varying the one parameter of thrust vectoring would have enabled an assessment of that parameter's value by itself, separated from other aircraft characteristics, capabilities, and performance. Although it was a good idea, this fratricidal fight was destined never to occur, unfortunately. There were, however, some other benefits in having another airframe in the program.

In the "low-cost" spirit, the team decided not to build an "Iron Bird"—a mockup of the actual aircraft in which each system is laid out in relation to the actual configuration of the aircraft and all the system components are installed in the same relative space as they would be in the actual aircraft. Using this tool, engineers can test the operation of the various systems, discover design problems with system integration, and study the consequences of different failures. Instead, the second aircraft was used for the same purpose.[45] Additionally, the program did not fund construction of a dedicated "loads-test" aircraft to be tested to failure or "ultimate load," which is normally at least 150 percent of the design limit load (which, for the X-31, was +9 g's and –4 g's). In the X-31 program, one of the aircraft was tested to 110 percent of the design limit load, which allowed that aircraft to still be used for actual flight tests. This procedure was agreed to by the various government agencies, the Navy, DARPA, and the German aeronautical certification agency.[46]

Wing construction was an MBB responsibility. The interior of the wing was a metal substructure with numerically controlled milling of the spars and ribs. This substructure was covered with a composite skin with fairing covers at the wing-root attach points to aerodynamically blend the wing with the fuselage. The wing had a 56.6° leading-edge sweep at the root, and the leading edge was "cranked," abruptly transitioning to a lesser sweep angle of 45° on the outboard panels. The wing was "dry" (i.e., containing no fuel), which ensured minimal "interfacing" problems with the Rockwell fuselage and enabled a lighter internal and external wing structure. Wing-mounted control surfaces included split trailing-edge elevons providing principle pitch and roll that were actuated separately. The actuators were contained in "bathtub"-like structures on the undersurface of the wing because there was not sufficient room within the mold-line of the wing to contain the trailing-edge actuators. Leading-edge flaps were positioned on both sections of the wing (56.6° and 45°) and were actuated by drives contained in the leading-edge structures borrowed from the F-16XL.

The thrust-vectoring paddles were also a responsibility of MBB and, as discussed previously, were constructed of carbon-carbon material instead of Inconel steel (as used on the F/A-18 HARV and the F-14 Yaw Vane Technology Demonstrator) to save on overall aircraft weight and to keep the airplane balanced with respect to its center-of-gravity margins. In contrast, the Inconel-vane-equipped F/A-18 HARV required a large amount of nose ballast, somewhat reducing its potential performance. The fabrication of the paddles was subcontracted to SIGRI GmbH, and the paddles were ground tested on an F/A-18 (which used the same F404 engine as the X-31) at the Naval Air Test Center. Designers originally limited the maximum paddle deflection to 26° but subsequently increased this to 35°, which produced a thrust-vector change of 16°. The three carbon-carbon paddles weighed a total of 103 pounds. The aft-fuselage frame supporting the paddles was 28 pounds, and support for the vectoring hardware was 30 pounds. Flight control system components weighed 79 pounds. This sums to a total of 240 pounds, comparing very favorably to the 400-pound fully axisymmetric nozzle used on the later F-16 MATV program. Additionally, use of paddles on the X-31 rather than a multiaxis thrust-vector nozzle saved, by itself, approximately $60 million in development costs.[47]

Rockwell was responsible for fabrication of the fuselage, vertical tail (fin and rudder), and canards. Again, composite materials were used for major sections of these components (some of the skin panels on the fuselage, rudder, and vertical tail skins). The single fuel tank in the fuselage held the total fuel load of 4,500 pounds. In addition to the engine, airframe- mounted accessories, cockpit, and landing gear, the fuselage also housed the avionics, digital flight control system (DFCS) computers, air data computers, and specialized flight-test instrumentation. Two panel-type speed brakes flanked the sides of the fuselage near the tail.

Rockwell's most impressive accomplishment during fabrication of the fuselage was its use of "fly-away tooling." In conventional aircraft manufacturing, a set of external tooling fixtures are manufactured and fixed in place on the manufacturing hall floor, external to the structure of the airplane. This tooling precisely holds various pieces or subcomponents and assemblies of the aircraft in place while fasteners (such as rivets or bolts) are installed to hold the various parts together in the proper location and alignment. The cost of this external tooling is typically quite expensive, but it is amortized over the production of many aircraft. In the case of X-31, only two aircraft were going to be constructed, meaning that such construction could add so much cost to the program as to endanger its continuance. Thus, Rockwell devised the concept of fly-away tooling. Rockwell began by manufacturing the fuselage frames as numerically controlled machined parts. Normally, the "fly to buy" ratio of machined parts for aircraft makes them prohibitively expensive for large use in aircraft except where absolutely necessary (like in engines, landing gear, etc.).[48] Since only two X-31 aircraft were to be built, it was decided to very accurately machine the fuselage frames using aluminum, aluminum-lithium, steel, and titanium, depending on frame location and loading, with the higher-temperature-tolerant materials used in the aft engine areas. Then, a simple frame-holding tool was constructed and attached to a rigid and stable floor. The fuselage frames were then very accurately loaded and rigidly locked into the holding fixture using survey equipment (today, it is done with laser sighting equipment). At that point, the 15 major frames became the tooling for substructure and skin assembly. Thus, there was minimal need for external tooling for the fuselage, saving greatly on cost, and when the aircraft flew, the "tooling" took to the air as well.[49] This manufacturing concept, while not often touted as an output from the X-31 program, was undoubtedly one of the most useful product spinoffs of the program.

The canards were another responsibility of Rockwell. They were symmetrical airfoil designs that allowed both right and left sides to be identical, again reducing costs and time by ensuring that the four surfaces (two per aircraft) were interchangeable. Rockwell actually considered using the B-1B's structural mode control vanes (two of which were located on the nose of the "Bone" as load- and ride-alleviation devices) as the X-31 canards, but these proved to be too heavy to meet the lower weight requirement of the X-31. However, the forged spindles of the B-1B vanes were used as the core of the canards with much more material machined away to save weight.[50]

Back in Germany, MBB was busy working on the flight control laws. While not a structural component, this element of the airplane was really the heart of making it work. This area was also probably the toughest area in terms of the Rockwell-MBB shared teamwork, largely due to the philosophical differences in the approach to control law development. The German approach was to use a mathematically "predictive" model of the aircraft's flightpath to determine the appropriate control surface responses to different pilot commands and flight conditions. The American approach, on the other hand, was to have a more "reactive" type of control law in which control surfaces would be deflected based on pilot commands, flight conditions, and aircraft behavior and reaction that were actually measured. The difference in philosophy, coupled with MBB's desire to not divulge much of their control law development techniques due to proprietary concerns, caused some friction between the two teams. This friction soon dissipated as the German control laws proved themselves in preflight simulations and as the Rockwell engineers became more familiar with the logic and reasoning underlying the MBB approach.[51]

A conventional fighter-type stick and rudder pedals constituted the interface between the pilot and the flight control system. Longitudinal stick (pitch inputs) commanded load factor (n_z) at high airspeeds and angles of attack below 325 knots calibrated airspeed. There was a "soft" stick stop at 30° angle of attack that limited the angle there unless a "post-stall" switch located on the stick was engaged. If the post-stall switch—essentially, a "permission switch"—was engaged, the aircraft was above 10,000 feet (ft) minimum altitude, thrust-vectoring was engaged, and the engine was in minimum afterburner setting, then the angle of attack could be commanded to exceed 30° nose-up angle.[52] Lateral stick would command roll rate, but this was roll rate around the velocity vector, not the fuselage axis. Thus, from the pilot's perspective, at very high angles of attack, the use of lateral stick would seem to be producing yaw, not roll.

In parallel with the fabrication of the two aircraft in Germany and at Palmdale, several significant ground tests were conducted to support construction and the future flight-test effort. As discussed previously, various wind tunnel tests were conducted at the NASA Langley Research Center, and a 0.27-scale model of the X-31 was fabricated to be drop tested from a helicopter. The purpose of this test was to determine the "out-of-control" characteristics of the airplane. The computer simulations in use would simply freeze when the aircraft went very far out of control, and engineers wanted to understand the behavior of the aircraft when it departed controlled flight at extremely high angles of attack. The drop-test model revealed a "violent roll departure" that was undetected in previous simulations and wind tunnel tests, enabling designers to develop control laws and to build in control authority sufficient to overcome this problem.[53] (The ability of the flight control system to attempt to regain control after an out-of-control situation would be inadvertently demonstrated following a pilot ejection during the flight-test program, as discussed subsequently.) In all, 25 flights—the longest of which was 128 seconds—were flown with the drop-test model. The final flight was flown without a vertical stabilizer.[54] As well as these aircraft-focused efforts, Rockwell developed an X-31 flight simulator inside a 24-foot dome at Downey, CA (where the Apollo and Space Shuttle were built), that could

X-31 drop-test, July 1991. (NASA LRC)

be "flown" by project test pilots to support flight testing by providing realistic handling in post-stall maneuvering.[55]

Unique to the X-31 were several key items necessary for high-AOA flight testing. The high-temperature-resistant thrust-vectoring paddles controlled by an integrated flight and propulsion digital control system (including the floating canard) were a "first." Additionally, the articulating inlet cowl (which could open to a maximum deflection of 30°, depending upon the angle of attack, to ensure adequate airflow to the engine) was also a first. Not unique, however, was the tendency for the aircraft to grow in weight as construction progressed, a traditional problem in aircraft design that was made more critical by the employment of a single F404 engine in the aircraft. The weight escalated to nearly 16,000 pounds, reducing the thrust-to-weight ratio to about 1 to 1. This seriously endangered the program, for earlier simulation studies of the EFM concept had shown that the aircraft needed a thrust-to-weight ratio of at least 1. This weight growth caused program officials to delete some planned operational features, such as radar, air-refueling capability, and the ability to carry fighter-type weapon load-outs. Therefore, the X-31 would have to fly simulated combat missions "clean"—without the air-to-air weapons used in operational fighter training. All of this was perhaps a reasonable tradeoff; however, the lack of refueling capability meant that flight-test missions would be very short, reducing the amount of data that could be acquired from any particular flight. Actually, according to Mike Robinson, an aerial refueling capability was never seriously considered. The typical sortie duration would be slightly less than an

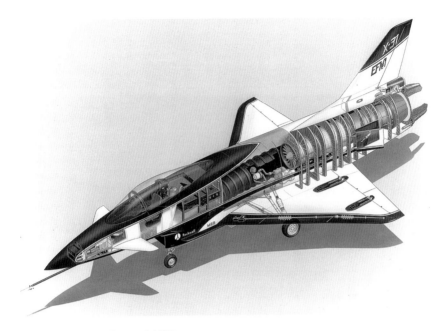

X-31 internal details. (Rockwell-MBB)

hour, and closer to half an hour if afterburner was used, and afterburner was required if thrust-vectoring was to be employed.[56]

Also, as is typical of many aircraft programs, the schedule slipped. In the case of X-31, the total schedule slip in the Phase III construction phase was a full year. The major contributor to this slip was, unsurprisingly, the integrated flight and propulsion control laws and the associated verification and validation (V&V). Another potentially major event that, thanks to workarounds, turned out to be a less-impacting factor occurred when one of the wing skins, while being manufactured at MBB, was dropped late on a Friday and damaged beyond repair. Here, the international teamwork spirit greatly minimized the impact. Rockwell had significant experience with composite manufacturing, including repair and substitution techniques. By Saturday evening, an experienced Rockwell manufacturing manager was en route from Palmdale to Munich. The team collaborated and determined that the least-impacting approach was to remove a skin from Ship 2's substructure by "back-drilling" the 1,200 attachment rivets. Thus, the skin from the second wing was removed and substituted, yielding an overall schedule loss of 3 months for Ship 2. It had only about a 3-week impact on Ship 1—quite minimal considering the calamitous nature of the event. There were also bottlenecks with the use of the second airplane as an "Iron Bird" for software integration, as well as several other small problems that all contributed to an eventual year-long delay.

X-31 development team and Ship 1 prior to rollout. (Rockwell)

Despite these difficulties, finally, on March 1, 1990, the aircraft was rolled out at Rockwell's Palmdale facility. With just a few more months of preparatory work, it would be ready to fly.

Endnotes

1. Dennis R. Jenkins, Tony Landis, and Jay Miller, *American X-Vehicles: An Inventory—X-1 to X-50* (Washington, DC: NASA SP-2003-4531, 2003), pp. 5–38.
2. Lane E. Wallace, *Nose Up: High Angle-of-Attack and Thrust-vectoring Research at NASA Dryden 1979–2001*, Number 34 in the *Monographs in Aerospace History* series (Washington: NASA SP-2006-4534, 2006), pp. 1–2.
3. Robert F. Dorr, "Rockwell/MBB X-31," *World Airpower Journal* 24 (spring 1996): p. 35.
4. Messrs. Hochgesang, Betcke, and Walter were the first operational pilots to experience simulated 1-versus-1 combat with a fighter that had post-stall capability.
5. Deutsche Aerospace, *Roll Out—Palmdale, USA, 1 March 1990—A German View* (Munich: Deutsche Aerospace AG, 1990), pp. 6 and 33.
6. Helmut John, "From Stable Towards Unstable Configuration—Drag Optimization," in Ernst Heinrich Hirschel, Horst Prem, and Gero Madelung, eds., *Aeronautical Research in Germany: From Lilienthal Until Today* (New York: Springer Verlag, 2004), pp. 495–496.
7. Jon Lake, "Eurofighter Typhoon," *World Airpower Journal* 35 (winter 1998): pp. 56–63.
8. Wallace, *Nose Up*, pp. 5.
9. Deutsche Aerospace, *Roll Out—Palmdale, USA*, pp. 12–13.
10. For the MBB side, see Helmut John, "Controlled Flight in the Presence of Flow Separation," in Hirschel, Prem, and Madelung, *Aeronautical Research in Germany: From Lilienthal Until Today* (New York: Springer Verlag, 2004), pp. 498–510.
11. Jay Miller, *The X-Planes X-1 to X-45*, Third Edition (Hinckley, England: Midland Publishing, 2005), p. 318.
12. AFFTC, *X-31 Enhanced Fighter Maneuverability Program Final Report*, Volume I, Videotape Record (Edwards AFB: Multimedia Center, n.d.).
13. Deutsche Aerospace, *Roll Out—Palmdale, USA*, pp. 14–15; Miller, *The X-Planes*, p. 318.
14. President's Blue Ribbon Commission on Defense Management, *A Formula for Action: A Report to the President on Defense Acquisition* (Washington, DC: GPO, April 1986), p. 20.
15. Public Law 99-145, which, with the Defense Appropriations Act, U.S.C. Title 10, section 2350A, "provided funds to promote cooperative programs with U.S. allies"; see U.S. Dept. of Defense, Office of

the Inspector General (OIG), *Audit Report: International Cooperative Research and Development*, Report No. 93-009 (Washington, DC: DOD OIG, Oct. 21, 1992), p. i; Miller, *The X-Planes*, p. 318.

16. Wallace, *Nose Up*, p. 35.
17. AFFTC, *X-31 Enhanced Fighter Maneuverability Program Final Report*, v. 1.
18. John, "Controlled Flight in the Presence of Flow Separation," pp. 510–512.
19. Miller, *The X-Planes*, p. 318.
20. "Flat-wrapped skinning" requires minimal tooling, thus reducing manufacturing costs.
21. Daniel P. Raymer, *Living in the Future* (Los Angeles: Design Dimension Press, 2009), pp. 258–259.
22. Wallace, *Nose Up*, pp. 34–35.
23. John, "Controlled Flight in the Presence of Flow Separation," p. 511.
24. Raymer, *Living in the Future*, p. 256.
25. Ibid., p. 256.
26. Michael Robinson, telephone interview by Douglas A. Joyce, May 31, 2011.
27. Deutsche Aerospace, *Roll Out—Palmdale, USA*, p. 12.
28. See James E. Tomayko, *Computers Take Flight: A History of NASA's Pioneering Digital Fly-by-Wire Project* (Washington, DC: NASA SP-2000-4224, 2000).
29. Lane E. Wallace, *Flights of Discovery—60 Years at the NASA Dryden Flight Research Center* (Washington, DC: NASA SP-2006-4318, 2006), pp. 105–111.
30. Dorr, "Rockwell/MBB X-31," p. 40.
31. Ibid., p. 38.
32. Miller, *The X-Planes*, p. 319.
33. See Joseph R. Chambers, *Partners in Freedom: Contributions of the Langley Research Center to U.S. Military Aircraft in the 1990's* (Washington, DC: NASA SP-2000-4519, 2000), pp. 213–224.
34. Ibid., pp. 216–219.
35. Harvey Schellenger, e-mail to Douglas A. Joyce, January 25, 2012.
36. Ibid., pp. 219–221; see also Miller, *The X-Planes*, p. 318.
37. Robinson interview; there were even foam inserts emplaced around the canopy to insure the similarity.
38. Wallace, *Nose Up*, p. 37; Dorr, "Rockwell/MBB X-31," p. 42.
39. Jeffery W. Sappington and Lt. Cmdr. Robert L. Thompson, USN, "F-14 Yaw Vane Demonstration Program," in SETP, *1987 Report to*

the Aerospace Profession (Lancaster, CA: The Society of Experimental Test Pilots, 1987), p. 193; Raymer, *Living in the Future*, p. 258.

40. Robinson interview.
41. Wallace, *Nose Up*, p. 37; Miller, *The X-Planes*, p. 319.
42. Ibid., p. 319.
43. Wallace, *Nose Up*, p. 38.
44. Deutsche Aerospace, *Roll Out—Palmdale, USA*, p. 16.
45. Wallace, *Nose Up*, pp. 37–38.
46. Deutsche Aerospace, *Roll Out—Palmdale, USA*, p. 26.
47. Nozzle costs and deflection data from John, "Controlled Flight," p. 511.
48. Robinson interview.
49. Deutsche Aerospace, *Roll Out—Palmdale, USA*, p. 23.
50. Dorr, "Rockwell/MBB X-31," p. 40.
51. Wallace, *Nose Up*, p. 38.
52. Dorr, "Rockwell/MBB X-31," p. 40.
53. Wallace, *Nose Up*, pp. 38–40; and Chambers, *Partners in Freedom*, pp. 219–221.
54. Miller, *The X-Planes*, p. 319.
55. Dorr, "Rockwell/MBB X-31," p. 40.
56. Ibid., p. 41.

The X-31 initiating a Herbst turn during a 1994 test flight. (NASA)

CHAPTER 2

Into the Air:
Initial Flight Testing

With the end of fabrication and roll out, planning for the first flight tests had been under way for some time. The initial airworthiness testing was originally going to be undertaken under Phase IV funding with the rest of the flight-test efforts.[1] Like at the end of Phase II, the funding cycle (on either side of the Atlantic) did not match the initial phaseology, however, so the program adapted to reality and performed the initial testing as part of Phase III. Additionally, when MBB negotiated their contract with BWB, BWB added some initial flight testing to their Phase III as proof that Phase III was successful. This flight testing would clear the conventional flight envelope and consist of the normal flight-test disciplines of pitot static calibrations, flutter testing, load testing, and flight control system testing. Flight control testing was of particular importance because this airplane was statically unstable and relied on the flight control system to maintain the basic stability of the aircraft. The "normal flight envelope" for the aircraft was a 9-g design limit load factor with a dynamic pressure limit of 800 pounds per square foot, up to a Mach number limit of 0.9. The flight control system would initially provide g-limiting of 7.2 g's, which is 80 percent of the design limit when travelling faster than the corner airspeed of approximately 325 knots calibrated airspeed.

As discussed previously, when static ground-load testing of the aircraft was accomplished, the decision was made to test the airplane to 110 percent of the design limit load. This was done on one of the aircraft that was to be flown and not on a dedicated static test article; therefore, the airborne load limit for the airplane was 80 percent of the design limit load, or 7.2 g's (80 percent of 9 g's)—which, ironically, is the F/A-18's g-limit.

The plan for this stage of testing was to use the Air Force Flight Test Center (AFFTC) airspace, with the airplanes based out of the Rockwell facilities at Palmdale, CA, on the Air Force Plant 42 airfield. Interestingly, the Navy had earlier bailed a Vought RF-8G aircraft (the reconnaissance version of the esteemed F-8 naval fighter) to Rockwell for experiments unrelated to the X-31 (but under Mike Robinson's management). Since the plane was still at Rockwell

X-31A over Palmdale's Plant 42 with its RF-8G chase. (Rockwell)

and was being well supported, it was decided to use it as the chase airplane in this portion of the flight-test program.

Preflight Preparations Through Initial Flight Exploration

In the low-cost mode, the flight-test planning targeted a fly rate somewhere between the then-recent YF-16 and X-29 flight-test programs. Initially, the YF-16 program achieved an average fly rate of about 0.8 flights per day, with 100 flights in the first 125 days after first flight. The X-29 program achieved about 0.075 flights per day, with 30 flights accomplished in the first 400 days after first flight. It is important to note that the YF-16 was a prototype-aircraft flight-test program, whereas the X-29 was an experimental, or research, flight-test program. It would be expected that a prototype effort in which the airplane is closer to a production flight article would have a higher flight rate than an experimental aircraft program. At this stage, the planned fly rate for the X-31 was about 0.30 flights per day, or 100 flights in the first 325 days after first flight. Needless to say, this was a very aggressive flight-test schedule for an entirely new experimental research aircraft design. Flight-test support was to be provided through the use of a Rockwell flight-test control room at Palmdale and the Rockwell resources at Palmdale and El Segundo for data reduction. As mentioned in the previous chapter, a flight simulator using a 24-foot dome was available at the Rockwell Downey facility to support flight testing. The two X-31 aircraft were equipped with identical flight-test instrumentation suites that could provide real-time and near-real-time data to the control room.[2]

At this juncture, the test team planned to clear the aircraft's conventional flight envelope and then to move on to do an incremental expansion of the post-stall envelope. The post-stall envelope would include flight up to 70° angle of attack, with rolling maneuvers at 70° angle of attack and "dynamic entries" into the high-AOA regime. Dynamic entries would be aggressive, mimicking the urgency of air combat, with rapid-g-onset maneuvers to the 70° AOA limit. The flight-test organization was a combined test team composed of a Rockwell team leader and an MBB deputy team leader. Members of the flight-test team came from both contractors as well as from the U.S. and German governments. Following the establishment of an adequate post-stall flight envelope, the test program was to move to NAS Patuxent River for the portion of flight test that would involve the evaluation of tactical effectiveness during close-in air-to-air combat. The overall objectives of the flight tests following envelope clearance were to demonstrate and measure Enhanced Fighter Maneuverability performance and to accomplish an evaluation of the X-31 during close-in air-to-air combat. At this time, first flight was scheduled for February 1990. There were to be about 600 flights from both locations (Palmdale and Patuxent River), and the entire program was to be completed in 2 years.

Initial ground testing illuminated a number of technical challenges that needed to be solved prior to the start of taxi testing. These challenges were by no means unusual for the initial checkout of a brand-new aircraft design; however, they did require troubleshooting and the development of appropriate fixes before first flight could occur. The first issue was encountered when the flight control system was engaged for the first time. The flight control surfaces entered a 5° deflection at 4 hertz (Hz). Ground vibration test data showed a 4 Hz "on-gear" pitching mode, and analysis indicated that this mode was coupling with the flight control system to cause the oscillation. The fix to this problem was to stiffen the rate-gyro mounting platform (perhaps surprisingly, given the "high-tech" nature of the program, simple ½-inch marine plywood was used). The oscillation disappeared.

During initial ground testing of the flight control system, the flight control surface motion was jerky, especially with large control surface movements. An interesting solution was devised for this problem. A smoothing filter was used to quiet the control surface motion, but this produced a bandwidth issue with the flight control surfaces, so a digital lead filter was installed upstream of a digital-to-analog converter, followed by an analog lag filter after the digital-to-analog converter. This combined filter fix had no effect on the frequency response of the flight control system, but the jerky surface motion was at least "smoothed."

A potential flight safety issue arose regarding flight control redundancy. The primary source of angle of attack and angle of sideslip for the flight control system was a single-ring laser gyro. The flight control system's redundancy-management system depended upon an internal flag in the inertial navigation unit (INU) to cause the system to switch to the alternate sensing of angle of attack and angle of sideslip that came from the aircraft noseboom. The problem was that this "flag setting" took as long as 200 milliseconds after an INU failure, whereas flight-hardware-in-the-loop simulation testing had shown that the aircraft had a likelihood of controlled-flight departure after only 20 milliseconds of bad data were input to the flight control computers. The fix here was to compare INU body rates and accelerations to flight control system sensors and to reject the INU data in the first instance that it was out of tolerance. With this fix to the INU's redundancy management, the airplane was ready to start its taxi tests.

Taxi testing commenced on June 20, 1990, with a low-speed test. During the test, some flight control computer anomalies arose, as well as a rudder problem. Two medium-speed taxi tests to 80 knots and 85 knots followed, accompanied with steering evaluations. These also uncovered some flight control computer issues and a problem with the "weight-on-wheels" logic—an important input to the aircraft's computer systems. There was objectionable directional sensitivity both with and without nosewheel steering. At about 70 knots, the aircraft started a zigzag oscillation that was deemed unacceptable by the pilot. Both nosewheel steering and rudder pedal response were felt to be too sensitive. Since the X-31 was using an F-16 nosewheel steering control box, it was modified to produce only 10° of deflection, and its sensitivity was also reduced. This became the new "normal" mode. Pilots could still select the original F-16 nosewheel steering mode (±30°) for hard turns. Rudder sensitivity was fixed by lowering the effective rudder pedal to rudder-surface deflection gain at speeds below 110 knots. This seemed to be adequate during subsequent medium- and high-speed taxi tests. The taxi tests progressed to higher speeds with two medium-speed taxi-steering evaluations to 105 knots, including a taxi in the R3 flight control reversion mode to 70 knots. These also identified an R1 reversion-mode problem because the X-axis acceleration-sensing threshold was set too tightly and there was a leading-edge flap failure.

Often in the development of a new aircraft, the test team will avail itself of the services of one of Calspan Corporation's variable-stability Learjets. These are experimental aircraft in which the flight control system has been modified to be programmable to simulate the flight dynamics of the aircraft under development—in this case, the X-31. The test pilots can then fly the variable-stability Learjet and actually observe the flight dynamics of what they can expect to see in the test aircraft. This is a particularly useful tool in preparation for a first flight. Rockwell Chief Test Pilot Norman K. "Ken" Dyson strongly advocated for this resource, but it was not made available due to funding. Dyson did spend many hours in the Rockwell flight simulation dome in preparation for the first flight.[3] Finally, a high-speed taxi test was accomplished on October 3, 1990, that included a drag chute deployment. There were some minor problems with the flight-test instrumentation's data link. This was the final flight readiness test in preparation for first flight.[4]

The first flight of Ship 1 (U.S. Navy [USN] Bureau Number 164584) took place on October 11, 1990, with Ken Dyson at the controls. Dyson was a retired USAF test pilot who had participated in the flight testing of the Lockheed XST Have Blue project, an early stealth demonstrator aircraft and progenitor of the F-117 stealth fighter and many other noteworthy airplanes, including his "low-g fighter," the B-1B. The first flight lasted 38 minutes and attained a little over 300 knots calibrated airspeed and reached an altitude of 10,000 feet mean sea level (MSL). Dyson reported that the aircraft's flying qualities were excellent and matched ground simulation predictions. He cycled the landing gear, and flying qualities were evaluated in both power-approach and cruise configurations. Subsystem performance matched preflight expectations, and after landing, he had only minor maintenance discrepancies to report.[5] The X-31 program was now a flight-testing reality. It should be noted that the X-31 was flown without the thrust-vectoring paddles on this first flight and for several of the initial flights. This was done because an inadvertent hardover of a thrust-vectoring vane on takeoff could cause loss of aircraft control

First landing of the X-31, followed by a T-38 chase airplane. (Rockwell)

and because thrust-vectoring-vane ground clearance during takeoff rotation was critical. Once the thrust-vectoring redundancy management was validated and takeoff and landing tail clearance was observed, the thrust-vectoring vanes were installed.

On November 6, 1990, MBB Chief Test Pilot Dietrich Seeck flew Ship 1 for the first time, followed on November 15, 1990, by Fred Knox, a former Navy fighter pilot and test pilot who had joined Rockwell as an engineering test pilot. In the meantime, Ship 2 (USN Bureau Number 164585) was progressing toward first flight with its series of ground tests and taxi tests. A disturbing event occurred during the first taxi test of Ship 2. As the aircraft accelerated to a relatively high speed, a divergent oscillation occurred in pitch. Two of the flight control system's rate gyros had been wired backward. It was a surprising anomaly, and one that should not have occurred. Previously, other high-performance aircraft had been lost because of installation errors involving control gyros, including a Lockheed A-12 Blackbird and, years later, the first production F-117A stealth fighter. The aircraft was slowed to a stop with no untoward effects. On January 19, 1991, Ship 2 took to the air with Dietrich Seeck at the controls. The very first international X-plane was now an airborne accomplishment!

Assessing the X-31's Basic Flying Qualities

Once the redundancy of the thrust-vectoring system was assured and ground clearance of the vanes on takeoff and landing was determined, the vanes were installed and then flown on the 10th flight of Ship 1 on February 14, 1991, with Ken Dyson at the controls. The vanes were not used to vector thrust on that flight. The initial test with the thrust-vectoring vanes installed consisted of flying with the vanes in a commanded fixed position out of the exhaust plume to validate that vibration, acoustic levels, and temperatures were within thrust-vectoring vane specifications. Following this checkout and postflight evaluation, the X-31 flight-test team would be better positioned to plan the first use of vanes in the exhaust to enhance agility.

With Ships 1 and 2 both active, the program moved quickly along with new international and American pilots. On March 15, 1991, Karl Lang of the Wehrtechnische Dienststelle-61 (WTD-61) at Manching flew the X-31 for the first time.[6]

Following the start of flight envelope clearance, the X-31 test team undertook initial Government Performance Evaluation (GPE) flights even though it was still relatively early in the test program. The concept of a Government Performance Evaluation began as a Navy process whereby a Government pilot would fly an aircraft that was involved in a contractor flight-test program to

X-31 Initial test pilots at Plant 42: (left to right) Fred Knox, Dietrich Seeck, Ken Dyson, and Karl Lang. (Rockwell)

gain an early evaluation of the performance, flying qualities, and systems operation of the aircraft, but only within the flight envelope already cleared by the contractor pilots. In the case of the X-31, U.S. Marine Corps test pilot Maj. Bob Trombadore undertook the first GPE flight on April 24, 1991. German Air Force Maj. Karl-Heinz Mai followed this with a second flight on April 30, 1991, and the two pilots undertook two more flights on May 2 and 3, 1991, to complete the first series of GPE tests.

Initial use of the thrust-vectoring paddles occurred on a test flight on May 31, 1991, with Dietrich Seeck at the controls. These missions were known as "plume line" flights, during which Seeck moved the vanes up to 15° at altitudes from 10,000 to 40,000 feet MSL. The vanes were moved to map the jet plume line as a function of nozzle area and nozzle pressure area. This sort of data was required to produce a table for the flight control computers so that nozzle effects could be included in the flight control computer calculation, a requirement for an integrated flight and propulsion control system. Flights with the vanes automatically tracking the plume line showed that there was no effect on aircraft handling and no uncommanded aircraft movements.

Fred Knox subsequently reported that these early evaluations during the first year of flight testing indicated that the X-31 had excellent handling qualities, particularly in the power-approach configuration; its measured flight-test performance was well matched to preflight ground simulations; it was shown to be a reliable aircraft, easy to fly and operate; and its GE F404 engine was flawless in its operation.[7]

In contrast to Rockwell, however, the German view of the X-31's reliability was less positive. German test team members believed that, despite the use of many "off-the-shelf" components (all of which were flight-certified), flight testing had uncovered many weaknesses and problem areas that needed to be resolved. The majority of flight maintenance squawks or discrepancies in the first 63 flights (representing nearly a year of flying) related to the environmental control system, flight control system hardware and software, and flight-test instrumentation.[8] Since the flight control system was pushing the state of the art in combining flight and thrust control, it is perhaps not surprising that this system should have some difficulty in attaining maturity. Also, since flight-test instrumentation for a given aircraft type is usually a "one-off" design for just that specific aircraft flight test, it is not unusual for there to be flight-test instrumentation problems early in a flight-test program. Maintenance problems did require parts from one airplane to be "borrowed"—or "cannibalized," as the military terms it— more often than was desired. Despite this occasional cannibalization, Rockwell and the Navy consistently provided parts quickly and efficiently through their normal supply channels.

Initial flight clearance limits for the aircraft were set by Naval Air Systems Command, the Navy being DARPA's agent for the program. These initially were an AOA limit of 30°, an altitude limit of 30,000 feet MSL, a Mach limit of 0.67 (365 knots true airspeed), and a structural load limit of just 4 g's. These were gradually expanded to approach the desired conventional envelope of the aircraft, which was an altitude limit of 40,000 ft MSL, Mach limit of 0.9, a structural limit of 7.2 g's, and an AOA limit of 30°.[9] Throughout the clearance of the conventional flight envelope, pilots reported excellent handling qualities; Level 1 handling qualities were reported up to 30° angle of attack with and without use of thrust vectoring. (Flying qualities are reported in varying levels as defined in a military specification, with Level 1 being the best and indicating "[f]lying qualities clearly adequate for the mission flight phase."[10]) While some flying quality anomalies were found in this first year of flight testing, they were not so significant as to impede the ever-so-important envelope expansion. Some of these anomalies are discussed below.

While conducting initial flutter testing, pilots discovered a roll-response asymmetry: there was more roll rate and acceleration to the right than to the left, and roll sensitivity to the right was unacceptable. This sensitivity reflected an almost full-right roll-trim requirement above 300 knots calibrated airspeed that was caused by the flight control law's lateral trim mechanization. This problem was fixed by adjusting the trailing-edge flap rigging to minimize lateral trim requirements and roll-response asymmetry. This provided acceptable roll response and allowed flutter testing up to 500 knots calibrated airspeed. A subsequent software change that modified trim inputs from rate commands to direct position bias was tested in simulation and applied as a permanent fix to the roll-response asymmetry problem.

Overall, project test pilots felt that the pitch and roll response of the aircraft was, in their terms, "snappy" above 300 knots calibrated airspeed. After examining damping, frequency, and bandwidth in the pitch axis, project engineers made adjustments to the stick mechanization. Also, roll-time constants seemed normal, but after a permanent fix to the roll-trim issue, this was evaluated further to determine if a software change would be required to reduce roll-rate onset at high dynamic pressure.

The X-31 had three reversionary modes built into its flight control system because there was limited redundancy in three critical measurement channels. There were only two means of sensing angle of attack and angle of sideslip. Additionally, there was only one inertial navigation unit. Therefore, it was important not only that the reversionary modes operate properly with good handling qualities, but also that there were essentially no transient responses when transitioning from a normal mode to a reversionary mode. The "R1" reversionary mode handled inertial navigation unit failures, the "R2" reversionary mode handled failures of angle-of-attack and angle-of-sideslip sensing, and the "R3" reversionary mode handled air data failures. Intentional flight-test events plus unintentional anomalies allowed assessment of these modes. (There was one failure of the angle-of-attack/angle-of-sideslip sensing that required a landing in the R2 reversionary mode.) On July 12, 1991, Fred Knox was flying a flutter-data-focused flight when an unresetable sideslip data failure caused an R2 request. Fred slowed the airplane and selected R2 with no apparent transient responses. He configured for landing and performed a brief flying qualities evaluation that was satisfactory. Due to relatively high crosswinds on the only available runway at Palmdale and the fact that the X-31 had a fairly high weight due to the high remaining fuel load, the decision was made to land at Edwards AFB. The landing was made uneventfully and the airplane was ferried back to Palmdale 2 days later. These reversionary modes all exhibited Level 1 flying qualities.

During a level deceleration in the R1 reversionary mode (which is the INU failure mode), a 13-Hz surface oscillation occurred as the X-31 passed through 200 knots calibrated airspeed. Postflight analysis revealed a coupling of the noseboom (which furnished secondary AOA sensing) structural mode to the flight control system in the R1 mode. This did not appear in the normal (i.e., INU operating normally) mode because the INU acts as a low-pass filter for the boom signal. This was initially filtered out with a low-pass filter to allow continued expansion of the high-AOA envelope, with the final fix being a notch filter at 13 Hz.

Flutter testing was conducted out to the limiting dynamic pressure of 800 pounds per square foot. The 800-pounds-per-square-foot dynamic pressure line is along the 485 knots equivalent airspeed line, which is equal to 485 knots calibrated airspeed at sea level and Mach 0.9 at approximately 10,100 feet MSL. The flutter excitation was provided by direct electrical commands to the actuators of individual flight control surfaces through a flutter-test box that was a part of the flight-test instrumentation system. This is a normal mechanization on an aircraft with an electronic flight control system. Flutter margins were as predicted and pilots observed that the aircraft's ride quality in turbulence was excellent, allowing for continuation of flutter testing even when atmospheric conditions were somewhat turbulent, as is characteristic of the hot desert afternoons around Edwards AFB and the R-2508 airspace complex.[11]

Flight at high angles of attack while using thrust vectoring was the heart of the X-31's reason for being. As discussed in the first chapter, the program's object was to demonstrate departure-free operations with thrust vectoring on or off (initially at 30° angle of attack or below). Having demonstrated this, the same departure-free characteristics were then to be demonstrated between 30° and 70° with thrust vectoring on. Additionally, the thrust-vectoring system had to exhibit "fail safe" operation above 30° angle of attack. Initially, AOA expansion was conducted to 30° with thrust vectoring off, then with thrust vectoring on. Testing of the thrust-vectoring system started at Mach 0.6 and proceeded to both lower and higher speeds. Since the low-speed side of the flight envelope was as important as the high-speed side, this was a true "build-up" technique to expand the thrust-vectoring envelope. The integrated flight and propulsion control system provided identical flying qualities with thrust vectoring both on and off below an angle of attack of 30°. No differences in flying qualities were expected and, in fact, none were noted once flight testing explored this environment. Instead, the pilots reported that the airplane felt the same whether thrust vectoring was engaged or not. Testers evaluated the X-31's high-AOA handling qualities using the standard flight-test maneuvers of doublets, rolls, steady-heading sideslips, and windup turns. Before flight, engineers had predicted that the X-31 would demonstrate Level 1 handling qualities, and they were validated in full-flight, again confirming the basic fidelity of the preflight modeling and simulation to actual flight-test results. At elevated angles of attack above 13°, the airplane showed light buffet. Rapid pitch step inputs to 20° angle of attack or above produced small, rapid wing drops. Control of angle of attack was reported as precise, and angle of sideslip remained at 4° or less during maximum deflection rolls at 20° angle of attack.

Roll performance at 1 g and elevated g was termed outstanding. As the airplane decelerated to slower flight speeds, the thrust vectoring provided increasing amounts of control power in comparison to the control power generated by its conventional aerodynamic controls. Test pilots characterized the X-31 as "comfortable and solid" during this phase of testing, all the way up to 30° angle of attack.[12] The final test of the integrated flight and propulsion control system was to complete a 360° roll around the velocity vector, which the aircraft executed with extreme accuracy.[13]

Having cleared the conventional envelope, it was time to penetrate the stall barrier and enter the post-stall envelope. On November 21, 1991, during Ship 2's 36th flight, Fred Knox flew the airplane to 40° angle of attack. This was near the maximum lift coefficient for the aircraft and is most critical because sudden airflow detachment or a vortex "burst" at that point could cause real surprises. Unfortunately, a computer failure triggered the automatic recovery mode, terminating post-stall flight before Knox could explore this regime in detail.[14]

The day before Knox's foray to high AOA, a new series of GPE flights began. U.S. Navy Cmdr. Al Groves joined the test team, and between November 20, 1991, and December 13, 1991, Groves and Lang completed seven GPE flights. At this stage, there were seven pilots that had flown in the two-airplane test program and, though this was an unusually high number of pilots for a program involving only two aircraft, even more pilots were soon to be added. A large number of pilots on a program of this size has its plusses and minuses. On the plus side, pilots representing all of the stakeholders (contractor and government [NASA, Navy, USAF, German Air Force]) have an opportunity to fly and comment on the airplane. This is ultimately good for the test team, which is trying to obtain data that often takes the form of pilot commentary. On the minus side, it is difficult for the pilots to maintain "currency" of recent experience in flying the test airplane. This can be mitigated by having the pilots also fly often in similar-type aircraft. It has been the author's experience that often there are too few pilots rather than too many, and if one gets sick or is reassigned, a scheduling crisis must be averted.

Whither X-31? Program Relocation to Dryden

As the year 1991 drew to a close, the program and its testers could take great satisfaction in what they had accomplished, including a final flight that year in the post-stall envelope up to 52° angle of attack. At this point, the two X-31 aircraft had flown 108 flights in 428 calendar days, roughly 1 flight every 4 days.[15] But while this was, at first glance, a pretty impressive fly rate, it was still much less than the projected 100 flights in 325 days—0.30 flights per day—that was originally projected during test planning. Thus, though much had, in fact, been accomplished, there was a feeling within the X-31 program office and test team that it was moving too slowly. It had taken over a year to achieve conventional envelope clearance and post-stall flight up to 52° angle of attack.[16] While the engineers and test pilots were gradually expanding the envelope by flying in a controlled fashion well beyond the stall, the managers in Washington were struggling mightily to keep the program alive.

There were two fundamental reasons program personnel believed that the program was in trouble. As mentioned previously, the Navy (through NAVAIR) granted clearances for each test flight, starting with the very minimal envelope of 30,000 feet MSL, Mach 0.67, and 4 g's that were set early in the program. The Navy's procedure for flight-test clearance was largely developed for testing prototypes of operational aircraft, and the process was focused on minimizing program risk by taking a careful, incremental approach, building up only gradually to maximum performance. Rockwell, MBB, and DARPA all felt that this process was too slow for a purely experimental airplane program and that the slowness of progress itself was putting the program at risk, as there was a fear that program funding would dry up.

Furthermore, the Navy, while initially anointed with the job of military agent for DARPA in the X-31 program, had many overriding fiscal priorities that had a more immediate impact on their operational fleet aircraft, particularly in dealing with its aging F-14 Tomcat fleet (which was being converted to "Bombcats" after the Gulf War) and shepherding advanced models of the F/A-18 into service. So even as the X-31 flight-test program plodded along in 1991, there was a funding crisis developing, one in which the Navy could not be expected to go to any great lengths to support the tiny jet in the desert.

As a consequence, the DARPA program manager, Tack Nix, initiated talks with personnel at the NASA Ames-Dryden Flight Research Facility (now known as the Dryden Flight Research Center) about moving the X-31 flight-test program from Palmdale to the Dryden facility at Edwards AFB. Moving to Dryden had support from both DARPA and the German test establishment (WTD-61). Dryden possessed extensive flight-test facilities, including specialized control rooms and data-reduction facilities, and was in the midst of constructing a new building specifically designed for the integration of research teams and research components. This facility, the Integrated Test Facility (ITF), was designed specifically to support development of hardware and software, and the testing, analysis, and flight qualification of advanced aircraft having highly integrated flight and propulsion control systems. Another advantage was that this building offered a facility where program management, engineering support, and even the aircraft all could be located under one roof.

Other advantages to testing at Dryden were that the program would remain out west and have the benefits of the great weather and expansive R-2508

NASA Dryden Integrated Test Facility, 1991. (NASA DFRC)

flight-test range airspace that was available at Edwards AFB. In addition to the fact that the weather, on average, was poorer at NAS Patuxent River than at Edwards AFB, there also was the problem that the focus at Patuxent River was on programs that could have a direct bearing on higher-priority operational fleet aircraft, whereas the main focus at Dryden was on testing unconventional research airplanes. Therefore, in the daily scheduling battle for flight-test resources, the advantage would be at Dryden, where testing this type of aircraft was the primary mission of the Center and not simply an "add on" to existing (and likely higher priority) operationally focused flight-test programs. The ultimate type of testing that the X-31 would perform (i.e., dogfighting) was not something that Dryden typically did. They were used to performing in a more "pure research" mode. Dryden also was focused on data quality, not schedule pressures and airplane fly rate.

Very apparent to DARPA, which had just completed the X-29 program with NASA, was the financial benefit of testing at Dryden; this constituted, in fact, the biggest advantage of moving to Dryden. In the early 1990s, there were two different methods of accounting, or "charging," for resources used in a flight-test program. One method was known as "institutional" funding, in which an organization received an annual budget amount for its operation and the organization's managers determined how to support the various programs that were assigned to them. The other method was a "reimbursable" method whereby the flight-test customer was charged for each test resource as it was used.

The reimbursable method was often known as "full cost accounting" and was intended to provide managers and funding authorities (like Congress) with the knowledge of the real costs of a program. This method also expanded into charging program partners for the "services" provided to a program.

The institutional method was the method in use at that time for many NASA Centers, including Dryden. The method used by the military, including NAS Patuxent River and contractors, was the reimbursable method. Therefore, Dryden could absorb the overhead cost of its personnel and support services into its institutional overhead, saving the X-31 program an enormous amount of money. When the International Test Organization (ITO) was created for the X-31, Dryden Director Ken Szalai could decide what charges to pass through to the ITO. For example, there were no charges to the ITO for building space, NASA engineers and test pilots, or NASA chase aircraft and their fuel costs. The ITO was charged, though, for the additional computers required to build the X-31 simulator at Dryden and any necessary new equipment that was specific to the X-31 program.[17] It has been noted that, through Dryden, NASA contributed the equivalent of $14.9 million to the X-31 program in terms of indirect (personnel and support services) support.[18]

As might be expected, the Navy's flight-test community was less happy with the plans to move to Dryden, as they had expected to undertake post-stall envelope expansion at Patuxent River. At this time, the plan was still to move the aircraft back to Patuxent for the tactical utility portion of the program. As noted above, DARPA and WTD-61 were in favor of the move, but Rockwell and MBB had some hesitancy with the prospect of going to Dryden. Rockwell's experience with Dryden during the HiMAT program, and both companies' close observation of the X-29 program, was that NASA could become so involved in the details of doing the research that schedules and progress often slowed considerably. On the other hand, Dryden had considerable experience in conducting flight tests of nonproduction research aircraft, and since flight clearance authority was to transfer from the Navy to Dryden, it was felt that the flight clearance process could potentially proceed much faster than the rate being experienced.

Even so, there were a few even within NASA who remained unconvinced that moving the X-31 to Dryden was a good move. This minority felt that the tactical utility emphasis of the X-31 made the program a better fit for the military test community rather than NASA, whose main interest (in their view) was pure research data gathering. However, NASA Dryden—and the NACA High-Speed Flight Station that had preceded it—had long engaged in programs directly related to tactical utility, including the extensive pitch-up studies NACA had undertaken on combat aircraft such as the F-86 in the 1950s. At the time this minidebate occurred, Dryden was in the midst of two

Grumman X-29 forward-swept wing test bed. (AFFTC)

other high-AOA programs: the X-29 forward-swept wing, which had just finished its flights, and the F/A-18 High Alpha Research Vehicle. The X-29 was a DARPA research program with Dryden as the responsible test organization that had as its primary objective an understanding of the benefits and risks of aircraft configurations having forward-swept wings. While flight at high angles of attack was not the primary objective of this program, the X-29 was operated at angles of attack up to 52°.

The F/A-18 HARV was an F/A-18 modified with paddles similar to the X-31's; however, the installation on the F/A-18 HARV was very heavy, and while the F/A-18 HARV did yeoman work in exploring the high-AOA regime, including three-dimensional thrust vectoring, it did not have the performance of the X-31. The X-31 had a 40 percent higher thrust-to-weight ratio, a 35 percent lower wing loading, a 30 percent higher maximum g-limit, and twice the thrust-vectoring control power of the F/A-18 HARV. Thus, the X-31 offered NASA engineers the ability to explore areas of thrust-vectoring flight at very high angles of attack that they could not achieve with either the X-29 or the F/A-18 HARV. This was the part of the X-31 program that was attractive to the Dryden engineers.[19]

As the test team at Palmdale was slowly expanding the flight envelope for the X-31, DARPA in mid-1991 had made the decision to move the program to Dryden and make both NASA and the Air Force partners in the program.

NASA F/A-18 High Alpha Research Vehicle, 1996. (NASA DFRC)

On January 20, 1992, both X-31 aircraft flew in formation, piloted by Fred Knox and Dietrich Seeck, on a ferry flight from Palmdale to the Dryden facility at Edwards AFB, just 40 miles away. It would turn out that this was the only time that both aircraft were flown together.[20]

Shortly after the move took place, the reticent industry members' resistance melted away. This was because of two NASA managers who saw the reticence and understood why it was there. These two, Ken Szalai (director of Dryden) and Gary Trippensee (the designated NASA X-31 program manager), dedicated themselves to doing things differently to support the X-31 goals and objectives. They deftly managed their own team to change to the "new" approach and proved true to their word, becoming stalwarts of the program.

Program Expansion: Probing the Post-Stall Environment

With the addition of NASA and the USAF as X-31 partners, things had become even more complicated. The X-31 team now consisted of contractors (Rockwell and MBB), governmental agencies (DARPA, NASA, and the German MOD), military services (the U.S. Navy, USAF, and the German Air Force), and flight-test agencies (Dryden, WTD-61, NAS Patuxent River, and the Air Force Flight Test Center). In order to manage all of this, the various partners established an official International Test Organization that attempted to promote cooperative decision making with no single person as the "chief." The logo that was developed was an oval shape with no single entity at the "top." The structure of this organization will be discussed in later sections.

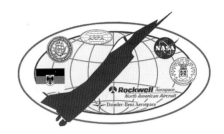

X-31 International Test Organization logo. (NASA DFRC)

The move to Dryden brought with it a change in the responsibility for aircraft maintenance from Rockwell to Dryden and for flight clearance authority from NAVAIR to Dryden. It now took even more time for the aircraft to be inspected and the systems to be understood by Dryden personnel so that the flight clearance activity could be started. By April 1992, the aircraft was deemed ready for its first flight under the auspices of the ITO. On April 23, 1992, Karl Lang took to the air in Ship 2 for a systems-checkout flight that included flying qualities in all three reversionary modes.

The X-31 program was still very fragile. Funding was always a concern, and for this reason DARPA managers wanted to move forward with some deliberate speed. Col. Michael Francis, USAF, who had replaced Tack Nix as DARPA program manager, was concerned that "the flight safety community wanted to baby-step us," which would lead to delay and complication.[21] But NASA had sound reasons—including flight safety and data-reduction quality—for not rushing along. However, the financial reality was that delays could cause the program's cancelation. There was the constant pull and tug of finding the right balance between "safe," "perfect," and "good enough" that plagues all flight-test programs, but perhaps affects research programs to a greater extent.[22] In an attempt to address safety concerns and to develop some milestones for the post-stall envelope program, Francis held an offsite meeting in nearby Lancaster, CA, between May 19 and 20, 1992. This planning session reviewed the program goals and the current program status, prioritizing the following flight-test objectives for the post-stall envelope expansion:

- Demonstrate dynamic post-stall flight,
- Assess unique EFM technologies (agility, the vehicle, human-machine interface), and
- Prepare for the tactical evaluation.

Test planners discussed the maneuvers that needed to be demonstrated to complete the dynamic post-stall flight envelope clearance, acknowledging that the envelope had to be gradually expanded so that areas of concern were adequately characterized. They named these demonstration maneuvers "maneuver milestones," and these consisted of the following:

- Deceleration to 70° angle of attack at 1 g;
- Full deflection, 1-g rolls at 70° angle of attack (executing this maneuver contractually completed Phase III of the program);
- Dynamic, level turn entry to post-stall from corner speed; and
- Turn-optimized/gravity-assisted post-stall maneuver to 180° heading change (this maneuver would subsequently receive the moniker, the "Herbst turn").

Planners also discussed concerns over insufficient roll control at high angles of attack, along with the planned addition of strakes on the aft fuselage as a fix. The above maneuver milestones assumed that this roll-control problem would be fixed by the strake installation. There was some discussion of the methodology for conducting the follow-on tactical evaluations. Interestingly, it was agreed that, ideally, flying one X-31 against the other with only one of the aircraft using thrust vectoring would provide the best technical assessment of the program (though, as mentioned previously, this subsequently did not take place).[23]

Since Dryden and the Air Force Flight Test Center were now partners in the test effort, it was time to get their test pilots checked out in the airplane. Rogers Smith from Dryden flew his first checkout flight on June 4, 1992, followed by Lt. Col. Jim Wisneski, USAF from AFFTC, on June 9, 1992.

As the post-stall envelope expansion continued, testers evinced continuing concern that the effectiveness of the trailing-edge elevons was different than had been predicted before flight. This had been noted in the initial testing at Palmdale, as was discussed previously.[24] This was a serious issue because most delta-wing aircraft (including the X-31) do not have separate ailerons (for roll) and elevators (for pitch). Rather, they use a single surface called an elevon (for *elev*ator-aile*ron*) that combines both functions. Operated differentially, an elevon furnishes roll control; operated symmetrically, it furnishes pitch control. The difference between the predicted and actual trailing-edge elevon deflection necessary to hold a trim angle of attack at increasingly high angles was as much as 10° greater than predicted.

This problem meant that there now was insufficient elevon control authority left to provide adequate roll control. Elevon deflections available for roll control were reduced by 50 percent. The nose-down aerodynamic safety margin was also reduced. How could the preflight prediction have been so out of synch with postflight reality? It was discovered that the X-31 wind tunnel model was connected to the wind tunnel's mounting device by two attachment rods located along the aft fuselage of the model. These rods themselves contributed a nose-down pitching moment to the wind tunnel model. Since the actual aircraft did not have these rods, the airplane did not have the nose-down pitching influence of the rods. Langley engineers quickly provided a fix to this problem. They designed two aft strakes that were 4 feet long and attached to the aft fuselage between the trailing edge of the elevons and the nozzle area. These strakes were tested on the existing 19-percent scale model of the X-31 in the NASA Langley 30- by 60-foot wind tunnel, which validated that the strakes indeed returned the pitching moments to the required values.[25] The strakes were fabricated out of plywood sandwiched between two metal sheets and then covered with fiberglass. The initial flight with the strakes attached

X-31 without aft fuselage strakes, 1992. (NASA DFRC)

X-31 with aft fuselage strakes. (NASA DFRC)

was flown on September 10, 1992, with Navy test pilot Al Groves. Flight-test results confirmed the new tunnel predictions, and testing was now able to safely continue expanding the post-stall envelope to 70°.

The X-31 achieved its maximum design angle of attack of 70° during a flight by Groves on September 18, 1992. Groves decelerated and stabilized the aircraft at 70° angle of attack for approximately 40 seconds. This was subsequently repeated by Karl-Heinz Lang and Rogers Smith on the same day. Additional aircraft controllability was demonstrated on September 22, 1992, when Fred Knox performed 30° bank-to-bank rolling maneuvers at 70° angle of attack.[26] The goal now was to demonstrate "agility" at high angles of attack, which is the ability to energetically and rapidly maneuver from one flight condition to another. This was accomplished on November 6, 1992, during a flight by Fred Knox in which he performed 360° rolls about the velocity vector while the airplane was flying at 70° angle of attack.[27] With this particular accomplishment, the X-31 had truly entered a regime of flight where no other conventional aircraft had been.

During the expansion to high angles of attack, the pilots noticed several "lurches," or dramatic changes in roll rate with a constant roll command on the stick. Engineers experimented with fixing this by placing "grit strips" (strips with a sandpaper-like surface to activate airflow in the boundary layer around the forebody) on the radome and on the noseboom. They suspected that vortex shedding off the radome or noseboom was causing these lurches and hoped to control it with the grit strips. The results were mixed. In some cases, no lurches were noted while in others, the change in roll rate was substantial.

The next area to explore was the so-called "dynamic entry." Researchers realized that in actual combat, fighter pilots would enter the high-AOA regime in an aggressive manner, likely with relatively high rates of g-onset. The high-AOA testing of the X-31 to date had been with relatively slow decelerations to the desired angle of attack. The same approach was used in rolling the aircraft, whereby the airplane would be slowed to achieve the target angle of attack and would then be rolled through the desired roll angle. As noted, Fred Knox reached 360° of roll at 70° angle of attack. Now it was time to achieve post-stall flight with a dynamic entry more representative of what would be encountered in an actual combat-maneuvering entry.

The method of achieving a dynamic entry was to roll the airplane inverted and then abruptly apply full-aft stick to attain the desired angle of attack as set on the AOA limiter. Naturally, if an angle of attack in excess of 30° was desired, the post-stall switch on the control stick had to be actuated. The first attempt at a dynamic entry was flown by the Air Force member of the team, Jim Wisneski, on November 25, 1992. This first entry was to attain an approximately 2-g post-stall entry and was followed by some other maneuvers.

X-31 in high-AOA flight, 1994. (NASA DFRC)

Then a rude and unanticipated surprise occurred. As reported by Rockwell flight-test engineer David Rodrigues,

> The first maneuver was performed at 35,000 feet / 0.4 Mach and consisted of a full aft pitch input from inverted flight with maximum afterburner set and the angle of attack limiter set at 45° (a split S maneuver). This maneuver was repeated for additional data. The angle of attack limiter was then set to 60° angle of attack for the next split S. During the next maneuver, PST was inadvertently disengaged, limiting the angle of attack to 30°. A recovery was made and the aircraft set up to repeat the split S to 60°. This maneuver was again at 35,000 feet / 0.4 Mach with afterburner set. *The aircraft stabilized momentarily at about 60° degrees but was yawing to the right and continued to departure from control with increasing angle of attack and yaw rate.* [Emphasis added.] The pilot initiated recovery with forward stick as a recovery call was issued from control. The aircraft immediately responded to the forward stick and with angle of attack reduction, the yaw rate damped to zero, completing recovery of the aircraft to controlled flight. No failures were noted in the aircraft and no engine or other system anomalies were noted during the departure.[28]

The departure came as a shock to mission planners, for the X-31 was designed to avoid doing just that! Fortunately, the aircraft recovered after 320° of turn due to the excellent nose-down pitch authority provided by the thrust-vectoring system.[29] Analysis showed that the departure was probably caused by a large, unexpected yawing moment that was generated from the forebody of the airplane, a problem encountered on earlier programs such as the Northrop F-5E Tiger II development effort and the early F-15E Strike Eagle program (the former because of forebody shape and the latter because of an asymmetrically offset flight-test pitot noseboom). Wind tunnel tests at NASA Langley showed that the X-31's nose configuration could have very nonlinear and unstable yawing-moment characteristics due to the influence of asymmetric vortices coming off the nose. These vortices could impart asymmetric drag, effectively "pulling" the nose to one side or the other and triggering a departure from controlled flight. This testing also showed that rounding of the nosecone on the airplane and the addition of 20-inch strakes along the nose would provide adequate directional characteristics above 50° angle of attack.[30] Grit strips were also added to the nose, as had been done previously to help make the vortices more uniform and predictable in behavior.

Postflight analysis of the incident from a flight control perspective resulted in changes to the flight control software to prevent sideslip buildup as well as to increase the thrust-vectoring control power.[31] Technicians increased thrust-vector vane travel from 27° to 34°, allowing a greater amount of thrust deflection.[32] The 27° limit prevented the vanes from hitting each other during operation.[33] (It should be noted that changes to the flight control software are not unusual in flight-test programs, and, indeed, the X-31 had 32 software releases over the course of the program; such is the nature of research aircraft programs in the electronic flight control era.)[34] On February 9, 1993, Jim Wisneski again took the X-31 into the elevated-entry regime with a buildup of split-S maneuvers to 50°, 55°, 60°, 65°, and ultimately 70° angles of attack. No problems were encountered on any of the elevated-g tests, even at the higher AOA marks.[35]

Harvey Schellenger, a Rockwell engineer who joined the program early on as it moved from Columbus to Los Angeles and later became chief engineer and then acting program manager of the EFM program, recalled to the author that solving these high-AOA vortex-shedding issues constituted an "interesting story":

> The low speed wind tunnel model had a nose with a small radius. The aircraft also had a small radius, but after correcting for scale, the wind tunnel model radius was larger (on the order of a large marble at full scale). We saw no indication of large yaw asymmetries in the wind tunnel tests, but the aircraft had a yawing departure in flight. Back into the Langley [30- by 60-foot] tunnel with a bit of clay to sharpen the model nose, and the asymmetry showed up. We rounded the noses of the aircraft to match the original w-t [wind tunnel] model—plus a little, to about a golf ball. We also added strakes as sized in the tunnel but I think that just rounding would have been enough. The approach was to hit it with a big hammer and make sure it would not return, so it was rounding with strakes and back in the air. Aircraft 1 was rock steady from then on, but A/C 2 still showed a little "nervousness" in yaw at high AoA. Because of this the pilots started calling it the "evil twin". We were about to give up on A/C 2 and concentrate on just A/C 1 ops when I noticed that we had somehow not rounded 2's nose as much as 1's. How we missed this I can't explain, but we did. And the strakes didn't cover it up – not completely. We're talking pretty small differences here. From way back in the memory bank: the original radius was about 0.1", the final was ≅ 0.7", and the evil twin was initially ≅ 0.4. Changing A/C 2 to match A/C 1 completely eliminated the "nervousness" and we had a two plane program again.[36]

Illustrating the criticality of nose shaping, Patrick "Pat" Stoliker, an engineer on the X-31 at the time and now deputy director of Dryden, recalled, "The two aircraft had different grit strip configurations (Ship 2 needing a longer strip). Ship 1 had 20-inch strakes while 47-inch strakes were used on Ship 2."[37]

As testing progressed, changes in the air data–sensing system were made as well. Since the pitot-static-sensing function (as well as the angle-of-attack and angle-of-sideslip vanes) was expected to be unreliable at the high angles of attack anticipated for X-31 operations, the INU was used to provide estimated angle-of-attack, angle-of-sideslip, and dynamic pressure figures. Postflight data analysis showed large errors in angle of attack, angle of sideslip, and airspeed due to wind shifts. While this did not degrade flying qualities, it did make the monitoring of flight control system performance difficult, and it caused several maneuver aborts through erratic data input. Consequently, testers decided to modify the noseboom to provide usable data. With the original boom, the AOA vane was usable to 70° angle of attack, but the sideslip vane had large oscillations at 60° angle of attack. Indicated airspeed was always at the minimum of 48 knots when the airplane was above 60° angle of attack. The design change resulted in the installation of the Kiel airspeed probe at a 10° nose-down attitude. Additionally, technicians mounted the sideslip vane on a wedge to provide it with a 20° nose-down attitude. Therefore, at 70° angle of attack, the sideslip vane remained below 60° and pilots no longer saw the sideslip oscillations.

The new noseboom configuration provided good angle of attack, angle of sideslip, and airspeed throughout the X-31 envelope, including post-stall flight to 70° and –5° angles of attack.[38] At the time, there was not a heated

Kiel probe canted to compensate for high angles of attack. (NASA DFRC)

Kiel probe "collar" to "collect" pitot pressure at high AOA. (NASA DFRC)

version of the Kiel probe. The test team made the decision not to wait to have a heated version manufactured; therefore, in changing the noseboom configuration, technicians installed the new "canted" noseboom knowing that it was not heated. This was not considered to be problematic because the X-31 only flew in clear-sky day testing. This later would have dire consequences, highlighting yet again that in flight testing and flight research, one cannot be too careful in preflight mission planning and instrumenting research airplanes.

Since MBB engineers had the responsibility for flight control law development, and because their technique (which differed from the American approach) relied largely on mathematical prediction of the aircraft's response, it was important as envelope expansion progressed for the German test contingent to understand the values of the aircraft's aerodynamic parameters. Aerodynamic parameters are called "coefficients" and are determined by measuring various forces and moments produced by the aircraft and then normalizing them by dividing by dynamic pressure, a reference area (usually wing area), and, in the case of moments, a reference length. Such calculations naturally depend on accurate measurements of the forces and moments acting on the airplane. As might be expected, the accurate and repeatable measurement of these forces and moments in the post-stall arena proved to be difficult due to the very dynamic and nonlinear nature of aerodynamic flow conditions above stall speed. Several different techniques were employed to establish these coefficient parameters. Researchers tried both closed- and open-loop time-history matching, as well as maximum likelihood estimators.[39]

The problems in aerodynamic parameter identification arose from the fact that the airplane was unstable, making it difficult to merely integrate the mathematical state equations for the aircraft. Additionally, aircraft parameters and control parameters are highly correlated, so individual parameters often cannot be estimated independently. There was a large amount of noise due to vortices shedding from the aircraft nose forebody that contaminated the data further, complicating data acquisition and reliable analysis. Finally, the aircraft motion was not often sufficiently excited for parameter identification because the excellent flight control system suppressed all undesired motions, such as sideslip onset and excursions. So, somewhat ironically, the data gathering was actually hampered by the superior design of the flight control system![40] In the end, no single technique for parameter identification was particularly effective; however, combining the results of all of the techniques (coupled with good intuitive engineering judgment) provided usable estimates of the aerodynamic coefficients. Nevertheless, as a consequence, the analysis and design of a flight control system optimized for post-stall flight conditions was very challenging due to the difficulty of accurately determining aerodynamic coefficients. This forced a less desirable and necessarily more imprecise design capable of handling the large unknowns in aerodynamic coefficients encountered during the X-31's high-AOA flights.[41]

Human-factors issues posed a parallel concern during envelope expansion. These involved both physiological and spatial orientation issues. Early in the design of the aircraft, designers were concerned that flight motions might be unacceptable for the X-31's test pilots and that the seat's motion restraints would be insufficient given the high pitch, roll, and yaw rates that the airplane was likely to develop. However, test pilots reported that body-axis yaw rates of 50° per second at 70° angle of attack proved comfortable and required little adaptation, even though these approximated maximum-rate body-axis roll at the maximum angle of attack. Pilot restraints were also deemed adequate. Spatial disorientation during the very dynamic post-stall maneuvering was also an early design concern; however, again pilots did not have a problem maintaining orientation and, hence, situational awareness. Since the aircraft was flown in visual conditions, good visual ground reference plus the use of the F/A-18-derivative head up display (HUD) with some minor format modifications were adequate for maintaining good spatial orientation. Some pilots wanted improved velocity vector cueing during post-stall maneuvering. As discussed subsequently, this and other display issues led to tests of a special helmet-mounted display (HMD) and a three-dimensional audio system on the X-31.[42]

The final "maneuver milestone" to be accomplished was the awkwardly named "turn optimized/gravity assisted post stall maneuver to 180° heading change," which came to be known as the "Herbst turn," after the man whose dream of flying controllably beyond the stall limit had led to the X-31. The Herbst turn is difficult to describe in words or even in diagrams and really needs to be seen to be appreciated. The maneuver starts at relatively high speed (Mach 0.5 or greater). The aircraft is then decelerated very rapidly by pulling up and increasing the angle of attack. The airplane exceeds the conventional stall limit of maximum coefficient of lift and requires thrust vectoring to maintain control. Angle of attack is increased (in the case of the X-31, to the maximum limit of 70°). At this point, the aircraft is at a pitch attitude of about 70° as well, but the velocity vector is nearly parallel to the horizon. The pilot then commands a roll around the velocity vector, changing the heading of the aircraft 180° and thus reversing the heading of the airplane. The pilot then lowers the nose and, using the high thrust-to-weight ratio of the airplane, rapidly accelerates to high-speed flying in the opposite direction from which the maneuver was initiated. German test pilot Karl Lang from WTD-61 first performed a Herbst turn on April 29, 1993, demonstrating that it was more than just wishful thinking.[43] With the accomplishment of the Herbst turn, the X-31 had ushered in a new spring in aeronautical agility. It had met its final maneuver milestone. Now, ahead loomed the tactical evaluation.

X-31 initiating a Herbst turn, 1994. (NASA DFRC)

Endnotes

1. Dietrich Seeck and Ken Dyson, "An Introduction to the X-31," in SETP, *1989 Report to the Aerospace Profession*, (Lancaster, CA: The Society of Experimental Test Pilots, 1989), p. 112.
2. Ibid., p. 120.
3. Ken Dyson and Fred Knox, interview by Douglas A. Joyce, March 24, 2011.
4. Fred D. Knox, "X-31 Flight Test Update," SETP, *1991 Report to the Aerospace Profession* (Lancaster, CA: The Society of Experimental Test Pilots, 1987), pp. 88–90.
5. Ibid., pp. 90–92.
6. WTD-61 is an abbreviation for the German Technical and Airworthiness Center for Aircraft, which is subordinate to the Bundesamt für Wehrtechnik und Beschaffung (Federal Office for Defence Technology and Procurement, BWB).
7. Knox, "X-31 Flight Test Update," p. 90.
8. Deutsche Aerospace, *X-31—From Roll-out to Tactical Evaluation—A German View* (Munich: Deutsche Aerospace AG, n.d.), p. 8.
9. Dorr, "Rockwell/MBB X-31," p. 43.
10. Jan Roskam, *Airplane Flight Dynamics and Automatic Flight Controls—Part I* (Lawrence, KA: Roskam Aviation and Engineering Corporation, 1979), p. 536.
11. R-2508 is the airspace used for Edwards flight test. See R-2508 Joint Policy & Planning Board, *R-2508 Complex Airspace Briefing* (Edwards AFB, CA: AFFTC, April 23, 2010), *http://www.edwards. af.mil/shared/media/document/AFD-090812-039.pdf*, accessed September 28, 2011.
12. Knox, "X-31 Flight Test Update," pp. 90–93.
13. Deutsche Aerospace, *Roll-out to Tactical Evaluation—A German View*, p. 9.
14. Ibid., p. 10.
15. Fred Knox, Cmdr. Al Groves, USN, Rogers Smith, and Lt. Col. Jim Wisneski, USAF, "X-31 Flight Test Update," SETP, *1993 Report to the Aerospace Profession* (Lancaster, CA: The Society of Experimental Test Pilots, 1993), p. 102.
16. Dorr, "Rockwell/MBB X-31," p. 43.
17. Rogers Smith, e-mail to Douglas A. Joyce, June 28, 2011, author's personal files.
18. Wallace, *Nose Up*, p. 41.
19. Ibid.

20. Ibid.
21. Dorr, "Rockwell/MBB X-31," p. 44.
22. Wallace, *Nose Up*, p. 43.
23. DARPA Memo, "X-31 Flight Test Planning Offsite Results," May 20, 1992, DFRC Archives.
24. Deutsche Aerospace, *Roll-out to Tactical Evaluation—A German View*, p. 12.
25. Knox, Groves, Smith, and Wisneski, "X-31 Flight Test Update," p. 104.
26. NASA Memorandum for Correspondents, September 28, 1992, DFRC Archives.
27. Miller, *The X-Planes*, p. 320.
28. David Rodrigues, "X-31A Flight 2-73 Report,"(November 25, 1992), p. 1, DFRC Archives.
29. Knox, Groves, Smith, and Wisneski, "X-31 Flight Test Update," p. 104.
30. Ibid.
31. Rockwell International Memorandum, "Yaw Control Prior to 2-73 Departure," December 11, 1992, DFRC Archives.
32. Wallace, *Nose Up*, p. 44.
33. Dorr, "Rockwell/MBB X-31," p. 45.
34. Wallace, *Nose Up*, p. 44.
35. David Rodrigues, "X-31A Flight 1-106 Report," (February 9, 1993), DFRC Archives.
36. Harvey Schellenger, e-mail to Douglas A. Joyce, January 3, 2012.
37. Patrick Stoliker, e-mail to Douglas A. Joyce, August 17, 2012.
38. Knox, Groves, Smith, and Wisneski, "X-31 Flight Test Update," p. 105.
39. Ibid., p. 106.
40. S. Weiss, D. Rohlf, E. Plaetschke, "Parameter Identification for X-31A at High Angles of Attack," Deutsche Forschungsanstalt für Luft und Raumfahrt (DLR) Institute of Flight Mechanics (n.d. circa 4th Quarter 1992), DFRC Archives, p. 3.
41. Knox, Groves, Smith, and Wisneski, "X-31 Flight Test Update," p. 106.
42. Ibid., p. 106.
43. Wallace, *Nose Up*, pp. 45–46.

The X-31 rolling inverted over Edwards Air Force Base. (NASA)

CHAPTER 3

Expanding the X-31's Research Program

The tactical evaluation would either prove or belie the fundamental tenet of the program—that post-stall maneuverability would provide a significant close-in-combat (CIC) air-combat advantage that was heretofore unattainable. This segment of the X-31 program was key to its success. Identifying the utility of post-stall maneuvering to the tactical fighter pilot was arguably the most important end result of the program. As envelope expansion was progressing from 1991 to early 1993, preparations were being made for the tactical utility testing. The first effort during the X-31 program that explored dogfighting with a thrust-vectored airplane was a piloted simulation conducted in Munich, Germany, at the Industrieanlagen Betriebsgesellschaft (IABG) Ottobrunn dual-dome facility. The IABG facility was another low-cost approach to the program; since it already had been used extensively in early PST development, the amount of work required to configure the simulation was minimal. In fact, the same facility had been used to demonstrate PST to key U.S. players during the effort to get the initial feasibility contract sold. The IABG simulation included aircraft noise as well as visual projection of aircraft motion. Two cockpits were housed in separate domes for use by the evaluator pilots, and the facility included a control and briefing system.

This initial X-31 tactical evaluation simulation effort was conducted in September and October 1991, even before the test program moved to Dryden. The objectives of this piloted simulation included the following:

- Have the X-31 evaluated by tactical pilots from the U.S. Navy, U.S. Air Force, and German Air Force (GAF).
- Develop a method and requirements for the tactical evaluation of a demonstrator aircraft that does not have any avionics (i.e., sensors such as infrared, radar, etc.) or armament provisions.
- Fly close-in-combat engagements against a dissimilar opponent, the F/A-18.
- Determine postflight analysis tools.
- Develop starting conditions and suitable post-stall tactics and maneuvers.

- Develop rules of engagement for the safe conduct of the evaluation flights.

Four pilots (one Navy, two USAF, and one GAF), as well as operational analysts from MBB and Rockwell, participated in this simulation effort, which came to be known as "Pinball I." The results of this simulation testing were very encouraging and provided input for the development of an Integrated Simulation and Flight Test Plan that was developed by the ITO team following the move to Dryden.[1] Early in the following year, a Pinball II simulation was conducted to establish a database and to define the upcoming tactical utility flight tests to be conducted by the X-31.

The Pinball Simulations

The Pinball I testing identified four principal setup conditions for starting a CIC engagement. These included the following:

- Defensive—Starting airspeed of 325 knots calibrated airspeed, with adversary having a nose-on position toward the X-31 at 3,000 feet range.
- Offensive—Starting airspeed of 325 knots calibrated airspeed, with the X-31 having a nose-on position toward the adversary aircraft at 3,000 feet range.
- High-Speed Line-Abreast—Starting airspeed of 400 knots calibrated airspeed, line-abreast in same direction of flight separated by 6,000 feet range.
- Slow-Speed Line-Abreast—Starting airspeed of 250 knots calibrated airspeed, line-abreast in same direction of flight separated by 3,000 feet range.

Planners believed that these starting conditions would allow post-stall flight during engagements that could be used and evaluated over a range of initial conditions.

Since the X-31 was not an operational weapons system with radar, infrared missiles, and an onboard gun system, it was necessary to establish what conditions constituted a "kill" for evaluation purposes. This "rule of thumb" (ROT) weapons system (as it came to be known among X-31 insiders) established parameters such as the minimum tracking time required for a kill, the missile's maximum allowable off-boresight angle, the missile's maximum allowable angle of attack, and the minimum and maximum ranges for both gun and missile engagements.[2] For example, the ROT required that the X-31's simulated gunsight (the pilot's view through the HUD) had to dwell on the target for 1 full second to be scored as a gun kill.[3]

Even prior to Pinball I, the X-31 test team had decided that the principal adversary aircraft would be the F/A-18. The F/A-18 was a standard Navy and Marine Corps fighter in service with several foreign air forces, and it typified an advanced fourth-generation fighter configuration. If the tactical testing was done at Patuxent River, the ready availability of F/A-18 aircraft would make its use as an adversary a virtually foregone conclusion. Additionally, it served as a high-performance research test bed and chase aircraft for the NASA Dryden Flight Research Center, thus making it a convenient research associate for the X-31 if the program remained at Dryden.

Ideally, the best evaluation would have been flying one X-31 that was using thrust vectoring against the other X-31 that was not using thrust vectoring. In this situation, the only variable other than pilots' skill would be the use of thrust vectoring, and this would have constituted a convenient means of assessing the value of thrust vectoring as a singularity in air-combat maneuvering. But the record of "simultaneous" research aircraft had been poor since the earliest days of the X-series, and the X-31 proved no exception to this. As the early flight-test program progressed, the X-31 test team realized that it would be very difficult (i.e., cost and schedule inefficient) to have both X-31 aircraft available for flight at the same time.[4] This was due to the frequent maintenance inspections required on these experimental aircraft, the various modifications and other normal maintenance actions required, and the use of the aircraft to perform necessary ground tests in support of flight testing. Another factor was the limited availability of spare parts—technicians often had to "cannibalize" parts from one aircraft to keep the other flying. Another important consideration was the potential for a midair collision, which is always a possibility when participating in close-in-combat evaluation or training. If a midair involving the only two X-31 aircraft in existence occurred, the program would be ended once and for all.[5]

Both the NASA F/A-18 and the X-31 had to be instrumented for the tactical utility testing by equipping them with C-band beacons to improve their tracking by ground-based radars. This was necessary because Edward AFB (and NAS Patuxent River, for that matter) was not equipped with the air combat maneuvering instrumentation (ACMI) range that is typical of tactical fighter training ranges such as Nellis Air Force Base, NV. An ACMI range had airborne equipment aboard the aircraft (usually installed in a pod of similar dimensions to an AIM-9 missile and mounted on an AIM-9 wingtip or underwing missile station) as well as ground-based receiving and display systems, where the results of aircraft in tactical combat situations (i.e., dogfighting) can be observed in real time as well as in playback. Lacking this type of system at the flight-test location, NASA engineers had to develop a "pseudo-ACMI" capability with the C-band tracking beacons as well as the onboard aircraft parametric data (pitch, roll, yaw, heading, altitude, airspeed, etc.).

NASA F/A-18 safety chase and mission support aircraft. (NASA DFRC)

Initial Pinball I testing showed that the conventional performance capability of the single-engine X-31 was inferior to that of a "clean" (tank- and missile-free) twin-engine F/A-18. This would cause difficulties in testing because it tended to inhibit the air-to-air engagements from progressing to the low-speed arena, where the X-31's post-stall capabilities could be assessed.[6] In order to establish a more even start point for the engagements, the simulation researchers uploaded the F/A-18 with a centerline external fuel tank and two wing pylons in an attempt to more closely match the conventional flight performance of the X-31 and the F/A-18.[7]

Thus, the Pinball I simulations consisted of dual-dome engagements between an X-31 utilizing post-stall capability and either an F/A-18 configured with a matching conventional performance or an X-31 lacking post-stall maneuver capability. Many combinations of adversaries and "fight's on" setups were evaluated to assess the effectiveness of a post-stall aircraft versus a non-post-stall aircraft and to develop procedures for conducting flight tests, as noted in the objectives above.[8]

The flight envelope to be used during the tactical utility testing was a subset of the envelope that had been cleared for post-stall maneuvering prior to the start of tactical utility testing. To review, at this stage of the program, the cleared *conventional* flight envelope was 800 pounds per square foot dynamic pressure ("q" in engineering shorthand) to Mach 0.9 up to 40,000 feet MSL and 1 g at 30° angle of attack. The *post-stall* envelope was defined as 5.3 g's at 70° angle of attack up to Mach 0.7 and 40,000 feet MSL and 1 g at 70° angle of attack. For tactical testing, the maximum speed was selected as 225 knots calibrated airspeed with a minimum airspeed of 70 knots true airspeed, which was selected because that was the lowest airspeed that the air data computer could calculate. The maximum altitude was selected to be 30,000 feet MSL because engagements were planned to start at 23,000 feet MSL and 30,000 feet was the maximum altitude expected in the engagements. The minimum altitude was selected as 13,000 feet MSL to enable recoveries from post-stall to less than 30° angle of attack prior to reaching 11,000 feet MSL. It was assumed that a recovery from post-stall maneuvering to the conventional envelope (30° angle of attack) would take approximately 2,000 feet. The 11,000-feet requirement was based on the rule that post-stall flight could only be flown above 10,000 feet above ground level (AGL) for flight safety reasons.[9]

Pinball II, the second piloted simulation effort supporting the X-31 flight-test program, was also conducted at the IABG dual-dome facility, or Dual-Flug-Simulator (DFS), between April 19 and 30, 1993, both adding to the statistical database of post-stall engagements and serving as an efficient tool for test planning of the Tactical Utility Flight Test (TUFT) program. The objectives of Pinball II were to support the Tactical Utility Flight Test program by

- validating the starting conditions for the engagements to be used in the TUFT program;
- validating/training optimum maneuvers to be used to demonstrate tactical utility;
- verifying rules of engagement, safety limitations, and training requirements;
- training pilots and engineers for TUFT;
- analyzing the X-31's tactical utility by comparing its performance with and without post-stall technologies while flying against the F/A-18; and
- evaluating how proposed modifications to the X-31 that provided it with an improved "high-lift" configuration contributed to tactical utility.

The X-31 was simulated in four variations: in baseline configurations, both with and without PST, and in "high-lift" configurations with and without PST. The F/A-18 was modeled in a configuration that was thought to be representative of an F/A-18 that had completed a bombing run and was egressing the target area. The configuration of the F/A-18 (for T/W-ratio and drag purposes) had a starting weight of 34,000 pounds and had external stores of two AIM-7 Sparrow air-to-air missiles and five empty weapons pylons. This F/A-18 configuration came to be known as the "modified fighter escort" (MFE) configuration. For simulation purposes, the X-31 had an initial weight of 14,600 pounds. The F/A-18's weight corresponded to a fuel fraction of 66 percent, and the X-31's weight corresponded to a fuel fraction of 50 percent. These fuel fractions were set to represent equal amounts of fuel burned from takeoff to the start of the engagements.[10] Again, as in Pinball I, simulation planners sought to model the "conventional" F/A-18 and the X-31 aircraft in the assessment to have similar basic performance characteristics so that the fight would quickly degrade to the slow-speed, high-AOA "knife-fight in a phone booth" arena where post-stall thrust-vectoring utility could be evaluated.

The Pinball II tests identified four principal setup conditions for starting a CIC engagement:

- Defensive—Starting airspeed of 325 knots calibrated airspeed, with the adversary having a nose-on position toward the X-31 at 3,000 feet range
- Offensive—Starting airspeed of 325 knots calibrated airspeed, with the X-31 having a nose-on position toward the adversary aircraft at 3,000 feet range
- High Speed Line-Abreast—Starting airspeed of 325 knots calibrated airspeed, line-abreast in the same direction of flight separated by 3,000 feet range
- Slow Speed Line-Abreast—Starting airspeed of 215 knots calibrated airspeed, line-abreast in the same direction of flight separated by 1,500 feet range

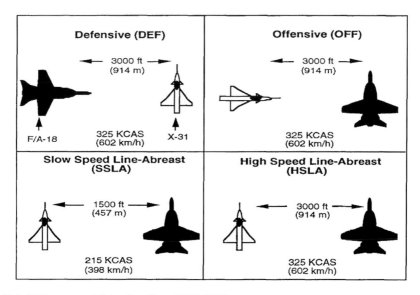

Pinball II Engagement Setup Condition. (NASA DFRC)

Later, as the evaluation developed and "guest pilots" were brought in, a "butterfly" setup was suggested in which both aircraft started out line-abreast, executed a heading-change turn away from each other, and then reversed to approach head-on with about 1,000 feet of lateral separation. The "engagement" portion of a butterfly setup starts when the aircraft pass line-abreast and each attempts to turn onto the tail of the other, resulting in a closing spiral that quickly goes to high g, low speeds, and high AOA. There is no evidence that this butterfly setup was used in the Pinball II evaluation, but a butterfly setup is very typical of an engagement setup used during actual fighter close-in-combat tactical training. (Readers should note that the Pinball II starting conditions were slightly different from the Pinball I starting conditions.)[11] The rationale for this change is not documented; however, because the change reduced the range separation in the high-speed line-abreast setup from 6,000 feet to 3,000 feet, one can surmise that it was done in an effort to force a close-in dogfight.

The Pinball II evaluation was undertaken by eight pilots, which included the six X-31 International Test Organization pilots as of April 1993 as well as two new "guest pilots," who were not test pilots but were experienced fighter pilots from the operational fighter community in the USAF and U.S. Navy. The pilots were Fred Knox, Rockwell International, ITO pilot; Rogers Smith, NASA Dryden Flight Research Center, ITO pilot; Cmdr. Al Groves, USN, ITO pilot; Lt. Col. Jim Wisneski, USAF, ITO pilot; Maj. Quirin Kim, German Air Force, ITO pilot; Karl Lang, German Federal Ministry of Defense, ITO pilot; Maj. Derek Hess, USAF, guest pilot; and Lt. Steve Schmidt, USN, guest pilot. The ITO pilots, while experienced test pilots, were also former operational fighter pilots. The guest pilots came directly from the operational fighter community with very recent fighter experience.

In scheduling the pilot simulator sorties, the eight pilots were divided into two groups, with one group flying the first week and the second group flying the second week. During a given week of participation, the first 3 days were spent on pilot training and the remaining 2 days were spent conducting CIC engagements. The training component included aircraft familiarization flights, single-ship tactical maneuver training, and basic fighter maneuver (BFM) training using a cooperative target. The following 2 days included unlimited CIC engagements. The altitude for all starting conditions was 20,000 feet MSL. Six CIC cases were examined during Pinball II—three with the baseline X-31 configuration and three with the improved "high-lift" configuration. These six configurations consisted of the following:

- Baseline X-31 with post-stall technology versus the F/A-18 MFE
- Baseline X-31 with post-stall technology versus the X-31 without post-stall technology
- Baseline X-31 without post-stall technology versus the F/A-18 MFE
- High-lift X-31 with post-stall technology versus the F/A-18 MFE

- High-lift X-31 with post-stall technology versus the high-lift X-31 without post-stall technology
- High-lift X-31 without post-stall technology versus the F/A-18 MFE[12]

As mentioned in the discussion of Pinball I, since the X-31 did not have any sort of offensive capabilities, a rule-of-thumb weapons system that included simulated weapons and delivery envelopes needed to be created so that the engagements could be scored. For Pinball II, the simulated weapons were four short-range air-to-air missiles (assumed to be infrared-seeking, such as the AIM-9 Sidewinder) and a rapid-firing cannon with 200 rounds of 27-millimeter ammunition like the Mauser BK-27, the cannon employed on the Panavia Tornado and the Eurofighter Typhoon. The "sight picture" firing criteria for the cannon was a minimum tracking time of 0.2 seconds before trigger squeeze, with the F/A-18 located within the 2-millimeter gunsight pipper on the HUD. Additionally, two snapshots would equal a kill. For the missile, the minimum tracking time was 0.5 seconds after trigger squeeze, with a maximum angle of attack of 30° and a maximum off-boresight angle of 30°. The gun envelope was further defined by the rule that head-on gun attacks would not be permitted, thereby denying target aspects in the 0° to 45° range. For guns within the envelope of a target aspect of 45° to 180°, evaluators imposed a minimum range of 500 feet and a maximum range of 3,000 feet. Likewise, for the missile on a head-on aspect of 0° to 20°, a minimum range of 9,000 feet was imposed, as was a maximum range of 6 nautical miles. In the target aspect range of 20° to 60°, a minimum range of 5,000 feet and a maximum range of 6 nautical miles were imposed. For a target aspect range of 60° to 120°, a minimum range of 3,500 feet and a maximum range of 4 nautical miles imposed. Finally, for the tail-on aspect of 120° to 180°, a minimum range of 2,000 feet and a maximum range of 2 nautical miles were imposed. Thus, the parameters for weapons "employment" for the X-31 were defined. These weapons-loading and firing envelopes were nominal for the types of gun and short-range (infrared) missiles in use in the early 1990s.[13]

As is accepted international practice in military air-to-air training, testing, and evaluation engagements, mission planners developed a set of rules of engagement, primarily for safety reasons, even though this was just a simulation. One might question the validity of some of these rules since the X-31–F/A-18 encounters were "just" a simulation; however, one of the objectives of this simulation was to "verify Rules of Engagement, safety limitations, and training requirements" for the Tactical Utility Flight Test program.[14] A maneuver floor of 10,000 feet AGL was imposed for the duration of the simulation—the same floor used in actual flight testing over Edwards AFB airspace. The X-31 tactical utility flight testing was to occur in a unique test area at Edwards AFB comprised of three designated spin areas within R-2508 north of the base.[15] The following rules of engagement were implemented:

- Opposing aircraft were to come no closer than 500 feet range to each other (during the simulation, this would result in a simulation freeze).
- No head-on gun attacks would be allowed (i.e., the target aspect angle had to be less than 45°).
- On a head-on pass, both aircraft were to clear to the right (i.e., a left-to-left pass). If unsure, the pilot was to call his intentions.
- The aircraft with the higher nose position was to go high if there were an approach to the same airspace.
- The downhill "chaser" aircraft would be responsible for monitoring the altitude of the fight.
- No "blind" lead turns would be allowed.
- If situations required a ballistic flightpath for one aircraft, the pilot was to call it and the other aircraft was obligated to maneuver away.
- Any aircraft that loses sight of the other aircraft was to call "lost sight" immediately.
- Anyone could call a "knock-it-off" (terminate the fight) for any reason.

During the actual in-flight tactical utility flight test, two additional rules of engagement were added as an extra precaution:

- The aircraft that is up-Sun would be responsible for collision avoidance.
- A "knock-it-off" was to be called for any of the following occurrences:
  - A non-participating aircraft entered the engagement area.
  - A stalemate in the fight developed.
  - The test objectives for the engagement were met, or no more useful testing could be attained from the engagement.
  - The minimum altitude was reached by either aircraft.
  - Any aircraft lost its radio capability (known as a "NORDO" situation). In this case, the NORDO aircraft stopped fighting and maintained 1-g flight while rocking its wings.
  - An aircraft was overstressed.
  - Bingo fuel was reached ("Bingo" fuel is the fuel state at which a return to base must be initiated).[16]

During the simulation exercise, there were 12 different pilot combinations available. Since four pilots would be flying in each week of simulation, a "pilot combination" would be when one pilot was flying the F/A-18 (or X-31 without post-stall technology) against the other three pilots flying the X-31 with post-stall technology. Thus, there were four groups with three pairings of pilots in each group, giving an overall total of 12 pilot combinations in each week. With 12 pilot combinations flying each of the four starting conditions, it was possible to fly 48 engagements for each of the six cases that had been developed. A total of 240 engagements were flown with the baseline X-31 configuration, and 192 engagements were flown with the X-31 in the modified high-lift configuration.

During the evaluation of the results of this simulation testing, several primary and secondary measures of effectiveness were developed to allow for the analysis of the engagements. The first of the primary measures of effectiveness was the exchange ratio, defined as the number of "Red" losses divided by the number of "Blue" losses, in which the Red aircraft were defined as either the F/A-18 or the X-31 *without* post-stall technology, and the Blue aircraft was the X-31 *with* post-stall technology. Exchange ratio will be the only measure of effectiveness discussed herein. A weapon kill was scored when the rule-of-thumb weapons system criteria and envelope were met for the weapon selected. In addition, a "ground kill" was scored when the target aircraft penetrated the 10,000-feet AGL hard deck. This was based on the assumption that the target aircraft's pilot must have been forced into the "ground" by his lack of situational awareness or aircraft energy due to the threat presented by the opponent.[17]

As summarized below, when the X-31 was pitted against the F/A-18, the overall simulation results showed that the use of post-stall technology provided a clear improvement in CIC. The exchange ratio for the X-31 without post-stall technology against the F/A-18 was 0.37, and the exchange ratio improved to 1.83 for the X-31 with post-stall technology against the F/A-18.

The post-stall technology gave the X-31's pilot the capability to quickly change his maneuvering plane relative to the F/A-18 to reduce his turn radius inside that of the F/A-18, and the increased nose-pointing ability of the X-31 with post-stall technology allowed the pilot to threaten the F/A-18 to the point where the F/A-18's pilot had to abandon the close fight to ensure survival.

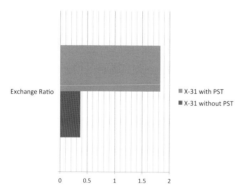

X-31 exchange ratio versus NASA F/A-18. (Joyce)

Simulations of the X-31 with post-stall technology against the conventional F/A-18 that examined the individual start conditions in greater detail provided further insight into both the dynamics of the encounters and the advantage of PST. Whenever the X-31 with post-stall technology began the fight in a defensive position, the exchange ratio was only 0.36. (This starting condition was defined as 325 knots calibrated airspeed at a nose-on range of 3,000 feet, with the F/A-18 aggressor in firing range.) Even though the X-31 has the ability to maneuver immediately, it is at a distinct disadvantage because the F/A-18 is able to shoot immediately.

But when the X-31 with post-stall technology was in the offensive position, again immediately within range to fire, the statistics changed dramatically; the X-31 garnered an 8.5-to-1 exchange ratio, approximately equivalent to the air-to-air advantage enjoyed by the North American F-86 Sabre over the Soviet MiG-15 in the Korean War, though that historic exchange ratio was driven more by differences in opposing pilot quality than by differences in opposing technologies (the Sabre did, however, have a much better flight control system). The post-stall technology allowed the X-31 to maneuver into the F/A-18's vulnerable rear quarter without overshooting, and the additional pointing capability provided by the post-stall technology provides early and frequent shot opportunities.

During the slow-speed line-abreast starting condition (with the two opposing aircraft on parallel line-abreast flight tracks 1,500 feet apart at 215 knots calibrated airspeed), both aircraft began in a neutral position inside the so-called "phone booth" that fighter pilots use to refer to a slow-speed, close-in fight. In this case, the X-31 with post-stall technology achieved a spectacular 16-to-1 exchange ratio, all the more impressive since this simulation reflected "fights" between superlative pilots who could be expected to exploit every advantage of their opposing airframes. Again, the starting conditions gave the X-31 the opportunity to exploit the post-stall technology advantages of a small turn radius, high turn rate, and high velocity vector roll rate, which were most advantageous in this condition because it would otherwise be considered "neutral" compared to aircraft with equal conventional performance. This starting condition essentially turned what might be considered a "neutral" start into an "offensive" start.

When the line-abreast starting condition was changed to the "high-speed line-abreast" (with a starting airspeed of 325 knots calibrated airspeed and a separation range of 3,000 feet), the results showed more evening, with an exchange ratio of 0.86 for the X-31 with post-stall technology against the F/A-18. Here the greater speed and greater separation ranges afforded by this starting condition (since the X-31 is at a much higher speed than allowed for post-stall flight) kept the fight on a more conventional basis, decreasing the number of post-stall maneuvering opportunities for the X-31. In this starting arena, the F/A-18's conventional performance advantages effectively equalized the X-31's post-stall performance advantage, highlighting that PST technology, on its own, was insufficient to offset a high-performance conventional design. PST thus had to be incorporated as an integrated element of aircraft design.

Fokker Dr I triplane, the world's first supermaneuvering aircraft. (National Museum of the USAF)

In effect, this was the "rediscovery" of a nearly 80-year-old lesson dating to the Western Front during the Great War. Then, the famed Fokker Dr I triplane was capable of supermaneuvering post-stall pointing and shooting, but pilots of conventional fighter aircraft such as the British S.E. 5a and the French SPAD XIII learned to offset it by exploiting the greater power and speed of their fighters to extend and attack in slashing strikes that nullified the Fokker's maneuverability advantage, thus denying it the ability to pick and choose the time and place of conflict, and even the ability to break off a fight once it had engaged with the foe.[18]

Overall, combining all starting simulation conditions, the X-31 with PST demonstrated a 1.83-to-1 exchange ratio over the F/A-18—an impressive accomplishment by any measure. But when the post-stall technologies were

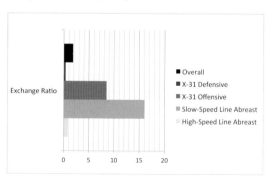

Exchange ratios at differing start conditions with PST. (Joyce)

taken away, the overall exchange ratio dropped to 0.37, a testimony to the basic mediocrity of its underpowered design as compared to the more powerful F/A-18, which had a more suitable high-lift dogfighting wing planform.

For the X-31 without post-stall technology, the defensive exchange ratio dropped to just 0.2, the offensive to 1.25 (little better than parity), the slow-speed line-abreast to 0.25, and the high-speed line-abreast to 0.85. This change clearly demonstrated the advantage of having post-stall technology in the X-31 and how much it contributed to the close-in-combat effectiveness of the X-31. Additionally, a look at the probability-of-survival and probability-of-kill data shows that the use of post-stall technology nearly doubled these probabilities for the X-31.

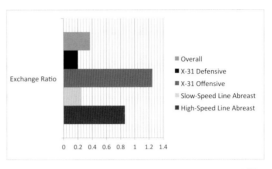

Exchange ratios at differing start conditions without PST. (Joyce)

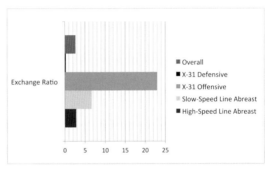

Exchange ratios at differing start conditions, X-31 with PST vs. X-31 without PST. (Joyce)

One obvious question inspired by these simulation results is, "What if the X-31 with post-stall technology encountered an X-31 without it?" As with the engagements against the F/A-18, simulations of a PST X-31 versus a non-PST X-31 clearly demonstrated the advantage of having post-stall technology. When the X-31 with post-stall technology is in the defensive position, the exchange rate is 0.27, again due to the very disadvantageous starting condition. But the offensive starting condition resulted in a *23-to-1* exchange ratio. Here, the X-31 with post-stall technology not only had a very advantageous starting condition, but it also afforded its pilot the ability to maneuver to great advantage. In the so-called "neutral" starting conditions of slow-speed line-abreast and high-speed line-abreast (which would be expected to be equal—1.0—for equally performing aircraft), the exchange ratios were 6.67 and 2.8, respectively, which clearly highlights the advantage of having PST when all other factors are equal. Overall, the X-31 with post-stall technology demonstrated a 2.67-to-1 combined kill ratio against the identical X-31 lacking PST, nearly three times better than the "conventional" fighter variant.[19]

It is interesting to compare the differences in the results between Pinball I and Pinball II (note that the data available was for exchange ratio in all engagements). For the "defensive" starting condition, Pinball I gave an exchange ratio of 1.2 while Pinball II gave an exchange ratio of 0.47. This was attributed to a difference in the use of post-stall technology on the initial move because in Pinball II, use of post-stall technology was limited during the initial move. The use of post-stall technology was prevalent during the initial move in Pinball I, however, thus contributing to the better exchange ratio. The data from the offensive starting condition was nearly identical, with 22 for Pinball I and 23 for Pinball II. For the slow-speed line-abreast starting condition, the Pinball I results showed 20 while the Pinball II showed 6.67. The high-speed line-abreast starting condition gave a 1.5 exchange ratio in Pinball I and a 2.8 exchange ratio in Pinball II.[20] While some of the differences in these simulations were a bit surprising, they portended that there would be a lot to learn from the upcoming flight tests.

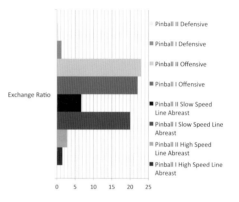

Exchange ratio, Pinball I vs. Pinball II. (Joyce)

Flight researchers recognized that an X-31 in a high-lift (HL) configuration could have dramatically increased lift below 30° angle of attack. Without post-stall technology, the HL X-31 would perform better than the baseline X-31 against the F/A-18. On the other hand, simulations showed that the HL X-31, even with post-stall technology was slightly less effective against the F/A-18 because pilots were giving up post-stall opportunities by trying to fly in the high-lift mode. Pilots with the ability to exploit high lift would fly in the post-stall mode until the fight went low, then they would fly below 30° angle of attack and use high lift to avoid hitting the 10,000-feet hard deck. In this condition, the fight would progress into a conventional (i.e., below 30° angle of attack) fight where high lift was helpful. However, since the high-lift advantages did not show up in the post-stall-flight part of the engagements, and since the primary advantage of the X-31 was in post-stall flight, the international X-31 test community decided not to spend the time and money required to implement high lift on the X-31.[21]

Starting Condition	Exchange Ratio Increase with Post-Stall Technology over non-Post-Stall Technology
Defensive	80%
Slow-Speed Line-Abreast	6,300%
Offensive	580%
High-Speed Line-Abreast	244%

Exchange ratio increase, PST vs. non-PST. (Joyce)

From Pinball to TUFT

In an attempt to provide meaningful flight-test recommendations from Pinball II for use in the flight-test portion of the tactical utility flight test, the various starting conditions were thoroughly analyzed to determine which provided the most efficient and useful setups. Any starting condition that demonstrated little or no improvement in effectiveness was eliminated, thereby tightening the focus and increasing the efficiency of the flight-test program.

The data from Pinball II, when taken as a whole, indicated that each starting condition provided a unique opportunity to demonstrate the tactical benefits of post-stall technology. Exchange ratio data showed an 80-percent increase with post-stall technology relative to non-post-stall technology in the defensive starting condition, increasing to a remarkable *6,300-percent* increase in the slow-speed line-abreast starting condition. The offensive and high-speed line-abreast scenarios showed increases of 580 percent and 244 percent, respectively. (This might be expected because the slow-speed line-abreast starting condition was intuitively the most "neutral" of the starting conditions and is, in a separation/airspeed arena, most conducive to forcing the fight into a slower, turning engagement.) Of course, the flight-test planners had to consider other "real world" factors that would be present during flight tests but were not present in simulations. These included flight-envelope restrictions, safety-of-flight issues, the ease of test and technical setup, and post-stall tactical use.

These real-world factors all constituted important inputs into the tactical utility flight-test planning as well. As an example of an envelope restriction, the actual X-31 aircraft was restricted to a post-stall entry speed of 225 knots calibrated maximum airspeed, whereas the maximum during the Pinball II simulation had been a much faster 325 knots calibrated airspeed. This restriction alone resulted in a 30 percent reduction in post-stall use compared to what was experienced in Pinball II. Only the slow-speed line-abreast condition was not significantly affected by the 225-knot calibrated airspeed restriction. Overall, the Pinball II data analysis resulted in the following priority for tactical utility flight-test starting conditions: slow-speed line-abreast, defensive, high-speed line-abreast, and offensive.[22]

The slow-speed line-abreast held the highest priority as a starting condition. It was the only one not affected by the 225-knot-calibrated-airspeed post-stall entry restriction, and in Pinball II it was the starting condition that provided the greatest difference in results when comparing post-stall technologies to non-post-stall technologies. It was the starting condition that was most likely to show that post-stall maneuvering would allow the X-31 to turn a losing condition (if the X-31 was restricted to non-post-stall-technology use) into a winning condition (provided post-stall technology was used). Pinball II results showed that the X-31, when limited to non-post-stall technology, would lose four out of five engagements, yet the exchange rate would flip to 16 to 1 with post-stall technology. Therefore, it could be assumed that the X-31 would have a high likelihood of beating the F/A-18 in a slow-speed line-abreast starting condition. One caution that was noted with this starting condition was the increased risk of midair collision due to both the slow speed and the fact that in this starting condition, the initial move tends to force both airplanes to immediately head toward each other despite an already-small separation distance.

Use of post-stall technology in the defensive starting condition during Pinball I showed significant potential, but the results from Pinball II were not as promising. The exchange ratio for the X-31 using post-stall technology against the X-31 not using post-stall technology was 1.2 in Pinball I versus 0.47 for Pinball II. This was attributed to the inconsistent way that post-stall technology was used for this starting condition in Pinball II. During Pinball I, a standard initial move was used that usually neutralized the attacker's advantage and turned the defensive start into an offensive situation for the X-31. This initial move was used only occasionally in Pinball II, however, so the results were not as favorable for the X-31 using post-stall technologies. Again, if the fight started at 325 knots calibrated airspeed, it was above the 225-knot calibrated airspeed maximum post-stall-entry speed, thereby limiting the ability to demonstrate the benefits of post-stall maneuvering for this starting condition. Also, it is important to note that both the offensive and defensive starting conditions are difficult to set up in flight. Since the crossing angles are 90° and the closure rates are high, it takes considerable timing to achieve a specific separation range at 90° aspect angle at a given airspeed. The attacking airplane often ends up in a less-than-exact starting condition in a turn with considerable bank angle, and thus the attacker may be in an even more advantageous position.

In a simulation, of course, the starting conditions can be set up exactly prior to "unfreezing" the simulator's computer at the "fight's on" call.

Due to the high airspeed and significant separation range, the high-speed line-abreast starting condition generally led to a conventional fight, resulting in a series of near-neutral head-on passes. Using post-stall technology, a J-turn could often be performed at one of the neutral passes. The J-turn is essentially the Herbst maneuver described in a previous chapter, and it allows the post-stall-capable X-31 to rapidly reverse its flightpath to gain a 6-o'clock advantage over an opponent. During Pinball II, pilots were able to use this maneuver at the first pass above 225 knots calibrated airspeed with some success. In flight tests, it was postulated that use of this maneuver at the second head-on pass could allow the pilot to remain within the 225-knot calibrated-airspeed restriction, but that each succeeding head-on pass would allow the F/A-18 to gain energy and therefore a tactical advantage. Pinball II analyzers felt that the post-stall airspeed restriction, coupled with the F/A-18's better conventional performance, would limit the demonstration of post-stall tactical utility for this starting condition.

The offensive starting condition also demonstrated the increased effectiveness of post-stall technologies during the Pinball II simulation, but this starting condition did not really stress the post-stall capability of the X-31. The use of post-stall technologies in the offensive starting condition was primarily used in the mid-AOA region (i.e., 30° to 45°), which was used to increase lift and drag in order to maintain a position behind the target aircraft. This condition did not really emphasize the total post-stall capability, which, at these conditions, is most obvious at very high angles of attack (up to 70°) with a velocity roll. The advantages of post-stall technologies were also much more obvious when the X-31 started from a neutral or defensive position from which the use of post-stall technologies resulted in a win. Given a limited number of flight-test engagements, program planners felt that it would be difficult to statistically quantify the increase in winning between conventional performance and post-stall technologies. Regardless, the Pinball II data analysts did not suggest eliminating this starting condition.

Pinball II recommended that a minimum of 24 flights be flown in the tactical utility flight tests, with each of the six ITO pilots flying in each of the starting conditions. It was assumed that three or four engagements would be flown on each flight, with one or two of these identified for data-analysis purposes. It was strongly suggested that the test conditions for the 24 flights be as close as possible to the conditions flown during Pinball I and Pinball II so that the vast amount of data obtained in all three campaigns could be validated and statistically compared. It was recommended that there be a set of defined initial maneuver options established for each starting condition.

This was recommended in an effort to force the fight into the post-stall regime quickly and to prevent a conventional dogfight from occurring. It was suggested that these maneuvers be rehearsed in a domed simulator.[23]

NASA Dryden did not have a domed simulator; the IABG was the only facility in the X-31 program that had a twin-dome facility at a single location. However, Rockwell Downey and Patuxent River each had single-dome facilities. Rockwell's dome had been used in support of the X-31 since the start of the program. Patuxent River's facility was regularly used to support the X-31 and the F/A-18, as well as other programs.[24] It was recommended that these two facilities be linked together via computer networks. The advantage of having this type of facility available would be the large increase in available data points. In particular, the more detailed assessment of the impact of post-stall entry speed (225 knots calibrated airspeed, as limited by the post-stall flight-test envelope, or 325 knots calibrated airspeed, as used in Pinball II) would be possible. It was hoped that this capability would make flight testing more efficient and enable better starting setups while eliminating many surprises that might be experienced due to entry-speed restrictions. At this juncture, there was talk of incorporating a helmet-mounted display into the test program because the availability of a twin-dome capability would allow for an evaluation of the helmet-mounted display and for the development of a statistically significant amount of data using this helmet display to support eventual flight tests. The concept of linking the Downey and Patuxent River domes was proven in 1993; however, there still were significant equipment problems, and this potential capability was never used in support of the program.

The Pinball II simulation resulted in several recommendations concerning the maneuvers to be flown during the tactical utility flight tests. Of the planned maneuvers that evolved during the X-31 test program, three were felt not to stress the post-stall capability of the X-31 and two were judged not to contribute to the tactical utility of post-stall technology. For these reasons, the Pinball II team recommended that such maneuvers be eliminated from the flight-test portion of the tactical utility demonstration. The first three maneuvers were the "optimum loop," the "split-S (at maximum pitch rate)," and the "split-S (at tactical rate)." The optimum loop is a maneuver in which the aircraft is pulled up into a loop at a moderate g-rate (3 g's in this case) and a moderate angle of attack (for the X-31, 15° to 17°) and then, when the aircraft is inverted, is pulled to 70° angle of attack. A heading-change velocity roll can also be performed on the back side of this loop. The split-S maneuvers resemble the classic aerobatic split-S (starting from inverted flight with a pull to level flight upright—e.g., one half of a loop) except that they are done at different pitch rates. The primary value of these maneuvers was as a means to demonstrate some of the post-stall capability of the X-31 to new pilots, although X-31 neophytes could not be familiarized with the entire range of capabilities presented by the aircraft. Since split-S maneuvers are highly stylized, two-dimensional, single-axis exercises that are not typically seen in air-combat maneuvering (which is usually much more focused on the dynamic blending of pitch, roll, and yaw), they could not familiarize pilots with the multiaxis, three-dimensional, post-stall capabilities available to the X-31 for BFM and CIC engagements, as would be expected in the tactical utility flight tests.

In addition to the significant flight-test guidance provided by the simulations, the flight-test planners also rejected such crowd-pleasing maneuvers as the Hammerhead Turn and the Pugachev Cobra. Neither had been incorporated into the Pinball II simulation effort, and they were eliminated from the tactical utility flight-test evaluation as well. The Hammerhead Turn was a classic aerobatic maneuver, a quarter loop to the vertical followed by a 180° yaw (either to the left or right) to nose-fully-down and then completion of the turn. The Cobra was a maneuver popularized by Sukhoi design bureau test pilot Victor Pugachev that demonstrated the power and control capability of the Su-27 Flanker. At various airshows, he and other Sukhoi pilots would rapidly pitch-up a Flanker to angles of attack in excess of 90° and then, just as rapidly, pitch down to recover into level flight by using the combination of power and control to avoid a nose slice or falling off into a spin. Both the Hammerhead and Cobra are impressive maneuvers for airshows, but neither had tactical utility. In any case, the Cobra maneuver was impossible for the X-31 to perform due to the combination of its 70° AOA limit and its 25°-per-second pitch-rate limit.[25]

The tactical maneuvers that were selected for use in the flight-test portion of the tactical utility phase were the pitch-rate reserve, J-turn (the Herbst maneuver), helicopter (helo) gun attack, and the flat scissors.

The "pitch-rate reserve" maneuver affects what fighter pilots often refer to as "nose pointing authority," which is the ability to further increase the angle of attack from the current flight condition to allow a gun-firing or missile-firing solution. The difference with the X-31 was the great change in angle of attack available from the 30° maximum conventional angle of attack to the 70° post-stall angle of attack. Compare this to a typical fighter of the time, the F/A-18, for which a normal maximum angle of attack might be 20° to 30°, with the ability to momentarily pull into a higher angle of attack (the F/A-18 has been up to 52°) to achieve a firing solution. But the F/A-18 could not maintain this increased angle of attack for any great period of time, and it could not perform the carefree maneuvering at that condition that the X-31 could. In the case of the F-16, another typical fighter of the time, the angle of attack was limited by the electronic flight control system to a maximum load factor, g, or (at slower speeds) angle of attack. So an F-16 pilot flying "on the limiter" at maximum angle of attack cannot further increase the plane's angle of attack to increase its nose-pointing authority. These limits were designed into its flight control computers to prevent the F-16 from getting into a high-AOA, out-of-control condition, based on early flight-test experience with the YF-16 and F-16A full-scale development (FSD) airplanes. In contrast, the X-31 had the capability of going all the way to 70° angle of attack. Thus, if the X-31 pilot was flying at the conventional limit of 30° angle of attack but was unable to bring the nose to bear on the adversary aircraft, the nose could be pulled all the way to 70° in the post-stall envelope to achieve a firing solution—a 40° increase in nose-pointing authority!

During X-31 flight testing, two types of pitch-reserve maneuvers were used. The "guns reserve" allowed the X-31 to increase the angle of attack to achieve a guns-tracking solution. The "missile reserve" required the X-31 to increase the angle of attack to be able to pull lead on the target so that the angle of attack could then be reduced to 30° (the maximum for a missile shot under the rule-of-thumb missile envelopes in use during the X-31 flight tests). It must be noted that, since the X-31's flight tests, maximum AOA firing envelopes have increased dramatically, particularly with newer, 50+ g, hard-maneuvering air-to-air missiles (AAMs) such as the French Magic, Israeli Python, and the especially impressive thrust-vectoring French MICA and Russian R-73 Vympel.

Pilots reported encountering one problem while flying these maneuvers. The X-31 had relatively high stick forces, especially when flying in the post-stall arena, which caused pilots to have a tendency to induce pitch overshoots when performing these maneuvers. This tendency could be managed with a moderate amount of pilot compensation ("learning and adapting"). In any case, the X-31's nose-pointing authority was a dramatic improvement over the typical fighters that the X-31 test pilots had previously experienced (which, for this group, included such stalwarts as the Canadair Sabre, F-104 Starfighter, F-4 Phantom II, F-14 Tomcat, F-15 Eagle, F-16 Fighting Falcon, and the F/A-18 Hornet).

The J-turn (Herbst maneuver) was the final "maneuver milestone" in the envelope expansion portion of the flight test. This maneuver, to refresh the reader's memory, consists of a rapid pitch up to a high angle of attack, followed by a rapid-velocity vector roll to perform a 180° heading change, then a rapid acceleration to increase speed. In the tactical utility flight tests, this maneuver would allow the X-31 to complete a turn well inside the turning radius of the F/A-18 target, thereby achieving a gun- or missile-firing solution. Experience with using this maneuver in flight also showed that it was a great setup maneuver for initiating the "helo gun attack." In this attack, the X-31 performs a high-AOA velocity vector roll, allowing the pilot to acquire and track the target. This maneuver looks much like a helicopter performing a "pedal turn," in which all the motion is in yaw. Picturing the X-31 at 70° angle of attack, one can imagine how a velocity vector roll would have much more of a yaw than roll component when viewed from the body axis of the airplane. The considerable difference in stick forces for roll control versus pitch control induced a control harmony problem that project test pilots quickly identified. It was much easier to precisely control roll with the stick than to control angle of attack with the stick; it required nearly 3 inches of lateral stick to obtain full roll control command, whereas only very small changes in longitudinal stick (with attendant high stick forces) caused large variations in angle of attack. Therefore, the lateral (roll) acquisition and tracking task required less pilot compensation than the pitch reserve maneuver. Also, pilots found that the lateral acquisition and tracking task could be executed with great precision. Rockwell test pilot (and ITO pilot) Fred Knox commented to the author that when the X-31 was pirouetting inside the target's turning circle during a helo gun attack, "I can gun track you." (He also commented that, in comparison, other current fighters, such as the F-22, were "softer" [i.e., less precise] in their own lateral-acquisition and tracking abilities).[26] But overall, while the X-31's control-harmony problem could be compensated for by the highly experienced project pilots, the control system as designed would not be desirable for a production airplane, which would be flown by less experienced (at least at first) pilots.

The final tactical maneuver selected for the flight phase of tactical utility was the classical "flat scissors." A flat scissors develops when two opposing aircraft are close to one another, flying at low airspeed, and travelling in approximately the same direction. They turn toward each other, resulting in overshooting flight-paths, and then reverse direction of flight as each attempts to maneuver behind the opposing aircraft, seeking to gain a favorable firing solution. Thus, their flightpaths resemble wavy, overlapping, back-and-forth trajectories. Success in this flight regime requires the ability to fly slower than the target aircraft and rapidly reverse and change flightpath, which requires high roll rates. The flat scissors is typical of slow-speed aerial combat, so it was logical to include this maneuver in the X-31 tactical utility flight-test repertoire. This was yet another flight regime in which the X-31 excelled compared to contemporary fighter aircraft—though, again, it had its own nuances and quirks. For example, the X-31 could easily decelerate behind the F/A-18 using its high-AOA capability. However, at very high angles of attack, its high drag caused it to sink below the F/A-18 in altitude. While the high velocity vector roll rates that the X-31 could generate were also an advantage in performing this maneuver, the high nose attitude attained by the X-31 during these maneuvers hindered the pilot's ability to maintain sight of the target airplane. This became one of the first important lessons learned from the comparative program: maintaining sight of the target and situational awareness during high-AOA fighting was an area that future designers would need to address. As a consequence, testers planned evaluations of helmet-mounted displays that would improve situational awareness in the X-31. This aspect of the program will be discussed in the next chapter.

As mentioned previously, there was no readily available ACMI range to provide situational awareness to evaluators on the ground or to use to debrief aircrews after the engagements, as was done, for example, in the Air Force's Red Flag and Navy's Top Gun fighter training programs. Even so, the X-31 test team realized that they had the ability to obtain the desired visualization because the X-31 had C-band tracking beacons and real-time telemetry that furnished other parameters, such as pitch, roll, yaw, airspeed, etc., thus enabling flightpath and vehicle-attitude reconstruction. McDonnell-Douglas (now Boeing) had previously developed a program called "Agile Vu" for the Navy to use for aircraft agility studies. Agile Vu could display more than one aircraft simultaneously, and it presented a number of different display options that furnished various viewpoints, scaling, time history plots, etc. Originally envisioned as a postflight debriefing tool, Agile Vu was adapted by ITO technicians (Dryden, Navy, and contractor) to operate in real time, and it was subsequently used by Dryden mission control for tactical, basic fighter maneuver, and close-in-combat simulation missions. Since the range between aircraft could be displayed, this tool was helpful in establishing the starting conditions for the engagements. Agile Vu, together with a Rockwell-developed program called "Flight Images," furnished valuable postflight analysis and debriefing information, and taken together, the two comprised a powerful information-acquisition and -presentation toolset. Thanks to the integration of these two tools, the X-31 program effectively had an "ACMI-like" capability for real-time test control as well as postflight data analysis. While not as sophisticated as ACMI, this capability was certainly useful for X-31 "1-v-1" flight testing, which was made possible because both aircraft—the X-31 and NASA's F/A-18 aircraft—were instrumented to present aircraft position, altitude, and attitude versus time (this data was not available on the "guest adversary" aircraft used later in the program).[27]

PST Aloft: Proving the X-31 "1-v-1"

In the flight portion of the test, tactical maneuvers were first flown by the X-31 pilot against a "cooperative" F/A-18 followed by basic fighter maneuvering and then the final close-in-combat phase against a "hostile" Hornet. Toward the end of the close-in-combat phase, fighter aircraft other than the F/A-18 were used as well. Moving from tactical to basic fighter to close-in-combat maneuvering followed a typical flight-test buildup philosophy. The AOA limiter, which had been used during most of the envelope expansion to attain precise control of the angle of attack, was not used in this phase of flight testing. Tactical maneuvering provided familiarity with the X-31's handling in a less structured environment than the very precise flight-test maneuvers performed during envelope expansion. The F/A-18 was flown as a cooperative target using prebriefed initial maneuvers. The X-31 pilots could then practice the pitch-rate reserve, J-turn, helo gun attack, and flat scissors maneuvers, thereby gaining an appreciation of the X-31's unique capability in performing these maneuvers before proceeding to the more dynamic basic fighter maneuvering and the free-for-all maneuvering of close-in combat. Because the "cooperative target" phase comprised short, scripted experiences in post-stall maneuvering, they were actually flown before the 225-knots calibrated-airspeed envelope had been cleared. The tactical maneuvers were initially flown using the 185-knots calibrated-airspeed and 18,000-feet MSL minimum-altitude post-stall envelope with a minimum separation of 1,000 feet maintained at all times.[28] The first tactical mission was flown on June 10, 1993, by NASA Dryden test pilot Rogers Smith, followed by USAF Flight Test Center test pilot Jim Wisneski on the same day. Interspersed with the tactical mission tests were the X-31 checkout flights for Quirin Kim. Kim was an experienced fighter pilot in the German Air Force and had participated in both Pinball I and Pinball II.[29]

X-31 with NASA F/A-18 with centerline tank. (NASA DFRC)

(Kim flew just two pilot checkout sorties in the X-31 before flying his first tactical sortie, an indication not only of his own skills but of how rapidly an operational fighter pilot could adapt to the X-31 and, in particular, to the very high AOA regime in which this experimental aircraft operated.) After gaining confidence in the X-31's post-stall maneuvering, the team proceeded on to basic fighter maneuvers.[30]

Basic fighter maneuvering differed from the tactical maneuvering flights in that the BFM targets were unpredictable and the scenarios less scripted. During the tactical maneuvering flights, the F/A-18 target basically maneuvered so that it provided the X-31 with maximum opportunities to practice attacking. During BFM, the target-aircraft pilot prebriefed his initial move (e.g., "going high" or "going low"), but after the first move both pilots were free to maneuver their aircraft at will. As with the tactical maneuvering flights, the primary objective was training. For this reason, the fights were allowed to last more than 90 seconds and up to a maximum of 120 seconds. Also, a weapon solution (i.e., a "kill") did not constitute a requirement for ending the engagement. BFM engagements proceeded from the "fight's on" call until the X-31 pilot had achieved his training objectives, until the minimum "hard deck" of 13,000 feet MSL (10,000 feet AGL) had been reached, or until the engagement ran out the clock at 120 seconds. The starting conditions for the BFM engagements were those that had been refined during the Pinball I and Pinball II twin-domed simulations. The first BFM flights used 185 knots calibrated airspeed as a starting condition because envelope expansion was not yet finished. On these flights, only the offensive starting condition was used. The test team followed the rules of engagement developed and validated during Pinball II, with a minimum aircraft separation of 1,000 feet, until pilots were sufficiently experienced to reduce the separation distance to 500 feet.

Setting up the starting conditions in a real flight test proved much more difficult than in the simulations. In the static world of simulation, the offensive and defensive starting conditions for the aircraft could be specifically defined to furnish evaluation pilots with a wings-level starting condition at the correct separation distance and airspeed. In the dynamic world of flight testing, the pilot of the attacking aircraft had to attempt to set up a 90° crossing angle at the correct airspeed and separation distance within seconds against a constantly shifting opposing airplane. This typically required the attacking aircraft to turn into the target with a nearly 2-g turn such that the attacker was usually at about 60° bank angle and turning at the start of the fight, a possibly test-skewing advantage for the attacking airplane. Another important difference between the simulation and flight test was the allowable airspeed envelope for the starting conditions. In Pinball II, the X-31 pilot could use post-stall capability any time his airspeed was below 325 knots cali-brated airspeed, or Mach 0.7. In the BFM flight program, tests started at 325 knots calibrated airspeed, except "slow-speed line-abreast," which started at 215 knots calibrated airspeed. The X-31 pilot had to decelerate to 225 knots calibrated airspeed in order to maneuver into the post-stall regime above 30° angle of attack because of a post-stall entry limitation in the software.

There were a number of pilot-aircraft interface issues that were noted during the BFM phase of flight. Notwithstanding these issues, the pilots characterized the flying qualities of the X-31 as reflecting "carefree maneuver-ing." The excellent performance and flying qualities of the X-31 highlighted the benefits of thrust vectoring during close-in air-to-air engagements, but with some irony, the overall excellence of the X-31 induced challenges of its own. Pilots found that the buffet level of the X-31 at 12° angle of attack was comparable to that at 70° angle of attack. In fact, the flying qualities at high angles of attack were so good (i.e., without the typical noise, airframe buffet, or wing rock common in fighters of the day, all of which served to warn a pilot of impending high-AOA departure) that pilots indicated that they might want an aural tone or some other cueing device to indicate the airplane's angle of attack. (A form of audio cueing was tested later in the pro-gram.) Stick forces and harmony was also an issue (as noted previously). The airplane had relatively high longitudinal (i.e., pitch) stick forces, particularly when beyond the "soft stop" at 30° angle of attack. This caused pilots to fly with both hands on the stick. The engagements were flown with the engine in maximum afterburner, so there was no need for the pilots to have a hand on the throttle for power manipulation. However, the microphone button was on the throttle, so pilots did have to remove their left hand from the stick to depress the microphone button. This constituted a nuisance during the high-intensity BFM engagements because frequent radio calls are required between aircraft to maintain situational awareness among the aircraft during such tests. The rules of engagement required calls such as "blind," "going high," "lost sight," or "knock-it-off," so the need to use the radio during BFM was not infrequent.

The third issue noted was inadvertent pilot use of the rudder pedals. The X-31 was designed such that rudder command controlled sideslip and faded out during flight at angles of attack above 30° to 45°. Sometimes, pilots inadvertently made rudder input while trying to twist their bodies around to keep the aggressor aircraft in sight in the rear hemisphere, or "checking six" in fighter pilot vernacular (i.e., looking in the 6 o'clock position, or directly behind the aircraft, for attacking aircraft). This inadvertent deflection of the rudder pedals normally occurred when the pilot pushed on the rudder pedal on the opposite side of the direction they were looking. That is, looking around over the left shoulder resulted in an inadvertent push of the right rudder pedal, where the pilot was merely trying to get some leverage to twist his body. Some pilots with previous background in the F-4 had the instinctive habit of making left or right rudder-pedal inputs while rolling the airplane left or right at high angles of attack because the F-4 required rudder input (rather than stick-controlled aileron input) for roll at high angles of attack and, over time, this had become reflexive. The automatic fade out of rudder command at higher angles of attack fortunately made this a minor issue.

Basic fighter maneuvering flights began on August 31, 1993, with Kim, the German Air Force pilot, flying the first sortie.[31] They continued until October 14, 1993, with all six of the ITO pilots participating in this phase.[32] On September 28, 1993, Rear Adm. Riley D. Mixson, the director of Air Warfare for the U.S. Navy, flew in the NASA F/A-18 aircraft that was being used as a BFM target. After that mission, Mixson wrote a letter to Dr. Gary L. Denman, the director of ARPA (formerly DARPA), stating in part the following:

A DFRC F/A-18 during hard maneuvering. (NASA DFRC)

> I recently had the opportunity to visit the ARPA sponsored X-31 program at NASA/Dryden. As a part of that visit I was able to fly simulated air combat in an F/A-18 against the X-31. In short I was very impressed! The X-31 was able to turn inside me and gain firing solutions long before I would have been able to fire on him. The X-31 appears to be leading the way to a new high payoff form of air combat.[33]

With the completion of the tactical and basic fighter maneuvering phases of the X-31 flight-test program, the X-31 and the ITO team were poised to enter the realm of simulated air combat with an experimental airplane, an arena never before entered by an X-plane. In parallel

The X-31 rolling inverted. (NASA DFRC)

with the tactical maneuvering evaluation, basic fighter maneuvering, and close-in-combat evaluations, flight tests were continuing on envelope expansion, flutter, and initial evaluations of helmet-mounted displays. (Testing of the helmet-mounted displays is discussed in the following chapter.) The last basic fighter maneuvering sortie was flown on October 14, 1993, by Kim, who also flew the first close-in simulated-combat sortie less than a month later, on November 5. The F/A-18 adversary pilots for this phase were three NASA pilots from Dryden (one was also an X-31 pilot), all of whom were highly experienced in fighter aircraft. As explained previously, accurate position data for both the X-31 and F/A-18, combined with telemetered data on altitude, attitude, and airspeed—along with weapons-select indications, firing commands, and angle of attack—enabled real-time scoring of the missile engagements using the rule-of-thumb weapons parameters that were developed in simulation. However, pilots had to score their own gun kills because the parameters were too tight for them to be scored from the ground. After each flight, analysis of the HUD tape would either confirm or deny the claimed kill. Out of all the engagements, only one claimed gun kill was denied.[34]

There were nine major test blocks accomplished during the tactical utility flight tests. The test team conducted a post-stall close-in-combat evaluation with the X-31 fighting a NASA F/A-18 to obtain a baseline post-stall capability.

The F-14 Tomcat variable-sweep naval fighter. (NASA DFRC)

The F/A-18 Hornet lightweight naval fighter. (USN)

The F-15 Eagle, the jet age's most successful air-to-air fighter. (USAF)

The F-16C Viper lightweight fighter. (USAF)

This was followed by an evaluation in which the X-31 was limited to only 30° angle of attack—in other words, the conventional envelope. This was accomplished to validate that the conventional performance of the X-31 and F/A-18 were indeed similar. An evaluation was then conducted using the guest pilots from the U.S. Air Force and Navy that had participated in the Pinball II twin-domed air-combat simulation to see if operational fighter pilots could easily employ post-stall technology.

Later evaluations included flights against then-current front-line fighters—the Navy's F-14 Tomcat and F/A-18 Hornet, and the Air Force's F-15 Eagle (most successful of all American post–World War II fighter aircraft) and F-16 Fighting Falcon (more popularly known as the "Viper")—to determine the X-31's post-stall technology benefit against operational aircraft.

Testers then undertook an evaluation with the X-31's post-stall entry speed increased to 265 knots calibrated airspeed to determine if the increase made any significant difference. They also completed an evaluation with the X-31 restricted to 45° angle of attack to determine the benefit of going from 45° to 70° angle of attack. Two other evaluations simulated the impact of "improved" air-to-air short-range missiles, one with a higher AOA launch capability and another with both a higher AOA and off-boresight launch capability.[35]

In the initial post-stall close-in-combat campaign, five ITO pilots from the X-31 test team flew 21 sorties that resulted in 94 scorable engagements and 9 nonscorable ones. A nonscorable engagement resulted from conditions such as low fuel, aircraft malfunction, and the like. There were 70 neutral starting conditions flown: the high-speed line-abreast and the low-speed line-abreast. Twenty defensive conditions were flown in which the X-31 was being attacked, and four offensive starting conditions were flown in which the X-31 had the initial attacking advantage.

For the neutral starting conditions, 6 percent of the engagements ended in a neutral outcome or a draw; test managers defined a neutral outcome or a draw as occurring when 90 seconds of "combat" expired without a winner or when one of the aircraft descended below the 13,000-feet MSL (10,000-feet AGL) hard deck. Of the rest, beginning from a neutral starting condition, the F/A-18 won 3 percent of the engagements while the X-31 won 91 percent.[36] Put

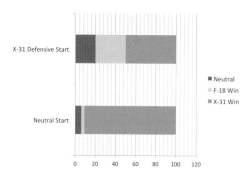

Comparison of X-31 and F/A-18 flight test winning engagements. (Joyce)

another way, the X-31 won 64 out of 66 engagements for a whopping 32-to-1 exchange ratio.[37] When the X-31 was in a defensive position (which was flown for 20 engagements), the F/A-18 won 30 percent of the time, 20 percent of the engagements ended up neutral, and the X-31 won 50 percent of the time despite having started from a very disadvantaged position. These results definitively confirmed the anticipated benefits of post-stall maneuvering technology for close-in combat.

Interestingly, the results from this initial campaign of a "real world" post-stall capable X-31 versus an F/A-18 were significantly better than what had been seen during the Pinball I and Pinball II twin-domed simulations of computer-modeled and -generated opponents. The differences were so great that engineers and analysts on the ITO were concerned that the F/A-18 may have been overly handicapped by requirements that it carry a centerline fuel tank and two wing pylons. Therefore, seven follow-up sorties were flown with the X-31 restricted to its 30° maximum angle of attack conventional envelope.[38]

During this later evaluation, 28 scorable engagements and 8 nonscorable ones resulted from 26 neutral starting conditions (defined as high-speed line-abreast or low-speed line-abreast), 1 offensive, and 1 defensive starting condition. Here, the results were notably different. Overall, 36 percent resulted in neutral outcomes; the F/A-18 won 46 percent of the time and the X-31 won only 18 percent, for an exchange ratio of 2.6 to 1 in favor of the F/A-18.[39] If only neutral starting conditions were considered, the F/A-18 won 12 out of 16 engagements for a 3-to-1 exchange ratio.

The "adversaries" before setting up a fight. (NASA DFRC)

This data indicated that the performance of the F/A-18 with a centerline tank and two wing pylons was similar in conventional performance to the X-31 limited to 30° angle of attack. The F/A-18 did have a slight instantaneous-g turning advantage over the 30°-limited X-31 because the F/A-18 had an available nose-pointing authority up to a range of 40° to 50°.[40] So it was shown that, without post-stall technologies, the X-31 and F/A-18 were generally similar in performance. More importantly, when comparing the X-31 with post-stall technology to the X-31 without post-stall technology, the great advantage of the former was readily evident.

Since one hoped-for flight-test objective was to show that operational fighter pilots can easily adapt to post-stall technology and its unique capabilities in a reasonable period of time, the next question researchers desired to answer was, "Do fighter pilots require special training to employ post-stall technology?" To answer that question, two "guest pilots"—Derek Hess, USAF, and Steve Schmidt, USN—flew the aircraft. Hess and Schmidt had participated in the X-31 twin-dome simulation in Pinball II, so they were generally familiar with the X-31 and its capabilities, but this could not compare with experiencing the dynamic conditions of PST in real flight. In February and March 1994, each completed three "familiarization" flights in the X-31 aircraft then undertook close-in-combat evaluations. This resulted in 26 scorable engagements, with 20 from neutral starting conditions and 6 from defensive ones. The neutral starting conditions were the familiar high-speed line-abreast and slow-speed line-abreast, and the butterfly starting condition was also added to the neutral-start mix. The F/A-18 achieved all its kills from the X-31's defensive starting condition (remember, the F/A-18 is already within firing parameters at the onset of the engagement in this starting condition). However, with neutral starting conditions, there was only one neutral outcome, with the X-31 winning *all* of the other engagements! Overall, then, the X-31 won 19 engagements when beginning from neutral starting conditions, lost 6 when beginning from defensive starting conditions, and had just one engagement that started from a neutral position and ended in a neutral outcome. This gave an exchange ratio of over 3 to 1 in favor of the X-31 with pilots that previously had only three training sorties in the airplane.[41]

This evaluation by two operational fighter pilots

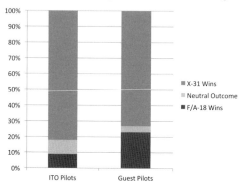

ITO pilot vs. guest pilot performance. (Joyce)

served to introduce the post-stall capability to the U.S. fighter community and certainly showed that an X-31 pilot did not need to be a trained test pilot or have extensive PST training to effectively fly and fight post-stall-technology-equipped aircraft.

Shortly after the evaluation flights by Hess and Schmidt, another "guest pilot" was added to the roster: Ed Schneider, the primary NASA F/A-18 adversary pilot. Even though this was not a part of the initial planning, Schneider was selected to fly the X-31 for two reasons. First, he was the primary NASA adversary pilot (the others being Rogers Smith, one of the X-31 ITO pilots, and Steve Ishmael, a NASA pilot who only flew a few F/A-18 adversary sorties) and his comments on flying the X-31 were desired after he had fought the airplane so much in the F/A-18. Second, Dryden had a history of giving "qualitative evaluation" flights to supporting NASA pilots who were not project pilots on a given project. Ed's job as the principal F/A-18 adversary pilot was to go against each one of the X-31 pilots in the F/A-18 and make them fly the X-31 to the limit in order to beat him. Having flown so often against all the X-31 pilots, Ed felt like a project stakeholder—and he certainly was. Even though Ed only flew the X-31 on four sorties, his experience in both airplanes makes for interesting commentary. Ed also was the project pilot on the F/A-18 HARV, another Dryden high-AOA airplane. Here are his comments to the author on flying the X-31 against the F/A-18, an airplane of which he was an expert close-in-combat pilot:

> The X-31 was a very easy airplane to fly and fight. The thrust vectoring was engaged up and away and disengaged prior to landing. Button hook loops, J turns, and helicopter gun attacks were easy to do in the airplane, and you quickly became adept at slow speed maneuvering and utilizing the agility (nose pointing capability) of the airplane. The standard X-31 tactic was to maneuver as necessary to bring the nose onto your opponent and keep it there. That forced the F-18 into a low speed energy deficient state. The X-31 could always get on the inside of the turning circle and relatively quickly get to a weapons solution. Because the X-31 was so comfortable in this environment, you had to take care of watching your rate of descent, and the hard deck altitude. With an airplane like the F-22 which has a significantly higher thrust to weight, you go a long way towards eliminating a clear X-31 deficiency, viz., being able to rapidly accelerate out of a knife fight towards corner velocity. I got to fly two flights using a helmet mounted sight. Adding this capability coupled with an AIM-9X/AA-11 weapon makes the airplane nearly unbeatable in a low speed fight.

When I was flying as an adversary, I always looked for any opportunity to catch the X-31 arcing vice pressing me, so I could unload and try to get to corner speed. The Hornets were always configured with a centerline tank as well as AIM-7 carriage hardware on the fuselage stations to run-up the drag count. Additionally, we started the engagements at 250 KCAS [knots calibrated airspeed] with a head on pass, so it was tough to gain energy with the X-31 pressing you. I tried to force a two-circle fight in the Hornet so that I could have more separation between aircraft in the hope of getting a shot after we came around and went nose to nose again. I did win a couple of engagements when I was allowed an unknown vice a scripted first move. I went vertical at a relatively low speed, came over the top with a lot of nose rate, unloaded for a simulated AIM-9 shot and got a kill. This didn't happen very often. When the word quickly got out that I wasn't reluctant to go over the top, the X-31 guys, who liked to dictate a horizontal fight, used nose pointing to threaten me from the bottom of the circle, and negated my ability to get the AOA generated at the top of the circle reduced to get into the missile or cannon AOA envelope. It proved very frustrating for me.

When the X-31 went against the operational guys in F-15s and F-14B, they were against airplanes that would go high in the vertical and could stay there above the X-31. This negated the X-31 nose-up pointing tactic. It also gave lots of nose to tail separation against the -31, and shot opportunities against it. If the -14s or -15s got into the phone booth with the -31 they got hammered.[42]

The only other F/A-18 opponent pilot to fly the little test bed was Dryden ITO X-31 pilot Rogers Smith. The orientation to the X-31 was particularly important for an opponent pilot. As recalled by Rogers Smith,

Eddie [Schneider] was a main player in the program during the air-to-air final evaluation for the merits of integrated T/V in close in combat. He and I were the only NASA pilots cleared to fly the adversary F/A-18 (configured with a centerline tank and our main adversary aircraft). Since we flew with a 500-ft bubble as an ROE, we needed pilots who were capable and who were proficient. You could not "just sign up" on the daily board, as an adversary pilot. Mistakes were potentially very costly. On one sortie with me in the X-31 and him in the F/A-18, we made such a mistake in a near vertical (likely 60° climb) engagement. I called "am going 'high'" and attempted to cross-over him. What does 'high' mean in this nose-high climb? Well, it meant something different to each of us. We did cross with much less than 100-ft clearance, close enough to feel the "bump" (air kind, mercifully) of the other aircraft. We knew it, no one else did. We de-briefed a close call and reviewed our collective understanding of our calls. All the engagements were analyzed in Germany. A few weeks later, my friend from Germany showed me the data: *very* close![43]

The next step in the evaluation was to pit the X-31 against current operational fighters. This served to demonstrate the X-31's close-in-combat capabilities against these adversaries as well as to expose the operational community to the post-stall enhanced fighter maneuverability capability of the X-31. The first service unit to participate in this part of the evaluation was VX-4, the Navy's West Coast operational test and evaluation (OT&E) squadron based at Point Mugu Naval Air Station, CA, which operated both the F-14D Tomcat and F/A-18C Hornet aircraft. Operational evaluation squadrons are tasked with operational flight testing of new weapons systems and tactics development for the employment of these systems. They are typically crewed with test pilots and highly experienced operational fighter crewmembers who have extensive background in their assigned aircraft. VX-4 flew against the X-31 in April 1994.[44] Six sorties were flown against the F-14D resulting in 20 scorable and 3 nonscorable engagements. The sorties were flown by three VX-4 pilots and one VX-4 radar intercept officer (RIO, roughly equivalent to a USAF weapon systems officer [WSO]). There were 19 neutral starting conditions flown—including high-speed line-abreast, slow-speed line-abreast, and butterfly—and 1 offensive (for the X-31) starting condition. Of the 20 scorable engagements, the X-31 won 16 engagements (80 percent) and the F-14D won 2 (10 percent), with an additional 2 (10 percent) turning out

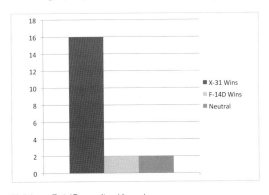

X-31 vs. F-14D results. (Joyce)

neutral. The overall exchange ratio for the X-31 against the F-14D was thus 8 to 1 in favor of the little experimental jet. These results showed that the offensive potential of the X-31 was sufficient to overcome the assumed conventional superiority of the F-14D over the X-31.[45] One caveat, however, was that the X-31 pilot had to aggressively drive the fight from the beginning to take the initiative away from the F-14D crew, thus placing them on the defensive and in a reactive, not proactive, mode.

VX-4 also challenged the X-31 with a clean F/A-18C. As previously mentioned, in the Pinball simulation exercises and during flight test against the NASA F/A-18 aircraft, the F/A-18 was configured with stores to make the conventional performance of the X-31 and F/A-18 more similar. The engagements with VX-4 used "clean" F/A-18Cs that were clearly superior in basic conventional performance to the X-31. Two VX-4 pilots flew these engagements, resulting in 16 scorable and 2 nonscorable engagements. There were 12 neutral starting conditions (high-speed line-abreast, slow-speed line-abreast, and butterfly), 3 defensive starting conditions for the X-31, and 1 offensive starting condition for the X-31.

Of the 16 scorable engagements, the X-31 won 12 (75 percent) and the remaining 4 (25 percent) ended up neutral. In short, despite all of its advantages and the expertise of its operationally focused pilots, the F/A-18C did not win any of the engagements. The margin of winning was smaller—75 versus 80 percent—for the X-31, but the

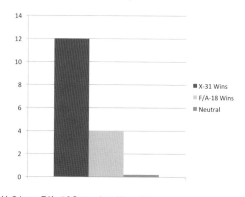

X-31 vs. F/A-18C results. (Joyce)

X-31 kept the initiative by using its great nose-pointing authority early in the fight to "trap" the F/A-18 in the "phone booth."[46]

By May of 1994, the international X-31 test team had expanded the post-stall entry envelope to 265 knots calibrated airspeed. During the Pinball simulations, many of the starting conditions were at 325 knots calibrated airspeed, but in actual flight tests, the envelope limit was 225 knots calibrated airspeed. An obvious question was, "What is the *desired* post-stall entry airspeed?" Four sorties were flown to answer this question, with six neutral starting conditions and four defensive (for the X-31) starting conditions. The X-31 won all the neutral starting conditions and two of the four defensive starting conditions. Testers observed that the X-31 could use the vertical axis more, and in a defensive situation, the higher entry speed reduced the missile-launch opportunities for its opponent. Higher post-stall-entry speeds were helpful if a quick deceleration was necessary, and the consensus was that a post-stall entry speed of around 300 knots constituted a good design point for future aircraft.[47]

Another question intriguing high-AOA investigators was, "How much angle of attack capability is enough?" The X-31 had a maximum post-stall angle of attack of 70°. Was this too much? Could the X-31 do as well with a lower maximum angle of attack? To answer these questions, the X-31 test team flew six sorties from March through July 1994, with the X-31's angle of attack limited to 45°. These sorties were interspersed with the VX-4 adversary evaluation, the 265-KCAS post-stall entry investigation, further envelope expansion, helmet-mounted sight evaluation, the quasi-tailless investigation, and other events (these and other events will be discussed in the following chapter). The 45°-AOA-limited sorties produced 16 scorable outcomes, with the X-31 winning 14 and losing 2 for a highly respectable exchange ratio of 7 to 1. It was observed, though, that the fight was not as "close-in" as the X-31 would prefer to be able to take maximum advantage of its post-stall technology. Also, since the F/A-18 was capable of flying well above 30° angle of attack (the highest that had been seen was 52°), the X-31 pilot had to employ all of its velocity vector roll capability to obtain maximum maneuver advantage, and even this did not automatically provide an overwhelming superiority. The X-31's velocity vector roll rate capability above 30° was still high enough for close-in-combat maneuvering and remained virtually unchanged up to 70° angle of attack.[48] It was felt that since the technical requirements and associated costs were the same for 45° and 70° AOA post-stall maneuvering, and since the benefits of 70° AOA capability were greater, no sensible design tradeoff existed on an AOA limit.[49]

The test force conducted evaluations from August to November 1994 to evaluate the advantages of having a missile-launch capability above the 30° limit established by the rule-of-thumb weapons-employment envelopes that were developed during the Pinball II simulations. Four sorties produced 20 scorable engagements: the X-31 won 15 and lost 1 engagement from a neutral starting condition and won 2 and lost 2 engagements from a defensive (for the X-31) starting condition. It was noted that with a high-AOA missile capability, both opponents tried to stay close to each other; thus, for the X-31, PST enabled its pilot to force the fight into gun range. Another outcome was that in butterfly setups, the X-31 needed sufficient instantaneous turn performance to gain an initial advantage and then slow to enter the post-stall maneuvering envelope.[50] Some of these missions were flown with a helmet-mounted display (discussed in the following chapter).[51]

While the high-AOA missile evaluations and helmet-mounted display evaluations were both being flown in September 1994, the X-31 faced guest adversaries from the USAF. The adversary aircraft and pilots were from Air

Combat Command's 422nd Test and Evaluation Squadron (422 TES), based at Nellis AFB, NV. The 422 TES was composed of very experienced operational fighter pilots flying the most modern USAF fighters. Their mission, like the Navy's VX-4, was to conduct OT&E and develop tactics. The aircraft that the 422 TES brought to the evaluation were the F-15C Eagle equipped with the Pratt & Whitney 220 engine and the F-16C Block 52 with the Pratt & Whitney 229 engine. Both of these airplanes had a considerable thrust-to-weight advantage over the X-31 (and over the Navy's F-14D and F/A-18C as well), and the 422 TES pilots used this capability to their advantage. For the first time, close-in-combat engagements now favored the X-31's adversaries. The X-31 pilots were unable to dictate the fights by using post-stall technology to force the F-15 and F-16 to deplete energy and enter the short-range gun "killing ground." In short, the up-engined F-15 and F-16 aircraft had sufficient engine power to remain outside the phone booth. Instead, the 422 TES aircraft used their considerable thrust-to-weight advantage to establish an altitude sanctuary where the X-31's post-stall technology could not be used offensively.

Among the lessons learned from this evaluation was that an aircraft with post-stall technology must also have thrust-to-weight capability comparable to its adversaries. Post-stall technology is not a replacement for other fighter performance capabilities but is rather an addition to them. Furthermore, testers noted that an advanced short-range air-to-air missile is a clear requirement for an aircraft operating in a post-stall envelope. One wonders what the outcome would have been if the F-15 or F-16 had post-stall technology, perhaps with moveable 2-D nozzles (such as the F-22) or X-31-like petals. During November and December 1994, additional close-in-combat evaluations were conducted using an X-31 that was equipped with high-AOA short-range missiles and a 60° off-boresight launch capability. As of the publication date of this work, no unclassified results have been released from this evaluation.

PST in the Dogfight Arena: Concluding Observations

Overall, the tactical utility flight test was an incredible program. Out of 87 total sorties flown in this portion of flight testing, 80 sorties were scored. These resulted in 407 engagements, of which 325 were scored (nearly 80 percent).[52] These found that post-stall technology definitely provides smaller turning radius, superior weapons-pointing at slow speeds and high angles of attack, and superior velocity vector roll capability at slow speeds and high angles of attack. These characteristics also provide departure resistance and carefree handling, and all are essential for success in close-in combat. The tactical utility flight testing has shown that proper and timely employment of post-stall-technology maneuvering in close-in combat significantly improved combat effectiveness, or kill ratio, in both offensive and defensive maneuvering.[53]

The tactical utility flight testing qualitatively and quantitatively showed continuous dominance for the X-31 with post-stall technologies in the close-in-combat environment. This was demonstrated through increased kill ratios and increased survivability. The technical feasibility and tactical utility of post-stall technology capability had been proven. The X-31 had superior maneuverability and agility that gave it considerable advantages against a conventionally equal opponent in the close-in-combat arena.[54]

It is important to note that the X-31's tactical test program affirmed that post-stall technologies only supplement, and certainly do not replace, conventional performance capability. This was definitively shown when the 422 TES exploited the superior thrust-to-weight ratios of their F-15C and F-16C to maintain an altitude sanctuary above the "phone booth." The evaluation also showed that the use of post-stall technologies at the wrong time resulted in the adversary getting the first shot opportunity. The main advantages of the X-31 with post-stall technology were the apparent high "directional nose-pointing rate" (in actuality, this was the yaw rate capability, or its velocity vector roll capability at high angles of attack) and its very high nose authority in pitch. When properly exploited, these led to positional advantage and decreased the time required to reach a weapons solution. Other old rules of air combat were also relearned: small aircraft, like the X-31, are hard to see; aircraft flying out of the Sun are hard to see; and if you lose sight of the adversary, you will lose the fight, and likely your life.[55]

The results of the tactical utility flight testing can thus be summarized as follows:

- Post-stall technology close-in combat at 70° angle of attack had overwhelming success.
- Flying the X-31 in a conventional environment limited to 30° angle of attack showed that the benefits of post-stall technology were greater than expected.
- Operational guest pilots with minimal training were able to effectively fight with the X-31 using its post-stall technologies.
- The X-31 was very successful against the then-frontline Navy fighters, the F-14D and F/A-18C.
- When faced with opponents with superior thrust-to-weight ratios, namely the USAF F-15C and F-16C, the X-31 was far less

successful, since its opponents would not enter the close-in-combat arena and escaped to an altitude sanctuary.

- A higher post-stall entry airspeed, 265 versus 225 knots calibrated airspeed, was slightly better, with 300 knots being desirable for future fighters.
- Limiting the X-31 to 45° angle of attack showed that this was insufficient; 70° angle of attack should be used.
- Advanced short-range air-to-air missiles with greater angle of attack and off-boresight launch capability are highly desirable for an aircraft with post-stall technology.
- There were some notable differences between the Pinball simulations and flight-test results. Simulators, like other ground tests, are no substitute for actual flight tests, and the X-31 results prove this.

In the crisp blue skies over Edwards, post-stall thrust-vectoring technology had proven its worth through a dogfighting X-plane!

Endnotes

1. Deutsche Aerospace, *Roll-out to Tactical Evaluation—A German View*, pp. 19–20.
2. David E. Canter and Cmdr. Allen W. Groves, USN, "X-31 Post-Stall Envelope Expansion and Tactical Utility Testing," AIAA-1994-2171, Seventh Biennial Flight Test Conference, Colorado Springs, CO, 1994, p. 130.
3. Dorr, "Rockwell/MBB X-31," p. 46.
4. Fred Knox, e-mail to Douglas A. Joyce, July 6, 2011.
5. Canter and Groves, "X-31 Post-Stall Envelope Expansion and Tactical Utility Testing," pp. 129–130.
6. Knox, Groves, Smith, and Wisneski, "X-31 Flight Test Update," p. 107.
7. Dorr, "Rockwell/MBB X-31," p. 46.
8. Knox, Groves, Smith, and Wisneski, "X-31 Flight Test Update," p. 107.
9. Canter and Groves, "X-31 Post-Stall Envelope Expansion and Tactical Utility Testing," p. 129.
10. David A. Eubanks and Robert E. Bitten, "X-31 Pinball II Tactical Utility Summary," *Rockwell International Report NA-93-1256* (Los Angeles, CA: July 1, 1993), pp. 2–3, Dryden Archives.
11. Ibid., pp. 3–5.
12. Ibid., p. 3.
13. Ibid., pp. 4–6.
14. Ibid., p. 2.
15. International Test Organization, "X-31 Enhanced Fighter Maneuverability Program: Synopsis of Tactical Utility Evaluation" (October 1995), p. 5, Dryden Archives. It is important to note that this "floor" was the altitude above ground level (AGL), not altitude above sea level (MSL). Edwards AFB is 2,300 feet MSL in altitude, so a floor at 10,000 feet MSL would be only 7,700 feet AGL.
16. Eubanks and Bitten, "X-31 Pinball II Tactical Utility Summary," p. 7.
17. Ibid., 8–9.
18. In one such dogfight, the famed German fighter ace Werner Voss was shot down by several S.E. 5 aircraft that prevented him from breaking off the fight, fatally running him out of fuel.
19. Eubanks and Bitten, "X-31 Pinball II Tactical Utility Summary," pp. 10–20.
20. Note that in Pinball I, this starting condition was 6,000-feet-separation line-abreast at 400 knots calibrated airspeed while in Pinball II this starting condition was 3,000-feet-separation line-abreast at 325 knots calibrated airspeed. This was used as justification that the

Pinball II high-speed line-abreast starting condition was better for use in flight testing.

21. Eubanks and Bitten, "X-31 Pinball II Tactical Utility Summary," pp. 21–22.
22. Ibid., pp. 30–32.
23. Ibid., pp. 33–35.
24. David E. Canter and Cmdr. Allen W. Groves, USN, "X-31 Tactical Utility—Initial Results," (Lexington Park, MD: Naval Air Warfare Center Aircraft Division, ca. mid-1993), p. 12.
25. Eubanks and Bitten, "X-31 Pinball II Tactical Utility Summary," pp. 36–37.
26. Notes from Joyce, Dyson, and Knox interviews.
27. Canter and Groves, "X-31 Post-Stall Envelope Expansion and Tactical Utility Testing," pp. 131–132.
28. Ibid., p. 132.
29. Deutsche Aerospace, *Roll-out to Tactical Evaluation—A German View*, p. 21.
30. Miller, *The X-Planes*, pp. 324–325.
31. Canter and Groves, "X-31 Post-Stall Envelope Expansion and Tactical Utility Testing," p. 132.
32. Miller, *The X-Planes*, p. 324.
33. Rear Adm. Riley D. Mixson, USN, letter to Dr. Gary L. Denman, ARPA, October 22, 1993, Dryden archives.
34. Canter and Groves, "X-31 Post-Stall Envelope Expansion and Tactical Utility Testing," p. 133.
35. ITO, "X-31 Enhanced Fighter Maneuverability Program: Synopsis of Tactical Utility Evaluation" (Edwards, CA: NASA DFRC, October 1995), p. 6, Dryden archives.
36. D. Eubanks, R. Gutter, and B. Lee, "X-31 Close-in-Combat (CIC) Flight Test Results," briefing to the Full Envelope Agility Workshop, Eglin AFB, FL, Air Force Materiel Command Air Armament Center, March 1995, slide 5.
37. Canter and Groves, "X-31 Post-Stall Envelope Expansion and Tactical Utility Testing," p. 133.
38. Ibid., p. 133.
39. Eubanks, Gutter, and Lee, "X-31 Close-in-Combat (CIC) Flight Test Results," slide 6.
40. Canter and Groves, "X-31 Post-Stall Envelope Expansion and Tactical Utility Testing," p. 133.
41. Eubanks, Gutter, and Lee, "X-31 Close-in-Combat (CIC) Flight Test Results," slide 7.

42. Ed Schneider, e-mail to Douglas A. Joyce, November 28, 2011.

43. Rogers Smith, e-mail to Douglas A. Joyce, August 22, 2011.

44. ITO, "X-31 Enhanced Fighter Maneuverability Program: Synopsis of Tactical Utility Evaluation," pp. 6 and 7.

45. The F-14D was a re-engined, and hence much more powerful, variant of the F-14 Tomcat that more closely approximated the F-15E than the older F-14A (which also had a lower thrust-to-weight ratio).

46. Eubanks, Gutter, and Lee, "X-31 Close-in-Combat (CIC) Flight Test Results," slides 8 and 9.

47. Ibid., slide 11.

48. Ibid., slide 12.

49. ITO, "X-31 Enhanced Fighter Maneuverability Program: Synopsis of Tactical Utility Evaluation," p. 7.

50. Eubanks, Gutter, and Lee, "X-31 Close-in-Combat (CIC) Flight Test Results," slide 13.

51. ITO, "X-31 Enhanced Fighter Maneuverability Program: Synopsis of Tactical Utility Evaluation," p. 7.

52. Eubanks, Gutter, and Lee, "X-31 Close-in-Combat (CIC) Flight Test Results," slide 14.

53. ITO, "X-31 Enhanced Fighter Maneuverability Program: Synopsis of Tactical Utility Evaluation," p. 8.

54. Eubanks, Gutter, and Lee, "X-31 Close-in-Combat (CIC) Flight Test Results," slide 17.

55. Canter and Groves, "X-31 Tactical Utility," p. 133.

The X-31 climbing away during a "go-around" test. (NASA)

CHAPTER 4

The X-31 Follow-On Program

While the "tactical evaluation" was under way, there were many other efforts progressing in parallel with it in the X-31 flight-test program. If tactical utility flight testing could be considered the "baseline" program, the X-31 managers sought to employ the X-31 in research efforts that were not part of the original plan.[1] The potential uses of an HMD discussed in the previous chapter were being evaluated in parallel with the close-in-combat tactical utility flight tests. Since the X-31 had such expanded high-AOA capability, a program to evaluate handling qualities at high angles of attack while using standard maneuvers was undertaken. Some parameter-identification flights were conducted to provide data for the Langley Research Center, and the aircraft's flight envelope was being expanded into the supersonic regime. An initiative to support another military program by evaluating the ability to control the airplane using thrust vectoring without a vertical fin was conducted. And finally, there was talk of taking the airplane to the Paris Air Show and showing her to the world. But disaster would intervene.

Of HUDs and Helmets

As early as the conceptual phase of the program, engineers and managers wondered if and how the pilots of an X-31 could operate in the dynamic environment while transiting rapidly back and forth from conventional flight and post-stall flight. Moreover, they were concerned over how, at 70° angle of attack, pilots would maintain situational awareness while dogfighting at such an extreme angle of attack. In these early days, a series of human-factors experiments were conducted to see if insight could be gained about pilot performance in this new environment. Perhaps the most notable experiment was conducted at the Naval Air Development Center (NADC) in Warminster, PA. According to Mike Robinson, "The pilot disorientation issue was an early concern as you allude. Very early on we actually did a series of physiological and psychological tests regarding rapid onset and offset of maneuver state (hi agility) and hi alpha maneuvering with and without HMD (read heavy helmets). These were done at the manned 6-dof [degrees of freedom] centrifuge at NADC in Warminster, PA. The only result was that the residual Coriolis effects of the centrifuge messed up your eye-butt senses to the point it caused the pilots to get sick."[2] As implied in prior paragraphs, the pilots had no problem with handling the dynamic or high-AOA conditions.

On the other hand, the pilot's view at high angles of attack was not an idle concern; when flying at 70° angle of attack, the velocity vector (i.e., where the plane "is going") is pointed almost directly downward (i.e., *below*) from the pilot's seat. So, when looking through the HUD on the cockpit glare shield, the pilot's line of sight was nearly 70° from where the plane was actually heading and, consequently, likely 70° from where the target aircraft was. Furthermore, the target's movements and attitude (and thus, likely intentions) were masked by the intervening aircraft structure that obscured the pilot's direct line of sight. Since the HUD thus had limited value at best, researchers wished to evaluate an HMD. An HMD could be developed to present the aircraft's performance information (e.g., airspeed, altitude, g-loading, angle of attack, weapons information, etc.) as well as weapons-targeting information (i.e., a weapon's "sight") directly on the helmet visor, or on another optical device attached to the helmet. This information would therefore be available to the pilot wherever he was looking, whereas otherwise the pilot had to look "heads down" into the cockpit at instruments or displays or "heads up" through a HUD that was fixed in alignment with the longitudinal axis of the fuselage and provided only a limited, telescope-like view over the nose of the aircraft.

Helmet-mounted displays had been used and evaluated as early as the 1974 to 1978 timeframe, when a very primitive helmet-mounted sight was fitted to helmets flown in the Department of Defense Research and Engineering's (DDR&E) Air Combat Evaluation (ACEVAL)/Air Intercept Missile Evaluation (AIMVAL) program on air-to-air weapons and tactics.[3] Other initiatives followed in the United States, European, Soviet, South African, and Israeli militaries. Early in the X-31 program, MBB engineers had proposed installation of an HMD in the aircraft because the technology was available, even if not yet in a mature form.[4] This was proposed to improve pilot information and pilot orientation during post-stall maneuvering. Sometimes called "own ship situational awareness," HMD availability of this information eliminates the need for pilots to look inside to the instrument panel or through the head-up display for aircraft information and then back out of the cockpit at the target.[5] Hopefully, the pilot would be able to reacquire the target aircraft quickly, but there was always the risk of losing sight of it. Remember one of the old air-to-air combat lessons learned, or relearned, from the X-31 close-in-combat post-stall technology evaluation that was discussed in the previous chapter: "If you lose sight of the adversary, you will lose the fight."

MBB wanted to provide the pilot with better information about his flightpath relative to the aircraft body-axis system when at high angles of attack, but there was not a suitable helmet available to MBB at the time, and cost was an issue. As an alternative, MBB developed special display symbology and implemented it on an existing head-down display (HDD) manufactured by AEG/Telefunken that would be mounted on the instrument panel. This HDD was tested in the Rockwell Downey simulator but could not be fitted into the X-31 due to physical incompatibility with the existing display hardware, which was derived from an F/A-18 instrument panel.

Tests of three HMDs with possible application to the X-31 started in late 1992. The first was a German design that was discarded early in the evaluation because it was deemed too heavy and cumbersome, a problem that remains a quarter-century later in the age of the F-35 Lightning II Joint Strike Fighter. (In the 1980s, researchers from the USAF's Aeronautical Systems Division Avionics Laboratory at Wright-Patterson AFB had designed a multifunction helmet that offered remarkable capabilities, given the state of avionics and optics developments at the time, but which was likewise too cumbersome and heavy for use.) The

Luftwaffe Maj. Quirin Kim wearing the GEC Marconi I-NIGHTS HMD. (NASA DFRC)

second was a design with binocular optics called the Interim-Night Integrated and Head Tracking System (I-NIGHTS), which had been developed for night-vision work by GEC Marconi but also had some day capability.[6]

In March 1993, the ITO partners held a meeting during which they agreed to incorporate the I-NIGHTS helmet into the X-31 and test selected symbology on a noninterference basis with other research. This system performed well but was considered too heavy, and its center of gravity was too far forward. There was concern that during an ejection the pilot's head would be pulled forward and down, thus jeopardizing safe ejection; even with an "ordinary" helmet, the abrupt snap-down of the head during high-g vertical ejection acceleration could generate serious injury, as exemplified by an Air Force A-10 test pilot who experienced a fractured vertebra during an ejection (fortunately, he recovered to fly again).[7] The third tested design was the GEC Marconi Viper helmet, which offered the same capability as I-NIGHTS but had a monocular vision display rather than a binocular one. By the time Ship 2 was ready to fly with an HMD, GEC had the new monocular Viper helmet ready to fly.[8]

GEC marketed the Viper as a low-cost, lightweight, monocular, visor-projected HMD. The system projected information directly onto the visor of the pilot's helmet using a high-efficiency miniature-cathode-ray-tube display that used an optical relay assembly. A standard aircrew visor was used, with the addition of only a neutral-density reflection coating to ensure a high-outside-world transmission without coloration. The system weighed 3.8 pounds (excluding the oxygen mask) and had a field of view greater than 20°. The Viper display module could be fitted to any existing USAF or Navy helmet (which, at the time, were the ubiquitous Gentex HGU-53P and HGU-55P lightweight helmets). The design was such

Rockwell test pilot Fred Knox wearing the GEC Marconi Viper HMD. (NASA DFRC)

that the image remained stable on the visor even if the visor was raised slightly to permit the pilot to perform the ear-clearing Valsalva maneuver (pinching the nose and blowing hard). The system had both day and a night capabilities with sensor-image projection available. Of course, in the X-31 application, only the system's day capability was employed.[9]

The Viper system, as modified for application to the X-31, was first worn by NASA Dryden ITO pilot Rogers Smith on December 16, 1993, followed by German Air Force ITO pilot Quirin Kim on the same day.[10] The first flights using the Viper HMD in simulated close-in combat were flown on January 6, 1994, with the first flight being flown by Kim and the second by Fred Knox, the Rockwell ITO pilot. The display that was tested used new symbols designed specifically to show angle of attack and other aircraft performance information.[11] AOA awareness was especially important to the X-31 pilot due to the airplane's extreme AOA capability and the relative lack of other aerodynamically produced cues, like buffet, that typically accompany its attainment. Initial pilot comments on the Viper system were very positive, including: "the symbology is crisp and clear," "I can get the information while looking off-boresight," and "[Viper] is the CIC display of the future."[12]

In addition to the HMD, the X-31 program also experimented with audible cues to indicate angle of attack. Other production fighter aircraft, most notably the F-4, have used audible cues to warn of increasing angle of attack. A proposed follow-on effort to the display of aircraft performance parameters on the HMD visor was to display "virtual computer generated adversaries" on the display, so that post-stall maneuvering could be evaluated against multiple targets. One of the arguments made against the fidelity of the X-31's close-in-combat evaluations to the "real world" of air combat was that most real-life scenarios involve multiple adversaries. A virtual adversary capability may have allowed that concern to be addressed; however, this effort was never funded.

One other area that was addressed with the HMD was the advantage of off-boresight missiles. The then-new AIM-9X missile (intended for the upcoming Lockheed F-22A Raptor program, whose developmental prototype, the YF-22, was then undergoing flight testing at the AFFTC) had a significant off-boresight launch capability. The debate that ensued was whether it was better to make the *aircraft* missile platform more maneuverable or to make the *missile* have better off-boresight capability so that it could launch from an aircraft pointed away from the target, maneuver to acquire the target, and kill it. Missile effectiveness deteriorated as angle off the target (and off the launch platform) increased, and X-31 proponents argued that the right combination was a more maneuverable aircraft *and* missile. The X-31's HMD experiments thus allowed exploration of the potential combination of a highly maneuverable aircraft with a highly maneuverable missile.[13]

X-31 Handling Qualities and Close-In Combat

As the close-in-combat evaluations were nearing the completion of their objectives and this phase of flight testing was winding down, the X-31 test force initiated a structured high-AOA handling-qualities flight-test program built around a series of "standard evaluation maneuvers" (STEMs) that were used to assess longitudinal and lateral gross acquisition and fine tracking at high angles of attack.[14]

Three separate simulations were used in preparation for the flight testing of high-AOA handling qualities. The first was a piloted simulation that was a six-degrees-of-freedom nonlinear simulation employing a fixed-base (i.e., no motion) cockpit mockup equipped with flight hardware. The cockpit incorporated the pilot displays and controls, and a 5- by 6.5-foot flat-screen projection provided the pilot with a limited field of view out of the cockpit of approximately 30° laterally and 20° vertically. A target aircraft could be projected onto this screen, and its trajectory could be controlled to allow pilot training with a target that makes repeatable maneuvers. The second simulation was a batch version of the six-degrees-of-freedom simulation and was used to generate models of the aircraft flightpath. These models could be used with the third simulation—a linear simulation—to generate transfer functions for use in handling-qualities evaluations.

The cockpits of the actual X-31 airplane and the piloted simulation had a HUD that incorporated a conventional pitch ladder and heading display as well as digital displays of altitude, rate of climb/descent, Mach number, and calibrated airspeed. On the left side of the display were two "tape displays" that showed angle of attack and load factor, and this data was also shown digitally at the top of the tape. The current AOA command limit (i.e., where the AOA limiter was set, if used) was shown by an arrow next to the AOA tape. There was also a 2-milliradian fixed pipper depressed 2° from the aircraft centerline with an inner 20-milliradian reticule and an outer 40-milliradian reticule. The HUD displays could be video recorded for data-analysis and debriefing purposes.[15]

During the close-in-combat phase of flight testing, ITO pilots had conducted an informal evaluation of handling qualities, and afterward there was a general consensus among the pilots that the X-31 had good to excellent handling qualities (Level 1 or Level 2 on the Cooper-Harper rating scale [CHR]) in the high-AOA close-in-combat regime.[16] It was important to keep the pilots' subjective opinions of the aircraft's handling qualities in mind during this phase of flight testing because, of necessity, the pilots were required to successfully accomplish gross target acquisitions and perform fine tracking in order to score a successful "kill" against the opponent. All of this was accomplished in the very-high-gain environment of close-in combat or dogfighting at very high angles of attack.

Evaluating handling qualities during close-in combat is particularly challenging because it is a very dynamic environment where angle of attack is constantly (and considerably) changing. X-31 testers therefore sought a more structured type of flight test to validate the subjective judgments of good handling qualities that were reached during the close-in-combat tests. Engineers at the Flight Dynamics Directorate, Wright Laboratory, and McDonnell-Douglas Corporation, in cooperation and participation with pilots and engineers at the NAS Patuxent River Naval Air Warfare Center, Edwards AFB Air Force Flight Test Center, and the Wright-Patterson AFB 4950th Test Wing, had developed a series of standard evaluation maneuvers encompassing 20 standardized maneuvers that could be used for flight-test evaluation of handling qualities.[17] For the X-31's structured-handling-qualities evaluation, testers employed STEM 10 (the STEM high-AOA longitudinal-gross-acquisition module), STEM 2 (the high-AOA tracking module), and STEM 3 (the high-AOA lateral-gross-acquisition module). In a manner similar to tactical testing, a NASA Dryden F/A-18 chase aircraft served as the target. Data were collected from postflight interviews, reviews of in-flight HUD video recording, telemetered data showing aircraft parameters, and pilot rating sheets that were completed immediately after each maneuver. In an effort to emulate the acquisition and tracking tasks that were accomplished during the close-in-combat phase, an additional evaluation maneuver was flown using the slow-speed line-abreast starting condition that had been used in the close-in-combat evaluation. This setup enabled the accomplishment of acquisition and tracking tasks over a range of angles of attack.[18]

Formal handling-qualities flight testing started in June 1994 and continued through October 1994. Nineteen flights were flown in this evaluation. Five ITO pilots—Knox, Lang, Smith, Kim, and Capt. C.J. "Gus" Loria, U.S. Marine Corps (USMC)—participated in this phase of flight testing. Loria was a new addition to the team of ITO test pilots who replaced the Navy member of the ITO pilot team, Al Groves, who was retiring. Loria was a graduate of the USAF Test Pilot School at Edwards AFB and flew for the Naval Air Warfare Center Aircraft Division at NAS Patuxent River, MD. He had been working on the X-31 program since March 1991, when he participated in the planning for the X-31's tactical utility evaluation. Loria arrived at Dryden on August 22, 1994, and immediately started simulator and ground-school training. He flew his first X-31 flight on August 30, 1994, and after two familiarization flights, he was flying a close-in-combat practice test mission against an F-15 from Nellis AFB. His first STEM mission was on October 13, 1994. At this stage in the program, the German government had allowed Quirin Kim and Karl-Heinz Lang (the latter, the WTD-61 pilot) to remain on the X-31 project even though they had been slated for replacement or reassignment.[19] Additionally, Jim Wisneski had left the program, retiring from the Air Force on April 1, 1994. His last flight was a close-in-combat test mission on February 10, 1994, and the USAF did not seek to replace him due to the relatively short time remaining until program completion.[20]

STEM 10 evaluated the longitudinal gross acquisition task, as stated in the Wright Labs and McDonnell-Douglas STEMs descriptions:

> This maneuver is intended to isolate the flying qualities characteristics of an aircraft during a high AoA longitudinal capture task. The evaluation aircraft begins in trail of the target aircraft, approximately at 3,000 feet range. The target enters a constant angle of attack descending turn, with control of bank angle to maintain speed. The evaluation pilot allows the target to attain a predetermined angle-off and then rolls into the target's maneuver plane and sets the throttle to test position. The evaluation pilot must hesitate until the lag position is such that the capture will occur at the test angle of attack. This does require some practice.

The acquisition should be aggressive and result in a capture within an 80 mill horizontal band. After capture, the pilot unloads and allows the target to drift to some offset (value controls angle of attack at capture) and repeats, thus allowing several acquisitions from one setup. Target flight path can be steepened to increase evaluation airspeed.[21]

As is readily apparent, while this type of maneuvering is not nearly as random and variable as air-to-air combat, it is certainly not a pure and easy type of maneuvering to fly. As mentioned above, at the start of the maneuver, the X-31 trailed the target F/A-18 for 3,000 feet. The F/A-18 pilot began the maneuver by selecting maximum afterburner and starting a turn at a constant 20° angle of attack, maintaining 200 knots indicated air speed (KIAS). After delaying for 4 seconds, the X-31 pilot selected maximum afterburner (which was required for its post-stall technology to function) and rolled in plane with the target, performing a rapid pull to capture the target within 25 milliradians of the pipper and at the desired angle of attack. The target's airspeed and angle of attack, as well as the "capture requirement," changed slightly as the X-31's angle of attack was increased. For instance, at 60° angle of attack for the X-31, the F/A-18 target flew at a 25° angle of attack and 170–180 KIAS, and the capture requirement was within 40 milliradians of the pipper. These tests were performed at a desired angle of attack of 30°, 45°, and 60°, with the X-31's Mach number varying from 0.45 at the initiation of the maneuver to 0.6 at 30° angle of attack and 0.5 at 45° and 60° angle of attack. The AOA limiter was not used, as was common in envelope expansion. It is readily apparent that careful setup was critical to ensure that all the parameters came together as the maneuver progressed.

The lateral gross acquisition task is derived from STEM 3 and is a similar setup except the acquisition is attempted using only lateral control stick. The target and the X-31 started out in an echelon formation with 1,500 feet of separation. The target maneuvered in a turn away from the X-31. The X-31 pulled to the desired angle of attack and, when the target was at a predetermined angle away from the X-31's nose, the X-31 pilot aggressively maneuvered the X-31 while attempting to use only lateral stick to capture the target using "capture requirements" that were similar to those used in the longitudinal gross acquisition. In this maneuver set, the AOA limiter was used to set the desired angle of attack.

The fine-tracking evaluation was based on STEM 2, with the X-31 trailing the target F/A-18 by 1,500 feet. The target again rolled into a turn and the X-31 rolled in plane and attempted to track it, but this time the task was to move the pipper on the target aircraft, nose to tail for longitudinal tracking and wingtip to wingtip for lateral tracking. The AOA limiter was not used. This fine-tracking evaluation was done in two phases. Phase 1 testing was done at angles of attack of 10°, 15°, and 20° to provide a reference and basis for other, more conventional AOA evaluations and subsequent testing in the post-stall regime. Phase 2 testing was done at angles of attack of 30°, 45°, and 60° and included fine-tracking tasks in both the longitudinal and lateral axes.

A combined maneuver was flown on one flight because there were perceived differences between the handling qualities observed during STEMs and during close-in-combat evaluations. The starting conditions for the combined maneuver were the same as those used for the slow-speed line-abreast setup during the close-in-combat evaluation. The X-31 and F/A-18 started side by side at 215 KIAS and 25,000 feet MSL altitude, separated by 1,500 feet. The aircraft initially turned toward each other, with the X-31 going over the target aircraft and then reversing. The F/A-18 made a single heading reversal and then maintained a steady turn at 30° angle of attack and 170 KIAS. The X-31 maneuvered as required to acquire and track the target, with multiple acquisitions achieved by repeatedly lagging off and reacquiring the target. The desired performance was to aggressively acquire the target within 25 milliradians of the pipper, with no overshoot for gross acquisition, and to fine track within plus or minus 5 milliradians for 50 percent of the task and within 25 milliradians for the remainder of the task.

Results for the longitudinal gross acquisition showed that the Cooper-Harper ratings given by the pilots increased from CHR 2 to CHR 4 as angle of attack increased from 20° to 65°.[22] In the case of longitudinal gross acquisition for the X-31, CHR 2 meant "good, negligible deficiencies where pilot compensation was not a factor for desired performance," and CHR 4 meant "minor but annoying deficiencies where desired performance requires moderate pilot compensation." These pilot ratings were assigned with high confidence and were recorded both immediately after the maneuver and at debrief following the mission. The first and second CHR given were generally the same. Ratings were also assigned for pilot-induced oscillation (PIO), which is an indication of an unwanted sine-wave-like motion induced by the pilot's own stick and/or rudder movements that is typically indicative of some over-sensitivity, lack of damping, or control-input lag in the flight control system. PIO ratings were assigned using a rating scale published in the military handbook, MIL-HDBK-1797A, that was similar to the Cooper-Harper rating scale. The PIO scale ranged from 1 to 6, where 1 represented "no tendency for pilot to induce undesirable motions" and 6 represented "disturbance or normal pilot control may cause divergent oscillation—pilot must open control loop by releasing or freezing stick."[23] Sixty-four percent of the tasks received a PIO rating of 1, with the remaining 36 percent receiving a PIO rating of 2, which indicated some undesirable motions that did not compromise task performance. These ratings generally matched the expectations from the close-in-combat evaluations. Relative to the increased difficulty as the angle of attack increased, one pilot commented, "Thirty is the critical point. It's better [for the evaluation] to be above 30; below 30 is too easy." For flight in the post-stall regime at angles of attack above 30°, pilots consistently noted that stick forces were too heavy and stick motion was too large, as was observed during the envelope expansion and the close-in-combat evaluations. Also, pilots noted a lateral disturbance above 45° angle of attack that tended to complicate the task. This was also noted during envelope expansion and was attributed to asymmetric forebody cores that changed as a function of the angle of attack.[24]

The lateral gross acquisition task was considerably more difficult. In the longitudinal gross acquisition task, the aircraft motion was essentially confined to one plane after the X-31 was banked into the correct plane to track the target. The lateral gross acquisitions required motion in multiple axes, greatly complicating the geospatial positioning of the aircraft. First, at high angles of attack, the aircraft must perform velocity vector rolls for lateral acquisition. These result in significant coning motion that is complicated by the fact that the velocity vector settles downward during the maneuver, resulting in a perceived "yaw-like" maneuver when roll control is used for lateral gross acquisition. This task required significantly more practice before proceeding to data runs. Again, higher CHRs were found as the angle of attack was increased. This time, the CHRs increased to 8, meaning "major deficiencies where considerable pilot compensation is required for control." The task did not emulate the lateral acquisition tasks that were performed during close-in combat, during which the X-31 was typically maneuvered within the turn radius of the target aircraft with the velocity vector straight down in the typical "helicopter gun attack." The close-in-combat testing did not indicate a tendency for the higher CHRs seen in the STEM testing for this task. Testers concluded that it was not clear that the STEM task was representative of the maneuvering that pilots might be required to perform when dogfighting in the post-stall flight regime.

Reflecting on the X-31's close-in-combat maneuvering at high angles of attack, Jim Wisneski said, "I believe it would be unanimous that the ability to control the aircraft in the post stall environment was a pleasant surprise to all—very precise control was available throughout the flight envelope. Nose-pointing both in 'pitch' or 'roll' (roll about the velocity vector) was responsive and easy to start/stop without overshoot."[25] However, for the STEM maneuvering task, PIO ratings also increased with angle of attack, with two cases showing nondivergent oscillations and receiving a PIO rating of 4. One pilot reported, "Lots of them. Many overshoots; borderline PIO at the end," noting that the task was "very difficult."[26]

Clearly then, there were major differences between X-31 pilot perception when dogfighting in a free-for-all close-in-combat environment versus doing a structured STEM task for a handling-qualities evaluation. When dogfighting, the pilots generally liked the aircraft's handling, but when performing STEM 2 with the X-31, they had difficulty. This was likely due to the design of the STEM 2 maneuver rather than to the aircraft itself. While STEM was an accepted model to obtain handling qualities in the conventional fighter operational envelope, the X-31 results indicated that STEM would need significant adaptation to be a reliable tool in the post-stall operational regime.

Tracking Tasks in the High-Alpha Arena

Fine-tracking tasks were performed in both the longitudinal and lateral directions. Initially, quite a bit of practice was required for the pilots to become accustomed to the performance of these tasks. One early difficulty in performing the tasks was the amount of time spent tracking. The planning for this event had allowed 4 seconds of tracking; however, in actual practice, the pilots were spending 20 seconds or more performing the tracking task, which caused significant variations in flight conditions, particularly angle of attack. For instance, in one case when the pilot was directed to track at 30° angle of attack, the actual tracking occurred between 30° and 23°. Afterward, the pilot commented, "There were two distinctive airplanes. When I was at the initial AoA around 30°, it was quite a bit harder to track than when I settled in. My rating will be associated with the initial values of the tracking."[27] Thus, fine tracking at the higher angles of attack was more difficult, as confirmed by subsequent Cooper-Harper ratings. For angles of attack less than 30°, the CHRs were consistently 3 or less, indicating Level 1 handling qualities. Between 30° and 50° angles of attack, the ratings ranged between 3 ("Fair: some mildly unpleasant deficiencies") and 7 ("Major deficiencies" with "adequate performance not attainable with maximum tolerable pilot compensation"). The highest ratings at the highest angle of attack showed Level 2 (CHR 3–5, the "border" between Level 1 and Level 2), with two ratings of Level 3 (CHR 7 or worse) near 50° angle of attack. Additionally, the setup of the tracking tasks changed, with the initial separation reduced to 1,500 feet from 3,000 feet and the X-31 "start maneuver" based on angle off rather than time from the start of the target maneuver. For the gross acquisition task, the separation was 3,000 feet and the start maneuver criteria were based on a delay time. This resulted in the X-31 getting considerably outside the circle of the maneuvering target, so the separation was reduced to 1,500 feet and the start of the X-31 maneuver was based on angle off. This resulted in more repeatable tasks.

The confidence classifications also changed with angle of attack. Confidence-class ratings were used to evaluate the effectiveness of using a maneuver to rate the aircraft's handling qualities. Changing the initial conditions or increasing practice time with the maneuvers would tend to improve the confidence-class ratings. A rating of "A" meant the CHR was assigned with a high degree of confidence. "B" meant that the CHR was assigned with only a moderate degree of confidence because of uncertainties introduced by moderate differences in environmental conditions, aircraft configurations, aircraft states, or task performances from what was desired. A "C" rating meant that the CHR was assigned with minimum confidence because of important differences between the desired and actual environmental conditions, aircraft configurations, aircraft states, or task performances that required considerable pilot extrapolation.[28] All confidence classifications were "A" for angles of attack below 30°. For angles of attack in the post-stall regime, 10 were given confidence class "A" and 6 were given class "B." PIO ratings also tended to increase with angle of attack for this task, ranging from 2 to 4, which indicated that there were undesirable motions and oscillations throughout the post-stall range.[29]

The initial intent was for the pilot to perform nose-to-tail tracking on the target aircraft, but in actuality, since there almost always was a difference in the maneuver plane of the X-31 and the target's plane of symmetry, the pilots necessarily made both lateral and longitudinal stick inputs to run the pipper from nose to tail on the target. Therefore, test planners changed the instructions to not attempt nose-to-tail tracking but rather to use only pitch inputs, using appropriate aircraft features as a reference. The pilots still often inadvertently made diagonal stick inputs. One test pilot commented, "The tracking we're trying to do here is kind of dynamic-pitch tracking and not the kind of tracking we typically did during the end game, which tended to be more in matching yaw rates."[30] Clearly it is hard to "decouple" actual target tracking in the close-in-combat sense into a longitudinal task and a lateral task.

If the "longitudinal-only tracking task" proved difficult, so too did the "lateral-only tracking task." Again, the trend was in higher Cooper-Harper ratings as angle of attack increased, and higher-AOA tasks earned confidence class ratings of "B" while the lower-AOA tasks earned an "A." PIO ratings also were comparable to other tasks in that higher angles of attack produced higher ratings and more reported oscillations. Several pilots commented that, "The more aggressive you are, the harder time you have tracking." Again, pilots needed to make diagonal inputs to the stick in order to track using the wingtip-to-wingtip task. When the task was modified to require only lateral inputs, pilots still had a natural tendency to use diagonal stick inputs.[31]

As mentioned above, a "combined maneuver" was also evaluated. This maneuver used the starting conditions of the slow-speed line-abreast close-in-combat evaluation and consisted of one cycle of a flat scissors maneuver with the target maintaining the final turn and allowing the X-31 to track. In this maneuver, the longitudinal and lateral tasks were not decoupled; however, gross acquisition and fine tracking were rated separately. Unlike in the attempt to decouple the longitudinal and lateral tasks, in this maneuver the results and the pilot satisfaction seemed to be better. The resulting Cooper-Harper ratings were borderline between Level 1 and Level 2 for both acquisition and fine tracking. No PIO tendency was noted during gross acquisition, and any motions that were detected did not affect the task during fine tracking. One pilot reported, "The [slow-speed line-abreast] SSLA setup was an excellent starting condition to evaluate handling qualities in the PST regime."[32] Perhaps trying to decouple the maneuvers was not the right approach in the first place. Pilots also commented on control forces and control harmony, which they had also noted earlier during envelope expansion. Pilots considered stick forces to be too heavy and stick displacement to be too large. With respect to harmony, while pitch was sensitive, roll was clearly less so.

The bottom line was that pilots liked this combined maneuver better than the decoupled "longitudinal" and "lateral" tasks and felt that it was more representative of the flying done in the close-in-combat evaluations. They believed this type of maneuver could provide a better means of evaluating handling qualities in the post-stall regime. However, from a flight-test engineer's viewpoint, the varying flight conditions make this maneuver of limited value at best for analysis or design purposes. Afterward, NASA engineers Pat Stoliker and John Bosworth concluded the following:

> The Standard Evaluation Maneuvers (STEMs) provided repeatable tasks that could be compared with analytic and nonlinear simulation results. With suitable initial conditions and practice, gross acquisition and fine tracking could be performed at the desired angle of attack (AoA). Pilot comments indicated that these maneuvers were not consistent with the types of maneuvers performed during the close-in-combat (CIC) evaluations. This testing identified problems that may not be significant in actual tasks. Further testing is needed to resolve these differences.[33]

Even with the problems identified in trying to decouple longitudinal and lateral motion for pilot evaluation and design data in the post-stall regime, the X-31 program had taken an important step in developing methodology for high-AOA handling-quality evaluation.

Continuously "Predicting" Aerodynamics

As discussed previously, the MBB approach to flight control law development was to use a mathematically "predictive" model of the aircraft's flightpath to map the appropriate flight control surface deflections (and thrust vectoring) to pilot commands and flight conditions, whereas the American approach was typically a "reactive" control law in which control surface deflections and thrust vectoring would be based on pilot commands, flight conditions, and, most importantly, the aircraft's behavior and reactions as actually measured by sensors on the aircraft. The predictive approach required an accurate aerodynamic "model" of the aircraft. While this can be relatively easily done for aircraft flown at moderate angles of attack, modeling the aerodynamic parameters (commonly called stability derivatives and control derivatives) for an aircraft flying at high angles of attack is considerably more difficult. The reasons for this are many. First, the basic airplane is unstable, which complicates finding the mathematical solutions of the aircraft's state equations via integration. Second, the aircraft's states and controls are (obviously) highly interrelated; however, this means that the aerodynamic parameters cannot be estimated independently of one another. Third, the presence of forebody aerodynamic vortices causes significant "noise" in the data that are obtained from flight or wind tunnel testing. Fourth, in attempting to perform standard flight-test maneuvers, such as a control "doublet," the superb flight control system suppresses undesired motion (e.g., directional sideslip is kept close to zero), so the aircraft's response is very damped and well behaved. Finally, in the X-31, lack of high instrumentation accuracy meant that thrust, weight, and center-of-gravity location could not be known with sufficient accuracy to permit reliable modeling. For these reasons, flights for "parameter identification" (PID) were accomplished throughout the flight-test program. As the program was winding down in the summer of 1994, some flights were flown at the request of NASA Langley researchers to investigate nonlinear and unsteady effects.[34]

The X-31 and JAST's Quest for "Quasi-Tailless" Flight

In the early 1990s, there were a number of programs in the Air Force, Navy, and DARPA that looked at potential future fighter technologies and designs. DARPA had two programs: the Common Affordable Lightweight Fighter (CALF) program and the Advanced Short Takeoff/Vertical Landing (ASTOVL) program. On February 23, 1993, the Department of Defense initiated a bottom-up review (BUR) to define a strategy for defense planning in the post–Cold War era. While this review (which encompassed the entire defense establishment) concerned primarily grand strategy and policy direction, it also influenced future fighter development because one of its outcomes was the initiation of the Joint Advanced Strike Technology (JAST) program. The mission of the JAST program office, established on January 27, 1994, was to define and develop aircraft, weapon, and sensor technologies to support the future development of tactical aircraft. These technology studies eventually led to the Joint Strike Fighter (JSF) program, which oversaw development of two competitive technological demonstrators—the Boeing X-32 and Lockheed Martin X-35—that were flown during JSF concept definition. Ultimately, the X-35 was selected for subsequent development, leading to the Lockheed Martin F-35 Lightning II.

The X-31 played a small but significant role in this effort because one of the technologies JAST program managers pursued was controlling aircraft without a vertical fin and rudder simply by using thrust vectoring.[35] Reduced tail size has many potential advantages, including reduced drag, weight, structural complexity, and radar cross section. Since JAST was a multiservice program, the Navy was particularly interested in understanding the handling of a completely tailless aircraft during an aircraft carrier approach, where precise flightpath control throughout touchdown and hook engagement is an absolute necessity. All these potential advantages had to be traded against the added complexity, weight, and reliability requirements of a thrust-vectoring system. The latter was a particular concern because if the reliability of a thrust-vectoring system could not be guaranteed to a sufficient level, some sort of emergency backup system (such as a retractable fin) might be required. Also, landing approach maneuvers often require low power settings (particularly in a configuration like the X-31), while vectored thrust effectiveness increases (and/or the thrust-vector angle is less for a given control effectiveness) at high power settings. So, using vectored thrust during a carrier landing approach may require larger drag devices, such as speed brakes, so that power settings can be established at a higher level and then maintained throughout the approach, with the flightpath modulated by application of aerodynamic braking via the speed brakes.[36]

The B-2 Spirit, a pure flying wing tailless aircraft. (NMUSAF)

The B-2 demonstrated that a complex tailless aircraft could be safely flown and introduced into operational service. It was, of course, a subsonic aircraft, whereas JAST program managers were interested in the application of tailless technology in the supersonic regime up to Mach 1.5 and above. The X-31 had been designed as a supersonic airplane to demonstrate the "relevance" of the design for supersonic fighter-like airplanes. Karl Lang had first flown the X-31 supersonically on November 24, 1993, achieving Mach 1.08 at 37,500 feet MSL altitude, and in the subsequent week, the flutter envelope was expanded to Mach 1.28.[37] X-31 program managers were looking for money to keep the program moving, there was a (fortuitous) connection within DARPA to JAST, and Rockwell liked involving the X-31 with JAST because it would provide a close and perhaps beneficial association with a program that was eventually going into production. Thus, the stage was set for the X-31 to demonstrate the tailless technologies of interest to JAST advocates. To this end, artists altered photographs to show how the X-31 sans its vertical fin might appear. As events turned out, however, the X-31 would not suffer the physical loss of its vertical appendage.[38]

Rockwell's X-31 staff gave a well-received advocacy briefing to the JAST program office in October 1994 that was followed with a "JAST and X-31 ITO Work Agreement and Research Plan for Quasi-Tailless Experiment" document on November 7, 1994.[39] Just 9 days later, the X-31 ITO, the JAST Flight Mechanics Integrated Product Team, and several other Government and contractor representatives met at Dryden to agree to demonstrate "quasi-tailless" (QT) flight.[40]

X-31 tailless concept, 1994. (NASA DFRC)

What is the "quasi" in quasi-tailless? How can one simulate a tailless airplane without actually removing the tail? The concept proposed by the X-31 program was to use the rudder control surface to cancel the stabilizing effect of the fixed vertical fin, in effect "playing" one moveable surface (the rudder) against the other fixed one (the vertical fin). With the vertical surface thus effectively "neutralized," the airplane could then be controlled by yaw commands to the thrust-vector system. For example, as sideslip is developed, the rudder is used to cancel out the stabilizing effect of the vertical fin so that the effect is, in essence, negative stability. Now the thrust vectoring can be used to stabilize the airplane by driving sideslip to zero; moreover, the thrust vectoring can be used to control the desired amount of yaw when a velocity vector roll is commanded. The gains applied to the rudder destabilization effect can be varied, thereby producing differing levels of directional stability in flight with no need to physically reduce the size of the vertical tail. As an added benefit, if the thrust vectoring fails to control the aircraft, the pilot can revert to "conventional" mode (i.e., using the fin and rudder) to return safely.[41]

Throughout the following quasi-tailless discussion, there will be reference to the amount of the tail that is effectively removed (0 to 100 percent). The reader must remember that the specifics are only relevant to the X-31, which was never designed as a tailless or reduced-tail-size vehicle. The relevance to general design solutions is the amount of directional instability that a given amount of thrust vectoring can overcome combined with the amount of control that the vectoring system can impart. The tests described herein thus provide a data resource that will provide future designers with insight into the amount of thrust vectoring required for various critical "mission points" of aircraft that are designed from the start to have no or a reduced vertical tail. The X-31 pilots selected the quasi-tailless mode by first inputting the desired percent of simulated vertical tail removal into the plane's status/test panel. This panel took these entries on a "QT Index." For example, a QT Index of 0 represented 0 percent vertical tail removed, a QT index of 2 represented 40 percent vertical tail removed, a QT index of 3 represented 50 percent vertical tail removed, a QT Index of 4 represented 60 percent vertical tail removed, and a QT Index of 6 represented 80 percent vertical tail removed. Once the pilot had entered the desired test percentage into the status/test panel, he saw a display of the index on the panel and a corresponding indication on the HUD. At the commencement of the test during flight, the pilot would depress a "QT Select Switch" on the throttle. An indication of "QT 3 ENGAGED" would simultaneously appear on the status/test panel and in the HUD. The pilot could manually disengage the quasi-tailless mode by again depressing the QT Select Switch on the throttle or by engaging a "paddle switch" on the lower forward part of the stick. Additionally, automatic safety disengagement occurred if specified envelope parameters, such as sideslip or g-load, were exceeded.[42]

The first phase of flight testing the quasi-tailless concept involved a flight by Rogers Smith during which the quasi-tailless mode was engaged and the airplane was flown up to Mach 1.2. During this flight, Rogers exercised the quasi-tailless mode with standard flight-test maneuvers (doublets, bank-to-bank turns, and windup turns) with the quasi-tailless setting in the 0-percent-tail-off mode.[43] The second flight of the series was flown by Karl Lang on the same day, March 10, 1994, with the airplane tested at 10-, 20-, and 30-percent tail off. Karl commented, "The QT de-stable mode did not show any noticeable destabilization."[44] Rogers flew the last flight of the day. Initially, this test point was flown in the destabilized-only mode with up to a 20-percent tail reduction programmed. Rogers commented that "the 20 percent destabilized cases clearly showed reduced directional damping with several overshoots observed."[45] On March 17, Rogers flew a flight with up to 70-percent tail reduction and stability provided by the thrust vectoring. When the full quasi-tailless mode was selected with the thrust-vector system engaged and used to restabilize the airplane at this simulated tail reduction, Rogers concluded that "the aircraft response was satisfactory for all [tested] values of tail off."[46] This flight envelope point represented a supersonic cruise condition in which a reduction in the size of the vertical tail (e.g., on a future supersonic commercial air transport) results in large drag savings. Of course, eliminating the vertical also saves structure and weight and, for military applications, it reduces radar cross section.

Clearly, the use of thrust vectoring to stabilize the simulated-tail-off airplane was working. Much of the work during this phase of flight testing was actually accomplished prior to the formal signing of the program tasking in Washington, DC. This actually saved much time and allowed the test team to get a head start on implementing a quasi-tailless control law for the second phase of testing to support the JAST requirements. This required a much larger subsonic envelope.

The next tasks selected to support the JAST program were a simulated carrier-approach landing task and a ground attack profile. Two factors complicated preparations for the carrier-approach and ground attack testing. The first was accurately determining the location and magnitude of the jet exhaust plume in the vicinity of the thrust-vectoring vanes. Determining where the exhaust plume was required the pilot to slowly move the thrust-vectoring vanes into the jet plume while flight-test engineers on the ground monitored the total flow field and jet efflux pressures at the aft end of the paddle and the sensed load upon the paddle actuator. These parameters were used to judge the location of the jet plume, which was required so that the jet-plume deflection of a given control moment command could be known for implementation of the control laws. In parallel with these efforts, the thrust-vectoring vanes were removed from Ship 1 for modification. Ground-based simulation had shown that a hard-over failure of the paddles would result in unacceptable handling qualities, so the paddle actuators were modified to allow faster removal of the paddles from the jet plume in the event that such a failure occurred.

Additionally, the Operational Flight Controls Program (OFP) also required modification. The flying qualities noted with the original OFP were generally quite good, but even so, the aircraft displayed sideslip buildup during mild maneuvering and, very noticeably, during full lateral-stick-deflection aileron rolls and bank-to-bank rolls. Simulation and analysis also showed that there was a considerable difference between commanded and actual jet-plume deflection. These issues prompted an update to the OFP. The second factor that complicated preparation for the subsonic carrier approach and ground attack testing was that the flight envelope for this aggressive maneuvering had to be expanded from the 14,000-feet MSL floor used in close-in-combat testing to the 2,300-feet MSL of the surface at Edwards.[47] (There was already talk of trying to participate in the Paris Air Show, so this clearing for a lower altitude operation definitely was a step in the right direction.) On November 8, 1994, Gus Loria, Fred Knox, and Karl-Heinz Lang started testing the new OFP and expanding the envelope down to lower altitudes. Since time and money were very limited at this juncture of the X-31 program, the envelope expansion focused on the carrier-approach and ground attack evaluations.

The X-31 "Goes to Sea"

For the carrier-approach evaluation envelope, testers examined the power approach configuration with landing gear down, high-lift devices engaged, on-speed approach airspeeds defined as 170 to 220 knots calibrated airspeed, and at altitudes from the surface to 10,000 feet AGL. For the air-to-ground evaluation, they studied the cruise configuration from 360 to 420 knots calibrated airspeed at altitudes from 1,000 feet AGL through 10,000 feet AGL. The new OFP software proved up to the task, with Loria noting, "The new configuration was a success. The aircraft exhibited delightful handling qualities throughout the envelope!"[48]

Aside from the fact that the JAST program's Navy contingent was curious about the potential of tailless aircraft that could operate from carriers (a tailless aircraft could have lower space requirements for "spotting" on a deck, thus increasing the number of aircraft in a carrier's air wing and, hence, its combat projection power), the carrier-approach task also provided the X-31 pilots and engineers with an opportunity to evaluate a demanding mission profile, one requiring the pilot to maintain very precise control of the airplane's angle of attack, glide slope, speed, and lineup simultaneously. The landing task required large control surface deflections and large control moments, especially for roll control. These large roll-control requirements led to additional demands to minimize yaw, which presented an acute challenge for a tailless thrust-vector-for-yaw-only control system. Carrier approaches are typically flown at a constant angle of attack on the "backside" of the power curve—a region of "reversed command" where throttle is used to maintain proper glide slope (e.g., add power to reduce descent, retard power to increase descent) and pitch attitude is used to modulate airspeed (e.g., nose low, increase speed; nose high, reduce speed). This requires very dynamic throttle movement with largely varying amplitude and frequency. Lacking the in-house technical capability and requisite insight, the X-31 ITO prudently solicited input from the Navy's Shipboard Suitability and Landing Systems Department (located at the Naval Air Warfare Center Aircraft Division at NAS Patuxent River) to help design the flight-test portion of the carrier-landing evaluation.

The X-31, having not been designed as a carrier airplane, presented challenges to its use in a carrier-landing evaluation. First, the X-31 had an approach speed of approximately 170 knots calibrated airspeed, reflecting its sharply swept fixed-delta planform. Typical carrier aircraft are designed for an approach speed of 140 knots calibrated airspeed or less. The X-31's high approach speed resulted in high closure speeds on the landing area, and thus in less time for the pilot to make flightpath corrections on final approach, which was exacerbated by a low-drag configuration that necessitated low approach power settings. This could have been a problem because, by its very nature, thrust vectoring requires relatively high power settings. Additionally, low power settings made glide-slope control more difficult due to slower engine response. Low power settings also resulted in poor go-around, or "wave-off," performance. An automatic disengage feature was incorporated into the software when the power-lever angle (i.e., throttle angle) dropped below 55° to avoid quasi-tailless operation at insufficient thrust levels. The high approach speed also caused high rates of descent on final approach at the normal carrier approach glide slope of 3.25°.

Another issue that made the X-31 challenging was its delta planform. Delta aircraft have an inherently higher-than-average angle of attack during landing approaches that, in extreme form, can compromise the pilot's ability to see the runway (this was why, for example, the Concorde SST had a so-called "droop" nose that lowered for takeoff and landing). The X-31's planform gave it a carrier-approach angle of attack of 12°, affording its pilot a barely acceptable over-the-nose field of view. Higher approach angles were thus not possible due to visual field-of-view problems and unacceptable visual distortion through the windscreen.

The X-31 team conducted the carrier-approach evaluation in two phases. The first phase evaluated the X-31's basic control system during the precision approach tasks. The second phase evaluated the control system in "quasi-tailless" mode. This evaluation consisted of formation-flight tasks in the power-approach configuration as well as actual field carrier approaches ("field" refers to the fact that the team conducted these approaches at an airfield rather than an aircraft carrier at sea). X-31 pilots undertook the formation tasks at altitudes of 10,000 feet MSL and 5,000 feet MSL in the power-approach configuration (i.e., with landing gear down, high-lift devices deployed, and speed brakes open). These formation tasks were performed at higher altitudes to enable the initial evaluation of power-approach quasi-tailless flying qualities while in a relatively safe altitude environment, well away from the ground. The team evaluated two formation tasks. The first was a slot-position formation with an F/A-18 and an X-31, the latter in a power-approach configuration flying in the familiar in-trail slot position. Lt. Cmdr. Robert Niewoehner (a member of the JAST Flight Mechanics Integrated Product Team) had recommended this task as a means of further investigating the directional stability of the X-31 in a quasi-tailless configuration. The second formation task was the standard parade or "fingertip" formation position in which the X-31 would fly in the wingman position off of an F/A-18 leader aircraft. Researchers grappled with developing demanding test plans that would force the X-31 pilot to undertake both gross- and fine-tracking tasks without endangering flight safety. The answer was provided by one of the ITO X-31 pilots, NASA Dryden's Rogers Smith. He had spent much of his career involved with flying-qualities testing methodology in a series of ever-more complex jet fighters, from the first-generation F-86 to the fourth-generation F/A-18. Smith proposed that the lead F/A-18 pilot perform mild maneuvering in pitch and roll, with the X-31 flying normal formation in either the slot or fingertip positions. With the X-31 in the fingertip position, the F/A-18 pilot would perform an unexpected (to the X-31 pilot) pitch input of ±5°, with the X-31 pilot's task being to reacquire the desired formation position as rapidly as possible. With the X-31 in the slot position, the F/A-18 pilot would make an unannounced roll input of ±10°. These unexpected deviations required an immediate and high-gain task to reacquire the desired formation position, where the "desired criteria" was ±1 foot and "adequate criteria" was ±5 feet. The parade-position formation tasks received Cooper-Harper ratings of 3 with a 40-percent tail reduction. The slot position task did even better, receiving a Cooper-Harper rating of 2 with a 40-percent tail reduction. The pilot, Gus Loria, commented on the slot position evaluation, saying, "The aircraft was extremely well behaved during this evaluation, handling qualities were actually better than for parade position."[49]

Following completion of the formation tasks, the evaluation continued with field carrier approach trials. Due to the X-31's high approach speed and descent rate, testers set the initial glide-slope setting at 2.75° rather than the Navy's standard 3.25–3.5° setting. On a carrier, a Fresnel Lens Optical Landing System (FLOLS) is used in conjunction with the landing signal officers (LSOs) to provide glide-slope indication to the pilot. One of these devices was set up at Edwards for this purpose. For both fidelity and expertise, the X-31 team employed a Navy LSO to provide feedback to the X-31 pilot and to act as a safety observer. In addition, the X-31 pilot would make intentional deviations from the lineup or glide slope. The LSO would then command corrections unexpectedly at different portions of the approach. This would require the X-31 pilot to reacquire the lineup or glide slope at very high gain, thus providing a high-gain task for handling-quality evaluation. There were no actual landing touchdowns made during this portion of the flight testing. Since the X-31 landing gear was not as structurally strong as a carrier aircraft, it could not sustain touchdown at a constant angle of attack as a naval aircraft does. Thus, all approaches terminated in a wave-off or go-around at a minimum of 100

X-31 flying a simulated carrier approach at Edwards AFB using a Fresnel Lens Optical Landing System reference system. (NASA DFRC)

feet AGL. This part of the flight testing was flown exclusively by the program's two carrier-experienced pilots, the Marine Corps' Loria and Rockwell's Knox (a former Navy aviator). Interestingly, the LSO assigned by the Navy to support the X-31 testing was Lt. Mark Kelly (later a NASA astronaut and eventual commander of STS-134, the final mission of Space Shuttle Endeavour in 2011).[50]

The formation tasks that had been developed with the help of Rogers Smith and Robert Niewoehner required high-gain pilot inputs and proved to be good tasks for evaluating the quasi-tailless mode. Evaluating the quasi-tailless X-31 in the carrier-approach mode proved to be much more difficult because glide-slope control with the X-31 was very difficult. This was attributed to the very low power settings it required and the sensitivity of the flight control system in the pitch axis. The low power settings resulted in poor power response, thus requiring the pilot to make longitudinal stick inputs to accomplish glide-slope corrections. As discussed previously, this is counter to the normal carrier approach "backside" technique of power for glide-slope control and pitch variation for airspeed control. Exacerbating the problem was the sensitivity of longitudinal stick inputs in the X-31, a problem that has been mentioned previously. This sensitivity often caused the pilots to overcontrol in pitch, resulting in deviations above and below the glide slope (i.e., a slightly wandering flightpath characterized by excursions above and below the path, somewhat like a sine wave but without its periodicity of frequency or predictable amplitude). Pilots were rarely able to recapture the glide slope once a deviation had occurred, and they thus rated the X-31's approach handling qualities as very objectionable. They decided not to intentionally make glide-slope deviations or attempt to reacquire. Only lineup deviations would be made, while the pilot simply tried to stay on the glide slope. Another problem that resulted from these low power settings was that the quasi-tailless control laws caused an automatic disengage of the quasi-tailless mode at low throttle settings. Initially, in the carrier-approach evaluation, the large changes in throttle caused disengagement of the quasi-tailless mode on almost every approach!

The X-31's high approach airspeed was nearly double that of conventional carrier-based aircraft such as the F/A-18 or F-14 at that time, resulting in half the time on final approach, or "in the groove." Thus, there was much less time during final approach for corrections and evaluation. As mentioned previously, attempts were made to increase the approach angle of attack from the normal 12° to 12.5° and 13° in an attempt to reduce the X-31's final approach sink rate and approach speed while requiring an increase in average power settings. Clearly, changes were required to make the X-31's carrier approach tasks more mission-relatable in terms of workload and performance while still providing reliable data.

The test force considered adding drag-increasing devices to the airplane, but they rejected this idea after determining that physical modifications to the existing drag devices like the speed brakes were not reasonable given the short period of time available to conduct the tests. Project pilots flew approaches with the speed brakes both retracted and extended, after which the test team decided to employ extended speed brakes for the actual quasi-tailless flights. But this posed an additional problem because the contribution of landing gear, landing-gear doors, high-lift devices, and speed brakes resulted in much higher lateral instability than had been predicted by merely adding the instability contributions of each of these alone. Therefore, testers elected to select a QT Index of 3 instead of 4 for the precision glide-slope testing, which was equivalent to removing 50 percent of the vertical tail in recognition that, in the power-approach configuration with speed brakes fully extended, the target value of directional instability could be achieved with a QT Index of 3.

Since testers had selected an approach glide slope of 2.5° versus the normal carrier-approach glide-slope angle of 3.25°, the X-31 had a reduced sink rate of 700 feet per minute, increasing the average required approach power setting. The final approach distance was increased from 0.75 nm to 1.5 nm, with intentional deviations and corrections, on the call of the LSO, occurring between the 1.5 nm and 1.0 nm positions. This approach-distance lengthening resulted in the pilots having approximately the same amount of time on final approach, in the groove, as was typical of a daytime, visual meteorological condition carrier approach of 18 to 20 seconds.

Key cockpit instrumentation was modified or added. A flight-test throttle detent was installed at a power-lever angle of 56°. This then served as a quasi-tailless "flight idle" position and gave the pilot an indication of his proximity to the quasi-tailless throttle-disengage position of 55° power-lever angle. An AOA indexer was installed on the left-hand side of the head-up display. An AOA indexer is a simplified display of "on-speed" angle of attack as well as fast and slow indications, and it is arguably more useful on final approach than the HUD AOA display. An "indexer" was the primary source of AOA data for most carrier airplanes of the day. Finally, the test team decided that glide-slope control was difficult enough without any intentional deviations. Since lateral-directional behavior was of primary concern, the test team decided that only intentional deviations from lineup would be explored, with the pilots attempting to maintain glide slope.

As was just described, it took a lot of nonstandard thinking and innovation to allow the X-31 to demonstrate something so far out of its initial design regime. But that said, the program was up to the challenge, and the quasi-tailless evaluation during the carrier-approach testing was very successful.

In summary, during the formation testing, pilots found that the rapid, unexpected step-roll inputs by the F/A-18 provided ample opportunity for aggressive lateral-directional captures. The fingertip formation did not exercise the lateral-directional aggressive maneuvers but did allow evaluation of pitch-input sensitivity, low throttle settings, and slower engine response times. These exercises were flown both with the basic X-31 control system (with thrust vectoring on) and with the quasi-tailless control laws representing a reduction of 50 percent of the vertical tail! Additionally, carrier approaches were flown simulating a 50-percent reduction of the vertical tail (the QT Index 3 setting). Lateral deviations from runway centerline, normally about 50 feet, were flown with aggressive corrections to recapture the centerline. These corrections were made on the call from Kelly, the LSO, with the pilot simultaneously attempting to maintain angle of attack and glide slope while aggressively correcting lineup. Pitch sensitivity and problems with glide-slope control were still present, but the pilots were able to separate out the lateral-directional axis for evaluation. Evaluations that compared the basic X-31 control laws to the quasi-tailless control laws detected no appreciable handling qualities differences between the two. Indeed, the Cooper-Harper Handling Qualities Ratings for both sets of control laws on the X-31 were similar to CHR ratings for current Navy fixed-wing jet carrier aircraft performing the same task—predominately 4s and 5s representing Level 2 flying qualities. Pilots did not note any combined lateral-directional oscillations (i.e., "Dutch roll") or other objectionable flying qualities. Importantly, there was adequate control power available when comparing the basic X-31 to the quasi-tailless X-31. Engine power settings averaged 5° above the 55° power-lever angle set for automatically disengaging the quasi-tailless control laws. Interestingly, when this automatic disengage occurred a few times during the evaluation, the flying qualities were so similar, with no transients noted during the disengage, that the first realization of disengage by the pilot was when he received a call from the control room! Up to one half of the available thrust-vectoring capability was used in both the formation and carrier-approach tasks. There was sufficient thrust-vectoring capability despite the low power settings, and no degradation of flying qualities was noted.

Though the field carrier-landing task had been modified from what was originally envisioned, it still provided an excellent means of evaluating the X-31's quasi-tailless control laws. The program was not attempting to evaluate the X-31 for carrier suitability but was evaluating a flight control system configuration applicable to tailless aircraft. The X-31 took an important first step in evaluating the capability of thrust vectoring in the carrier-approach environment. This was an important part of assessing the feasibility of tailless configurations in the carrier-approach environment. The tests also highlighted the usefulness and flexibility of the X-31 research aircraft that was used as a test

The X-31 executing a go-around following its simulated carrier approach; note the FLOLS in the lower left of the photograph. (NASA DFRC)

bed for integration of thrust vectoring into operational airplanes. The X-31 was not designed for the precision carrier-approach task but was able to fly in that environment and provide prodigious amounts of high-quality data.[51]

The X-31 as a Quasi-Tailless Ground Attacker

Evaluation of the ground attack arena involved three typical air-to-ground attack profiles. ITO pilots Fred Knox, Quirin Kim, and Gus Loria developed three profiles to satisfy JAST program requirements: a representative 45° dive attack, a 15° glide or strafe attack, and a low-level ingress with a pop-up to a 15° dive attack, all of which were typical of NATO strike aircraft weapon-delivery profiles.

The 45° dive attack began from a 90° base leg at 18,000 feet AGL at an airspeed of 250 knots calibrated airspeed. After rolling in on the target, the throttle was positioned at the quasi-tailless cruise-flight-test idle stop of 63° power-lever angle. This lower power setting provided the "worst-case" conditions for the flight control and thrust-vectoring control system. During the dive, the target would be tracked down to a simulated weapon release altitude of 12,000 feet AGL at approximately 400 knots calibrated airspeed, at which time the pilot would execute a 4- to 4.5-g pull off the target with the throttle left at 63° power-lever angle. The gross target-acquisition task was to acquire the target within the outer HUD ring. The performance goals were to have no overshoots for a "desired performance" rating and only one overshoot for an "adequate performance" rating. Fine tracking involved tracking the target within the inner HUD ring with the same performance goals: no overshoots permitted for desired performance and only one overshoot for adequate performance.

The 15° glide or strafe attack flew against NASA's Adaptable Target Lighting Array System (ATLAS), which was used for closed-loop tracking-task evaluations of aircraft handling qualities during ground attack profiles. ATLAS consisted of nine lights arrayed on the ground and illuminated in an unpredictable sequence. The pilot was required to rapidly shift his tracking from one lighted target to another as they changed.[52] During the 90° turn from base leg to final (i.e., rolling onto the attack run), all nine lights of the ATLAS were on brightly to evaluate gross acquisition. When established on final (i.e., during the attack run itself), the lights were individually lighted in an apparently random fashion as the pilot shifted his sight tracking to whichever light was illuminated. Gross and fine acquisition performance, both desired and adequate, were the same as the 45° dive attack. These attacks began at a 4,000-feet-AGL base leg at 350 knots calibrated airspeed, with a 4-g turn to final to perform a gross acquisition of the fully lit ATLAS target activated by the chase aircraft. The throttle was again set at 63° power-lever angle on final to reflect the worst case for the flight control/flight-vectoring system. On final, the lights began their preprogrammed cycling and the pilot attempted to track each light as it was lit. There were five to seven target shifts per run, which were flown down to 1,000 feet AGL at 400 knots calibrated airspeed. Different pilots used different techniques, with Kim using aggressive step-type stick inputs and Loria using smoother stick inputs and rudder to assist in lateral tracking.

The third task was the pop-up to a 15° dive attack. Ingress began at 1,000 feet AGL and 400 knots calibrated airspeed. The pilot initiated his pop-up with a loaded roll that resulted in a 4-g pullup with a 30° heading change and a 30° climb. As the X-31 neared the preplanned pulldown point at 2,500 feet AGL, the pilot unloaded to 0.5-g and then rolled the X-31 to place the lift vector on the target. The airplane was then pulled at 2.5 g's to acquire gross acquisition of the target in the HUD. The airplane was then partially unloaded and rolled to upright, and the target was tracked for about 15 seconds until the release conditions of 1,000 feet AGL and 400 knots calibrated airspeed were reached. Recovery was via a 4.5-g pull through the horizon. Again, gross acquisition and fine tracking were the same as for the other air-to-ground tasks: namely, gross acquisition within the outer HUD target reticule with no overshoots for desired performance and one overshoot for adequate performance, and fine tracking within the inner target reticule with no overshoots for desired performance and one overshoot for adequate performance.

Once the tasks were planned, envelope expansion to support these tasks commenced. Thirteen flights were flown to expand the envelope to allow the low-altitude maneuvering anticipated by the air-to-ground tasks. During air-to-ground data flights, the X-31 was flown to the target area using basic X-31 control laws. Once in the target area, a QT index of 4 was selected, which was the equivalent of having 60 percent of the vertical tail removed. Initial results from the air-to-ground tasks were disappointing. In general, pilots reported sluggish aircraft response, slow roll rates, and a general lack of crispness in the aircraft's response. Longitudinal response was sensitive, with some engine gyroscopic effects noted in the 45° dives. Thus, although its pilots found the X-31 capable of performing the assigned tasks, the airplane was deficient in its ability to fly air-to-ground tasks in an aggressive, mission-representative sense. Some changes needed to be made.

A meeting of the flight controls team, including pilots Loria and Kim, was convened to analyze the results of the first two data flights and to review the maneuver restrictions that resulted from the envelope expansion. For example, lateral stick displacement was restricted to half due to the sideslip buildup that was observed during envelope expansion when 360° aileron rolls were performed. However, for the air-to-ground attack profiles, only approximately 135° of bank-angle change would be required. Therefore, lateral stick input restrictions were modified to be no greater than 75 percent instead of 50 percent. Another restriction that inhibited roll response was the simulated idle throttle setting of 63° power-lever angle. This restriction was removed to allow up to military-rated power as required during the pop-up, pulldown, and gross-acquisition phases of the air-to-ground profiles. This was very important because the power setting directly affected the roll response when in the quasi-tailless mode using thrust vectoring to assist in velocity vector rolls. These changes were then evaluated in the simulator. The flight controls team was able to come to a consensus that the additional lateral stick deflection (up to 75 percent) and the additional power setting (up to military-rated) were allowable. A notable improvement in the mission representative sense of the air-to-ground tasks was observed when these changes were flown on *the very next day!* This is but one example of what can be accomplished with an experienced, dedicated test team in the research airplane environment.

It is worth noting once again that even before these changes to lateral stick deflection and power settings were made, the X-31 was able to perform the air-to-ground mission tasks, though not as well as desired. The original flight-test restrictions required worst-case control-power margins and engine response, and yet less than 50 percent of the available control power was used. With the additional lateral stick and engine power, the pilot was able to maintain the plane's energy state and aggressively maneuver the airplane. This gave the pilot increased control power, increased roll rates, and thus better performance. While this required a significant amount of control power from thrust deflection, it still was only approximately 66 percent of the control power available. Level One flying qualities were achieved for the fine-tracking tasks in all three deliveries, and gross-acquisition tasks were rated at Level Two, not for failure to achieve desired performance but rather for the pilot workload and compensation required.[53] As Loria stated, "Thrust vectoring and a QT index = 4 [60 percent vertical tail removed] are suitable for these tasks and [air-to-ground] mission based on this limited investigation."[54]

Some conclusions and design considerations that emerged from the X-31 quasi-tailless flight-test effort are worth noting. Loria stated that, "Based upon the results of this limited experiment, tailless aircraft designs are suitable for the strike fighter mission for the US armed forces."[55] Pat Stoliker, a NASA Dryden flight dynamics engineer (and subsequently, deputy director of NASA Dryden), commented, "Thrust vectoring is a viable control effector which can replace the function of a vertical tail and rudder control surface....An increased level of interaction between the engine and flight control system will be required for future reduced tail or tailless vehicles with thrust vector control." Loria, commenting on design considerations for future tailless aircraft, said, "Reduced tail and tailless tactical aircraft designs are feasible today with existing technology and hardware." And, on the subject of carrier approaches, he stated, "As proven in this limited investigation, a directionally unstable aircraft could be flown in the demanding carrier aviation environment." Both Loria and Stoliker cautioned, "To build an efficient tailless or reduced tail aircraft requires working from a clean sheet of paper, blending all facets of airframe, powerplant and control system design against the performance and flying qualities design objectives....Early integration of thrust vectoring into the design process maximizes the achievable results."[56] The X-31 program had once again pushed the envelope by flying a piloted aircraft in tactically applicable missions with a very great reduction of effective vertical-tail area.

Endnotes

1. Dorr, "Rockwell/MBB X-31," p. 45.
2. Mike Robinson, e-mail to Douglas A. Joyce, May 19, 2012.
3. Lt. Cmdr. James A. McKinney, USN, and J. Thomas McWilliams, "The ACEVAL-AIMVAL Joint Test Program," *1975 Report to the Aerospace Profession* (Lancaster, CA: Society of Experimental Test Pilots, 1975), pp. 128–37.
4. Deutsche Aerospace, *Roll-out to Tactical Evaluation—A German View*, p. 30.
5. Dorr, "Rockwell/MBB X-31," p. 45.
6. Not to be confused with Inites LLC of Boca Raton, FL, which is an information technology firm.
7. The pilot was Maj. Francis C. "Rusty" Gideon, who was seriously injured when he ejected from A-10A (s/n 73-01669) on June 8, 1978, following a double-engine flameout during a firing pass that was caused by gun gas ingestion. His efforts to restart were unsuccessful, and as a consequence he ejected at approximately 2,000 feet AGL shortly before aircraft impact. The Gideon accident resulted in major changes to AFFTC's test protocols regarding potentially hazardous tests, as well as an elevation of the center's safety office to an independent directorate. See AFFTC, *Semi-Annual Historical Report, 1 Jan–30 Jun 1978*, and *Semi-Annual Historical Report, 1 Jul–31 Dec 1978* (Edwards AFB: 6510 ABG History Office, 1978).
8. Deutsche Aerospace, *Roll-out to Tactical Evaluation—A German View*, pp. 30–31; Dorr, "Rockwell/MBB X-31," pp. 45–46.
9. GEC-Marconi Avionics, "Viper Helmet Mounted Display System," brochure, 1994, copy in Dryden archives.
10. Hallion, *On the Frontier*, p. 533.
11. Office of Assistant Secretary of Defense (Public Affairs), "X-31 Aircraft Tests Helmet-Mounted Display in Air Combat," news release, January 11, 1994.
12. Rockwell & GEC-Marconi Avionics, "Viper Helmet Mounted Display System Fact Sheet."
13. Wallace, *Nose Up*, p. 48.
14. Patrick C. Stoliker and John T. Bosworth, "Evaluation of High-Angle-of-Attack Handling Qualities for the X-31 Using Standard Evaluation Maneuvers," NASA TM 104322 (1996), p. 2.
15. Ibid., pp. 4–5.
16. Ibid., pp. 4–5. The Cooper-Harper Handling Qualities Rating Scale (CHR, after NACA-NASA test pilot George Cooper and Cornell

Aeronautical Laboratory [later Calspan] test pilot Bob Harper) is the global flight-test community's standard reference scale for the evaluation of aircraft handling qualities. A CHR of 1 indicates "excellent: highly desirable" aircraft characteristics, where "pilot compensation [is] not a factor for desired performance." A CHR of 2 indicates "good: negligible deficiencies" aircraft characteristics, where, again, "pilot compensation [is] not a factor for desired performance." Both reflect Level 1 performance. (For the record, a 10 is "major deficiencies: control will be lost during some portion of the required operation.") The CHR originated in the initial work of George Cooper in 1957. Cornell Aeronautical Laboratory's Bob Harper then clarified this first scale, subsequently coauthoring an influential paper with Cooper. This resulted in a request to both men by the Advisory Group for Aerospace Research and Development of the North Atlantic Treaty Organization (AGARD-NATO) to produce a standard pilot's handling qualities rating scale. The resulting scale was published as the Cooper-Harper Handling Qualities Rating Scale (CHR) in 1969, and its use has subsequently gone global. See Darrol Stinton, *Flying Qualities and Flight Testing of the Airplane* (Reston, VA: American Institute of Aeronautics and Astronautics, Inc., 1996), pp. 189–191.

17. Thomas J. Cord, David B. Leggett, David J. Wilson, David R. Riley, and Kevin D. Citurs, "Flying Qualities Evaluation Maneuvers," AGARD CP-548 (March 1994), pp. 18-3–18-7.

18. Stoliker and Bosworth, "Evaluation of High AoA Handling Qualities for the X-31," pp. 5–6.

19. Col. Michael S. Francis, USAF (X-31 Program Manager), ARPA letter to Oberstleutnant (Lt. Col.) Wolfgang Turnwald, Bundesministerium der Verteidigung (German Defense Ministry), October 27, 1994; Gary Trippensee (X-31 ITO Director), letter to Helmut Richter (X-31 Deputy Program Manager), September 6, 1994, Dryden archives.

20. James Wisneski, e-mail to Douglas A. Joyce, August 9, 2011.

21. Cord, Leggett, Wilson, Riley, and Citurs, "Flying Qualities Evaluation Maneuvers," pp. 18-3–18-6.

22. Stoliker and Bosworth, "Evaluation of High AoA Handling Qualities for the X-31," pp. 5–13.

23. The history of the PIO rating scale is not as well known or documented as the "gold standard" Cooper-Harper Rating Scale. MIL-HDBK-1797A, which is not generally available to the public, traces the PIO rating scale to an Air Force Wright Aeronautical Laboratory

report (AFWAL-TR-81-3118) that discuses a study of handling qualities performed by the Calspan Corporation to support large airplane flying qualities and the Space Shuttle program. This report says, "This scale is a refinement of scales used in past Calspan evaluations." Discussions by the author with the participants in the X-31 studies or the earlier Calspan studies did not uncover any further history from their memories.

24. Ibid., pp. 12–14.
25. James Wisneski, e-mail to Douglas A. Joyce, July 21, 2011
26. Stoliker and Bosworth, "Evaluation of High AoA Handling Qualities for the X-31," pp. 15–18.
27. Ibid., p. 20.
28. The history of the "confidence classifications" is even murkier than the PIO rating scale. Discussions with Dryden personnel at the time of this writing resulted in this comment to the author from Pat Stoliker, the author of the NASA STEM report: "All the handling qualities folks here agree that we've been using the confidence class ratings for at least two decades, but no one seems to be able to identify where it originated. *So* [emphasis from Stoliker] I would say it is a Dryden creation."
29. Ibid., pp. 7 and 19–20.
30. Ibid., p. 20.
31. Ibid., p. 24.
32. Ibid., p. 28.
33. Ibid., p. 30.
34. Weiss, Rohlf, and Plaetschke, "Parameter Identification for X-31A at High Angles of Attack," slides 2 and 10–11.
35. Wallace, *Nose Up*, p. 49.
36. John T. Bosworth and C. Stoliker, "The X-31A Quasi-Tailless Flight Test Results," NASA Technical Paper 3624 (June 1996), p. 1.
37. Miller, *The X-Planes*, p. 325.
38. Mike Robinson, e-mail to Douglas A. Joyce, August 23, 2011.
39. Rockwell, "JAST Technology Maturation Utilizing the X-31 Testbed," briefing, October 1994; and ITO, "JAST And X-31 ITO Work Agreement And Research Plan For Quasi-Tailless Experiment, Revision A," November 7, 1994, Dryden archives
40. ITO, "X-31/JAST FMIPT Meeting Briefing Slides," November 16, 1994, Dryden archives.
41. Bosworth and Stoliker, "X-31A Quasi-Tailless Flight Test Results," p. 7.

42. Capt. Christopher J. Loria, USMC, Lt. Mark Kelly, USN, and Ron Harney, "X-31 Quasi-tailless Evaluation," in *European SETP Symposium Proceedings* (Lancaster, CA: Society of Experimental Test Pilots, 1995), p. 4.

43. Rogers Smith, NASA Dryden, "X-31A Flight Report 2-214," pilot report, March 10, 1994, Dryden archives.

44. Karl Lang, WTD-51, "X-31A Flight Report 2-215," pilot report, March 10, 1994, Dryden archives.

45. Rogers Smith, NASA Dryden, "X-31A Flight Report 2-216," pilot report, March 10, 1994, Dryden archives.

46. Rogers Smith, NASA Dryden, "X-31A Flight Report 2-217," pilot report, March 17, 1994; Bosworth and Stoliker, "X-31A Quasi-Tailless Flight Test Results," p. 11, Dryden archives.

47. Loria, Kelly, and Harney, "X-31 Quasi-tailless Evaluation," p. 5.

48. Ibid., p. 6.

49. Ibid., p. 9.

50. Kelly retired as a U.S. Navy Captain and is also the husband of the courageous and inspirational former Congresswoman Gabrielle Giffords, who was gravely wounded on January 8, 2011, in a mass shooting in Tucson, AZ.

51. Loria, Kelly, and Harney, "X-31 Quasi-tailless Evaluation," pp. 6–12.

52. M.F. Schafer, R. Koehler, E.M. Wilson, and D.R. Levy, "Initial Flight Test of a Ground Deployed System for Flying Qualities Assessment," NASA Technical Memorandum 101700 (August 1989).

53. Loria, Kelly, and Harney, "X-31 Quasi-tailless Evaluation," pp. 6–12.

54. Capt. C.J. Loria, USMC, "X-31A Flight Report 1-290," pilot report, January 19, 1995, Dryden archives.

55. Loria, Kelly, and Harney, "X-31 Quasi-tailless Evaluation," p. 16.

56. Ibid., 16–17; Bosworth and Stoliker, "X-31A Quasi-Tailless Flight Test Results," p. 33.

The X-31 on takeoff during its Paris Air Show debut. (Rockwell)

CHAPTER 5

Desert Disaster, Triumph in Paris, and a New VECTOR

January 19, 1995, constituted a busy day for the X-31 program. Piloted by Gus Loria and Quirin Kim, Ship 1 flew the first two flights of that day, finishing two air-to-ground quasi-tailless missions and completing the QT evaluation for JAST. The third mission was a finish-up parameter-identification sortie expanding and completing the PID data mission flown the day before. The pilot scheduled for this mission was Karl Lang, who had also flown the previous day's PID data mission. The flight would be the last scheduled data flight for Ship 1. But more than this, it would essentially finish the funded flights for the X-31 program, although program advocates still planned to attend the Paris Air Show if they could obtain funding and final approval. The weather at Edwards that day was unusual, with significant moisture in the air and a 25,000-feet overcast ceiling. The PID data points were planned for 28,000 feet, so Lang and the test conductor conferred because the X-31 was restricted from flight in visible moisture (i.e., clouds). The engineers responsible for the PID data agreed that any altitude above 20,000 feet was sufficient for the data points. The air-to-ground flights had been flown at relatively low altitude, so the high cirrus overcast was not a factor for them. Karl Lang then went to the airplane and the test conductor went to the control room to meet the planned 1310 Pacific Standard Time (PST) staffing time. The X-31 was configured with a modified flutter test box (FTB) designed to provide excitation of individual flight control surfaces, thereby allowing an accurate estimation of aerodynamic parameters. On this flight, manual excitation through pitch, roll, and yaw doublets were to be performed in addition to automatic excitation through the flutter test box. Additionally, a new version of the flight control software was installed that had been developed to support the quasi-tailless evaluation. The data from this flight would allow correlation between the manual and FTB inputs as well as comparison between this software load and previous ones. These PID flights had been performed throughout the program as flight control changes were made in order to keep the aircraft's aerodynamic parameter database current. They were relatively benign missions as compared to the very-high-AOA envelope expansion, close-in-combat, and quasi-tailless missions.

A Matter of Pitot Icing…

Ship 1 took off at 1346 PST, followed shortly thereafter by its NASA F/A-18 chase aircraft flown by Dana Purifoy, with the X-31 flying preliminary data-correlation maneuvers during the climb to altitude. At 1350 PST, Lang began acquiring the PID test data in close coordination with the Dryden mission control room. These points were flown at altitudes between 20,000 feet MSL and 24,000 feet MSL. The chase pilot observed after the flight that the X-31 produced visible condensation in the wingtip vortices during much of the mission. Karl Lang was observing an uneven cirrus cloud base at approximately 23,000 feet MSL and he had no clear horizon, which, again, was unusual for Edwards. Lang prudently reached down to his right-side console and turned on the clearly marked pitot heat switch, commenting to the test conductor, "Okay, remind me…I just put pitot heat on, remind me to put it off."[1] The test conductor acknowledged this comment by saying, "Copy that."[2]

At this point, on the internal control room communications net, a program engineer commented, "The Pitot heat's not hooked up on the Kiel probe." The test conductor did not immediately relay this information to the pilot, and some of the control room engineers pulled their headsets aside so that they could have a sidebar discussion about pitot heating that was not carried on the internal control room intercom. The pilot then noted, "I'm at 277; I mean 207 knots at 20° angle of attack. Okay, pitch doublet…." The pilot had obviously noted a discrepancy between the airspeed and angle of attack, but the fact that he was pressing on with the data point by then calling "Pitch doublet" indicated that he did not pick up on just how important this discrepancy was. Rogers Smith, the NASA Dryden ITO pilot, commented years later, "Anybody that's been on the program (and lots of people [including Lang] had been on many years) would know that 20° angle of attack would be somewhere around 135 knots, 140 knots…it's not 207 knots."

So Karl Lang, busy with finishing the final points before landing, made a comment to the control room but missed the potential gravity of this problem, as did the chase pilot. If the X-31 was at 20° angle of attack, then the chase pilot should be seeing 135–140 knots in his airplane. However, the comment made by Lang to the control room was made via intercom, not air-to-ground radio, and telemetered to the ground. This was of particular significance to the X-31 program because the high longitudinal stick forces made it more comfortable for pilots to use two hands on the stick. The use of a telemetered "hot mike" allowed the X-31 pilot not to have to depress a mike switch on the throttle to communicate with the control room; instead, he just had to talk into the intercom. Normally in NASA chase aircraft, hot mike conversations between the test pilot and control room were retransmitted back to the chase aircraft via radio. This enabled the chase pilot to retain more complete situational awareness of what was happening. However, this retransmission system had been causing substantial static in the chase pilot's headset that was very distracting. So, on this mission, the retransmission of hot mike conversations from the X-31 was disabled. The chase pilot was only able to hear radio transmissions and he therefore did not hear the airspeed/AOA comment of the X-31 pilot.

After making the manual doublet inputs, Lang engaged the flutter test box (designed to inhibit inputs if the airspeed was over 200 knots calibrated airspeed) for the automatic flight control surface excitation. He said, "three, two, one, go...eh...it doesn't do anything."[3] It was another vital clue; the computer was calculating over 200 knots calibrated airspeed, so the flutter test box was inhibited from responding. This was clearly shown on the displays in the control room and in the cockpit on the HUD. The X-31 pilot also had an alternate airspeed display near his right knee in the cockpit. This display was attached to a separate, simple pitot tube. It probably would have indicated somewhat near the actual airspeed, but Lang never checked it. Recovery fuel status was reached just at the completion of the attempted flutter test box excitation, so the X-31 pilot and the control room started running the prelanding checklist, and the chase pilot started to rejoin on the X-31.

Events now moved rapidly toward a dismal conclusion. The test conductor started to make a comment regarding the pitot heat, but Lang interrupted, "I'll leave it on for a moment." The test conductor responded, "We think it may not be hooked up." Lang, somewhat sarcastically, replied, "It may not be hooked up... that's good...I like that." As a note, the entire test team had been briefed when the Kiel probe was installed at NASA that there was no longer pitot heat and that the cockpit switch had been disabled. Moreover, Lang had flown with the Kiel probe many times and early on had been specifically briefed about the change from the original configuration. In any case, as the airplane descended, the pitot tube became increasingly obstructed by ice. The airspeed was decreasing, which possibly had given Lang the feeling that pitot heat was working. However, the airspeed continued to decrease well below what is appropriate for flight safety. The flight control computers calculated flight control system gains based on the airspeed that the pitot static system was showing, which can go to a very low value, varying between 48 and 100 knots calibrated airspeed. This low airspeed mandated that the flight control gains be set at a very high value—far too high for the actual airspeed of 170 knots. This, in turn, would cause the aircraft to overrespond to inputs to the point of oscillating out of control. Two seconds after Lang's sarcastic reply concerning inoperative pitot heat, a warning tone sounded, the Master Caution light illuminated, and X-31 Ship 1 abruptly pitched up out of control. Lang saw a red flight control system warning light and reflexively tried to counter the rapidly increasing pitch-up with full-forward stick.

Lang was under no illusions as to the gravity of his situation. He had been with the X-31 since its earliest Palmdale days and had seen this happen in the simulator; it was inevitably catastrophic. Ten seconds after the initial warning tone—and at a pitch-up angle that already was 20° nose-up *past* the vertical—Lang ejected. To Dana Purifoy in his NASA F/A-18 chase aircraft, the wing-rock, dramatic pitch-up, and ejection was his first indication of any problem. Purifoy responded by calling the test conductor, "O.K. NASA 1, we have an ejection. We have an ejection." Then he said, "NASA 1, do you read?" The test conductor responded, "Yeah, we copy Dana. We copy." The chase pilot then narrated the last sad seconds of Ship 1: "The aircraft is descending over the North Base area. I have a chute. The pilot is out of the seat, and the chute is good." Karl Lang was descending in a parachute with a 17-feet canopy diameter. The size was typical for Navy aircraft that operate mostly over water; however, this small canopy chute had a relatively high descent rate of approximately 28.3 feet per second. Thus, upon impact on the hard playa surface, Lang was injured; fortunately, his injuries were not critical. X-31 Ship 1 was completely destroyed during impact and the subsequent explosion and fire as it broke apart on the desert floor.[4]

Ironically, by the time the X-31 impacted the desert floor, its flight controls—in the basic mode—were working correctly. Initially, the plane had pitched up and down wildly, reflecting the high control gains that the FCS presumed were necessary because of the faulty data it was receiving. But as the ice melted from the Kiel probe, the correct total pressure was sensed and the

Ship 1's accident site at Edwards's North Base. (NASA DFRC)

control gains began to match the real situation. As the gains approached the correct values, the plane stabilized before hitting the ground. This can be viewed from the video of the descent and crash recorded by NASA's ground tracking cameras.

Why did this happen? When the original pitot probe was replaced by the Kiel probe, engineers made a conscious decision not to equip it with pitot heat because they did not want to wait for a heated Kiel probe to be manufactured. This is typical of many instrumented aircraft at Edwards, where the low-humidity environment does not mandate provisions for pitot heat. However, there was no temporary operating procedure paperwork issued to aircrew members or control room personnel informing them of this change. Appropriate management briefings were accomplished following the change to the Kiel probe, but no mention was made in the briefing slides of the omission of pitot heat. However, the accident report states that the air data engineer who presented the brief stated that the inoperative pitot heat was discussed by the briefing attendees. The work order that was issued for the installation of the Kiel probe called for the collaring of the circuitbreaker, correctly rendering it inoperative; however, it did not call for the pitot heat switch in the cockpit to be placarded as "inoperative." The pitot heat switch thus remained clearly marked "Pitot heat."

As a result, incredibly, most X-31 pilots assumed that there was heat; at the time of the accident, four of the five active X-31 pilots believed that the pitot heat system was functional. System safety analyses dating back to the Palmdale days that were updated when the airplanes came to Dryden did not adequately highlight the hazard of having erroneous pitot information fed into the flight control system. It was felt that loss of accurate pitot data would be the result of an event, like a bird strike damaging the pitot probe, during which it would become obvious to the pilot that a backup flight control mode or "reversionary" mode needed to be selected.

There was such a mode built into the aircraft systems. The X-31's flight control system included the "basic" mode (which could include thrust vectoring when enabled), three "reversionary" modes designed to handle failures, and a "spin recovery" mode. In the basic mode, the flight control system gains were scheduled based on Mach number, pressure altitude, and angle of attack. Pitot pressure was required for accurate Mach number information, and the inaccurate sensing of this critical parameter was what caused the problem. The "R1" reversionary mode handled inertial navigation unit failures. The "R2" reversionary mode handled failures of angle-of-attack and angle-of-sideslip sensing. The "R3" reversionary mode handled air data failures. If the flight control system computers thought a reversionary mode was warranted, they would disable thrust vectoring if it was active, sound a tone in the pilot's headset, and cause the appropriate reversionary mode switch to illuminate and flash. The flight control system would then switch to an interim mode known as the "R-request" mode. The pilot could then enter the reversionary mode by lifting a switch guard and depressing the illuminated light.

But the flight control system was *not* designed to automatically select a reversionary mode under any circumstances. In the R3 case, the flight control computers picked a fixed gain set of two available gain sets that could be alternated by the pilot. Initially, the appropriate gain set was selected based on the flight control system's assessment of the last valid airspeed. This backup system was quite robust, allowing control of the aircraft from 450 knots calibrated airspeed right down to landing. During the early part of the flight-test program, several air data computer anomalies did result in transfers to the R3 mode and uneventful landings in that mode.

In the X-31 program, the proper operation of the reversionary modes had been tested and, on several occasions, an anomaly in the calculation of primary data caused an "R-request" in which, on coordination with the control room, the appropriate R button was depressed and the aircraft was recovered in the reversionary mode. In the X-29 program, a previous NASA Dryden program that also had computer-controlled flight control with reversionary modes, the airplane was often flown in the reversionary modes as a matter of course. In the X-31 program, this was not done. It was the norm that the decision to enter into the reversionary modes would be a coordinated decision between the control room and the X-31 test pilot. In fact, the pilot's manual for the X-31 did not even call for flight control reversion as an immediate action during emergencies. This culture of discussion with the control room first may have inhibited Karl Lang from just immediately selecting R3, but he obviously did not fully appreciate the dire consequences of the airspeed/AOA mismatch that he was seeing. Neither did the control room, and the chase pilot was not even aware of the issue.

In the X-31, pitot-static information from the pitot probe—in this case, the unheated Kiel probe—was sent directly to two air data computers. One air data computer sent information to two of the flight control computers. The other air data computer sent information to the other two flight control computers, one of which was a "tiebreaker" that adjudicated between the three flight control computers and the two air data computers. The air data computers also provided the data that was shown on the HUD and other cockpit instruments, except the small standby airspeed indicator near the pilot's right knee. Whereas disagreements in the computed values of the air data computers and flight control computers would cause a fault and an R-request, this was not the case if false pitot-static information was sent to the air data computers. The hazard analyses and system safety analyses done on this design assumed that false pitot-static information would be obvious (as mentioned previously), and they did not fully address a failure such as pitot ice, particularly on an unheated pitot probe because when the analyses were done the vehicle had a heated probe. One might ask, however, why there was not an updated hazard analysis when NASA installed the unheated probe.

The bottom line was that the air data computers and the flight control computers were incapable of determining the validity of the raw pneumatic pitot data as it entered the air data computers. Invalid pitot data from the probe would send the same inaccurate value to *both* air data computers, and this inaccuracy would therefore *not* be detected by the air data computers or the flight control computers. As stated in the X-31 Mishap Investigation Report, "Of critical note was the fact that the only means by which the FCS was designed to detect a failure or degradation of the air data was if the two ADCs [air data computers] disagreed. *There was a misconception among test team and system safety engineers that the FCS could identify or resolve abrupt changes in the air data signals* [emphasis in the original report]. No flight control code could be found which implemented such a safeguard, and the [Mishap] Board concluded that it did not exist."[5] Thus, the pilot and the control room minimized the problem until the airplane departed controlled flight, and then it was too late.

The Mishap Board identified the following causes of the accident:

- Erroneous total pressure data from the pitot-static system caused incorrect gain selection within the FCS for the flight condition. This led to aircraft instability and departure from controlled flight.
- Erroneous total-pressure data were caused by the slow accretion of ice in or around the pitot tube.
- The system safety analyses failed to identify the potential catastrophic consequences of a failure in the pitot-static system.
- Simulation results that clearly identified the catastrophic consequences of a failure in the pitot-static system failed to lead to any corrective action.
- The relatively high descent rate of the main parachute system used in the X-31 resulted in the mishap pilot receiving injuries on landing.

The following contributing causes were identified:

- The Kiel probe design was inherently susceptible to icing.
- The Kiel probe was not equipped with pitot heat.
- The configuration control process failed to disseminate the condition of the pitot heat.

The Mishap Board recommended that the system safety analyses be reaccomplished, with a focus on single-point failures; that a fix to mitigate the hazard of the loss of raw pitot-static data be found and verified in simulation; that all temporary operating procedures be reviewed and a process developed to control future temporary operating procedures; that all cockpit switches and displays be audited for proper functioning and labeling; that all program personnel be trained in the basics of system safety; and that the parachute be replaced with one that had a slower descent rate.[6]

Several test team members did not completely agree with the Mishap Report and felt that large airspeed errors and suspected pitot icing should have mandated a halt to test operations until the cause of the discrepancy was identified. Some felt that the pilot and engineers should have had a better understanding of the importance of the correct flight control system gains and the connection of correct airspeed to those gains. One team member said, "The test pilot and flight control engineers ought to understand the importance of the right gains." And another commented, "I don't care how safe the aircraft is, 70 kt errors and icing conditions are not acceptable for good flight tests." They were concerned that that Mishap Report did not place enough emphasis on the test team's flawed emphasis of flight-test methodology, saying, "They should have paused instead of pressing on to the next condition."[7] In a presentation on the accident to the 1996 Society of Experimental Test Pilots Symposium, Rogers Smith tellingly said:

If You Do Not Understand or It Does Not Make Sense:

SPEAK UP!

STOP THE TESTS AND THINK![8]

As emphasized in a video produced by Dryden 10 years later, Ken Szalai, who was the NASA Dryden director at the time of the accident, said, "The right response is, 'something is going on here; I don't understand it; let's call a halt here and let's just figure it out.'" He also emphatically stated, "In the case of any discrepancy, anything that doesn't sound right, feel right, smell right… let's stop and think it over."[9] These are important recurring lessons in aviation, and they again were sadly relearned by the X-31 program in the days following January 19, 1995.

On to Paris

Ironically, even as the program team was accepting the bitter loss of Ship 1, the X-31 had won Pentagon approval to fly in the Paris Air Show in June. With great optimism, Charles Johnson, the X-31 program manager at NAVAIR, said, "If the [X-31] is approved for the Paris Air Show, we do have one airplane working, and baring any problems we could still do that activity."[10] The X-31 test team would indeed have to work very hard to make that happen! The accident happened in January 1995 and the Paris Airshow was held in June of 1995; thus, the team had less than 5 months to recover from the accident, develop show routines, and get the plane to Paris. On top of this was a morass of significant administrative tasks, both U.S. (DOD and contractor) and French. These are things flight-test teams do not naturally relish or excel at, but they were necessary if the X-31 was to fly at the Air Show.

The X-31 team wanted very much to end the program on a high note, and while providing much engineering support to the Mishap Board, they also started working on preparing for participation at the Paris Air Show. The flight on January 19 was to have been the last funded flight in the X-31 program, notwithstanding the accident, so there was no funding to support a deployment and performance at the Paris Air Show. Ultimately, the two companies (Rockwell and MBB) and the U.S. and German governments agreed to share equally in the cost of having the X-31 perform at Paris. There was a lot of technical work to do. First, the recommendations from the forthcoming Mishap Report had to be implemented. As these recommendations emerged, even before the formal report was published, the team was developing means to comply with them. The approach was to incorporate aircraft hardware and software modifications to address the Mishap Board recommendations, revisit the System Safety and Hazard Analyses, revise the process for issuing temporary operating procedures, and train all program personnel on the basics of system safety.[11]

In addition, there were several features that would be required for operations in Europe, including accommodations for the absence of a normal flight-test control room capable of monitoring critical aircraft parameters and for operations on European runways that were much shorter than the venerable Runway 22/04 at Edwards AFB, which was nearly 15,000 feet long. The X-31, except for the quasi-tailless flights, had done all of its high-AOA maneuvering above 10,000 feet. Therefore, it would be a nontrivial feat to expand the post-stall maneuvering envelope down to 500 feet AGL for flight at 70° angle of attack in a defined set of post-stall maneuvers. Then, rehearsal flights for the airshow profile itself would have to be conducted and several practice flights flown for pilot proficiency. Since NASA had a policy of nonparticipation in airshow presentations, the X-31 ITO team also had to orchestrate the transition of flight clearance and safety responsibility to NAVAIR.[12] The logistics of transporting the airplane to Paris had to be resolved. All this had to be accomplished in just 5 short months.

Fred Knox and Quirin Kim were selected to be the primary pilots for the airshow, with Rogers Smith ready to fly a limited number of envelope expansion flights if required. Since NASA had a nonparticipation policy in airshows, Rogers would not be able to fly in the actual demonstration flights in Paris.

Quirin Kim and Fred Knox, primary pilots for the Paris Air Show. (NASA DFRC)

Additionally, for reasons that are no longer totally clear, the Navy could not take the responsibility of officially supporting the efforts while in Paris, nor could it allow its pilots to do so. It was planned that six flights would be flown at or above 13,000 feet MSL to revalidate post-stall flight with the new flight control system software prior to moving into new flight regimes. These flights would follow functional check flight procedures to validate proper systems performance after the almost-5-month stand-down on Ship 2. The envelope expansion maneuvers were to be evaluated by each pilot at 13,000 feet MSL/8,000 feet AGL, 5,000 feet AGL, and 2,000 feet AGL before proceeding lower. The X-31 had a spin chute as a last-ditch recovery mechanism for high-AOA work at altitude. This chute was modified to become a drag chute for use in Europe, owing to Le Bourget's relatively short runways, and after the envelope expansion at altitude with the spin chute installed, the drag chute was substituted and evaluated during landings at Edwards. Pilots were to develop and validate the flight demonstration routine during the stepdown envelope expansion. To prepare for flights in Europe without a control room, some flights were planned to be conducted with a silent control room.

Redundancy management changes that were made as a result of the accident were considered to be the biggest unknown. These were to be addressed with piloted simulation, verification and validation testing, and the six actual flights at 13,000 feet MSL. The airshow demonstration routine was composed of maneuvers that had been extensively performed previously at altitude; it was designed specifically to limit the effect of failures at low altitude, and the pilots had developed and practiced the routine in the simulators at Dryden and Rockwell Downey. The test team felt that the risks attributable to low-altitude maneuvering were in the areas of aircraft performance and handling qualities and precision-piloting tasks. The risks associated with post-stall operation of the X-31 at low altitude, as compared to close-in-combat flight at high altitude, were considered to be mitigated by four factors. First, the airshow's structured, preplanned maneuvers are much more benign than the free-for-all dynamics of close-in-combat flight. Second, the entry airspeed for post-stall was reduced to 240 knots calibrated airspeed from the 265 knots calibrated airspeed of close-in combat. Third, a large margin was to be maintained above the minimum airspeed limit of 70 knots true airspeed.

Lastly, the changes in vortex-induced asymmetries due to Reynolds Number changes (at lower altitude) were predicted to be small. Remember, Ship 2 was considered to be the "evil twin" of, and had less predictable vortex behavior than, Ship 1. The precision-piloting task was to be addressed by "practice, practice, practice" in the low-altitude environment.[13]

The accident and consequent need to make changes in redundancy management led to several changes in the revisionary mode philosophy for the X-31, which was the focus of the testing to be done at altitude. Since there still was limited redundancy in the single-source input sensors, like pitot pressure, the flight control computers were reprogrammed to provide automatic R-Request modes if anomalies in the single-source sensors were noted. These anomalies were to be detected by adding monitors to air data, maximum sideslip, and the inertial navigation unit, as well as an additional monitor on the exhaust nozzle area. Also, reversionary modes that could be selected by the pilot without discussion with the control room were provided because there would be no control room in Europe. And the pitot probe on the new Kiel air data probe was heated!

Other hardware changes included a fix to the hot mike retransmission problem so that, during the envelope expansion to low altitude, the chase pilots would now be able to hear a clear retransmission of hot mike discussions, and a replumbing of the standby and backup airspeed indicators so that the output of secondary airspeed was now in the upper scan of the pilot in the cockpit. The X-31 had a hydrazine-powered emergency air-start system that could only be used at high altitude. Since the only high-altitude flights for the airplane were planned to be ferry flights from the reassembly location to Paris, the test team decided to remove this system. This eliminated the potential problem of hydrazine leaks from this system. A VHF radio was also added because UHF was not available in Europe.

The initially planned airshow maneuvers included a 30° AOA aileron roll; a "cobra" maneuver, which was an abrupt pull to 70° angle of attack at 200 knots calibrated airspeed; a 50° AOA flyby; a post-stall split-S maneuver; and a loop with a 180° post-stall heading reversal. Several relatively simple low-altitude immediate-action procedures were developed for pilot initiation because control room help was not available. All of these maneuvers and procedures were tested and validated by pilots in the simulator.[14] Candidate airshow maneuvers were obliged to meet the following requirements: be within the previously cleared AOA and airspeed post-stall envelope, be repeatable, provide safe ground clearance, provide for a safe recovery after a failure, and fit within the airspace and maneuver restrictions at Paris. Pilots flying these maneuvers in the simulator identified some basic rules for post-stall maneuvers near the ground:

- The ability to recover from a high-rate-of-descent post-stall maneuver was required by 3,000 feet AGL.
- Low-altitude post-stall maneuvers below 1,000 feet AGL had to be such that the velocity vector remained level or above the horizon.
- Post-stall rolls below 1,000 feet AGL were required to be in the wings-up direction. In other words, the lift vector had to be pointed up.
- Extended post-stall maneuvers below 1,000 feet AGL had to be at 50° angle of attack or below.

Simulators were used extensively to screen candidate maneuvers, practice recoveries from failures, and link maneuvers for the final airshow sequence. The NASA Dryden flight-hardware-in-the-loop simulator was used for failure simulations, and the Rockwell Downey dome simulator was used for integration of the full airshow demonstration. Fred Knox, in a subsequent presentation to the Society of Experimental Test Pilots, stated, "It would have been impossible to develop the air show in the time and sorties allowed without high fidelity manned simulators."[15]

In parallel with the engineering and pilot preparations for the show, the team had to plan the logistics of getting the airplane to Paris. Two options were considered. One involved using the Airbus Beluga aircraft, which was a modified version of a standard Airbus A300-600 airliner with a greatly expanded fuselage to allow shipment of outsized parts and components. It normally ferried Airbus components and subassemblies from Airbus consortium partners to Toulouse for final assembly. The X-31 would fit in the Beluga without any disassembly, but just barely. The fit was very tight, so there was a risk of damage during loading and unloading. The Beluga had a gross weight limit such that the X-31 and all the spares and other equipment could not all be carried on the same airplane, so two airplanes would be required to take everything the X-31 needed to Europe. In addition, the Beluga was a new design at the time; it had not yet been certified, and shipment of the X-31 would constitute its *first* load. The plan with the Beluga would be to fly to Toulouse, France (the Airbus final assembly location), in a multileg flight from Edwards AFB.

The second option was to use a USAF C-5A cargo transport. The C-5 had a long history of transporting outsized cargo, and it did not have the Beluga's restrictive gross-weight limitation. As a result, only one aircraft was needed to haul everything the X-31 program needed, and it could fly from Edwards to Manching, Germany, in a day. Manching was the German flight-test center, so there was great support in terms of equipment, shops, manpower, airspace (for functional check flights and practice), and chase aircraft. Manching was also where the MBB factory was located. A C-5 flight to Manching seemed to be the natural choice except for one technical issue and one administrative issue. First, the C-5A had a relatively restrictive cargo compartment width compared to the Beluga, so one of the X-31 wings had to be removed to make the X-31 fit inside the C-5. The risk here, of course, was in the disassembly and reassembly of the aircraft prior to the airshow. Second, time was short and approval was needed from the USAF to obtain the C-5 mission reservation and get "hazardous load" authorization, and the cost of "hiring" a C-5 under the USAF's industrial [reimbursable] funding scheme was more than the team members' budgets would allow.[16] Ultimately, however, the C-5 was chosen and the plan was to assemble the X-31 in Manching, fly functional check flights to ensure proper system operation, and ferry the airplane to Paris. So while the test team initiated its efforts, Navy Program Manager Charles Johnson and DARPA Program Manager Mike Francis set about arranging a C-5 ride for the X-31. They finally found an east coast USAF reserve team at Westover Air Reserve Base (ARB) in Massachusetts that could accomplish the mission as a much-needed training flight. Thus, the program was alleviated of a significant fiscal burden.

Aside from the logistics of getting the airplane to Manching, weather was a challenge both for the ferry flight from Manching to Paris and for the flights during the airshow. The X-31 could not fly in clouds or instrument-only meteorological conditions, not only due to the potential of pitot icing but also because the airplane did not have adequate instruments and navigation equipment for flight in the clouds, and because the airplane essentially needed to remain a "dry airplane." Many of the airplane's compartments were not waterproof, and the thrust-vector vanes were sensitive to moisture. Since the airplane needed to remain clear of clouds on the ferry flight from Manching to Paris, the team decided to make a two-leg flight with an en route stop at Köln-Bonn (Cologne), Germany. A direct flight from Manching to Paris was at the limits of the X-31's range, so there would be little margin for deviations around clouds and rain. The stop in Koln-Bonn provided a larger margin for weather deviations, but now good landing weather was needed at three locations. The best possible weather forecast on the day of the ferry flight was to be ensured by conducting face-to-face weather briefings with the weather forecaster, with translations provided by the German Air Force chase pilots. A handheld GPS was installed in the X-31's cockpit to provide navigation assistance in the event that the X-31 became separated from the chase aircraft. Weather conditions in Europe were marginal at that time of year and rapidly changed from acceptable to unacceptable. Strict weather limits were established for the actual airshow during the workup at Dryden and they were not changed after arrival at Paris. These limits were as follows:

- 5,000-feet ceiling for the full demonstration routine
- 1,500-feet ceiling for the poor weather (low show) routine
- Crosswind limit of 10 knots with gusts to 15 knots
- Tailwind limit of 10 knots
- No rain
- 5-kilometer visibility[17]

On April 13, 1995, after over 4 months on the ground, X-31 Ship 2 took to the air to perform a functional check flight of the hardware and software modifications that had been generated as a result of the accident. The first flight of the day was flown by Fred Knox, who reported, "All FCF items completed. No problems with aircraft or software. Good Flight."[18] This flight was followed by a second FCF flown by Rogers Smith, who commented, "Generally the Aircraft performed beautifully. It was very symmetric on all the decels and pulls—truly an amazing aircraft."[19] These initial FCF flights were followed by validation of the aircraft's flying qualities with the new software and hardware installed. These flights were flown at 13,000 feet MSL using standard flight-test maneuvers (e.g., step inputs, doublets, bank-to-bank rolls, etc.) as well as airshow maneuvers. All the normal flight-test resources and procedures were used for these flights, including a chase aircraft, telemetry, a control room, and a spin chute. After a flight on April 17, Quirin Kim commented, "Throughout the maneuvers, the X-31 showed excellent handling qualities. The selected maneuvers could be performed without any problems. The simulator training in Dryden and Downey proved to be an excellent preparation tool. Ready to step down to next lower altitude."[20]

Following several flights at 13,000 feet MSL, the testing moved down to 5,000 feet AGL. Here, the spin chute was not armed because an inadvertent deployment was considered more of a risk than the benefits it may have provided. Each pilot flew each maneuver at 5,000 feet AGL before going lower, and each pilot was the final authority on when they were ready for a lower altitude. The X-31 was performing much better at lower altitude due to the greater thrust that was available. In fact, the thrust was such that the standard flight-test clinical maneuvers were difficult to perform, and high-AOA points were not possible because the steady state conditions produced very low airspeeds. The technique was therefore altered to enter these points from a 30° bank. These flights were also used to evaluate the airshow demonstration maneuvers. Some comments by Rogers Smith after a flight on April 22, 1995, follow:

> Very enjoyable flight. The new techniques for the clinical expansion points worked well and the demo maneuvers were interesting to perform.

> Comments on the demo maneuvers are:

> - 30 deg roll is likely not impressive from the ground and can leave the pilot with no margins if the roll rate is not achieved for any reason.

- High speed cobra has a good initial phase but the recovery is a little awkward and unimpressive (The MiG 29 and SO-27 [SU-27] do it better).

- The split-S takes too long and gets my first rate for elimination.

- The X-31 is truly an impressive vehicle, particularly at these lower altitudes—all the members of the team can be proud of this accomplishment.[21]

During testing at this altitude, a cautionary note was made relative to the 30° AOA 360° velocity vector roll by Quirin Kim: "During this maneuver, full lateral stick input at 30° AoA has to be used to complete the maneuver without any altitude loss. If the maneuver is performed with less than full lateral stick input an altitude loss of about 500 feet will occur. If this maneuver is performed at low altitude (500 feet AGL to 1,000 feet AGL), it is essential to perform this maneuver only with full lateral stick deflection to avoid an altitude loss."[22]

The test team now stepped down to 2,000 feet AGL. All maneuvers were to be flown over a marked runway, either the Edwards AFB main Runway 04/22 or one of the marked dry lakebed runways on Rogers Dry Lake at Edwards. A chase aircraft was not used because it was not possible or safe for one to remain in a close position and because a landing runway was very close. The control room was used for this part of the testing, however. After flying at this altitude (2,000 feet AGL), Rogers Smith commented, "Exhilarating flight; the X-31 performs beautifully at these altitudes. Love the break turn (our candidate 'signature maneuver'); don't like to 30 deg AoA roll (no margins) and I don't feel that the Split S or high speed cobra can compete with the other maneuver in the final set."[23] (And, indeed, the 30° AOA full 360° aileron roll, the high-speed cobra, and the split-S were eventually eliminated from the planned airshow routine.)

Operating a research airplane outside of its normal environment—having real-time telemetry and a control room staffed with many experts in a myriad of aeronautical disciplines—was a challenge for the X-31 team. The hardware and software changes mandated by the Mishap Board were part of the solution. Practicing the routine by stepping down in altitude was the team's way of ensuring that the flight control system was robust and that the airplane's flying qualities were safe and predictable. Flights were flown in conditions of relatively high winds and gusts. Since telemetry would not be available to provide safety calls for marginal maneuvers, such maneuvers were removed from the airshow routine. This was the case with the 30° AOA aileron roll, which was eventually eliminated. While new automatic redundancy-management

Drag-chute testing at Edwards in preparation for Paris. (NASA DFRC)

routines and cockpit display formats helped to reduce the dependency on a control room, a "mini monitor room" was developed to assist the demonstration pilot, if needed. This mini monitor room was a van with a radio and a small control room team that included an X-31 pilot, flight control expert, engine expert, and systems engineer. During the final airshow rehearsal flights at Dryden, this mini monitor room was used with the Dryden control room silently monitoring. This process worked so well that the mini monitor room was used for all subsequent flights in Europe.

The X-31 was not designed with operations from the shorter European runways in mind. All operations had been from Palmdale or Edwards with runway lengths in excess of 12,000 feet. The challenge of operating on the shorter runways in Europe involved the usual concerns of potential brake fires, antiskid failures, blown tires, energy absorption, and departure from the runway if the airplane was unable to stop. A drag chute had been developed to provide for safer takeoffs (with potential aborts) and landings in Europe on shorter runways of less than 10,000 feet in length.

The development of this system, which replaced the spin chute, took longer than expected, and testing revealed problems that had to be reengineered. Only six actual chute deployments had been performed before the airplane was shipped to Europe, so the test team developed an alternate "brakes-only" landing procedure. Analysis showed that brakes-only landings in Europe would place brake energies in the caution area. Takeoff aborts, emergency landings, or heavy weight immediately after takeoff would place the brake energy in the danger area, with a risk of brake failure. The testing that was done on the drag chute as it was developed verified the deployment/jettison functions, maximum deployment speed, minimum jettison speed, and crosswind limits. The drag chute would allow takeoff aborts and landings on runways as short as 6,000 feet. Additional braking tests were performed for the brakes-only option, and the performance of the antiskid system, brake energy capabilities, and brake system usage was validated. This allowed construction of accurate brake performance charts. These braking tests revealed that a reduction in landing speed of 8 knots calibrated airspeed was required for a safe landing on a 10,000-foot runway, so the normal 12° AOA landing was increased to 13° and was then flight tested without problems. All of this testing was done concurrently with the low-altitude airshow practice, with no additional sorties required. This testing proved that the X-31 could routinely operate on runways shorter than 8,000 feet with a drag chute and safely land on a 10,000-foot runway without a drag chute in the event of a drag chute failure.[24]

As the X-31 was expanding the envelope down to 500 feet AGL and preparing for focused airshow practice, the process of transferring safety responsibility from NASA to NAVAIR was in progress. Since time was very short, it was agreed that NAVAIR technical personnel who had previously worked on the X-31 program would be used to help expedite the process. NASA would retain safety responsibility until the low-altitude envelope expansion was complete. Frequent transfer of data from Dryden to NAVAIR via phone, Videocon, and fax was used to keep NAVAIR personnel constantly in the loop. A Navy flight-test engineer was deployed to NASA Dryden to facilitate the clearance process. Finally, the flight clearance was to be issued in two increments. An initial clearance was issued for operation at Edwards, and then a final clearance was issued for operations in Europe. During this final, low-altitude envelope expansion part of the preparation, Rogers Smith reported the following:

> X-31 is very solid at these altitudes. It's a great opportunity to be able to fly these expansion points. I was impressed with the X-31 from inside the cockpit and listening to the excited comments from our ground observers (who went out to the edge of the lakebed). I gathered that it was equally impressive from the ground. It's a great accomplishment for the team to get this far against all odds and obstacles—I think we have a real shot at impressing the Parisians![25]

For Rogers Smith, this was to be his last flight in the X-31. Due to NASA's nonparticipation policy, all the remaining flights, including those at Paris, were to be flown by Fred Knox and Kim. NASA Dryden completed the low-altitude envelope expansion on April 28, 1995, and requested flight clearance for further flights in support of airshow practice. The maneuvers requested were the 30° AOA aileron roll, the high-speed cobra, the low-speed cobra, the post-stall split-S, a loop with post-stall heading reversals, and a break turn to 70° angle of attack.[26] The first Navy flight clearance was received on May 4, 1995, with the first low-altitude airshow practice flight flown by Fred Knox, including an airshow practice, a silent control room, and a 13° AOA landing.[27]

The airshow practices were flown at the airshow altitude of 1,000 feet AGL down to 500 feet AGL. Once pilots were comfortable with each individual maneuver at 500 feet AGL, they began practicing the entire airshow routine at 2,000 feet AGL, stepping down to 500 feet AGL. The final practices of the demonstration routine were structured to be as close to the conditions of the Paris Air Show as possible. Airshow-level fuel loads, precise takeoff times, precise landing times, and a simulated 8,700-feet runway with a drag chute landing were all used together to make the final practices as realistic as possible for the pilots. From April 13 to May 16, 1995, Smith, Knox, and Kim had flown 36 flights in preparation for the Paris Air Show.

In parallel, the administrative efforts to get the X-31 accepted by the Paris Air Show authorities and cleared through customs were continuing under Rockwell's Mike Robinson. Robinson recounted the following story on this process:

> In filling out all the French paperwork they demanded a visa number for the responsible person (me). As you know US persons don't need visas to get into France. However, in following the show authorities' demand I went to the French consulate in Beverly Hills to get a visa. The folks there were adamant that I didn't need a visa and thus were not going to issue me one. Finally after wasting a whole morning and waiting them out for a "French lunch period" I talked (and showed the paperwork) to a person who took pity on me and issued me a visa on the spot. Without it I wonder if we would have gotten the plane into the show.[28]

Finally, after both the test efforts and administrative activities were complete, the airplane was disassembled, loaded onto a C-5, and shipped to Manching.[29]

Left to right: Dance of the Disassemblers: removing the right wing so that the X-31 could fit into a Lockheed C-5 for airlift to Europe. The X-31 being loaded into an Air Force Reserve C-5. All tucked away, nice and snug. (NASA DFRC)

This was no small logistics challenge; maintainers had to remove the right wing so that the rest of the X-31 could fit into the gaping cargo hold of the Lockheed C-5 Galaxy wide-body airlifter. The right wing was boxed and carried in the airlifter, together with the support equipment needed for its European flights.

The second Navy flight clearance was received on May 22, 1995.[30] After resolving a potential issue concerning regional electromagnetic interference with the flight control system, flight operations began in Manching on May 29, 1995. Following four checkout and airshow practice flights at Manching, the ferry flight to Paris—with a stop in Köln-Bonn (Cologne)—was made by Fred Knox on June 3, 1995. During the flight from Köln-Bonn to Paris, an "alpha

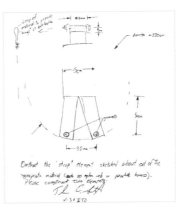

Pat Stoliker's X-31 strap drawing. (Stoliker)

fail" occurred that resulted in an R-3 landing at Paris. This problem was fixed by replacing the noseboom. There were continuing problems with deployment of the drag chute door, and technicians finally replaced it with a simple string/strap combination device designed by NASA engineer Pat Stoliker.[31] As he recalled,

The X-31 debuts at the 1995 Paris Air Show, bedecked with the French fleur-de-lis and the flag of Bavaria (home of MBB), along with the U.S. and German flags. Just visible at the top of the photograph is the Airbus Beluga, which had been considered as a possible X-31 transport. (NASA DFRC)

I designed the strap while we were in Manching doing the practice flights. The door was excessively complex and failed multiple
times. I sketched up a proposal, took it to the life support shop
at Manching and they manufactured two of them. I gave one to
Mike Bondi, the crew chief, and after the door failed on the first
landing in Paris, he installed it on the aircraft.[32]

An aircraft checkout flight and three airshow practice flights were flown by
June 9, 1995. President's Day, traditionally the first day of the Paris Air Show,
was on June 10. The X-31 was ready to fly—now it was showtime!

The X-31 Flies at Le Bourget

Ken Szalai, then the director of Dryden Research Flight Center, served as
NASA's senior aeronautics representative at the Paris Air Show.[33] Years later,
he recalled that when the show announcer broadcast that the X-31 was next
to fly, people began streaming out of the various chalets bordering the flight
line to watch its debut.[34]

Four basic X-31 signature maneuvers comprised the X-31's Paris show routine: the post-stall loop with a 150° heading reversal, the Mongoose turn, the
Herbst turn, and a post-stall loop with a 180° and then 90° heading reversal.
Planners also designed a "low" show routine (in the event of a low cloud ceiling) consisting of two Mongoose turns and one Herbst turn. Thus, in the final

Into the air: the first X-series airplane in foreign skies. (Rockwell)

approved airshow routine, the aileron roll (which had received much pilot criticism), Sukhoi-like "cobra" maneuvers, and post-stall split-S maneuver were eliminated.

The first maneuver in the full "high" show was the post-stall loop with 150° heading reversal. The pilot pulled 2.0 g's and then maintained 20° angle of attack until the velocity vector passed the horizon inverted. At this point, the pilot would pull to 70° angle of attack and, upon reaching it, execute a 150° left post-stall velocity vector roll. Upon completion of the velocity vector roll, he would reduce the angle of attack to less than 30°.

The second maneuver was the Mongoose turn. The pilot would fly at 180 to 200 knots indicated airspeed, roll to 70° to 90° left bank and pull to 70° angle of attack, and continue the turn to the opposite heading before—while maintaining 70° to 90° left bank—executing a nose-up nose slice via a right velocity vector roll to a vertical nose position. The angle of attack was then reduced to 50° and the aircraft was flown straight out and accelerated.

The third maneuver was the now-familiar Herbst turn. For this maneuver, the pilot would stabilize at 30° angle of attack in level flight, then pull to 70° angle of attack. He would then reduce the angle of attack to 50° before commencing a left climbing turn, making a 150° heading change with a velocity vector roll, then returning to level flight and accelerating. (Compared to previous experience, this maneuver had been modified somewhat so that the plane maintained a profile closer to a "climbing turn" instead of the velocity vector roll typical of the end of a Herbst turn pull.)

The fourth and final maneuver was another post-stall loop, this time with 180° and then 90° or 180° heading reversals. The pilot would pull to 3.0 g's and maintain a 15° to 17° angle of attack until the velocity vector passed through the horizon inverted. The aircraft would then be pulled to 70° angle of attack and the pilot would execute a 180° left post-stall velocity vector roll, stop, and make a 90° or 180° velocity vector roll to the right. Upon completion of this roll, angle of attack would be reduced to below 30°.[35]

It is important to note that unlike most airshow routines, in which each maneuver flows into another maneuver (and, since the subsequent maneuver is dependent upon

The X-31 at high AOA in Paris; note the position of the canards. (Rockwell)

the previous one, energy management is very critical), in the X-31 routine each maneuver was performed separately. Thus, an emphasis on maneuver safety and quality could be more tightly focused. Each separate maneuver could be easily simulated and the failure matrix for each maneuver could be well defined. The whole objective of appearing at the Paris Air Show was to showcase X-31 thrust-vectoring technology, so the use of separate distinct maneuvers was not only the safest approach to the demonstration routine; it was also the most effective, from an observer's standpoint, in presenting what the technology could accomplish in flightpath modulation.[36]

John T. Bosworth, Dryden chief engineer at the time of the Paris Air Show, enumerated various lessons learned from the X-31's Paris experience:

1. Seeing is believing! I, as an engineer, tend to underestimate the impact of advertising. I liked to believe that an idea like thrust vectoring would sell itself on its technical merits through technical reports. Two events illustrate the impact of a big air show:

   • The sale of several F-15 aircraft to Egypt was made contingent upon the ability to upgrade to thrust-vectored engines in the near future.[37]

   • A science reporter who had been reporting on the X-31 over the last four years made the comment that "she never really understood the capability until she saw it."

2. The Aerospace Industry is truly a world market and Dryden is not necessarily at the center of it. We tend to overestimate the exposure the work we do at Dryden gets. It is in all the publications that we read, however, the average Joe "off-the-street" doesn't read *Aviation Week*.

3. Part of NASA's charter is to promote aeronautics and inspire today's youth to a career in a scientific field. Air shows provide an opportunity for this (although we may have inspired more French youth than American).

4. An air show is a public affairs expedition. Pictures, brochures, decals, patches, hats, t-shirts, etc. are as important as the technology demonstration itself. Bring lots of these along to give out.[38]

The X-31 proved to be an airshow crowd-pleaser. (NASA DFRC)

The comment about memorabilia is evidence of the crowd's intense interest in the airplane. Everyone wanted some remembrance of the show. An additional eyewitness review of the X-31's performance is provided by Rogers Smith, who, though not able to fly in the show, was on hand to provide support. According to Smith,

> [The X-31 put on a] fantastic air show, absolutely the most spectacular I've ever seen. I saw every one of them—I stood with the crowd on some of them and I was in the control tower on others and I was right underneath it at other times. But to deal with the crowd and watch even hardened veterans—military—who had no concept of what it could really do and [then] seeing it, was jaw dropping for the crowd. It was spectacular![39]

A couple of anecdotes related to the author by Mike Robinson further serve to illustrate the impact of the X-31 demonstration:

> While in the Rockwell Chalet (we had a prime show viewing location) I was approached by a gent in a flight suit with a huge video camera who introduced himself as part of the Russian delegation at the show. He asked if he could be allowed to film the X-31's flight from our porch. We accommodated him and little more need be said about the impression it made on the Russians.... Then there was the famous *Av Week* [*Aviation Week & Space Technology*

magazine] quote which went to the effect, "The X-31 was the hit of the show, every time it approached show center and initiated a maneuver everyone was amazed…but even more amazing was that immediately thereafter we didn't see the pilot in a chute."[40]

Four practice flights and eight airshow flights were flown at Paris. Luckily, the weather cooperated, and the first airshow performance on President's Day was a high show. The weather mandated only one low show performance, on June 13, 1995, and only one flight was canceled, due to a flight control computer power supply failure on power-up. June 18 was the last day of the airshow; the next day, the airplane was flown back to Manching, with a stop in Köln-Bohn. Over the next 5 days, technicians defueled the X-31, removed its thrust-vectoring vanes, Kiel probe, and right wing, and then loaded it onto a pallet. The X-31 was rolled aboard a USAF C-5 on June 24 and flown from Manching to Edwards the next day. There, the team had to wait for a fix to the C-5 before unloading because the C-5 would not "squat" to the unloading position. The X-31 was unloaded on June 27 and the wing was reattached on June 28. The airplane was placed in storage in Building 4826 at Dryden. By Friday, July 7, its engine had been removed and the X-31 team had been reassigned. It seemed that the X-31 had flown its last flight.

VECTOR for the Future

But the X-31 was not yet done with flight testing. The performance of the X-31 at the Paris Air Show was so impressive that it also attracted the attention of senior engineering and operations planners in the U.S. Navy. Moreover, the several Rockwell and MBB X-31 personnel had discussed taking advantage of the high-AOA control to significantly reduce landing speeds—a keen interest of the Navy, whose pilots operated from the decks of ships. Thus, both the Navy and industry were interested in determining whether thrust vectoring might enable very short landing distances, which can result from the very slow touchdown speeds that are made possible by approaching at very high angles of attack. The original Rockwell-MBB concept for a demonstrator was called the "Giraffe" owing to an extremely long (foldable) nose gear that allowed the plane to be landed at high angles of attack. But it soon became clear that such a concept was not very realistic for an operational system. In response, Steve Holowell and Mike Robinson had developed a totally different approach to both the landing and takeoff potential that was afforded by integrated thrust-vector control. This concept was called extremely short take off and landing (ESTOL), and it utilized thrust vectoring to rotate the aircraft early in takeoff and to "derotate" the aircraft from a high-AOA approach just before touchdown. Their study results showed that there were significant possible benefits from ESTOL, and they subsequently patented the concept.[41]

A new demonstration program subsequently emerged from this concept with keen Navy interest. Unlike the Enhanced Fighter Maneuverability program, this program did not include the participation of DARPA or Dryden. It was solely a NAVAIR-managed program

X-31 VECTOR team logo. (USN)

and was flown at the Naval Air Test Center at NAS Patuxent River. The contractors were Boeing (Rockwell) and the European Aeronautic Defense and Space Company (EADS), which now included the former MBB.[42] German government participation once again included the WTD-61 test center, BWB, and the Deutsches Zentrum für Luft und Raumfahrt (the German Aerospace Center).

The program was named Vectoring ESTOL Control Tailless Operations Research (VECTOR), and it explored the use of thrust vectoring to allow slower final landing approaches at higher-than-normal angles of attack.[43] Note that while the ESTOL patent addresses both the takeoff and landing phases of operation, the VECTOR program only addressed the most challenging segment: the landing. The advantages of ESTOL landings on production jet fighters, particularly carrier-based fighters, were many. There would be greater operational flexibility and lower life cycle costs because aircraft would not be punished by the extremely hard landings of current carrier fighters, and the "bring back" weight could be increased enough to eliminate the need for pilots to jettison ordnance or fuel in order to reduce the airplane's landing gross weight enough to be accepted by the carrier's arresting system. Aircraft could also land with less wind over the deck, thus providing the carrier air wing's commander with more flexibility in employing aircraft. Wear and tear on the carrier's arresting gear and deck would be less. Since ESTOL would provide lower structural weights, it would be easier for designers to provide lighter structures, thus providing more commonality for jointly developed airplanes for both the Navy and Air Force. The Marine Corps would benefit by having aircraft that could use very short runways or even highways, befitting its expeditionary nature.[44]

Obviously, the thrust vectoring that was demonstrated during the EFM program would be a major enabler in demonstrating these high-AOA, slow-speed landing approaches, but some other technologies also required development. The aircraft would have to be flown very close to the runway at a high angle of attack and "de-rotated" to a lower angle of attack just prior to touchdown so that the tail would not strike the runway. This required centimeter-level accuracy in aircraft position determination, including altitude. The IntegriNautics Company in Menlo Park, CA, had recently developed a specialized differential-GPS-based navigation system, the Integrity Beacon Landing System (IBLS). Ironically, it was developed and demonstrated in conjunction with United Airlines so that commercial aircraft could utilize the existing onboard GPS for precision landings in lieu of adding a new microwave landing system (MLS). Mike Robinson uncovered the concept through professional acquaintance with United's engineering director, Gordon McKenzie. Then Boeing's engineering staff, working with NAVAIR engineers and IntegriNautics engineers, adapted the concept to function with an autothrottle system from an F/A-18 and an autopilot developed by the VECTOR team. The landing was a fully coupled autoland during which the pilot remained hands off until the airplane was on the ground. Of course, the pilot could command a wave-off or go-around at any time, but early studies showed that the timing was so critical that pilots were not capable of reliably performing the derotation maneuver, so the team went to a fully automated landing system early in the program. One of the problems was that the new navigation system was more accurate than available ground-based measurement systems, such as ground-based lasers. This led to the approach of testing at altitude by simulating a landing on a virtual runway prior to attempting an actual landing.[45]

Another technology was also demonstrated on VECTOR: the advanced Flush Air Data System (FADS) that was developed by EADS Military Aircraft and Nord-Micro. This system involved flush pressure ports located around the tip of the nose cone that provided more accurate airspeed, angle-of-attack, and angle-of-sideslip measurements at high angles of attack. Initially, the array was known as the Advanced Air Data System (AADS) and was flown on the X-31 because of its high AOA capabilities; it had now evolved into the Flush-mounted Air Data System (FADS), a separate EADS experiment flown on the X-31 in parallel with VECTOR.[46] Interestingly, for initial flight-test data the original Kiel probe was installed—and this time it was heated. A smaller Rosemount Pitot probe was also mounted under the radome to provide an alternate source of air data, which was routed to an additional air data computer that monitored pitot data and would instruct the pilot to revert to fixed gains via the R-3 reversionary mode if a substantial error was detected in the primary air data from the Kiel probe. This Rosemount probe was also heated! Finally, redundancy in air data sensing was built into the X-31.[47]

In testing the FADS, the X-31 was flown through airshow-type maneuvers up to 70° angle of attack and a Mach number of 1.18 at 39,000 feet MSL. While supersonic, the test pilot—German Naval Reserve Cmdr. Rüdiger "Rudy" Knöpfel—induced combinations of angle of attack and sideslip to tax the FADS. After processing the data, engineers were able to declare that the FADS was performing as desired throughout the flight regime.[48] There were actually two versions of the FADS tested; one was a breadboard system tested for functionality and the other was a miniaturized version that was more representative of production. The Boeing VECTOR program manager, Gary Jennings, said of the FADS, "The advantage of the nose mounted FADS is to provide a full envelope from 70° angle of attack all the way out to supersonic speed. Almost all existing air data systems using probe sensors cannot be relied on above 30° angle of attack so inertial derived data must be used instead." The Navy program manager, Jennifer Young, commented, "This is a whole new way of collecting the data, from probes on the aircraft. This system is better in two ways. First it is miniaturized and doesn't interfere with the radome. Second, we've never gotten the algorithm right on a flush data system before and I have been very pleased with the result of this one." Jennings summed up the success of FADS by saying, "While others have achieved some of the same results within fairly narrow flight envelopes and at relatively moderate AOAs, the German FADS was extremely successful up to Mach 1.2 at 39,000 ft. The other significant part is we did air-show-type maneuvers, up to 70° angle of attack. So they have a device that has been demonstrated throughout and envelope most airplanes can't even fly in, to replace conventional systems. This is a single, solid-state, small device with a far more functional software system running behind it. This one little cone at the front end of the radome did it all."[49]

The VECTOR program was conducted in three phases. Phase I involved a functional checkout of the airplane, pilot familiarization, and thrust-vector calibration. Phase II evaluated ESTOL avionics, navigation performance of the IBLS, autopilot functionality, and the first version of the FADS. Phase III evaluated the ESTOL landings and tested the miniaturized version of the FADS. Originally, the VECTOR program was also to include tailless research, during which the X-31's tail would actually be removed altogether, thus greatly expanding the quasi-tailless work done in the EFM program. Funding limitations restricted this part of VECTOR to a paper study only. Initial VECTOR planning included the replacement of the thrust-vectoring paddles with an axisymmetric vectoring exhaust nozzle (AVEN) in cooperation with the Swedish and Spanish governments.[50]

Phase I of the VECTOR program was known as the Program and Requirements Definition Phase. The Navy signed a contract for Phase I with Boeing on February 18, 1998, with planned completion of the phase on August 14, 1998. This phase, in which Dryden participated, included multinational team negotiations for a Memorandum of Agreement, an X-31 aircraft parts count, a fit-check of a Saab JAS-39 Gripen fighter RM-12 engine (which was a derivative of the GE 404 engine used in the X-31 during the EFM program), and painting of the airplane.

The X-31 VECTOR over the southern Maryland countryside. (USN)

The RM-12 engine was to be used in what was envisioned as the demonstration of GE's axisymmetric nozzle—a U.S.-Swedish part of the program that never materialized. Phase I work began at Dryden on March 2, 1998, and included the engine fitcheck and aircraft parts count by VECTOR program partners. As the program evolved, participation by the Swedes, Spanish (who collaborated with GE on the nozzle), and Dryden ended and the program became a joint venture between the U.S. Navy and Germany's BWB, managed on the U.S. side entirely by NAVAIR. The contractors on the program were the European Aeronautic Defense and Space Corporation and Boeing Aerospace. Flight testing was conducted under the auspices of the Navy's VX-23 test squadron at Patuxent River. Modifications of the X-31 began in Palmdale by Boeing, and the airplane was moved to Patuxent River in April 2000 to undergo a major overhaul effort that took over 10 months to complete.

On February 24, 2001, X-31 Ship 2 flew for the first time since traveling back to Manching following the Paris Air Show. This flight was flown by Navy Cmdr. Vivan "Noodles" Ragusa.[51] Since this was a joint program with Germany, subsequent flights were also flown by Germany's Rudy Knöpfel. The X-31 flew 10 functional check flights in this phase of the program and achieved an altitude of 24,000 feet MSL and a speed of Mach 0.8. On April 6, 2001, Knöpfel engaged the X-31's thrust vectoring for the first time since the airplane had flown in the Paris Air Show. This was accomplished at 30° angle of attack, which is just below what is considered to be post-stall maneuvering. Knöpfel reported, "It was a very stable, smooth flight." He took the airplane to 5,000 feet and performed a series of pitch, roll, and yaw maneuvers while the thrust-vectoring vanes provided directional control in all three axes. In the following year, the X-31 was reconfigured for up-and-away ESTOL flight, and the FADS was also installed.[52]

Phase II started on May 17, 2002, with a functional check flight by Rudy Knöpfel. The X-31 had received a number of upgrades and modifications, including new flight control software, the F/A-18 autothrottle system, the IBLS, and the FADS. Technicians also installed a belly-mounted video camera to allow the pilot to view the runway for obstructions at the very-high-AOA approaches that were anticipated. "The airplane flew nicely and as predicted. I'm very confident for the future of the program," said Knöpfel following the flight. This phase focused on evaluating the ESTOL flight control software, the precision position measurement performance of the IBLS, the avionics integration of the triplex INS/GPS and triplex air data computers (a redundancy improvement over the EFM program), the new autopilot, and the ESTOL head-up display functionality. Test pilots and engineers also tested the advanced FADS air data system.[53] Following checkout of all the new systems, the culmination of Phase II was to conduct ESTOL landings on a "virtual runway" 5,000 feet in the air.

This was first accomplished on November 18, 2002, by Maj. Cody Allee, USMC, who engaged the X-31's ESTOL mode and made the project's first two ESTOL landings onto a virtual runway. These approaches were flown at angles of attack of 12° and 14°. Allee reported, "The landing went exactly as expected. If everything works as advertised, it is a fairly uneventful flight. It's a testament to all the hard work of the engineers, the programmers, and the designers who have spent years getting us to this point."[54] Allee had replaced Ragusa as the primary American test pilot on the program, and he was joined by Lt. Gerald Hansen, USN, a backup pilot whose only program flight occurred on November 19, 2002. Subsequently, five more ESTOL approaches were performed at altitude, reaching an angle of attack of 24°. Approaches were to be limited to 24° angle of attack for the following phase of testing, during which "ESTOL-to-the-ground" landings would be accomplished. The rationale for this was that at 24° angle of attack, the X-31 still had sufficient aerodynamic control power to complete the landing maneuver if there was a failure of the thrust-vectoring system during the landing.

The approach profile was complex. Final approach was flown at a higher-than-normal glide path and, of course, at angles of attack much larger than conventional aircraft. A derotation maneuver prevented the tail from hitting the ground prior to the main landing gear by dropping the aircraft onto its landing gear when its tail was just 2 feet above the runway. Due to this complexity, the landing was flown completely on autopilot. Due to the extreme precision required to accomplish this approach and landing, the X-31 was guided throughout the approach by the IBLS, which uses differential global positioning system data along with ground-based beacons to very accurately track the aircraft's position and altitude. Jennifer Young said, "We're getting excellent data. A year ago, we were talking about the theoretical; now we're proving things. These are not just ideas any more, they are products."[55] The final flights of Phase II were flown on March 22, 2003, by Knöpfel. He flew two supersonic flights to Mach 1.06 and 1.18, respectively, in full afterburner at 39,000 feet MSL. These final flights were to assess FADS performance at supersonic speeds.

Phase III began with preparation of the X-31 for the final "ESTOL-to-the-ground" test phase. The airplane received a new software load for its flight control computers. This load included the control laws for an actual ground landing. The VECTOR team was also making minor airframe modifications. The expectation was to accomplish all the VECTOR goals within

X-31 VECTOR landing just prior to derotation. Note the nozzle paddles far below the main landing gear. (USN)

14 flights, with the first actual ground landing occurring around the eighth flight. The first VECTOR flight to an actual ground touchdown occurred on April 22, 2003, and was flown by Rudy Knöpfel. He flew the airplane to an invisible engagement box in the sky, at which point the autoland system was engaged and Knöpfel monitored as the X-31 flew to touchdown, after which he took over control and lifted off again. On this first attempt, the thrust vectoring was engaged but the angle of attack was limited to 12°, which was the airplane's normal landing attitude. Following the flight, Knöpfel reported, "Everything worked perfectly and was just as we had done it in the simulator. There was a very smooth flare and touchdown. I must admit that it was a smoother landing than I can sometimes do."[56]

Follow-on landings increased the final approach angle of attack one degree at a time, up to a maximum of 24°. Of the higher-AOA approaches at a steeper glide path than conventional aircraft, Knöpfel commented, "[This is] a view that we have to get accustomed to."[57] This comment was made in reference to the fact that, at higher angles of attack above 15°, the pilot loses sight of the runway and must rely on a video camera in the belly of the aircraft to verify that the runway is free of obstructions. The final flight in Phase III was flown by Cody Allee to touchdown at 24° angle of attack (twice the normal 12°) at only 121 knots (31 percent slower than the normal 175-knot landing speed). Following touchdown, Allee needed only 1,700 feet of runway to slow the X-31 down sufficiently to make a turn-around in the middle of the runway and then taxi in a complete circle! This provided a significant contrast to the normal X-31 landing distance of 8,000 feet for a conventional landing. The resulting energy savings was over 50 percent, a factor of huge importance for the Navy. Energy is the key parameter for evaluating payoff to the Navy because it has a major impact on the design and construction of arresting gear on carriers, as well as impacts on the design and operations and support (O&S) of the aircraft.

This final landing was greeted by cheers in both English and German by the many VECTOR team members watching from the side of the runway. Commenting on the feel of landing at 24° angle of attack, Allee said that the world scrolled slowly by at a pace that was "almost sedate. From the start of the approach, it is very obvious that the aircraft is sitting at a pretty extreme angle. You are still at one g, but you're leaning way back in the seat with the nose pointed way up at the sky."[58] The team then had to finish celebrating and move into a data-analysis and reporting phase, creating what was essentially a how-to manual for thrust-vectored ESTOL and the other technology demonstrated in the X-31.

Gary Jennings, the Boeing Phantom Works manager for VECTOR, commented, "The high angle of attack landing was very exciting and dramatic. More importantly, we proved that an integrated flight and propulsion control system has potential for use in extremely short takeoffs and landings."[59] Jennings summed up the transition of the X-31 from EFM to VECTOR by saying, "We have taken a technology (an integrated flight propulsion control system), demonstrated it with close air-to-air combat techniques, and combined that with a precision navigation system-IBLS-to prove we can follow a very precise path through space to get us to that derotation point above the concrete. How many airplane [development programs] spend many millions of dollars trying to get 4 or 5 knots off their approach? We just took off 58 knots, with a total program cost of $80 million."

The X-31 had once again done what no other X-plane had done. It had finished one program, remained dormant in storage, and awoke to perform a significantly different research effort years later. At the time of the completion of VECTOR, the X-31 was the only crewed X-plane in flight. The Navy wrote that the X-31 is, in that sense, a "true" X-plane, being solely a tool to explore concepts and technologies. The Navy program manager, Jennifer Young, summarized the purpose of the X-31 best: "Our main product is knowledge."[60]

Following the VECTOR program, the X-31 did not again return to storage to await another program. By agreement between the U.S. and German governments, the X-31 was loaned to the Flugwerft Schleißheim of the prestigious Deutsches Museum, until a new display wing for experimental aircraft could be constructed at the National Museum of Naval Aviation at historic NAS Pensacola, FL.[61] As of this study, the X-31 remains on exhibit in Oberschleißheim, a tribute to both German and American aerospace engineering and research.

Endnotes

1. "Pitot" refers to the hypodermic-like instrumentation boom located on the nose (and sometimes the wing) of an airplane that measures dynamic air pressure. The name comes from French fluid dynamicist Henri Pitot, a pioneer in the study of fluid mechanics. Since a pitot tube can be blocked with ice, it is typically heated to prevent ice formation. In this case, alas, it was not.

2. X-31-1 flight transcript for flight on 19 Jan 1995 (Edwards, CA: DFRC Safety Office, 1995), n.p. copy in Dryden archives. All subsequent quotes from the communications on this flight are from this transcript. See also NASA DFRC Safety Office, "X-31 Breaking the Chain, Lessons Learned," video discussion of X-31 Ship 1 accident, 2005, copy in Dryden archives.

3. NASA DFRC Safety Office, "X-31 Breaking the Chain, Lessons Learned."

4. X-31 Mishap Board, "NASA 584 X-31 Mishap Investigation Report, Date of Mishap: January 19, 1995," final report (Edwards, CA: NASA DFRC, August 18, 1995), pp. 4-1–7-39, Dryden Archives.

5. Ibid., p. 7-3.

6. Ibid., pp. 8-1–8-6.

7. Michael A. Dornheim, "X-31 Board Cites Safety Analyses, But Not All Agree," *Aviation Week & Space Technology* (December 4, 1995): pp. 81–86.

8. Rogers Smith, "X-31 Accident: Lessons to be Learned," *40th Symposium Proceedings* (Lancaster, CA: Society of Experimental Test Pilots, 1996), p. 218.

9. NASA DFRC Safety Office, "X-31 Breaking the Chain, Lessons Learned."

10. Michael Sperling, "Crash Grounds X-31 Performance at Paris Air Show," *Defense News* (January 23–29, 1995), p. 10.

11. Paris Flight to Cap Busy X-31 Test Schedule," *Aviation Week & Space Technology* (June 12, 1995): p. 112; and "Turning Heads," *Flight International* (June 28–July 4, 1995), p. 31.

12. ITO, "X-31 AFSRB Brief," (April 6, 1995), slide 4.

13. ITO, "Envelope Expansion—Flight Planning Guidelines and Risk Management," ITO draft document (March 25, 1995), pp. 7–8, Dryden archives

14. ITO, "X-31 AFSRB Brief."

15. Fred D. Knox and Thomas C. Santangelo, "Taking an X-Airplane to the Paris Air Show," *39th Symposium Proceedings* (Lancaster, CA: Society of Experimental Test Pilots, 1995), p. 296.
16. ITO, "X-31 Technical Demonstration (C-5A to Manching/Beluga to Toulouse)," ITO briefing (March 24, 1995), Dryden archives.
17. Knox and Santangelo, "Taking an X-Airplane to the Paris Air Show," pp. 297–299.
18. Fred Knox, Rockwell, "X-31A Flight Report 2-232," pilot report (April 13, 1995), Dryden archives.
19. Rogers Smith, NASA Dryden, "X-31A Flight Report 2-233," pilot report (April 13, 1995), Dryden archives.
20. Lt. Col. Quirin Kim, GAF, "X-31A Flight Report 2-235," pilot report (April 17, 1995), Dryden archives.
21. Rogers Smith, NASA Dryden, "X-31A Flight Report 2-239," pilot report (April 22, 1995).
22. Lt. Col. Quirin Kim, GAF, "X-31A Flight Report 2-241," pilot report (April 24, 1995), Dryden archives.
23. Rogers Smith, NASA Dryden, "X-31A Flight Report 2-243," pilot report (April 26, 1995), Dryden archives.
24. Knox and Santangelo, "Taking an X-Airplane to the Paris Air Show," 298–300.
25. Rogers Smith, NASA Dryden, "X-31A Flight Report 2-245," pilot report (April 28, 1995).
26. Donald H. Gatlin, Acting X-31 ITO Director, letter to Commander, Naval Air Systems Command, April 28, 1995.
27. COMNAVAIRSYSCOM, message to SECDEF, May 4, 1995.
28. Mike Robinson, e-mail to Douglas A. Joyce, May 19, 2012.
29. Knox and Santangelo, "Taking an X-Airplane to the Paris Air Show," pp. 295–297.
30. Ibid., pp. 302–303.
31. Pat Stoliker is now the NASA DFRC deputy director.
32. Pat Stoliker, e-mail to Douglas A. Joyce, August 17, 2012.
33. Robert E. Whitehead, Acting Associate Administrator for Aeronautics, letter to Kenneth J. Szalai, Director of Dryden Research Flight Center, May 16, 1995.
34. NASA DFRC Safety Office, "X-31 Breaking the Chain, Lessons Learned."
35. Daimler-Benz Aerospace AG, "Paris Airshow X-31 Maneuvers," military aircraft brochure (1995), Dryden archives.
36. Knox and Santangelo, "Taking an X-Airplane to the Paris Air Show," p. 302.

37. For the record, this did not subsequently occur.
38. John T. Bosworth, "1995 X-31 Paris Air Show Trip Report," Dryden Flight Research Center (July 18, 1995), n.p.
39. NASA DFRC Safety Office, "X-31 Breaking the Chain, Lessons Learned."
40. Mike Robinson, e-mail to Douglas A. Joyce, May 19, 2012.
41. Mike Robinson, e-mail to Douglas A. Joyce, June 6, 2012. The patent was U.S. Patent Number 5,984,229, granted on November 16, 1999.
42. Boeing had acquired Rockwell in a merger, and what was once MBB became a part of EADS.
43. Wallace, *Nose Up*, p. 54.
44. AIAA, "X-31 Finds a Shorter Path to Success," *American Aerospace Online*, August 2003, *http://www.aiaa.org/aerospace/Article.cfm?issuetocid=392&ArchiveIssueID=41*, accessed on October 27, 2011.
45. James Darcy, "X-31 Makes ESTOL Landing on Virtual Runway," *Navy.mil*, November 22, 2002, *http://www.navy.mil/search/print. asp?story_id=4709&VIRIN=1586&imagetype=1&page=2*, accessed on October 27, 2011.
46. Boeing, "Boeing X-31 Takes Flight Again in New Multinational Program," news release, March 5, 2001, *http://www.boeing.com/news/releases/2001/q1/news_release_010305n.htm*, accessed on October 27, 2011.
47. Maj. J. Cody Allee, USMC, "Automating Safety in Flight Test," in SETP, *2003 Report to the Aerospace Profession* (Lancaster, CA: The Society of Experimental Test Pilots, 2003), pp. 93-102.
48. James Darcy, "X-31 Completes ESTOL Up-and-Away," *Navy. mil*, March 29, 2003, *http://www.navy.mil/search/display.asp?story_id=6566*, accessed on October 27, 2011.
49. AIAA, "X-31 Finds a Shorter Path to Success," *American Aerospace Online* (Reston, VA: AIAA, Aug. 2003), at *http://www.aiaa.org/aerospace/Article.cfm?issuetocid=392&ArchiveIssueID=41*, accessed on Oct. 27, 2011.
50. Boeing, "Boeing X-31 Takes Flight Again in New Multinational Program"; Wallace, *Nose Up*, pp. 54–55; Dryden Flight Research Center, "X-31 VECTOR Program Phase 1 Begins," news release, March 9, 1998, *http://www.nasa.gov/centers/dryden/news/NewsReleases/1998/98-09.html*, accessed on October 27, 2011; Col. Mike Francis, USAF (Ret), interview by Douglas A. Joyce, October 19, 2011.
51. Tragically, after retiring from the Navy and joining the Gulfstream Corporation, Noodles Ragusa perished with Kent Crenshaw, David

McCollum, and Reece Ollenburg in the crash of a Gulfstream G650 on April 2, 2011.

52. James Darcy, "VECTOR team completes first flight period for X-31," *Checkpoint Online*, April 29, 2001, *http://www.checkpoint-online.ch/ CheckPoint/J4/J4-0002-X-31CompletesTests.html*, accessed on October 27, 2011.

53. Boeing, "History: Products—Rockwell International X-31A Test Vehicle," at *http://www.boeing.com/history/bna/x31.htm*, accessed on October 27, 2011.

54. James Darcy, "X-31 Makes ESTOL Landing on Virtual Runway," *Navy.mil*, November 22, 2002, at *http://www.navy.mil/search/print. asp?story_id=4709&VIRIN=1586&imagetype=1&page=2*, accessed on October 27, 2011.

55. Ibid.

56. James Darcy, "X-31 Makes History with First Automated ESTOL," *Navy.mil*, April 25, 2003, *http://www.navy.mil/search/display.asp?story_ id=7075*, accessed October 29, 2011.

57. Ibid.

58. James Darcy, "Last Flight of X-31 Ends with 24-Degree ESTOL," *Navy.mil*, May 2, 2003, *http://www.navy.mil/search/display.asp?story_ id=7189*, accessed on October 29, 2011.

59. Boeing, "Boeing X-31A Vector Completes International Flight Test Program," news release, March 5, 2001, *http://www.boeing.com/news/ releases/2003/q2/nr_030507a.html*, October 29, 2011.

60. James Darcy, "X-31 Makes History with First Automated ESTOL," Navy.mil, April 25, 2003, *http://www.navy.mil/search/display.asp?story_ id=7075*, accessed October 29, 2011.

61. Col. Mike Francis, USAF (Ret), interview by Douglas A. Joyce, October 19, 2011.

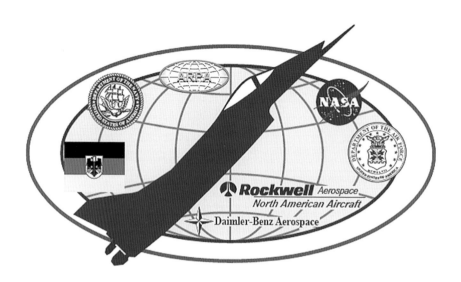

The X-31 International Test Organization logo. (NASA)

CHAPTER 6

Program Management and Direction

The X-31 program was extraordinarily complicated from a program management standpoint. As the first international X-plane program, it involved complex contractor, government, and military relationships with organizations in both the United States and Germany. Over time, some of the organizations involved changed their names or were involved in mergers or corporate acquisitions. In addition to all of this was the creation of a unique organization, the X-31 International Test Organization, to actually run the flight-test program after the move to Dryden. Couple this with a funding stream from two different nations and from multiple parties within each nation and one sees that the organizational interactions are indeed complicated. It is perhaps instructive to take a look at each organization independently to see where they fit into the total scheme of things; then, a review of the program costs after the program was over will provide a feel for the costs and benefits of the program.

The International Partnership

To recap, Messerschmitt-Bölkow-Blohm, or MBB, was involved in the early design conceptualization for a multipurpose fighter that would eventually become the Eurofighter, which was popularly known as the Typhoon. Dr. Wolfgang Herbst, an engineer for MBB, conceived of the idea that an aircraft capable of performing well in the post-stall region of flight would be best able to gain a tactical advantage in close-in combat. The effort to validate this concept is one of several factors that led to the Enhanced Fighter Maneuverability program. The X-31, of course, was the demonstrator aircraft that resulted from the EFM program.

During the Enhanced Fighter Maneuverability program, MBB was charged with the design and manufacture of the two sets of wings and the thrust deflector vanes. MBB would also develop the flight control laws for the flight control system, and it would define and analyze X-31 PST performance. Later in the program, MBB was tasked with developing a special display to avoid pilot disorientation during post-stall maneuvering. Of course, MBB was also a part-ner in the management, execution, and reporting of EFM flight tests, includ-ing participation in the Paris Air Show.[1] MBB evolved into being a portion of the larger European conglomerate, EADS. EADS was a major participant in the engineering and flight-test support for the follow-on VECTOR program.

By the start of the X-31 program, Rockwell International was completing the Space Shuttle production program and had survived President Jimmy Carter's cancellation of the B-1 program until President Ronald Reagan started the B-1B program. Additionally, Rockwell had continued North American Aviation's heritage of opening new horizons of flight with the HiMAT remotely piloted demonstrator aircraft. Mike Robinson, a program manager at Rockwell, had become acquainted with Wolfgang Herbst at various technical conferences and symposia and while both were supporting Saab in the JAS-39 Gripen's development. He was impressed with Herbst's vision of post-stall maneuver-ing and felt it was a nice compliment to the technologies that had recently been proven by the HiMAT program, although he knew that for PST to be accepted it would have to be flight demonstrated. As told in other chapters, this was the basis for Rockwell and MBB to team on the X-31. Rockwell had responsibility for the aircraft configuration, aerodynamics, vehicle construc-tion, simulation, redundancy management, and FCS hardware development. Later, of course, Rockwell was a major participant in the flight-test program. Finally, in the last stage of the X-31's life—the VECTOR program—Rockwell, having been acquired by Boeing, led development of the ESTOL and the enabling GPS-based precision approach and touchdown system. It was Boeing, through its St. Louis–based Phantom Works, that was responsible for the VECTOR program.[2]

Top-level management of the X-31 program within the U.S. Government resided in the Defense Advanced Research Projects Agency, an organization within the Department of Defense that was responsible for the development of new technology for use by the military. DARPA generally manages relatively high-risk military-oriented programs with the assistance of a military service that takes day-to-day management responsibility.[3] In the case of the X-31, this was the Navy through Naval Air Systems Command, which oversees all naval aircraft research, development, test, evaluation, and acquisition. The end of the EFM program in July 1995 marked the end of DARPA's participation in VECTOR, the X-31 follow-on program. This effort was led in the United States by NAVAIR.

However, concerns over NAVAIR's priorities (NAVAIR's focus, naturally, was on high-priority weapons systems for the fleet) and the length of time required to obtain flight clearances for envelope expansion (NAVAIR was used to working with mature systems, such as the F/A-18, that were nearly ready to be deployed, rather than one-of-a-kind research aircraft like the X-31) led to the transfer of many of NAVAIR's responsibilities to Dryden when flight testing moved there in 1992.[4] Upon completion of formal flight testing and in preparation for the Paris Air Show, these responsibilities again transferred back to NAVAIR because Dryden was not allowed to participate in airshow-type activities. Total program-management responsibilities fell on NAVAIR during the VECTOR program because DARPA was not involved.

During the early part of the X-31 program, Rockwell partnered with Langley for wind tunnel tests and helicopter-borne drop-model testing that explored the X-31's aerodynamics. When the insufficient nose-down pitching-moment problem arose, Langley helped identify a fix that used strakes on the X-31's aft fuselage. After the unexpected departure of the airplane during dynamic entries to high angles of attack, Langley analysis was instrumental in developing the nose-strake fix for this problem.[5]

These organizations were the major players at the start of the program in 1986, when the Memorandum of Agreement (MOA) was signed between DARPA and the German Ministry of Defense. The lines of authority were relatively standard, with the exception that there were *two* parallel lines of authority—one in the United States and one in Germany. The American contractor, Rockwell, interfaced with a U.S. Government program office at NAVAIR, which in turn was sponsored by DARPA. On the German side, the German contractor, MBB, interfaced with a German government program office at BWB, which in turn was sponsored by the BMV. Additionally, Rockwell and MBB negotiated an associate contractor agreement (ACA) to set protocols and procedures for day-to-day cooperation and dispute resolution. The ACA shared many of the fundamentals that were embodied in the government-to-government MOA but addressed the contractor-to-contractor relationship instead. The relationships and governing documents for the EFM program before it transferred to NASA/Dryden are shown on the figure on the right.

Just as important as the formal organization was the informal working model. Over time, it was best characterized by two factors: knowing one another and mutual trust. The best example of the success of this model was the weekly review that was run out of the Rockwell's

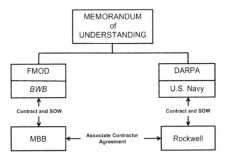

X-31 Governing Relationships Prior to Dryden Transfer

X-31 Governing Relationships Prior to Dryden Transfer. (R.P. Hallion)

"No Business as Usual" logo. (R.P. Hallion)

Palmdale facility but included appropriate players from DARPA, NAVAIR, BWB, and MBB—parties spread over nine time zones. Whichever party had prime responsibility for the issue at hand automatically took the lead for that part of the review. Even though the review was conducted over telephone (charts were faxed the evening before), there was no need to introduce the speaker; the team knew one another so well that voices were automatically recognized, even through many very heated and blunt discussions.

After the meeting, there were no hurt feelings, just a sense that everyone was doing their part to ensure success. Consistent with the program's goals of proving that international collaborative R&D can be cost effective and demonstrating low-cost prototyping, at the beginning of each week's review, John Priday (Rockwell's director of manufacturing for the X-31) presented a telling slide whose bold message soon was subscribed to by all team members:

NO BUSINESS AS USUAL

As described below, these same tenets prevailed after the program transferred to Dryden, albeit with additional players.

Contractor, Government, and ITO Responsibilities

A look into the share of work between Rockwell and MBB during the Phase II Preliminary Design phase provides insight into how the contractors worked together while receiving oversight from their respective government agencies and managers:

- Work was split into Rockwell work packages, to be performed at Rockwell with MBB local participation, and MBB work packages, to be performed at MBB with Rockwell local participation.
- Rockwell engineers working in Munich on MBB work packages reported to MBB management and vice versa.
- Close coordination ensured that there was no wasteful duplication of effort.

- There was no routine or regular transfer of funding between Rockwell and MBB except for specialized subcontracts.
- Overall, Rockwell had primacy for contractor program-management responsibility.[6]

This organizational arrangement worked well through Phase II Preliminary Design and Phase III Detail Design and Fabrication. The Phase III contract also included some flight testing, and this is where the organizational inefficiencies came to bring NASA Dryden into the picture. The long timeframe for processing envelope expansion flight clearances posed a serious and enduring concern for Rockwell, MBB, and even DARPA. It put future funding at risk, particularly because, though it was common practice for DARPA to "hand off" a program to one of the services once it had begun, the Navy from the outset said that they did not intend to pick up the flight-test program's funding. This motivated Tack Nix, the DARPA program manager, to seek other partners to keep the program afloat, which brought him to NASA. In late 1990, Nix began discussions with the Ames-Dryden Flight Research Facility about moving the X-31 to the Dryden facility at Edwards AFB.[7] The Ames-Dryden Flight Research Facility—now the NASA Dryden Flight Research Center— was NASA's premier flight-testing organization and the Agency's center of excellence for atmospheric flight operations, with a charter to develop, verify, and transfer advanced aeronautics- and space-related technologies.

As Dryden was being brought into the fold of X-31 program participants, so too was the Air Force through the aegis of the Air Force Flight Test Center. (The Navy had no issue with the USAF also participating so long as it funded its own participation.) In the correspondence to coordinate the draft EFM Memorandum of Agreement, the AFFTC agreed to provide four engineers and one test pilot to support the flight-test effort at Dryden.[8] The MOA tasked the AFFTC to

- participate in the planning of day-to-day operational control of the test team's efforts;
- participate in the activities of the Test Objectives Working Group;
- assist in the preparation and review of all test cards for flight safety and aerodynamic/system evaluation;
- participate in simulation studies;
- assist in developing air-combat-maneuvering-range instrumentation and data-reduction requirements and procedures;
- provide resources, on an industrially funded basis, to permit some proficiency flying for X-31 assigned pilots; and
- provide research pilots to the program.[9]

The Air Force Flight Test Center added the following additional responsibilities:

- Participate in all safety reviews;
- Conduct a formal technical review of military utility test objectives; and

- Author a Technical Report on the military utility of X-31 technologies.[10]

Typically, the Air Force Flight Test Center, in its role as a Participating Test Organization, would provide test pilots through its 6510 Test Wing (6510 TW) Research Projects Division. Ultimately, Jim Wisneski was assigned as the Air Force pilot for the X-31 EFM program. Engineering personnel were provided from the applicable engineering organizations and disciplines within AFFTC's test structure.

Having moved from Palmdale to Dryden, the X-31 test team thus added participants from NASA Dryden and the Air Force Flight Test Center to those from the transatlantic organizations discussed previously. Clearly, an organization had to be formed to integrate all of these players into an effectively functioning team. The team that was ultimately formed, known as the International Test Organization, was unique among American X-series flight-testing organizations (though not among other test programs).[11] The organizational structure emphasized consensual and cooperative management rather than a top-down directive style. It tried, as much as possible, not to have any one project manager, engineer, or pilot be the "chief" of any given area within the organization. The theory was that the team would count on cooperative and shared decision making, with team members encouraged to choose their own leaders in each research area.[12]

Accordingly, the ITO logo was originally designed as a circle to invoke the memory of the coequal "knights of the round table," though it finally became an oval—allegedly so it would fit better when painted on the two airplanes![13] All of the various international team member logos were arranged around the circumference of the oval so that no single organization had top billing. The organizational chart reflected a similar philosophy: within each of the organization's major subelements were identified a number of members from the contractors, the governments (U.S. and German), and the military services (Navy, USAF, and GAF), but no single person was placed "over" another. For example, in a December 1991 briefing, the Flight Research Engineering function included 28 Rockwell personnel, 19 NASA personnel, 10 MBB personnel, and 5 USAF personnel. All of the other functional areas—Aircraft Operations, Quality Assurance/Flight Safety, and Project Pilots—show a similar amalgam of personnel from all of the X-31 participating organizations.[14]

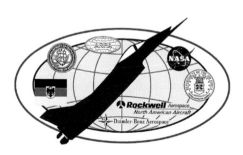

International Test Organization logo. (NASA)

Ken Szalai, the director of the Ames-Dryden facility, famously told the ITO team managers to put the organization chart in their bottom desk drawers, adding that if they ever had to consult the organization chart to solve a personnel conflict, their doing so would constitute ample evidence that they had failed.[15] Reflecting on the workings of the ITO, Lane Wallace wrote,

> The only thing likely to guarantee success for such a complex team was voluntary cooperation and mutual respect, especially when it came to conflict resolution. Flexibility was also important; it took an unprecedented and unconventional management approach to make the ITO work. Contractors reported to civil servants and vice versa, and if team members had insisted on hard-and-fast adherence to conventional contractor/government interactions, the project would have failed.[16]

There was some precedent for an integrated organization like this in flight-test management. In the 1970s, the Air Force had gone to the Joint Test Force (JTF), later called the Combined Test Force (CTF), concept in which all interested parties, development test personnel, operational test personnel, and contractors would work under one roof and share data from test flights.[17] In international programs such as the F-16, these organizations would sometimes include personnel from other services as well as allied nations. The Navy had also started to employ a similar organizational structure. The major difference was that in the CTF structure, while everyone worked under the same roof and participated together in planning and conducting tests, the organization was essentially a series of "stovepipes" with people from the various major organizations working together but reporting up a chain of command within each individual organization. Test reporting was also usually conducted independently by the major organizations. The "Integrated Product Team" has been noted as an analog within the manufacturing industry, but even in these organizations they are stovepiped or matrixed.[18]

Why did the ITO structure work so well? Initially, it took a little time for team members to develop mutual trust and respect for each other. However, DARPA, the Navy, Rockwell, BWB, and MBB already had developed strong and mutually supportive interrelationships from the earlier stages of the program. Language barriers had to be overcome and an understanding of the somewhat different engineering approaches to solving technical problems on both sides of the Atlantic had to be developed. Only "fog and friction" caused by the infusion of NASA and USAF members had to be overcome. Senior management within all the major participants was helpful in replacing individuals that did not seem to "fit" in this unique team structure. The fact that most of the team members were collocated in the Integrated Test Facility at

Dryden was a big help in facilitating team building.[19] Social activities such as a well-remembered "beer and bratwurst" party at Dryden were very helpful in building camaraderie. Shared loyalty to the X-31 program gradually superseded longstanding organizational loyalties that team members brought to the program, and thus the team became a true international test team. Cementing the team together was, in a word, *trust*. Thus, as the team grew, it become extraordinarily professional; former DARPA Program Manager Mike Francis recalled that the ITO "went from a dysfunctional high school football team, to a team of Super Bowl Champions."[20] There was some unraveling following the accident; however, as the success of expanding the envelope to very low altitude and developing a "jaw-dropping" airshow routine emerged, the team again consolidated and resolidified. As Harvey Schellenger, former Rockwell chief X-31 engineer, said, "nothing brings a team together like success."[21] And nothing, it might be added, tests and taxes a team more than disaster.

Perhaps the best indicators of the success of the ITO's organizational approach are the recollections by various participants. Alumni of the program invariably focus on *the team* and on what a great experience they enjoyed while being a part of that team. For example, upon completing the tactical utility portion of the flight-test program, the German contingent reported, "For the German participants this program resulted in a number of great achievements: It was a tremendous experience for the German team mates to work with their US colleagues on American soil [and many] lasting personal relations developed over the years."[22] At the completion of the quasi-tailless evaluation, Gus Loria, Mark Kelly, and Ron Harley concluded:

> To be successful in a dynamic organization and flight test program requires many things. The most important ingredient being the people involved. We were fortunate to be working with the best group of individuals we have ever had the pleasure of working with.
>
> From the highest ranks of management and leadership in the Navy, Marine Corps, the US Air Force, the German Air Force, NASA, ARPA, Rockwell International, and DASA right down to the individual fueling the aircraft, we worked with the best.
>
> In second place are three things often given lip service to, but which were actually realized at the X-31 ITO. They are trust, cooperation, and open minds. Not only were all the people involved given the opportunity to make their inputs, but they were all listened to and considered.

By virtue of this exchange of ideas, and innovative approaches we were able to brainstorm and maximize our talents.

The real success story here is not what was achieved with hardware or technology, but rather the people. Outstanding leadership and professionalism brought about this successful test program.[23]

Throughout the flight-test program at Dryden, an organization of senior members of the ITO known as the "ITO Council" conducted reviews of the flight-test program on a periodic basis (normally each quarter). During the last ITO Council meeting, held on August 29, 1995 (a little over 2 months after the last flight of the X-31 in Paris), action items for storage of the aircraft, return of spares, final financial settlements, aircraft disposition, and final reporting were assigned. The legacy of the X-31 International Test Organization was reflected in the minutes of this last ITO Council meeting:

Colonel Francis thanked everyone for contributing to the complete success of the first international experimental aircraft program in United States history. Special thanks went to the German Government and DASA (previously MBB) for their technical and managerial contributions to the success of the experiment. He invited everyone in the room to comment on their experiences in the program. If a consensus can be drawn from the comments it is that the *tenacity, selflessness, and camaraderie of individuals—working together as a closely knit international team—made the X-31 Program a complete success by achieving all the goals they set out to demonstrate* [emphasis added].[24]

As stated previously, the follow-on to the EFM program was VECTOR, and in the United States it was run by NAVAIR without DARPA or NASA having management roles. The organization reverted to something similar to the original EFM organization but without DARPA. Moreover, owing to the numerous mergers and name changes over the course of the program, by the time of the VECTOR program, the contractor team was familiarly known as "Boeing" and "EADS." Despite that, the team spirit that developed during the initial phases and in the ITO carried over, which certainly was a major element in the success of this final stage in the long life of the X-31. These relationships have sustained over the years, perhaps the best evidence of which is a reunion that took place in Munich on October 9, 2010, to commemorate the 20th anniversary of the X-31's first flight. Over 100 team members attended the event held at the Deutsches Museum, one of the world's premier museums of science and technology, which numbers the surviving X-31 among its aircraft collections. Team members from all major participating organizations (from technicians to testers to top management) took part, many having travelled from the United States just for the event.

Costs, Cost Analysis, and Program Funding

How much did the X-31 program cost? Available historical cost and funding documents are minimal, and some documents are in Deutsche Marks (DM) and thus must be converted to American dollars at contemporary exchange rates.

Cost documents from the Dryden archives that were prepared after Ship 1's accident and before preparations for the Paris Air Show indicate a cost of $173.3 million for detail design and construction of the two X-31 aircraft, plus an additional $55.3 million for flight-test support; these monies covered the 1991 through 1994 time period. Of the design and build money, $118.7 million was from DARPA and Nunn-Quayle, with an additional $54.6 million coming from the German government. While the original 75-25 split was only a target, the numbers came in close to that—closer than shown here. The U.S. contribution needs to consider the cost of the Navy and DARPA personnel, and the real cost to Germany in Deutsche Marks was lower, but exchange rates magnify their contribution on a percentage basis.

Interestingly, the majority of NASA and German funding for flight-test support was "indirect," with $14.9 million coming from NASA and $10.6 million coming from Germany. (Indirect funding means support that comes from personnel and facilities that are otherwise "institutionally" funded and therefore do not need to be reimbursed to the program.) The direct funding for flight-test support (all provided by the United States) totaled $55.3 million and was broken down as follows:

- $39.4 million from DARPA
- $3.0 million from Nunn Quayle
- $0.7 million from NASA (a relatively small amount of *direct* funding)
- $9.0 million from the Navy
- $1.6 million from JAST
- $1.6 million from the Air Force

All told, prior to the accident, a total of $254.1 million in direct and indirect funding was spent on the X-31 program.[25]

The X-31 program Close-Out Briefing given in November 1995 (well after the airplane was put into storage following EFM and the Paris Air Show) to Dr. Robert Whitehead, the NASA associate administrator of aeronautics, included an analysis of expenditures following each 100 flights. At the end of the first 100 flights, $183,355,700 had been expended (a cost of $1,833,557 per flight). On the second 100 flights, an additional $17,020,300 had been expended, so the additive cost per flight was $170,203. The analysis went on to show that the cost of the fifth 100 flights was an additional $5,057,700, resulting in a cost per flight of $50,577 for these flights. This analysis shows the dramatic benefit of flying as many productive sorties as possible on a research airplane (or any airplane for that matter) after the sunk cost of design and construction has been spent.[26] The X-31 flew a record 523 research flights (not counting the Paris Air Show effort or the VECTOR program), making it arguably the most productive X-plane to date in terms of sortie rate.

The accident flight of Ship 1 was the last research flight of the program as originally conceived. There was no more money to continue onward, and DARPA and the German government did not have any more "customers" or "sponsors" to continue funding the X-31's operation. There had, for some time, been interest in taking the airplane to the Paris Air Show. As discussed in the previous chapter, the technical and safety issues were worked out by an extraordinary effort on the part of the ITO team. Paying for all of this was another matter. The estimated total cost for the Paris Air Show effort was $2.4 million. Mike Francis convinced the four main participants in the X-31 program—Rockwell, MBB, the German government, and DARPA—to contribute $600,000 each to fund the preparation for the airshow, transportation of the airplane, and flight participation in the show.[27]

Details of the VECTOR program's funding are sketchy. Comments by Boeing's VECTOR Program Manager Gary Jennings give a rough insight into the total cost of the VECTOR program: "How many airplane [development programs] spend many millions of dollars trying to get 4 or 5 kt off their approach [speed]? We just took off 58 kt, with a total program cost of $80 million."[28]

Summarizing the cost information for the EFM program, Paris Air Show effort, and the VECTOR program, we find that a total of approximately $336.5 million was spent on the entire X-31 effort, including design, construction, and operation of two aircraft, as well as approximately 9.5 years of flying, well over 500 research sorties, and all support activities. Historically, then, this was a very cost-effective program.

Endnotes

1. Throughout this book, "MBB" has been used to refer to this contractor's participation in the EFM program, and "EADS" has been used to refer to its participation in the VECTOR program.
2. Throughout this book, "Rockwell" has been used to refer to this contractor's participation in the EFM program, and "Boeing" has been used to refer to its participation in the VECTOR program.
3. Defense Advanced Research Projects Agency, homepage, *http://www.darpa.mil*, accessed November 1, 2011.
4. Wallace, *Nose Up*, pp. 40–41.
5. See Chambers, *Partners in Freedom*, pp. 215–224.
6. Deutsche Aerospace, *Roll-out—A German View*, pp. 15–18.
7. Wallace, *Nose Up*, p. 40.
8. 6510 Test Wing Staff Summary Sheet, "Memorandum of Agreement for X-31" (Edwards AFB: Air Force Flight Test Center, May 9, 1991), Dryden archives.
9. DARPA, U.S., Navy, U.S. Air Force, and NASA Ames Dryden Flight Research Facility, "For Comment Draft Memorandum of Agreement for The EFM Flight Test Program," April 25, 1991, p. 8, Dryden archives.
10. 6510 Test Wing Staff Summary Sheet, "Memorandum of Agreement for X-31."
11. For example, in the late 1960s, NATO established a tripartite operational test and evaluation squadron among the British, Americans, and Germans to assess the military suitability of the Hawker P.1127 Kestrel, predecessor of the Hawker (later, British Aerospace) Harrier V/STOL ground support fighter.
12. Wallace, *Nose Up*, p. 42.
13. Mike Francis, interview by Douglas A. Joyce, October 19, 2011.
14. Kenneth E. Hodge, "X-31 Enhanced Fighter Maneuverability Demonstrator—Program Coming to Edwards AFB," briefing, NASA Dryden, December 17, 1991.
15. Rogers Smith, interview by Douglas A. Joyce, March 22, 2011.
16. Wallace, *Nose Up*, p. 42.
17. Col. Larry G. Van Pelt, *The Evolution of Flight Test Concepts* (Edwards AFB: AFFTC History Office, June 1982), pp. 27–49.
18. Mike Francis, interview by Douglas A. Joyce, November 6, 2011.
19. Wallace, *Nose Up*, p. 42.
20. Mike Francis, interview by Douglas A. Joyce, November 6, 2011; Wallace, *Nose Up*, pp. 42–43.

21. Harvey Schellenger, interview by Douglas A. Joyce, November 10, 2011.
22. Deutsche Aerospace, *From Roll-out to Tactical Evaluation—A German View*, p. 24.
23. Capt. Christopher J. Loria, USMC, Lt. Mark Kelly, USN, and Ron Harney, X-31 Quasi-tailless Evaluation" (Lancaster, CA: The Society of Experimental Test Pilots, 1995), p. 17.
24. X-31 International Test Organization Council, council minutes, August 29, 1995, Dryden archives.
25. "X-31 Total Estimated Development Costs" outline, copy in Dryden archives.
26. "X-31 Program Close-Out Briefing," presented to Dr. Robert Whitehead, NASA Associate Administrator of Aeronautics, November 3, 1995, copy in Dryden archives.
27. Wallace, *Nose Up*, p. 51.
28. AIAA, "X-31 Finds a Shorter Path to Success," America Online, August 2003, at *http://www.aiaa.org/aerospace/Article.cfm?issuetocid= 392&ArchiveIssueID=41*, accessed on October 27, 2011.

NASA vectored thrust aircraft (left to right) F/A-18 HARV, X-31, and F-16 MATV in formation flight over the Mojave, 1994. (NASA)

CHAPTER 7

The X-31 in Retrospect

In evaluating the place of the X-31 in aerospace history, it is useful to go back to the original program goals and to evaluate what was accomplished against those goals. This chapter will quickly summarize the various goals and level of achievement of each goal for the programs (EFM and VECTOR) that the X-31 supported. Appendix 7 will elaborate on these findings, should the reader desire further insight.

In Sum...

The X-31 was the flight demonstration asset for the EFM program, and four goals were established for that program at its outset.

1. The first of the EFM goals was *rapid demonstration of high agility maneuvering concepts.* Rapid is a relative term, since the program (like any Government-funded effort) was subject to the vagaries of the Government funding process and timing—in this case, it was subject to two governments' processes and cycles. In any case, the high-agility concept was validated by the spectacular performance of the X-31 during the close-in-combat evaluations and its breathtaking display at the Paris Air Show.

2. The goal to *investigate EFM benefits of the Enhanced Fighter Maneuverability (EFM) technologies* was highlighted by Rockwell's assessment of the success of the close-in-combat evaluations. The program demonstrated that multi-axis thrust vectoring and post-stall maneuvering improved close-in air combat effectiveness by a factor of six.

3. The goal to *develop design requirements and data base for future applications* was at least partially fulfilled. Without a doubt, the data exists, because there were a series of "final reports" produced for both the EFM program and the VECTOR program. However, one

can argue that these documents are not easily accessible. Whether a future designer of a multiaxis thrust-vectoring fighter could easily access this wealth of information is somewhat in question.

4. The final EFM goal was to *validate a low cost international prototyping concept*. When compared to other demonstration programs, it certainly can be claimed that this program was low cost and very cost effective. This was demonstrated in at least two fashions:

   a. The demonstrator's design, fabrication, and assembly were approximately half the cost of prior dedicated demonstration aircraft.

   b. The large number of flights and varied nature of the research program was very cost effective in terms of cost per flight and, more importantly, of data generated per unit of cost.

Aside from these four stated programmatic goals, there were many other facets to the X-31 program that benefited the aerospace sciences, and some of these drew wider interest and support on their own. One such goal was the "quasi-tailless" study program conducted toward the end of the X-31 EFM program, which was sponsored and funded by the Joint Advanced Strike Technology program. This "sub-program" was a lead-in to the Boeing X-32 and Lockheed Martin X-35 demonstrators that anticipated the DOD Joint Strike Fighter, the Lockheed Martin F-35 Lightning II. The objectives of the quasi-tailless evaluation were as follows:[1]

1. Investigate the level of directional stability reduction that can be handled with yaw/pitch thrust vectoring in a single-engine fighter under realistic flight scenarios.

2. Assess the maturation of modern integrated flight control technologies for application on future single-engine strike fighters.

3. Look into simple methods for assessing thrust-vector-control power sizing.

All three of these objectives were successfully attained, proving the viability of using thrust vectoring to control tailless strike fighter designs.

Taking the X-31 to the Paris Air Show in 1995 was not a typical "test program," although the low-altitude post-stall envelope expansion did serve to complete the technical exploration of multiaxis thrust vectoring and to expand the low-altitude database for future aircraft design. It also afforded an opportunity to showcase what American and German researchers had accomplished. Afterward, Rockwell concluded the following:

> The impact of demonstrating multi-axis thrust vectoring at the 1995 Paris Air Show was dramatic. The serious attention that the X-31 received from the world aviation community far surpassed the previous reach of the program. The technical achievements of the

program and the far reaching implications of the technology were clearly demonstrated to a vastly larger audience than ever before.[2]

The VECTOR program constituted a fitting end for the X-31 program, and it had a mix of challenging and intriguing goals. Upon its outset, its primary goals were demonstrating two new capabilities to meet operational needs: namely, ESTOL and the viability of tailless fighter and attack aircraft.

Additionally, from its outset it had secondary technology goals that related to the development of enabling technologies, including an Advanced Air Data System, an axisymmetric vectoring exhaust nozzle, and readying capabilities and technologies for operational application.[3] The applications envisioned for these technologies included new fighter and attack aircraft designs, unmanned combat air vehicles (UCAVs), and other future aircraft designs primarily focused on naval operations.

With the withdrawal of the Swedes and the Spanish from the VECTOR program due to lack of funding, the potential use of the AVEN nozzle went away. Also, the actual physical removal of all or part of the vertical tail was abandoned due to both safety concerns and a lack of funding. VECTOR's purpose was thus modified to reflect these changed realities.[4]

Overall, the X-31 VECTOR effort demonstrated several principles:

1. The ESTOL concept was workable and had significant payoff, especially for carrier operations.
2. An operational-type air data system was achievable in the AADS.
3. A simple GPS-based location system was a potential precision geolocation system for operational application, both ESTOL and conventional takeoffs and landings.

During the program, the X-31 flew a completely automated approach at 24° angle of attack with an automatic derotation and touchdown, an impressive accomplishment. It provided a 30-to-35-percent reduction in landing speed, with a corresponding 50-percent or more reduction in landing energy.

It is intriguing to contemplate, had additional funding been available, what higher-AOA approaches and landings the little canard delta might have executed. VECTOR was all the more remarkable because it involved an experimental research X-plane that was taken out of storage and restored to flyable condition to support a test program that had not even been considered when the X-31 was first designed, developed, and fabricated. This was something else never before done with an X-plane.[5]

Finally, the significance of the X-31 can be measured by the awards that the program and participants received. In 1995, Wolfgang Herbst posthumously received the AIAA Reed Aeronautics Award, the most prestigious honor an individual can receive from the AIAA for achievements in the fields of aeronautical science and engineering. That same year, the X-31 International Test Organization received the Smithsonian Institution's National Air and Space Museum Trophy for Current Achievement, an honor established to recognize extraordinary service in air and space science and technology. In making the award, Robert S. Hoffmann, the Provost of the Smithsonian Institution, stated the following:

> The X-31 International Test Organization is being awarded the 1995 Trophy for Current Achievement for an unprecedented record of engineering and flight exploration accomplishments in the past year. You have culminated a highly successful experimental program with a series of momentous "firsts" in aviation history, demonstrating the significant value of post-stall agility in close-in air combat, developing and demonstrating revolutionary helmet-mounted visual and aural pilot aids for situational awareness under WVR combat conditions, and conducting an epoch-making series of flights in which the X-31 employed its thrust vectoring to demonstrate the feasibility of tailless flight at supersonic speeds.[6]

Recognizing the significant international accomplishments of American and German cooperation in both the EFM program and the follow-on VECTOR effort, the International Council of the Aeronautical Sciences awarded both teams the von Kármán Award, presented for international cooperation in aeronautics. The award was presented "for over 20 years of successful Trans-Atlantic R&D (research and development) teamwork producing the first-ever International X-plane and significant breakthroughs in thrust-vectoring control."[7]

In 1994, the AIAA Aircraft Design Award was presented to five members of the X-31 team: Tack Nix (DARPA program manager), Hannes Ross (DASA program manager), Helmuth Heumann (German MOD program manager), Mike Robinson (Rockwell program manager), and Charles Johnson (NAVAIR program manager). This award was established in 1968 and is presented to an individual or team for an original concept or career contributions leading to a significant advancement in aircraft design or design technology. The citation reads, "For the innovative and original approach, conceptualization, and design of the X-31 aircraft, whose on-going flight test program is successfully demonstrating radically different, high payoff fighter capabilities."[8]

Also on the other side of the Atlantic, in 1996 the Deutsche Gesellschaft für Luft-und Raumfahrt made its first award of the "The Spire of Distinction of German Aviation" in memory of the German aviation pioneers Ludwig Bölkow,

Claudius Dornier, Ernst Heinkel, Hugo Junkers, and Willy Messerschmitt, to 17 German and American members of the X-31 team, including Wolfgang Herbst posthumously. The citation reads:

> In recognition of [their] outstanding achievements as...member[s] of the team that successfully accomplished the design, development, and testing of the German-American X-31 experimental aircraft. The X-31 has overcome traditional limits of maximum lift flight; using thrust-vectoring and fly-by-wire flight control, it opened a new field of controlled flight for highly maneuverable aircraft and contributed through outstanding aeronautical engineering to an outstanding technical advancement.[9]

Lessons Learned

The X-31 research program generated numerous reports, technical papers, and commentary, altogether furnishing many lessons learned—and, in some cases, relearned—pertaining to flight-test practice and safety, implications for future development, and the conduct of aerospace research. The International Test Organization and the companies, agencies, and services involved each drew particular lessons learned that may be examined through the prism of each organization.

The International Test Organization Perspective

At the conclusion of the X-31 program, the ITO members submitted inputs on lessons learned that were subsequently incorporated into a summary report issued by Rockwell.[10] The report constitutes a comprehensive listing of lessons learned from the inception of the program to the X-31's return from the Paris Air Show, organized by various topics. In their summary, the authors noted, "The X-31 program, as in all experimental aerospace programs, had the primary objective of passing lessons learned to government and industry.... There has been no attempt to emphasize the good and de-emphasize the bad. There were an overwhelming number of positive X-31 lessons, but we have included the negative as well and the corrective/mitigation actions already incorporated and/or recommended."[11] The complete lessons learned as reported in that report are included within Appendix 7 of this book. Only the most significant lessons are discussed in this chapter; they have been edited for clarity and importance and are listed by topic.

I. Engineering

Flight Control System

The use of existing modern flight control law theory from the all-digital, fly-by-wire MBB F-104 and the incorporation of existing Honeywell all-digital fly-by-wire AOFS HTTB design experience was one of the two primary engineering initiatives (software & thrust vectoring) which enabled the successful achievement of the basic X-31 Enhanced Fighter Maneuverability (EFM) demonstrated goal.[12]

The use of all-digital, fly-by-wire technology in prototype demonstrators is not new, however the use of the MBB modern flight control law theory as part of the technology to solve the post-stall, thrust vectoring control requirements is new and was a spectacular success!

Thrust Vectoring

The use of thrust vectoring control of the aircraft in pitch and roll/yaw at post-stall α [angle of attack] was the other of the two primary engineering initiatives contributing to the successful achievement of the basic X-31 EFM objectives.

When the concept of post-stall regime usage for fighter super maneuverability during close in combat was developed to the point of practical implementation, deflection of centerline engine thrust to achieve the required turning moments was the most viable option.

As a cost saving measure, thrust deflection was achieved in the X-31 design through the use of three vanes attached to the fuselage aft bulkhead. The cost savings vice an axisymmetrical nozzle were enormous at the time and made the program achievable.

Pilot Visual Aids in Post-Stall

The X-31 demonstrated that a helmet-mounted sight in conjunction with high-off-boresight capable missiles and high AoA close in combat capable aircraft would provide an overwhelming advantage to pilots of future super maneuverable combat aircraft.

Post-Stall EFM

The X-31 demonstration of precision controlled thrust vectoring at high α to enhance close in combat was shown to be an insurmountable advantage against the world's best fighters and combat pilots.

Quasi-Tailless Flight Demonstrations

The most dramatic lesson learned from the X-31 quasi-tailless demonstrations were the near-term technological, cost and schedule benefits accrued from using a free-air, piloted simulator to validate wind tunnel and ground manned flight simulator results. This first of its kind in the world achievement was a clever way to safely validate the thrust vectored control of a tailless, unstable aircraft without removing the tail.

FCS Redundancy

Limited hardware redundancy in the flight control system is more expensive to the program, in the long term. The money saved on initial hardware cost is more than spent on software redundancy management as the program is executed. Primary, flight critical, sensors should not be derived from a single source; initial savings in hardware will turn into multiple costs later.

FCS "Iron Bird"

Some limited "iron bird" capability is needed even for a research vehicle. Doing Flight Control System (FCS) integration on the aircraft itself delays final FCS development too long, could damage the aircraft and conflicts with other on-aircraft system test requirements. The program should have at least a representative test actuation system for each type of actuator on the aircraft. This would allow system integration and development on the FCS before the aircraft is ready to support the FCS.

Data and Telemetry

Use circularity polarized telemetry for an aircraft that is designed for maneuvers. This is both [for] the aircraft and ground station.

Simulation

The digital simulation allowed rapid testing of control law modifications. It also provided an easy to use tool for pre-flying the planned test cards without the requirement to bring up the full hardware simulation. The tool was much easier to use than a full up hardware simulation.

Flight hardware-in-the-loop simulation is an essential tool for development, verification, and validation of complex fly-by-wire flight control system software.

Helmet Mounted Display (HMD)

The tracker is a very important part of the HMD system and it was quickly discovered on the X-31 program that if tracker performance is poor the resulting action (for aircraft, planform stabilized symbology) is that the pilot finds the jitter and lag of the symbols (Flight Path Marker, Gun Piper) to be unusable and would de-clutter it.

Control Laws

LQR [Linear Control Regulator] control law design with gain scheduling was successful.[13]

Roll about the velocity vector and aircraft control via stick only (except for intended sideslip) at high α proved to be a very successful concept.

Aerodynamics

High angle of attack aerodynamic asymmetries need to be considered early in the design (a blunt nose and nose strakes tend to reduce high-alpha asymmetries considerably).

Mike Robinson, the Rockwell program manager, subsequently added, "As is typical, the wind tunnel mounting scheme (e.g. sting, or strut) had significant impact on the aerodynamics. In the case of X-31 where high AoA aerodynamics were critical, the mounting approach effects were exacerbated and like the "nose area" aerodynamics the after-body had a major impact in the pitch plane in particular. The drop model proved to be a very useful tool to guide the aero team through the high AoA aero design and validation. So again like any new aerodynamic design multiple models (in conjunction with CFD [Computational Fluid Dynamics] tools today) are necessary for both aero shaping and to gain data for digital control law development."[14]

Subsystems and Components

In general the X-31 subsystems and components, most of which were off the shelf, performed as expected, with as expected maintenance. Noteworthy exceptions are discussed in the following paragraphs:

Ejection Seat: The X-31 Martin-Baker ejection seat contains a 17-foot diameter parachute, designed for F-18 naval combat operations and the Navy pilots are trained for the relative hard landing owing to its relative small diameter. NASA Dryden is working to qualify a 24-foot parachute for use in the Martin-Baker ejection seats of their F-18 chase aircraft. That said the Navy has continued to use the 17-foot chute on its operational Hornets.

FCC Throughput: FCC throughput margin approached the point of concern, resulting in control room monitoring toward the end of envelope expansion. This was adequate for the recently completed program but does not afford the flexibility and increased throughput needed for projected modifications.

Mike Robinson added, "While not X-31 or EFM/ESTOL unique it was once again shown that on computer controlled aircraft both getting the highest capability computers during initial design and/or building in a computer growth capability is a high priority issue."[15]

Validity of Internal and External Loads Predictions

The X-31 was purposely designed and built without utilizing a Wind Tunnel Loads Data model—a low cost design decision albeit a quite non-traditional practice. The approach called for careful and conservative design using highly experienced design personnel. While probably not appropriate for a production design where weight and life cycle cost are drivers, the approach worked very well for a limited use demonstrator design. The predicted loads derived without wind tunnel data that the X-31 was designed to meet were extremely accurate. In addition, the aircraft structural design was very conservative, and the aircraft was limited to 80% of design limit load, throughout the program. As a result, no loads issues were encountered.

Design for Low Cost

The use of off-the-shelf major components was a key driver in successfully meeting the X-31 program goal of demonstrating a "low-cost" prototype aircraft; however some argue that the approach was taken too far—especially on 2nd and 3rd tier parts. Their use was often via the GFE system which afforded low priority to X-31 as compared to a combat aircraft situation of being grounded for lack of parts. This caused some delays, out of sequence (and other work-arounds) when equivalent parts could have been commercially acquired albeit at some-what higher initial cost.

On the other hand, the X-31 design very successfully incorporated a significant amount of off-the-shelf major components. This was one of the key Drivers in successfully meeting the "low-cost" prototype program objective.

The use of off-the-shelf major components was imbedded in the design of the X-31 from its inception. Rockwell, Daimler Benz and the customer, NAVAIR, worked as a team in the successful procurement of these components from ongoing production and prototype programs.

Additional advantages to this policy included in-place repair and replacement sources, minimal airworthiness requirements and in-place maintenance procedures.

The savings of this design policy as opposed to design, develop, and procurement from scratch would easily exceed the total cost of the X-31 program ($255M).

II. Operations

For a research flight test program it is essential that flight clearance be granted at the test location. The basic nature of the program requires change and remote clearance authority can significantly delay program progress.

Clear, specific program milestones and objectives are the key to test success and meeting schedule.

The benefits of an integrated team take time to realize, but as previously discussed had high payoff and have become the new standard for RDT&E testing.

Dual Dome Close-In Combat (CIC) Simulation: Simulation allowed tactics development and provided a much more efficient test program. That said effective use of post-stall in CIC was much easier in the aircraft than in the simulator.

In general the X-31 was easy to maintain, even though sustainability was not a strong design requirement. Once again the success of the X-31 in this regard can be attributed to use of highly experienced designers who knew where maintenance/replacement would be required and where it was unlikely for a test demonstrator. Noteworthy exceptions are discussed in the following paragraphs:

Control Surface Free-play Measurement Setup: The original periodic inspection test using a static measurement technique was very time consuming. A significant reduction in the time required was made at NASA Dryden by implementation of a dynamic technique.

Flight Control Computer (FCC) fiber-optic cable data links: Continual problems were encountered during the X-31 program keeping the FCC fiber optic data links clean and free from damage. Numerous cables and all of the FCC connectors were replaced due to cable fragility.

Flight Test Instrumentation (FTI)/Flight Control System (FCS): Some X-31 signals required for FCS operation are computed by the FTI system. This imposed undesirable support problems and in-flight risk.

Trailing Edge Flap Actuator Piston Wear: The use of trailing edge flap actuators with non-solid pistons caused premature wear, control surface free-play anomalies and time consuming delays. The pistons were replaced with a solid design which resolved the wear problem and allowed extension of the free-play interval.

Fuel Tank Gaging Inadequacy: The X-31 fuel tank capacitance probe gaging system provides inaccurate fuel quantity readings to the pilot at high α. This problem, caused by fuel slosh, consumed valuable flight time to level off and get accurate readings. The situation was improved by displaying a reading in the control room derived from integrated flow meter data.

The Benefits of Built-In Test (BIT): BIT reduced X-31 preflight time considerably. Rapid turn-around for multiple flight days would be impossible, without BIT. It is well worth the design and implementation cost, even on a low-cost demonstration aircraft.

Rapid Flutter Flight Data Analysis: During flutter envelope expansion to Mach 1.3 at NASA Dryden, the NASA automated wideband data reduction/analysis facilities were used. This reduced continued expansion flight clearance turn-around time from one week to one day.

X-31 Flight Test Meetings and Procedures (0800 Daily Status Meetings, ITO Bi-Weekly Program Reviews and Monthly ITO Council Meetings): These meetings were key to X-31 ITO communications and contributed to an extremely smooth running operation.

Mini-Technical Briefings, Technical Briefings, Flight Readiness Reviews (FRRs) and Airworthiness Flight Safety Review Boards (AFSRBs): These presentations to NASA-Dryden management were used to obtain clearance to proceed with new activities, to provide updated program status, to obtain new software release approvals, to proceed with anomaly corrective action and to proceed in flight with the corrective action incorporated. The clearance process was a great improvement over that used prior to moving to NASA Dryden.

Flight Crew Briefs, Flight Card Reviews, Weather Briefs and Flight Crew Debriefs: These are standard meetings developed by Rockwell and used with great success at NASA Dryden.

III. Program Management

General

The use of customer/contactor negotiated and agreed to limitations on specifications, drawings and procedures and rigorous tailoring of the ones that were required was the cornerstone achievement in successfully meeting the X-31 program goal of demonstrating a "low-cost" prototype aircraft on schedule (as limited by both U.S. & German budget cycles and associated vagrancies) and within cost.

The X-31 program success can be directly attributed to the relaxation of the overwhelming quantity of rigid specification, drawing and procedure requirements normally imposed on the development of a demonstration aircraft.

The use of limited and tailored specifications, drawings and procedures greatly reduced the time and expense required to design the X-31. In addition, the follow-on activities of fabrication, assembly, checkout and flight operations were greatly enhanced by this policy.

The use of streamlined configuration management, manufacturing planning, checkout/ramp and flight test planning methods reduced their cost and time to complete through first flight below that of earlier and contemporary prototype aircraft.

The Multiple Benefits of Successful International Teaming and Co-Location

The X-31 is the only international X-plane. The transfer of technical information between the German and American members of the team was constant and without inhibition. This multicultural exchange provided a fresh approach to the solution of difficult technical problems, was a basis for lowering the interorganizational cultural barriers of each participating nation, and resulted in a serendipitous increase in the value returned for each team member's investment.

When the X-31s were moved from Palmdale to NASA Dryden Flight Research Center (DFRC), the organizational members of the team became the X-31 International Test Organization (ITO) and were collocated in Bldg. 4840 furthering the same cooperative philosophy with even more organizations involved.

In reading these "lessons learned" decades later, Mike Robinson emphasized that the following three paragraphs are definitely "Foot Stomper" lessons learned from the EFM program.

Programmatics

In a program where numerous contract modifications and forms preparation are necessary to keep the program progressing smoothly, it is critical to establish a process, clearly defined and agreed to by the participants that is doable within an organization's structure without creating frequent stress and interference with other on-going programs.

Paperwork management is crucial considering current regulations and policy emphasizing reducing requirements. Program technical support personnel generally still conform to old methods of conducting acquisition programs and frequently utilize specifications which could be reduced in content and still meet safety requirements for a technology program. It behooves a program manager to work closely with them to encourage limiting requirements and to "tailor" to specific requirements for the project.

An example (utilized by X-31) is the elimination of most reliability/maintainability requirements when the aircraft is designed for limited life and does not have to meet the carrier/sea environment. What is imminently sensible and logical may not prevail. Push your technical staff to consider other and better ways to get the job done.

The test pilot and flight test engineer are valuable members of the initial design team and should be part of the initial design effort as well as throughout all program phases.

Program reports should be written on an incremental basis with periods not exceeding one year. Writing a final report covering a period of many years after most program personnel and budgets are gone loses much of the data.

Build at least two research aircraft when doing a flight test program. The second aircraft allows comparison and understanding of unique aerodynamic characteristics, provides backup if one aircraft is lost and allows a more productive test program by flying one aircraft while the other is being modified or maintained.

Up to six pilots at a time were active on the X-31 program. The large number of pilots had both good and bad points.

Each organization was able to have an active pilot in the program which enhanced team interest. The pilots were able to provide direct inputs on aircraft performance to their parent organizations.

The varied backgrounds and experience of the pilots added significantly to the technical expertise of the team.

At times it was difficult to provide adequate flying for each pilot. In general a simple rotation was used. During the CIC phase, pilot teams were rotated.

The relatively simple systems and excellent flight characteristics of the X-31 were the main reason the large pilot team was successful. A more complex aircraft or flight test plan may work better with a smaller pilot team.

Substantial support in obtaining ongoing funding support can be obtained from potential users of the technology.

Establishing advocates such as TOP GUN lends credibility to the importance of the program.

Unless cost factors are crucial or a contractor cannot obtain materials when needed, a program manager should attempt to require the contractor to provide all parts and materials. However, if the government is to provide all or some of the parts and materials, then establishing a high priority isn't enough. You must survey and place orders to ensure parts and materials are available when needed in the manufacturing/assembly process or serious delays and cost growth can ensue.

Again, Mike Robinson commented on this, saying, "There is a ton of controversy in the above paragraph and you will get as many on one side as the other. Probably a balanced and carefully considered approach to supplier management (including GFE) is the right answer. Engine, nozzle, canopy, cockpit structure, etc. were absolutely needed as GFE on X-31 to control cost and assure timely certification, but as previously stated it was probably carried a bit too far on X-31."[16]

> When several government agencies, including foreign government participation, are part of the program it is crucial to fully understand the philosophy of how each organization works and to determine if/how that process fits (or needs adapting) for the program to succeed.

> The X-31 program expanded the thrust vector-controlled 70° α post-stall envelope from 12,000 to 500 ft minimum altitude. No other aircraft has provided the aerospace community with precision high angle of attack control in this environment. This capability was dramatically demonstrated before the world at Paris Airshow '95. This was the technical highlight of the show and stimulated enthusiastic international interest to a far greater extent than the usual approach to advertising technological achievement. It can be a powerful program management tool.[17]

Rockwell's and MBB's Perspective

Rockwell stressed lessons learned from the design and operation of the X-31's various systems and use of off-the-shelf equipment. Of its flight control system, engineers noted:

> The flight control laws, redundancy management and software design and maintenance would have been greatly simplified if all flight critical sensors and actuators were all quadruplex or all triplex. The need for reversionary control modes would have been eliminated and the software to handle different levels of redundancy would not have been necessary. And flight safety would have been enhanced. A lot of effort was expended to provide failsafe capabilities for the simplex INU and the duplex air data sensors.[18]

Flight control laws were an MBB (DASA) responsibility, and upon conclusion of the program, Rockwell engineers acknowledged the great work of their German counterparts, noting that "DASA [MBB] did an excellent job in designing and developing the control laws as evidenced by the stunning results of the close-in-combat evaluations and the Paris airshow. This is the result of long-range planning, technical competence, and persistent pursuit of achieving a well-defined goal."[19] Under "redundancy management (RM)," the report discusses flight control actuator RM, air data and INU RM, and engine sensor monitors, concluding, "The flight hardware-in-the-loop simulation (FHILS) [was] critical in the development and evaluation of the redundancy management system. A thorough RM validation test matrix must be revised, reviewed and evaluated for each new software load to ensure that all flight safety concerns are addressed."[20]

Rockwell stressed the importance of early involvement by test pilots in the design and development process, particularly with regard to cockpit controls and displays, some of which were unique to the X-31 and developed for post-stall, quasi-tailless, and low-altitude flight. Engineers concluded, "The flight test pilots must be involved in the definition of the cockpit control functions early in the design cycle and as the flight test program develops to ensure success."[21]

Software development was of crucial importance to the satisfactory progression of the program, and Rockwell reported that during the X-31 effort, software loads were developed with a relatively quick turnaround, allowing high sortie rates in the flight test. In explaining how this was achieved, analysts concluded the following:

> The ability to achieve the high rate of X-31 flight tests at NASA Dryden [was] attributable to the co-location of the test engineers and the FHILS [flight-hardware-in-the-loop-simulation] simulation at the flight test site. Quick turnaround software overlays were defined, programmed in machine language, [and] debugged and validated in the FHILS. Turnarounds as short as 3 days from the time of CCB [configuration control board] approval to flight test release were achieved with some overlays. In spite of the quick turnarounds, there have been no failures that affected flight safety because of a software overlay error.[22]

Rockwell noted several lessons relative to off-the-shelf flight-qualified equipment. Though it constituted fully *43 percent of final weight*, the use of off-the-shelf equipment resulted in significant savings in program costs and schedule.

The off-the-shelf cables that were used for communications between the flight control computers were too fragile for aircraft use. Rockwell noted that fiber-optic cables "used for aircraft should be rated for rugged applications."[23] As discussed previously, flying the X-31 in Europe involved some significant electromagnetic interference (EMI) issues, and resolution of these issues required that the mission planners go back to the aircraft's EMI design to provide a baseline for determining clearances from high-power transmitters in Europe. EMI also proved to be problematic when the aircraft was flown at NAS Patuxent River in the VECTOR program. "When aircraft EMI levels are designed, entries/calculations should be included in the flight manual for separation required from high power transmitters (especially fly-by-wire aircraft)."[24]

An important fuel tank lesson specific to high-AOA designs had to be relearned on the X-31 (these issues had been known since the early 1950s): "Design of fuel tanks for high alpha flight should consider adequate use of baffles to prevent slosh and/or means to use fuel flow information over the full engine operational envelope to derive fuel quantity."[25]

For its part, the DASA (MBB) Final Report did not list "lessons learned" per se, but it did offer a considerable discussion on conclusions that could be drawn from the program. It can be assumed that many MBB lessons learned were incorporated into the ITO lessons learned presented previously. Overall, MBB noted with evident pleasure, "The X-31 EFM Program set several records for flight test efficiency and productivity and serves as a benchmark for future international cooperation and achievement."[26] This reaffirms the usefulness of cooperative international programs in technology demonstration, and while much of the media spotlight is on international cooperation in astronautical endeavors such as the International Space Station, it is a lesson worth learning from the X-31 program that international aeronautical programs are very useful as well.

The View from Dryden

Befitting its flight-research and flight-testing heritage, Dryden's focus on X-31 lessons learned embraced those dealing with the conduct of flight testing and, in particular, the shocking loss of Ship 1. Since Dryden was a flight-test organization that was primarily responsible for flight safety and clearance and not a management organization, it is natural to see that the lessons learned produced by Dryden deal with flight-test conduct. One lesson emphasized by the program— and discussed earlier—was the necessity of ensuring that flight-test clearance be controlled at the local level (i.e., at the test station itself). Otherwise, significant program delays could occur.[27] One of the major reasons for the move from the contractor's location at Palmdale to the research center at Dryden was the length of time it took managers at NAVAIR, across the country, to provide flight clearances to Rockwell during the early days of the program. Having flight clearance authority reside at Dryden was one of the reasons that the ITO, and ultimately the X-31 flight-test program, was so successful.

The loss of Ship 1 triggered intense self-examination and review at NASA Dryden, and it was the subject of a widely distributed video entitled *X-31 Breaking the Chain: Lessons Learned*. It resulted in a careful review of all mishaps to experimental aircraft over the previous two decades, as well as the explication of specific lessons learned from this particular accident. In the video, Dryden Director Ken Szalai noted that flight testers had a responsibility to "learn from all accidents, even close calls."

The X-31 accident reaffirmed the importance of careful configuration control and the danger of complacency. Analysts noted, for example, that the inoperative pitot heat switch had not been placarded on the instrument panel, an action that, if it had been done, would have immediately alerted the pilot to the absence of pitot heating. While notices of the change had been sent out, there was no feedback process to ensure that the information had actually been received and read by the recipients. Investigators found that other single-point failures, including the pitot heat, were noted as early as 1989—6 years before the accident—but a complacency had crept into the test team and this information was not revisited and reviewed in the later years of the program. As John Bosworth, NASA Dryden chief engineer, pointed out, there used to be a sign posted in the control room that read, "Prepare for the unexpected and expect to be unprepared." The complacency was reinforced by the nature of the flight itself: it was the *last* scheduled data mission for Ship 1, it was the *last* data point on that mission, and it was the *last* mission of that day. People started relaxing, thinking that they were done...but they were not. When a flight-test team becomes "mature" and comfortable after years of testing a given airplane, they should look back and review their assumptions about the airplane and their procedures.

There were other issues as well. For example, there was no clear communication among those present in the control room, the X-31 pilot, and the chase pilot. Communication had become fragmented, with sidebar discussions among participants that dealt with the lack of pitot heat on the Kiel probe but did not involve the others present in the room. Due to problems with the retransmission of telemetered X-31 radio transmissions, the chase pilot lacked timely awareness of what was going on. Reliable communications among all parties, Dryden stressed afterward, is vital to a successful flight-test program.

Another lesson involved individual responsibility: analysts stressed that if something occurs that a member of a test team does not understand, they should call a halt until the issue is resolved. As Dryden research pilot Rogers Smith memorably stated, participants should "stop the train" when things do not seem right. Most importantly, *everyone* on the team should understand that they are a part of the potential "accident chain" and thus are responsible for safety of flight.[28] In September 1996, prior to production of the X-31 lessons learned video, Smith gave a presentation on the accident to the annual symposium of the Society of Experimental Test Pilots. In summarizing what had been learned, he emphasized the following:

If You Do Not Understand or It Does Not Make Sense:

1) SPEAK UP!
2) STOP THE TESTS AND THINK!
Communicate to all test players
In the face of the Unexpected, Know the Quick System Path to Safety
There is No Substitute for Good Flight Test Judgment
Accidents Do Not Just Happen to "THEM"...They Happen to "YOU"[29]

The NAVAIR Perspective

After the conclusion of VECTOR, NAVAIR engineers wrote a three-volume summary report on the program, each volume of which contained a section that explicitly enumerated lessons learned from the VECTOR program, ranging from program and facility access through the conduct of flight-test operations. The following are the programmatic and flight-testing lessons that the Navy drew from its experience with the X-31, primarily during the VECTOR evaluation effort.

I. Programmatic Lessons

Like the EFM program before, VECTOR reaffirmed that establishing mutual trust between multinational contractors and government agencies is essential to programmatic success, with analysts noting, "Your primary, pass/fail objective must include your partners pass/ fail objective and you must prioritize it as high as your own. Loyalty to joint objectives must be maintained. All necessary actions from open communications, to coaching personal interaction skills, to providing a little more effort then you have to, are required to sustain the program."[30]

Surprisingly, given its own extensive experience with international aircraft development and flight-testing partnerships,[31] the Navy seemingly had greater difficulties than the Air Force and NASA in dealing with the X-31's foreign participants, noting that in the future, testers should

Expect security issues to require a great deal more effort to work, especially when dealing with foreign nationals.

Allow considerable dedicated time if trying to set up anything unusual security-wise.

Never assume the security "system" will function properly to admit people onto the base, even when all entries of establishing the visit request and "scheduling" the visitor have been accomplished.[32]

Navy analysts found that the VECTOR program fell victim to the "requirements creep" typical of many programs, in which new requirements were generated and made a part of the program after a contract was awarded. In addition, delays in getting authorization to commence work and unforeseen maintenance and engineering issues caused the schedule to slip, with analysts noting, "It took much longer and cost much more than even the experts could predict."[33] In particular, the flight-test team noted that requirements creep affected the aircraft and its hardware once it arrived at Patuxent. Research aircraft are often built to the "intent" of Military Specification (i.e., "MIL-SPEC") requirements but not to the letter of the specification. For instance, because the X-31 was built as a research vehicle, many of its wiring and installations were not compliant with full MIL-SPEC requirements, and its structure was not as thoroughly proof-tested as a combat airplane would have been. NAVAIR's testers expended much effort in trying to make it MIL-SPEC-compliant, which resulted in cost growth and inevitable schedule slips and led NAVAIR to conclude that in the future, testers should "[c]learly define the ground rules for achieving a flight clearance and budget and plan accordingly."[34]

The X-31 VECTOR effort clearly had benefited from senior-level NAVAIR support. While the support of senior management for a program is always important, it is even more so when the type of program (e.g., a science and technology effort) is not perceived to be a "core" war-fighting-related mission (e.g., weapons-system development in the case of NAS Patuxent River). NAVAIR concluded, "Upper level management's vision and direction to support is needed repeatedly when conducting a non-traditional program. Without high-level intervention, the program would have been buried as a low priority and would have failed. Lack of working level support can kill a program, even when funding is available."[35] Despite senior-level support, however, funding limitations forced the VECTOR program to use part-time NAVAIR engineers to support their program. The conflict of priorities on these engineers' tasking dogged the program, and analysts concluded, "Relying on part-time USN engineering and suffering a severe lack of priority leads to schedule slides, lost productivity, lost flight test opportunities and 'just in time' delivery at best."[36]

Given that many of the subsystems in the X-31 were drawn from "off-the-shelf" components and items that were supported by various Government supply agencies, and realizing that spares were limited and that the program often had a lower priority than other users in the field, the X-31 reaffirmed that maintainers have to be creative in supply support. NAVAIR noted, "Unique aircraft parts will always be a risk to an experimental aircraft program. Identify before it's needed the unique vendors and untraditional sources of parts that may be necessary. Be creative."[37]

Regarding risk mitigation, NAVAIR noted that the X-31 program affirmed, "Risk mitigation will be the primary factor in setting requirements for scheduling, funding, and most importantly, design. Even when risk mitigation is fully addressed, those in oversight who maintain the highest risk aversion will still prevail, to the result that significantly greater effort will be required to address their concerns."[38] As program requirements evolve (as they inevitably do), it is crucial that changes be communicated to contractors in a timely manner. NAVAIR noted, "Delivering late requirements to contractors often results in cost overruns and schedule slides."[39]

Keeping test-team members apprised of the state and status of the program was naturally of great importance, lest flight-schedule requirements slip. Of particular importance were System Safety Working Group (SSWG) meetings. Reflecting after the program's conclusion, NAVAIR noted, "System [software] team members should have participated in as many SSWG meetings as possible. Each software team member should have each participated in at least one SSWG meeting early in the VECTOR program."[40] The use of online tools was still relatively new at the time of the VECTOR program; however, one of the VECTOR subcontractors made use of a secure Web site to provide visibility of plans and technical documents to all on the program.

The flight software architecture was not known to a degree sufficient to allow VECTOR engineers to understand all of the minor impacts of changes. Thus, any change required substantial testing or even retesting to ensure flight safety. This could have been mitigated by a better understanding of the software architecture, leading NAVAIR to conclude,

> Regression testing could have been tailored or focused more on the SW affected by each incremental build if it could have been demonstrated via SW "decoupling" scheme that specific retests were not required. Furthermore, requirements tracking would have been more precise, resulting in reduced effort during debugging or problem identification sessions.[41]

Simulation taught its own lessons. Because independent organizations were responsible for different simulation components of software (SW) and hardware (HW), the responsibility for simulation validation and configuration control were fractionalized, and engineers concluded, "A great deal of time was lost initiating formal tests in the lab due to the delays in identifying and tasking the responsible parties for specific SW or HW configuration anomalies."[42]

II. Flight-Test Lessons

Remembering that the X-31 was designed to be operated as a "dry" airplane without exposure to rain, adverse weather, or crosswinds greater than 10 knots, operations of the X-31 from Patuxent River—on the shores of the Chesapeake Bay in the variable weather of the salty tidewater—imposed many more challenges than did operations from the dry (if windy) desert environment of Edwards AFB. Not surprisingly, then, NAVAIR recorded that, "Weather played a major role, and was often times overly restrictive, resulting in a much less than expected sortie completion rate."[43] Nor was this all; being a Navy facility, Patuxent River had carrier-like arresting cables rigged on all of its runways. The X-31's wheels were not stressed for routinely rolling over arresting gear cables, which forced the cables to be "derigged" whenever it flew and led NAVAIR to conclude, with some barely disguised head-shaking, "The requirement to de-rig arresting gear by removing the cable from the runway added a level of management not often considered in most other flight-testing programs at Naval Air Stations."[44]

The X-31 was originally designed for operations from relatively long runways and Edwards 04-22 offered 15,000 feet of useful runway, plus an emergency runoff into the vast expanse of Rogers Dry Lake. In contrast, Patuxent River's runways were constrained by terrain and the waters of the Chesapeake Bay. Operations at Patuxent River (and Europe as well) required the installation of a drag chute for added safety, something made possible by modifying the X-31's spin chute into a drag chute. Even so, there was concern lest a failure of the drag chute occur. (Precautionary aerobraking after touchdown seemed a prudent mitigating procedure.) The threat of hot brakes from emergency stops necessitated prepositioning a fire truck near the runway at Patuxent River during X-31 flight operations, something not needed at Edwards. The limited runways at Patuxent River also influenced changes in X-31 takeoff procedures. Concern over the stopping distance during a rejected takeoff in afterburner (AB) led to conducting takeoffs in military (MIL) power (maximum non-afterburning power) instead. In several instances, fire truck placement and arresting-gear derigging were not always performed in a timely fashion, with test team members noting that for future practice, "it is extremely helpful to coordinate with all Patuxent River/NAVAIR divisions/branches on a daily basis to ensure efficient test conduct. While there is some central scheduling function performed at the Test Wing Atlantic level, it does not sufficiently include all the organizations involved in flight test."[45]

Simplicity in design, a hallmark of the X-31, resulted in the airplane having only a single fuel tank with limited fuel capacity, and no provision for air-refueling capability. Fuel-reserve requirements limited operations at Patuxent River, where alternate airfields were relatively distant. The fuel-reserve requirements were the same on weekends as during the week even though the chances of simultaneously closing both runways at Patuxent River were remote on the weekends. NAVAIR found, "Flight times rarely exceeded 45 minutes due to the 40% fuel reserve requirement. Flight-testing during weekend operations was no different, even though airfield traffic was much reduced if not non-existent and the risk greatly mitigated or mute [sic]."[46] Accordingly, testers recommended a greater fuel capacity for experimental aircraft operating from Patuxent River, together with relaxed fuel-reserve requirements for weekend operations.

Testing at Patuxent highlighted a variety of communications and data-link issues. The X-31 had a UHF antenna only on the bottom of the fuselage. There were no problems operating at Edwards, with its wide-open desert expanses, but operations at Patuxent River were troubled by limited line of sight due to the base's more convoluted topography and verdant foliage. Eventually, the Navy relocated the X-31's UHF antenna to the top of the fuselage to improve signal reception, noting the experience as an interesting and significant lesson learned. Data-link problems between the aircraft and pseudolites (GPS satellite surrogates located on the ground) that were used for accurate navigational positioning of the X-31 drew particular concern. NAVAIR noted, "While data links are a well-understood issue in aircraft, it is still very difficult to maintain high-continuity connections. This was a major source of dropouts for IBLS [the very high accuracy navigation system on the X-31 necessary for ESTOL landings]."[47]

As with many earlier test programs, the VECTOR test team benefited from conducting "dry-run" training flights in the simulator (with the simulator electronically linked to the control room) before commencing a test phase with a new aircraft configuration. All test pilots and control room team members participated in the simulation, with NAVAIR concluding, "The RTPS [Real Time Processing System; i.e., the control room]/Simulator link was extremely beneficial to the test team in helping prepare for future phases."[48]

Test-team engineers advocated the separation of documentation for aircraft configuration and flight clearances, stressing that "[f]light clearances should say where the aircraft can operate," and "[c]onfiguration description documents should say what the airplane looks like,"[49] an excellent lesson for future flight-test teams. They also recommended using engineering test builds of software for initial integration and validation rather than waiting for formal operational flight programs, noting that "[f]inding software design or implementation flaws earlier in the process provides the best chances for a successful formal delivery without setbacks and costly schedule impact."[50] There were cases where the same mnemonic "name" was used for different types of data in different flight control software versions. Understandably, this caused confusion and resulted in NAVAIR cautioning, "Using the same mnemonic to identify more than one parameter of data is confusing and unnecessary. Data presentations real-time and post-flight are easier to verify and manage when unique names are used that don't vary over time."[51] Flight control software testing was performed by three separate organizations. This was problematic because a direct and verifiable trace of testing could not be performed, and test-team members concluded, "A single process, under one entity for requirements review and tracking, test script or procedure review and test results verification would have provided more confidence earlier on the CSCI's [computer software configuration item]."[52]

In the wake of the loss of Ship 1, the surviving X-31 had been modified with redundant static pressure sensors that proved to have difficult calibration and fidelity issues because of their location in different regions of flow around the aircraft. Accordingly, NAVAIR concluded the following:

> The main lesson learned is that when an air data system is used for redundancy management, both the primary and the secondary systems should be located in the same [or] similar airflow region. In this case, the L-Probe [secondary static pitot probe] could have been mounted on the flight test boom. For this program the other alternative could have been the calibration of the static source differences between the primary and the secondary static sources. This calibration could have been accomplished during the initial flights of the EFM configuration at Patuxent River.[53]

As can be seen from some of the lessons above, the Navy was very proactive in the provision of redundancy in the aircraft systems (e.g., air data sensing). This was a notable improvement over the airplane configuration in the EFM program. One can, however, discern a distinct difference in the "culture" and circumstance of operations at NAS Patuxent River from that of Dryden at Edwards AFB. If an airplane is designed and constructed for operations at a dry, open, and large facility such as Edwards and then moved to a location with a much different environment, problems are likely to occur. This is seen in the contrast between lessons learned in the EFM program and those written following the VECTOR program. These would have likely been seen if the original plan for EFM had been realized and the airplanes had been moved to Patuxent River for the close-in-combat evaluation. Therefore, the environment for any possible testing location needs to be carefully factored into the planning for any test program, even those involving pure research airplanes such as the X-series.

Endnotes

1. Rockwell International, "X-31 Quasi-Tailless Flight Test Experiment Final Report," Rockwell Report TFD-95-1261 (June 9, 1995), Abstract.
2. Rockwell International, "X-31 Low Altitude Post Stall Envelope Clearance and Paris Air Show Report," Rockwell Report TFD-95-1510 (March 8, 1996), p. 13.
3. "VECTOR Program Briefing," NASA Dryden Flight Research Center, c. 1998, Dryden archives.
4. U.S. Navy and NAVAIR, *X-31 VECTOR Final Report, Volume I: The Program* (NAS Patuxent River, MD: Naval Air Warfare Center, October 16, 2003), p. 7.
5. However, a precedent existed for taking X-aircraft engines out of storage. When, for example, NASA began its lifting body research program, XLR-8 and XLR-11 liquid fuel engines that were already in museums were recalled for use in the exotic craft.
6. Robert S. Hoffmann, Smithsonian Institution Provost, letter to Col. Michael S. Francis, USAF, ARPA Program Manager, July 12, 1995. I thank Colonel Francis for making this letter available to me.
7. Jay Levine, "X-31A team captures von Kármán Award," *The X-Press* 45, no. 6 (August 29, 2003), p. 1.
8. AIAA, *Citation for the Aircraft Design Award* (Reston, VA: AIAA, 1994), n.p.
9. DGLR, *Citation for The Spire of Distinction of German Aviation* (Bonn: DGLR, 1996), n.p.
10. Rockwell International, *X-31 Enhanced Fighter Maneuverability Program Flight Test Final Report: Development of the X-31 Flight Test System*, Rockwell Report TFD-95-1563 (March 14, 1996), section 10.
11. Ibid.
12. Emray Goossen, an X-31 flight control engineer at Honeywell, argues that "AOFS HTTB" is a typo and should instead be "AFCS" for Aircraft Flight Control System. The High Technology Test Bed was an experimental C-130 aircraft funded by Lockheed Martin that was used to demonstrate innovative technologies, including modern flight control computers, for use in extremely short takeoff and landing missions.
13. Linear Control Regulator was an optimum control law method.
14. Mike Robinson, e-mail to Douglas A. Joyce, July 31, 2012.
15. Ibid.

16. Ibid.
17. Rockwell International, *Development of the X-31 Flight Test System,* pp. 10-1–10-15.
18. Rockwell International, *Development of the X-31 Flight Test System,* p. 3-1. In Rockwell's *X-31 EFM Flight Test Final Report,* the "Flight Control Section" details the architecture of the X-31's flight control system (basically, a triplex system with a tiebreaker used after the second failure of a flight critical function). The system had reversionary modes to handle failures of flight-critical sensors that are not quadruplex, such as the simplex INU or the duplex air data sensors.
19. Rockwell International, *Development of the X-31 Flight Test System,* pp. 3-1–3-2.
20. Rockwell International, *Development of the X-31 Flight Test System,* p. 3-3.
21. Rockwell International, *Development of the X-31 Flight Test System,* p. 3-4.
22. Ibid.
23. Rockwell International, *Development of the X-31 Flight Test System,* p. 6-4.
24. Ibid.
25. Rockwell International, *Development of the X-31 Flight Test System,* p. 6-5.
26. P. Huber, *X-31 Enhanced Fighter Maneuverability Final Report* (Daimler-Benz Aerospace: December 22, 1995), p. 32.
27. Rockwell International, *Development of the X-31 Flight Test System,* p. 10-9.
28. "X-31 Breaking the Chain, Lessons Learned," video discussion.
29. Rogers Smith, "X-31 Accident: Lessons to be Learned," *40th Symposium Proceedings* (Lancaster, CA: Society of Experimental Test Pilots, 1996), p. 218.
30. U.S. Navy and NAVAIR, *X-31 VECTOR Final Report, Volume I,* pp. 64–65.
31. For example, the A-4 and F-4 programs of the 1960s; the F-14 program of the 1970s; the E-2, AV-8B, and F/A-18 programs of the 1980s; and numerous helicopter programs.
32. U.S. Navy and NAVAIR, *X-31 VECTOR Final Report, Volume I,* pp. 53–54.
33. Ibid., p. 55.
34. Ibid., p. 61.
35. Ibid., pp. 56–57.
36. Ibid., p. 58.

37. Ibid., p. 59.
38. Ibid., p. 60.
39. Ibid., p. 62.
40. U.S. Navy and NAVAIR, *X-31 VECTOR Final Report, Volume III,* p. 142.
41. U.S. Navy and NAVAIR, *X-31 VECTOR Final Report, Volume I,* p. 66.
42. Ibid., p. 67.
43. U.S. Navy and NAVAIR, *X-31 VECTOR Final Report, Volume III,* p. 121.
44. Ibid., p. 122. Running over cables may seem a small issue, but it is not. Heavily loaded aircraft, and aircraft designed to operate from smooth runway surfaces, can have tire failures even from running across relatively small separation cracks between concrete slabs, or across small perturbations in a surface. For example, when McDonnell-Douglas first started operations of its (then experimental) F-15E Strike Eagle at the AFFTC, the heavily loaded Eagle was blowing its tires simply crossing the discontinuities between concrete slabs on the Edwards ramp, forcing changes to its tire design. Thus, the X-31 faced potentially serious problems confronting the cables at NAS Patuxent River.
45. Ibid., p. 135.
46. Ibid., p. 125.
47. Ibid., p. 139.
48. Ibid., p. 128.
49. Ibid., p. 134.
50. Ibid., p. 132.
51. Ibid., p. 136.
52. Ibid., p. 144.
53. Ibid., p. 141.

Epilogue

As this is written, a decade after the last flight of an X-31, there are no American or European aircraft using the thrust-vectoring paddle technologies and post-stall maneuver capabilities developed and demonstrated on the X-31.[1] During research for this work, an interesting comment was made in an e-mail sent from Boeing to Dryden concerning the legacy of the X-31:

> To our knowledge, only the Russians have embraced multi-axis thrust vectoring for their latest fighters. We believe that the F-22 is the only US aircraft with thrust-vectoring and it is pitch only, not multi-axis like the X-31.[2] Some other X planes have used single-axis thrust vectoring (pitch or yaw): X-32, X-36, and X-45 (all Boeing planes). No applications to commercial transports have been tried.[3]

The F-22 does indeed employ pitch-only thrust vectoring, and its prototype, the YF-22, first flew on September 29, 1990, just 2 weeks before the first flight of the X-31. Its propulsion design had been explored in the experimental F-15B STOL/Maneuver Technology Demonstrator that first flew on September 7, 1988. Since the nozzle technologies for the F-22 had been developed well before the X-31 even flew, the timing was not right for it to incorporate axisymmetric thrust vectoring. Thus, the production F-22A Raptor fighter that followed toward the end of the 1990s retained the two-dimensional pitch-vectoring nozzles of its YF-22 predecessor. The Boeing X-32 and Lockheed Martin X-35, which were precursors to the F-35, had moveable nozzles for vertical lift during short takeoffs and vertical landings (STOVL), but not in-flight thrust vectoring for air-combat maneuvering. The X-45 UCAV was a tailless aircraft and had yaw-only thrust vectoring, primarily to enhance its low-observable-radar characteristics. When asked why the F-35 did not have axisymmetric thrust vectoring when this technology had been developed prior to the final requirement definition for the airplane, Lt. Gen. George K. Muellner, USAF (retired), the first JAST program director, stated:

> The logic the requirements folks used was: "a stealthy airplane with excellent maneuverability at normal speeds and an agile

missile does not get much benefit from high maneuverability at slow speeds." Simulation and testing showed that P_K and P_S went up with tactics that did not allow airspeed to get that low. The additional cost and weight (in the very rear of the aircraft) could never be justified. It was the combination of highly agile missiles and helmet-mounted cueing systems that obviated the need for thrust-vectoring.[4]

Overseas, a Eurojet EJ200 engine that implements thrust vectoring with an axisymmetric nozzle has been marketed by the multinational Eurofighter Typhoon consortium but has not been taken up in actual production.[5] In Russia, the upgraded Sukhoi Su-27SM Flanker fighter has provisions for thrust vectoring. The Su-34 has also been tested with this engine.[6] The Su-35S Flanker E has an even newer afterburning turbofan developed by NPO Lyul'ka-Saturn that features new high- and low-pressure turbines, a new full-authority digital engine control (FADEC) system, and nozzles that furnish all-aspect thrust vectoring.[7] Finally, the new Russian Sukhoi T-50 prototype, a stealthy "Gen 5" fighter like the F-22, is powered by two Lyul'ka-Saturn afterburning turbofans with both FADEC and pitch/yaw vectoring.[8] Sukhoi has demonstrated the T-50 to the Indian Ministry of Defense and hopes for an eventual production rate for the new fighter in excess of 100 aircraft per year. Meanwhile, the F-22, a premier fifth-generation air-dominance fighter with pitch-only thrust vectoring, ended production with the roll-out of the 195th airframe (187 combat aircraft and 8 test aircraft) on December 13, 2011.[9] The complementary fifth-generation F-35, a multirole fighter/attack aircraft with no maneuvering thrust vectoring, is planned for many customers, including the USAF, Navy, Marines, and several foreign nations, though its production numbers are still in flux.

In a broader sense, it is perhaps important to look at the acceptance cycle of X-plane technologies. Since the Bell X-1 (the very first X-series airplane), it has taken 7 to 10 years for the demonstrated technology to gain any production implementation. This time lag is probably even longer today because there are many fewer new airplane systems being started today than in the late 1940s and early 1950s, which was the era of the X-1. Looking at all of the technologies demonstrated on the X-31, one can see that many are present in new systems and new acquisition organizations today. Some examples include the following:

- The international collaborative model: the F-35 (formerly JSF) even used the X-31 as a successful example in selling collaboration overseas.
- The ITO operating model for flight-test operations and management: again, seen in the F-35 program.
- The groundbreaking quasi-tailless work: one only has to observe the many tailless UAVs flying today.

- The HMD trials: present on the F-35 replacing the traditional HUD, but also being used on the F-15, F-16, and other fighters.
- The precision GPS (pseudolite) system developed for VECTOR: present in the Wide and Local Area Augmentation Systems (WAAS and LAAS, respectively) being implemented by the FAA today.
- The use of fly-away tooling: has been adopted in various incarnations on many aircraft production lines, including the Boeing 747.

Clearly, like the oft-cited national space program, the X-31 has spun off a long list of valuable technologies and benefits going far beyond the intentions of those who conceived it.

Endnotes

1. The Lockheed Martin F-22A Raptor stealth fighter does use thrust vectoring for maneuver enhancement, but it uses nozzle vectoring, not paddles. The Lockheed Martin F-35 Joint Strike Fighter incorporates nozzle vectoring and a lift fan for its Marine Corps' Short Takeoff and Vertical Landing (STOVL) variant.
2. A word of explanation: This does not, of course, include the vectored-thrust V/STOL McDonnell-Douglas AV-8 Harrier II, which uses a form of vectored thrust that is very different in form and purpose than that of the F-22, X-31, and the other aircraft to which the memo author refers.
3. Donald W. Tuegel, Boeing, e-mail to Karl A. Bender, DFRC, March 29, 2011.
4. George Muellner, e-mail to Douglas A. Joyce, November 22, 2011.
5. Eurofighter GmbH, *Eurofighter World: Programme News and Features* (Munich: Eurofighter GmbH, February 2010).
6. Yefim Gordon and Dmitriy Komissarov, *Russian Air Power: Current Organisation and Aircraft of all Russian Air Forces* (Hersham, Surry, U.K.: Midland Publishing, 2011), p. 278.
7. Ibid., pp. 337–338.
8. Ibid., p. 346. The International Institute for Strategic Studies estimates that there are 281 Su-27SM series fighters in the Russian inventory, with older versions being upgraded. There are 11 Su-35 aircraft in the inventory, with 48 on order as of 2010. See International Institute for Strategic Studies, *The Military Balance 2010* (2010).
9. "Empty Nest," *Aviation Week & Space Technology* (December 19/26, 2011): p. 61.

Disseminating X-31 Research Results and Lessons: A Review

On August 29, 1995, X-31 program parties held a final International Test Organization Council meeting "to formally declare successful completion of the X-31 [EFM] program and to direct final activities pursuant to deactivation of the International Test Organization."[1] Along with activities assigned for the storage of the airplane, disposition of spares, and financial reconciliation, responsibility was also assigned for the production of final reports. Dryden was assigned responsibility for collecting information on the Paris Air Show and assimilating it into an organized presentation. Also, it was determined that the *X-31 Program Final Report* would be produced, and that it would consist of the following parts:

- Video Volume
- X-31 ITO Final Written Report
- Tactical Utility Volume (including two volumes: an unclassified volume and a classified volume)
- Quasi-tailless Volume
- NASA Reports
- DASA (MBB) Reports

Since then, along with this formal report, a number of American Institute of Aeronautics and Astronautics papers, Society of Experimental Test Pilots papers, and even doctoral theses have been published discussing various parts of the X-31 program and analyzing data produced by the program.

The Video Volume ended up being approximately 1 hour in length, although initially there was some discussion about making it much shorter (10 to 15 minutes) because some felt that an hour was too long for many Members of Congress to view. Ultimately, the decision was made to produce an hour-long video that would be a better historical document and would be useful for Congressional staffers.[2] The Video Volume was produced by Corporate Video of Landover, MD, and was disseminated through the Edwards AFB

Multimedia Center. This volume encompasses the entire EFM effort and features discussions of the program from many program managers, key engineers, and test pilots from both Government and industry. It is particularly useful in documenting the program's early beginnings and its design and manufacturing phase, of which there is little currently available written documentation. One of the more interesting features of the film is a time-lapse sequence showing the assembly of one of the aircraft. Additionally, video documentation of the airplane in flight performing post-stall maneuvers is most enlightening, since it is very difficult to provide a written description of these maneuvers that is easily understandable. They need to be seen to be understood and believed! The end of the video is interesting because, in place of the "credits" typical of a full-length movie, the video contains a listing of people that participated in the program within their particular organizations.[3]

The final written report, tactical utility report, and quasi-tailless report mentioned in the final ITO council minutes were supplemented by reports on the low-altitude post-stall envelope clearance for the Paris Air Show, structures flight-test reports, a helmet-mounted-display and audio-cueing report, and an agile-warrior report. Ultimately, eight separate documents were written by Rockwell International:

- *X-31 Enhanced Fighter Maneuverability Program Flight Test Final Report: Program Summary*, Rockwell Report TFD-95-1564
- *X-31 Enhanced Fighter Maneuverability Program Flight Test Final Report: Development of the X-31 Flight Test System*, Rockwell Report TFD-95-1563
- *X-31 EFM Tactical Utility Flight Test Evaluation Synopsis*, Rockwell Report TFD-95-1348
- *X-31 EFM Tactical Utility Flight Test Final Report Appendix*, Rockwell Report TFD-1349, Classified SECRET
- *X-31 Quasi-Tailless Flight Test Experiment, Final Report*, Rockwell Report TFD-95-1261
- *X-31 Low Altitude Post Stall Envelope Clearance and Paris Air Show Report*, Rockwell Report TFD-95-1510
- *X-31 Structures Flight Test Report, Rockwell Report*, TFD-95-1140-1, -2, -3 vol. 1, -3 vol. 2, and -4.
- *Flight Test Results of X-31 Helmet-Mounted Display and Audio Cueing Systems*, Rockwell Report TFD-95-1100
- *Final Report of Agile Warrior Concept Study*, Rockwell Report TFD-95-1101

The *X-31 Enhanced Fighter Maneuverability Program Flight Test Final Report: Program Summary* (Rockwell Report TFD-95-1564) is an excellent overview of the flight-test program. While this report provides a brief background of the genesis of the program, it does not cover the initial phases of the program (Phase I—Concept Feasibility, Phase II—Concept Validation and Design, and Phase III—Fabrication, Assembly and Initial Flight Test) in any detail. The focus of this report is the development of the "flight-test system" and the accomplishments of the Phase IV portion of the program, which encompassed the EFM flight testing that followed the initial 12 airworthiness test flights. In describing the flight-test system, the organizational relationships between the contractor and Government flight-test entities both prior to and after the move to Dryden are discussed. The X-31 aircraft is discussed in some detail, including aerodynamics, the flight control system, and the thrust-vectoring system. A brief discussion of the envelope-clearance flight testing for both the conventional envelope (below 30° angle of attack) and the post-stall envelope (30° to 70° angle of attack) is included. Flight testing during the Tactical Utility phase of the program is covered in some detail, including discussion of the broad results of conventional (no X-31 post-stall technology used) and baseline (X-31 post-stall technology in use) close-in-combat evaluations. Guest operational pilot evaluations, as well as evaluations of close-in combat against guest adversaries (F-14, F-15, F-16, and F/A-18), are discussed. Also included is an explanation of some testing excursions that were conducted. Limiting the X-31's maximum angle of attack to 45° and allowing missile launches at higher angles of attack than allowed by normal rules were investigated, and general results are provided. Conclusions are presented with mention of the availability of the two volume (unclassified and classified) Tactical Utility Results reports.

Follow-on efforts such as the quasi-tailless evaluation and the advanced-displays (head-down, helmet-mounted, and audio) evaluation are discussed in some detail. "Agile Warrior," while not a flight-test effort, was studied as a concept-definition study for potential application to flight testing on the X-31.

The final section of this report covers the envelope expansion to low altitude for the Paris Air Show and the development of the airshow routine. Changes to the aircraft that resulted from the Ship 1 accident, as well as changes to allow post-stall flight at low altitude and operation without the benefit of telemetry, are discussed. The process for transferring flight clearance authority from Dryden to NAVAIR is covered. The use of simulation in support of low-altitude envelope expansion and airshow routine design is highlighted as an essential tool for this endeavor. Procedures for low-altitude operations, including emergency procedures and the absence of a control room, are covered. The process for clearing the envelope from 10,000 feet MSL down to 500 feet AGL is explained. The process for determining the airshow maneuvers and then practicing them in a simulated airshow environment is illustrated. Finally, the four basic X-31 signature maneuvers used in the airshow are explained and augmented through pictorial diagrams. The high show and low show (for use in case of low ceilings) are discussed. An interesting feature of the X-31 Paris Air Show routine was the use of individual maneuvers rather than a routine where each maneuver flows into another. The rationale for this approach as a means of enhancing safety and maneuver quality is emphasized. Last, the impact on the world aviation community of flying the X-31 at the Paris Air Show is underscored.[4]

The *X-31 Enhanced Fighter Maneuverability Program Flight Test Final Report: Development of the X-31 Flight Test System* (Rockwell Report TFD-95-1563) is a large tome nearly 2 inches thick that covers the Phase IV—Flight Test part of the effort in considerable detail. The report has 10 sections and 3 appendices that will be summarized below. An interesting feature is that figures within the report are obviously taken from briefing slides used earlier in the program. The name of this report, *Development of the X-31 Flight Test System*, is somewhat misleading, however, because flight-test "system" is largely referring to the *aircraft* that were flight tested, with only a minor treatment of flight-test operations and data collection provided. This report provides a very useful summary that mainly explains the details of the aircraft systems and subsystems. Flight-test operations are also covered, but only in a brief manner.

Section 1—Introduction briefly covers the program schedule and organization with a depiction of the major milestones in Phases I through IV, the ITO responsibilities, and the ITO organizational structure. The following Program Goals are provided:

- Rapid demonstration of high-agility maneuvering concepts
- Investigation of EFM benefits of the Enhanced Fighter Maneuverability technologies
- Development of design requirements and a database for future applications
- Validation of a low-cost international prototyping concept

The report states that these goals were stated early in the program and were not changed and that they provided clear guidance, focus, and purpose that contributed to the successes realized by the program. It also states that all four goals were achieved.

The major attributes of the X-31 aircraft are briefly explained and illustrated through a cutaway illustration of the airplane. The low-cost prototyping goal is stated to have been achieved by practical configuration elements (e.g., a dry wing, single fuel tank, standard structural materials, simplified fuselage geometry with straight element lines, and reduced part count), the use of existing equipment to the maximum extent possible, and simplified design procedures (compared to normal military projects). Also contributing to the low cost were manufacturing techniques in the areas of tooling, fabrication, assembly, and quality assurance, but the most innovative was no doubt the "fly-away tooling" concept that reduced cost by a staggering 80 percent. The success of the design effort is touted, but this brief overview is all that is covered on design, fabrication, and airworthiness flight testing in this particular report.

Section 2 is a "flight test summary" showing major milestones and significant events up to the accident flight of Ship 1. Low-altitude envelope expansion and preparation for the Paris Air Show is covered in a separate report. The flight envelope and flight conditions for dynamics test points are shown (structures loads clearance tests are shown in a separate report).

Section 3 is a quite detailed discussion of the flight control system. This system, of course, is key to successful operation in the post-stall regime. The system is described in some detail through computer memory utilization explanations, block diagrams, and figures showing the positioning of subsystems on the airframe as well as cockpit integration of controls and displays. Interestingly, this section starts the documentation of "lessons learned" that is carried through the report and culminates in a lessons learned section at the end.

Section 4 is a complete discussion of the simulation capabilities that were developed to support the program. The discussion follows the development of simulation capability at Downey and the migration of capability to Palmdale and later to Dryden. The explanation mainly focuses on the Aircraft Dynamic Simulation (ADS), comprised of batch-real and non-real time simulations, and the Real-Time All-Digital Simulation (RTADS). Dryden's capabilities in the areas of nonreal-time simulation, RTADS, and flight-hardware-in-the-loop simulations for software validation and verification are explained. Notable is the fact that the only flyable "domed" simulation capability was at Downey; however, actual integration of the simulation with flight hardware capability was at Dryden with the FHILS system.

Section 5 covers the aerodynamics of the X-31 airplane. The initial part of this section covers the aerodynamic design of the airplane, which was driven by its requirements. Later subsections cover the changes to the airplane's aerodynamics that were driven by discoveries during flight testing. These changes included the aft fuselage strakes, small nose strakes, and blunted nose radius due to the yaw departure on flight 2-73. Conventional performance improvement to better match that of the F/A-18 adversary, particularly during turning flight, is discussed. Range performance, which was not an issue for flying at Dryden, was a subject of some study during preparations for the operation in Europe, particularly the ferry from Manching to Paris. Discussion and figures are used to explain the understanding of the airplane's true range performance. Finally, a treatment of the parameter identification process is covered, including an explanation of how the PID process fed into aerodynamics model updates for the simulation model and flight control law gains.

Section 6 is a relatively lengthy explanation of the subsystems in the X-31 aircraft and is the longest section in the report. Subsystems covered include propulsion and secondary power (engine, accessory-mounted gearbox, emergency air-start system, emergency power unit, and fire-detection system), electrical power generation and distribution, hydraulic power generation and distribution, fuel, environmental control, landing gear, spin-recovery parachute (including the modification to make it into a drag chute system for the Paris Air Show), flight control (mechanical items only; software and architecture was covered in a previous section), flight-test instrumentation and data reduction, and crew systems (this refers to crew ejection seat systems). Embedded in the discussions and descriptions in this section are several "lessons learned" that were discovered as a result of the flight-test program. Mention of the use of military specifications only as guidelines is accompanied by an additional report reference on how this was accomplished (Rockwell Report TFD-87-1411L). Interestingly, it is noted that the use of "off-the-shelf" flight-qualified equipment in the airplane, while reducing program cost and schedule dramatically, resulted in a weight penalty of a whopping 43 percent of the final aircraft weight.

Section 7 covers the thrust-vectoring system and is remarkably short (one page) considering the importance of this subsystem to the operation of the aircraft. Reference is made to three documents: the *X-31 System Design Manual* (Rockwell document NA-87-1119 revision F); a paper presented at the High-Angle-of-Attack Projects and Technology Conference at NASA Dryden from April 21 to 23, 1992; and to DASA document DASA-TN-X-31-82.

Section 8 is a brief discussion of weight and center of gravity and includes an explanation of the issues related to high pitch attitudes on the center of gravity of an aircraft with an unbaffled fuel tank system.

Section 9 is a very brief discussion of flight-test operations that illuminates the duties of each person in the control room and includes the standard pre-mission aircrew briefing charts. Flow charts for spin recovery and engine restart are shown.

Section 10 is a very comprehensive review of the lessons learned during the X-31 EFM program from its inception to the return from the Paris Air Show. These lessons learned reflect the inputs from all of the members of the International Test Organization. The section has the following subsections: Introduction, Engineering, Operations, Program Management, and Summary. These were discussed in chapter 7 of this book and are expanded upon in Appendix 8.

Appendix A contains flight sortie information mainly through the end of the data flights and prior to the envelope expansion, routine development/practice, ferry flights, and demonstration flights at the Paris Air Show. There is a considerable amount of useful data in this appendix, including pilots and number of sorties flown, major "century" milestones (e.g., 100th flight, 200th flight, etc.), flight trivia covering unique happenings in the flight-test program, sortie/date correlation for each aircraft, and an ITO quick look at post-stall and tactical utility highlights. A correlation of weekly flights with sorties and hours is given for each aircraft and compared to the X-29 program, the nearest competitor to the X-31 in terms of sortie production. An interesting series of charts showing the dramatic reduction in dollars per flight is shown. This information was discussed in Chapter 6 of this book.

Appendix B includes the flight control block diagrams in great detail. The diagrams are printed on separate sheets that must be cut and pasted together to construct a complete block diagram for a given system, such as "longitudinal control."

Appendix C contains PID changes to the aerodynamic model. These are quite complete; however, the legend of the different data point plots is not explained well.[5]

The *X-31 EFM Tactical Utility Flight Test Evaluation Synopsis* (Rockwell Report TFD-95-1348) is the unclassified document that covers the real original purpose of the EFM program; that is, the evaluation of the tactical benefits of enhanced fighter maneuverability through the use of post-stall technologies. The report gives an overview of the X-31 program, the ITO team that conducted the flight tests, and the X-31 aircraft. The report then justifies the existence of close-in combat within the continuum of air combat based on the following factors:

- Dynamic merge (i.e., fighters end up in close proximity as they merge unless they are killed pre-merge)
- Low visual or electronic observability (which can allow aircraft to get close enough to require close-in-combat maneuvering)
- Optical and electronic counter measures (ECM) that allow aircraft to get close enough to require close-in-combat maneuvering
- Missile failure that requires use of the gun
- Fighting outnumbered, surprised, or defending fixed assets
- Limits on the numbers and types of weapons carried
- Rules of engagement (ROE) and target identification requirements

The point is made that the above reasons are validated by the fact that all the latest fighters are equipped with a gun, the ultimate close-in-combat weapon. Once engaged, the objective is to achieve a quick kill before the enemy can counter-fire and have sufficient energy to disengage.

One of the primary objectives of the X-31 EFM program was to demonstrate and quantify the benefits of thrust vectoring and enhanced-fighter-maneuvering technologies for post-stall maneuvering in close-in combat. The matching of simulation in domed simulators to results from flight tests is briefly explained. The differences in results are noted and the flight-test program is briefly explained.

The major tactical utility flight-test blocks (i.e., post-stall close-in combat, conventional close-in combat, guest pilot evaluation, guest adversary close-in combat, etc.) are shown with dates, sortie numbers, and numbers of scorable engagements. Due to the classified nature of most of the results, the *only* actual data shown is for neutral starting condition engagements of the X-31 against the NASA F/A-18 configured to match the X-31's conventional performance in terms of thrust versus drag. Without post-stall maneuvering, the X-31 won only 15 percent of these engagements, but with post-stall maneuvering the X-31 won a remarkable 91 percent of the engagements. The report very briefly explains the evaluations with a guest operational pilot, with a guest operational adversary, with the X-31 limited to 45° angle of attack in close-in combat, and with a combination of advanced missiles and post-stall technology in close-in combat. The report concludes with a statement that "proper and timely employment of post-stall technology maneuvering in close-in combat significantly improved combat effectiveness in both offensive and defensive maneuvering."[6] The great success of this flight-test program, coupled with other initiatives such as the quasi-tailless demonstrations, is underscored in the closing. The majority of the tactical utility results are contained in the classified companion volume *X-31 EFM Tactical Utility Flight Test Final Report Appendix* (Rockwell Report TFD-1349, Classified SECRET).

The *X-31 Quasi-Tailless Flight Test Experiment, Final Report* (Rockwell Report TFD-95-1261) is a stand-alone report covering the flight testing performed and results generated in support of the Joint Advanced Strike Technology Program's Quasi-Tailless Flight Test Experiment. This part of X-31 flight testing was an addition to the original objectives of the EFM portion of the X-31 program. The report is a very detailed technical discussion with a large amount of reduced data. The X-31 Aeromechanics Group prepared the report. The objectives of the quasi-tailless experiment were to investigate the level of directional instability reduction that can be handled with yaw and pitch thrust vectoring of a single-engine strike fighter under realistic flight conditions, to assess the maturation of modern integrated flight control technologies for application on future single-engine strike fighters, and to look into simple methods for assessing thrust-vector-control sizing. This report discusses the early engineering parametric studies that investigated the potential of using thrust vectoring for primary directional control. The report goes on to cover the quasi-tailless flight tests in which the vertical fin and rudder of the X-31 were used to destabilize the aircraft to a level that simulated various amounts of reduction in the size of the vertical tail. The thrust-vectoring system was then used to provide control of this simulated "tailless" aircraft. Quasi-tailless flight testing started in March 1994 with supersonic flight evaluations.[7] Then, on September 1, 1994, the first quasi-tailless test at subsonic speeds with the aircraft "destabilized" in the power approach configuration was conducted in preparation for the JAST-sponsored testing.[8] This final report summarizes the results of the subsonic quasi-tailless parametric studies and flight-test experiments. It is a very detailed report that presents considerable amounts of actual data. Also included in the report are detailed appendices covering the work agreement and research plan for the quasi-tailless experiment, background data and simulation parametric studies, quasi-tailless flight-test time histories, pilot reports, and a quasi-tailless flight-test electronic data set. This is definitely a useful report for archiving the initial quasi-tailless research done by the X-31 program. It will provide an important, detailed historical archive of information relative to flight of tailless aircraft that use thrust vectoring for stabilization and control.

If the Quasi-Tailless Flight Test Experiment report was a technically oriented report, then the *X-31 Low Altitude Post Stall Envelope Clearance and Paris Air Show Report* (Rockwell Report TFD-95-1510) is a more operationally oriented report. This report was written by Fred Knox—a senior engineering test pilot for North American Aviation (Rockwell), the third person to fly the X-31, and the Rockwell member of the ITO test pilot team. Knox introduces the subject by noting the following challenges in clearing a low-altitude post-stall envelope to allow flight at Paris:

- Recovering from the mishap (of Ship 1)
- Updating the control law gains for low altitude
- Modifying control law software/hardware redundancy management for low altitude
- Developing normal and emergency procedures for low-altitude post-stall

Also, the following issues needed to be resolved in order to participate in the Paris Air Show:

- Procedures for operating without a control room or telemetry
- Safety of flight responsibility in Europe
- Transportation of the X-31 aircraft to Paris

Knox's paper discusses each of these in detail. The test team organization, particularly with respect to safety-of-flight responsibilities, is discussed. To summarize,

- The NASA director remained as ITO director, and NASA Dryden retained safety-of-flight responsibility for the low-altitude envelope clearance flights at NASA Dryden;
- The Navy assumed the position as ITO director, and safety-of-flight responsibilities were transferred to the Navy for the airshow practices

at Dryden, shipment of the X-31 to Manching, and the ferry flights to and from Manching and Paris; and

- Rockwell assumed the position as ITO director and assumed safety-of-flight responsibilities for the flight operations (practices and demonstration flights) at Le Bourget Airport in Paris.

The report lists 7 hardware changes and 13 software changes that were recommended by the mishap board to return the X-31 to flight, were required to safely fly low-altitude post-stall flight, and were required to allow the aircraft to fly in Europe without telemetry. Each of these changes is discussed in some detail with explanations of the operational requirement for each.

The flight clearance process for flight of the X-31 following the accident is covered. The mishap required a complete NASA Dryden Airworthiness Flight Safety Review Board (AFSRB) prior to returning the X-31 to flight. Included in the report as an enclosure are the actual briefing slides used, which emphasize hazard analysis and accepted risks. The procedure of transferring flight clearance authority and safety-of-flight responsibility to the Navy (NAVAIR) is explained in some detail, including the exchange of information between NASA Dryden and NAVAIR. This involved some interesting personnel management, such as using staff at NAVAIR who had previously been on the X-31 program and having a Navy flight-test engineer at Dryden to facilitate the clearance process. The NAVAIR clearance process covered flight controls, flying qualities, structures, propulsion, subsystems, and systems safety. This system worked! The low-altitude envelope expansion flights were completed on April 28, 1995, and the Navy flight clearance to begin airshow practices was received at Dryden on May 3. Airshow practice flights at Dryden commenced the following day. Similarly, the team worked on solutions to potential electromagnetic interference issues in Europe that were not present in the relatively benign electromagnetic environment of the California high desert while the airshow practice was being conducted at Dryden and the aircraft was being shipped to Manching. Once a plan had been developed to avoid flight near high-powered devices (radars, etc.), NAVAIR flight clearance was again received on May 25, and the functional flight check of the airplane in Manching was conducted on May 29.

The essential need for simulation to support low-altitude envelope expansion and to evaluate candidate maneuvers for the airshow is underscored in this report. The low-altitude maneuvers were required to be within the previously cleared envelope—namely, 70° angle of attack, 265 knots equivalent airspeed maximum (later changed to 240 knots equivalent airspeed for the airshow), and 70 knots equivalent airspeed minimum. They also had to be repeatable, provide safe ground clearance, provide a means for safe recovery after a failure, and conform to the airspace restrictions at Le Bourget Airport. Simulation of these maneuvers identified the following basic rules for flying a post-stall maneuver close to the ground:

- Recovery from a post-stall maneuver with a high rate of descent was required by 3,000 feet AGL.
- When performing low-altitude (below 1,000 feet AGL) post-stall maneuvers, the velocity vector had to remain level or above the horizon.
- Post-stall rolls below 1,000 feet AGL were required to be in a wings-up direction (i.e., the lift vector had to be pointed above the horizon).
- Extended post-stall maneuvers below 1,000 feet AGL had to be at 50° angle of attack or below.

The simulators used in this effort included the Rockwell domed simulator at Downey, which was used for integrated airshow development, and the NASA Dryden hardware-in-the-loop simulation that was used for failure simulations.

Some very specific low-altitude procedures were required for low-altitude operations. These covered operations without a control room, with use of the drag chute, with updated flight control system software operations, at low-altitude per se, and flight operations that were unique to flying in Europe. Specific low-altitude immediate-action procedures were developed for a flight control system warning at low altitude, loss of thrust at low altitude, and loss of control at low altitude.

Fred discusses the step-down process used for the low-altitude envelope clearance beginning with initial testing at 13,000 feet MSL with progressive stepdowns in altitude, first to 5,000 feet AGL, then 2,000 feet AGL, then 1,000, and finally 500 feet AGL. This was followed by practice of the complete airshow routine at 2,000 feet AGL, which then proceeded to 500 feet AGL. The final four demonstration maneuvers are shown in diagrams. These were the post-stall loop with 150° heading reversal or "helicopter" loop, the Mongoose turn, the Herbst turn, and a second helicopter loop. Also discussed is the "low show" routine that was to be used in the event of low ceilings, which consisted of two Mongoose turns and one Herbst turn. The construction of the entire airshow routine using each of these maneuvers as a separate entity is stressed as a safety effort that, while enhancing safety, did not detract from the effectiveness of the demonstration routine.

Certain special aircraft performance issues are covered in some detail, such as the change of the airplane's spin chute to a drag chute for landing, as well as the testing done to enable the short takeoff and landing performance required for the much shorter runways in Europe than those at Edwards AFB. Another performance issue was the special considerations for ferrying the aircraft in Europe from Manching to Paris and back. Long-range flights were not a consideration for flying test missions in the Edwards area, but the distance from Manching to Paris was at the limits of the X-31's range at altitude, so range performance implications needed to be studied to plan for these ferry flights. Ultimately, a two-sortie ferry flight was used with an option for low-altitude flight in the event of low ceilings.

Special operations issues such as flight without real-time telemetry and a control room are covered, including the development of a "mini monitor room," which is essentially a van with a radio and a team of experts (X-31 pilot, flight control specialist, engine expert, and systems engineer). Operations during practice and during the actual demonstration flights at Le Bourget are discussed, with an emphasis on the daily routine during airshow operations.

Finally, the report covers the logistics considerations for a long-distance deployment to an airshow venue, as well as the public relations implications of having an airplane with great international interest. Interestingly, these two sections of the report show the importance of paying attention to the details. Issues such as a spares pipeline to home, cellular telephone availability, petty cash availability while deployed, "give away items" (e.g., hats, t-shirts, brochures), VIP visit requests, and photographic support are highlighted as very important details to plan ahead for.

In summary, Fred Knox writes, "The serious attention that the X-31 received from the world aviation community far surpassed the previous reach of the program. The technical achievements of the program and the far reaching implications of the technology were clearly demonstrated to a vastly larger audience than ever before."[9]

The X-31 Enhanced Fighter Maneuverability Final Report, Daimler-Benz Aerospace (now DASA), written by Peter Huber, one of the prime engineers for the Germans on X-31, is a very complete document that covers the program objectives, program management and work share, the approach to a low-cost aircraft, and flight control system development and system integration. This is probably the best final *written* report for coverage of the early phases (prior to flight testing) of the program. It is important to note, though, that this report is written from the German, and more specifically the DASA, perspective. The video volume discussed earlier in this appendix also covers the early phases of the program. The flight control system's development is well covered because MBB (now DASA) was responsible for this area of the airplane. All areas of this report are well linked to supporting DASA documents, which are enumerated in a "Reference and List of Documentation." Taken all together, these reports provide a very complete history of the German participation in the X-31 program. This report also has appendices that include an excellent set of photos providing a photographic history of the entire program. Also included is an appendix with a very comprehensive listing of Rockwell and MBB documents on the entire X-31 program.

Following this initial part of the report, the remainder of the document covers the flight-test phase of the program from first flight through participation in the Paris Air Show. The technical flight test is especially well treated.

Software versions and the flight envelope expansion, conventional envelope expansion, thrust-vector integration, and post-stall envelope expansion are covered. Especially useful is an explanation of the various flight control software loads, including what their purpose was and on which flights and aircraft they were flown. Conventional envelope expansion is discussed, including plots of flying qualities data in the military specification (MIL-SPEC) MIL-F-8785C format, and it is noted that although MIL-SPEC criteria were used only as guidelines, most of the specifications were met. Flutter and loads tests are mentioned, although Rockwell was primarily responsible for them. Reversionary modes are explained, and flying qualities in these modes are noted to be adequate for providing a safe fly-home capability.

Thrust-vectoring integration is explained, with a discussion of the initial integration on the aircraft and the increase of paddle-deflection limits to provide adequate control power. Changes required during post-stall envelope expansion and to support the quasi-tailless experiment are covered.

Post-stall envelope expansion, including the addition of aft strakes and the inadvertent departure that resulted in the forward strakes, is discussed. The change from a normal pitot probe to a canted Kiel probe with canted angle-of-attack and angle-of-sideslip vanes (to accommodate the very-high-AOA flightpath of the aircraft) is explained. There are some nice photos of the aft strakes, forward strakes, and canted Kiel probe. As might be expected since the flight control system was a German responsibility, Peter Huber expounds on flying qualities and post-stall maneuvers in some detail. This discussion is accompanied by excellent plots of significant parameters (e.g., angle of attack, angle of sideslip, roll rate, load factor, etc.) versus time and airspeed. They are a wonderful graphical description of what the X-31 is capable of doing.

Tactical utility flight testing is covered very briefly, as might be expected due to the classified nature of much of the results. There is reference to a classified and an unclassified DASA report, however. These unclassified and classified DASA reports are *in addition* to the two tactical utility flight test reports that were produced by Rockwell, so there are a total of *four* reports—two unclassified and two classified—on tactical utility assessments of post-stall technology, which was the main reason for the creation of the X-31 program. There is also rather extensive coverage of integration of the helmet-mounted display, including diagrams of the display symbology, because DASA was a major player in the development of these displays.

The area of "follow on activities" covers pilot-aiding technologies, the quasi-tailless experiment, flying qualities in the high-AOA regime, single-surface excitation for parameter identification, tactical utility assessment of high-AOA and high-off-boresight missiles, enhancement of performance by thrust-vectoring, and the Ship 1 mishap. Pilot-aiding was a precursor study to the Agile Warrior

Program that is discussed in a Rockwell report listed previously in this appendix. The feasibility of coupling virtual threats and a man-in-the-loop simulator with an airborne X-31 was studied in order to overcome some of the criticism that the X-31 tactical utility engagements were all one-on-one, whereas in the real world, the airplane would probably be facing multiple threats. Using virtual threats on the helmet-mounted display was intended to be a way to evaluate this and perhaps lead to a training tool. This technology was assessed in the domed simulator at Downey, and initially flight tests were planned for early 1995 before being cancelled due to time and money constraints.

The quasi-tailless experiment is discussed, with an explanation of control law development and flight demonstration. This coverage is much the same as in other reports but is not as extensive as the stand-alone Rockwell report on the same subject. It does contain some nice discussion of the development of control laws and the flight envelopes created for quasi-tailless flight.

Handling-qualities evaluations using the Standard Evaluation Maneuvers are covered briefly, as is the methodology for conducting parameter identification using single-surface excitation as well as pilot inputs. Both of these areas are covered briefly. STEM has been covered in detail in a NASA report, but the discussion of PID methodology is relatively unique.[10]

Since the evaluations of high-AOA missiles and high-off-boresight missiles, as well as the evaluation against USAF F-15 and F-16 aircraft from Nellis AFB, occurred in this timeframe, they are mentioned very briefly in this part of the report.

Other uses of thrust vectoring, such as reducing trim drag during cruise and increasing total lift during approach and landing, are mentioned with reference to a DASA report that covers this area in some detail. The mishap of Ship 1 is briefly mentioned, with reference to the NASA Mishap Report.

The efforts involved in participating at the Paris Air Show, including flight software modifications, aircraft modifications, and low-altitude envelope expansion, are discussed in some detail. The information on flight control software and the flight envelope that was generated are not found in other documents. Airshow-routine development, practice flights, and the flight operations in Europe are briefly covered.

The report mentions that simulation at DASA was re-implemented and updated following the Paris Air Show so that this simulation reflects the latest control law status of the X-31. In conclusion, Peter Huber states, "The X-31 EFM Program has shown that flight at and beyond the stall boundary is technically feasible. The stall boundary, a critical barrier throughout aviation history, has disappeared." The report closes with the statement, "The X-31 EFM Program set several records for flight test efficiency and productivity and serves as a benchmark for future international cooperation and achievement."[11]

There have been many NASA technical papers, technical memoranda, as well as several papers published by professional organizations such as the American Institute of Aeronautics and Astronautics and the Society of Experimental Test Pilots (SETP). Additionally, there have even been papers published as a part of academic doctoral theses that use X-31 information or data. A listing of the NASA and AIAA published papers is included in this book's Selected Bibliography. There also have been some papers written and presented at NATO's Advisory Group for Aerospace Research and Development (AGARD), and these are likewise presented.

Following the completion of the X-31 VECTOR program, a three-volume final report was produced by Boeing under contract to NAVAIR. These volumes were

- *VECTOR Final Report Volume I—The Program*;
- *VECTOR Final Report Volume II—The Technologies*; and
- *VECTOR Final Report Volume III—Flight Test*, all dated October 16, 2003.

Volumes I and III have significant and comprehensive "Lessons Learned" sections that should be of value to new test programs. These were discussed in Chapter 7 and will be covered in greater detail in Appendix 8.

Volume I—The Program is an excellent description of the VECTOR program. Following a brief discussion of the preceding EFM program, the report covers the program goals, initial planning for VECTOR, and the conduct of the program from a program management and schedule standpoint. The report then expands the discussion to cover the starting of VECTOR by reactivating X-31 Ship 2 and moving it to NAS Patuxent River. The process of software development—much of it new for the VECTOR program—is covered, along with the processes for technical risk management and the change of external mold lines to encompass the advanced air data system. Unusually for a technical report, the contractual relationships between the governments (U.S. and German) and their various contractors are explained in some detail. The important areas of logistics, program reviews, and configuration management are also expounded upon in some detail. Finally, the area of program security is discussed, with particular emphasis on the issues surrounding the control and escort requirements for foreign-national team members on a Naval facility. Some very unique solutions to these issues were found.

Volume II—The Technologies was not available from the Navy to summarize for this book.

Volume III—Flight Test is an extensive report with sections on flight testing and evaluation overview and background, technical risk management, aircraft instrumentation, flight readiness reviews, flight operations, and a "lessons learned" section. The largest section of this report, "Flight Operations," covers in some detail the history of the flight testing on the X-31 VECTOR. The test program involved four phases. The first phase dealt with reactivation, or getting the aircraft in a condition to perform the VECTOR-specific flight tests. The next two phases involved testing of the VECTOR-specific technologies at altitude using two separate operational flight program variations. The final phase was the testing of the VECTOR ESTOL technologies to actual touchdowns. Each phase is discussed in terms of the ground and flight tests that were performed to evaluate the aircraft and its technologies. This is a valuable "history" of the VECTOR flight-test program.

Information dissemination on the X-31 had a checkered history. There is no evidence of coordinated preparation and publication of any of the reports and papers associated with the X-31 program, and there was no coordinating entity such as a "research review panel" to oversee the publishing program or the preparation and dissemination of information related to the X-31. Documents were written independently to support conferences, symposia, contracts, or government requirements. Ironically, then, the lack of a central information-dissemination organization and process meant that it had to largely be left to individual initiative, which effectively limited the availability of information to the aerospace community that was a result of this very unique research aircraft program.

Most of the papers written for professional organizations such as AIAA and SETP were presented at conferences and symposia and were published in the conference or symposia proceedings. These papers, for the most part, were very focused in nature and dealt with narrow portions of the X-31 program. The same is true of the AGARD papers. It is worth noting that AGARD merged with another NATO group in 1996 to become the NATO Research & Technology Organization (RTO). Although all of these papers were published, their distribution was such that they were most easily obtained by members of the respective organizations; they were not easily obtained by the general public. The Rockwell final reports were produced as a contractual deliverable to NAVAIR (and ultimately DARPA) for the EFM program. For VECTOR, NAVAIR was the ultimate customer. The DASA final reports appear to have been produced for the German government, since they contain the statement "PREPARED BY GOVERNMENT ORDER." These contractor final reports are, by far, the most comprehensive documents published on the X-31 program because they cover the total scope of the program and have many references to other documents that cover more specific subjects in greater detail. Since they were produced to fill a contract requirement, in the case of Rockwell, or a government requirement, in the case of DASA, these final reports are not readily available to the general public, including the aerospace community. Interestingly, since Dryden was a participating test organization and not a management organization on this program, they are not available at Dryden. The same is true for their availability at the Air Force Flight Test Center, another participating test organization.

Endnotes

1. X-31 International Test Organization Council, council minutes, August 29, 1995, Dryden archives.
2. Mike Francis, interview by Douglas A. Joyce, November 6, 2011.
3. ITO, *X-31 Enhanced Fighter Maneuverability Program Final Report, Volume I*, videotape record (Landover, MD, Corporate Video, in association with the Edwards AFB AFFTC Multimedia Center, c. 1997).
4. Rockwell International, *X-31 Enhanced Fighter Maneuverability Program Flight Test Final Report: Program Summary*, Rockwell Report TFD-95-1564 (March 14, 1996).
5. Rockwell International, *X-31 Enhanced Fighter Maneuverability Program Flight Test Final Report: Development of the X-31 Flight Test System*, Rockwell Report TFD-95-1563 (March 14, 1996).
6. Rockwell International, *X-31 EFM Tactical Utility Flight Test Evaluation Synopsis*, Rockwell Report TFD-95-1348 (October 27, 1995).
7. S.G. Schmidt, "Enhanced Fighter Maneuverability, The X-31A Aircraft, Flight Test Report—March 1994" (March 21, 1994), pp. 30–34.
8. S.G. Schmidt, "Enhanced Fighter Maneuverability, The X-31A Aircraft, Flight Test Report—September 1994" (September 21, 1994), p. 50.
9. Rockwell International, *X-31 Low Altitude Post Stall Envelope Clearance and Paris Air Show Report*, Rockwell Report TFD-95-1510 (March 8, 1996), p. 13.
10. Stoliker and Bosworth, "Evaluation of High-Angle-of-Attack Handling Qualities for the X-31."
11. P. Huber, *X-31 Enhanced Fighter Maneuverability Final Report* (Daimler-Benz Aerospace: December 22, 1995), p. 32.

X-31 Flight Log

Flight No.	Date	Pilot	Purpose	Comments
1990				
1-001	10-11-90	Ken Dyson, Rockwell		Ship 1 first flight, 38 minutes long, 340 miles per hour, 10,000 feet. Flown from Palmdale.
1-002	10-17-90	Dyson		Air data computer (ADC) failures.
1-003	11-03-90	Dyson		Air intake disconnected; right landing gear weight-on-wheel (WOW) sensor switch (SW) during landing.
1-004	11-06-90	Dietrich Seeck, MBB		Right WOW SW during landing.
1-005	11-08-90	Seeck		ADC failure.
1-006	11-10-90	Seeck		ADC failure.
1-007	11-13-90	Dyson		ADC failure.
1-008	11-15-90	Fred Knox, Rockwell		
1-009	11-21-90	Knox		Cross-channel data link (CCDL) failure.

Flight No.	Date	Pilot	Purpose	Comments
1991				
2-001	01-19-91	Seeck	Airspeed calibration, subsystem checks, flying qualities (FQ)	Ship 2 first flight. Flown from Palmdale.
1-010	02-14-91	Dyson		
1-011	02-15-91	Seeck		
1-012	02-20-91	Knox		
2-002	01-22-91	Seeck		Discovered canard actuator failure after flight.
2-003	01-23-91	Knox		
1-013	02-27-91	Dyson		Flap switch discrete, flight control system (FCS) reset discrete.
1-014	03-12-91	Seeck	R2, R3 modes FQ	
1-015	03-15-91	Karl Lang, WTD-61		
1-016	03-28-91	Knox	Line flutter	Logic failure of the thrust vectoring system (LFTVS) flag set.
1-017	03-29-91	Dyson	Line flutter	Flight test instrumentation (FTI) clock failure.
1-018	04-03-91	Dyson	Line flutter	FTI clock failure.
1-019	04-05-91	Lang		
1-020	04-12-91	Seeck	Loads	
1-021	04-18-91	Knox	Line flutter	N_y-tiebreaker (TB) failure, resonance during trailing edge outboard (TEO) asymmetric flutter.

Flight No.	Date	Pilot	Purpose	Comments
1-022	04-19-91	Dyson	Line flutter	Same as flight 1-021.
1-023	04-23-91	Lang	Line flutter	Same as flight 1-021.
1-024	04-24-91	Capt. Bob Trombadore, USMC	Government performance evaluation (GPE)	
1-025	04-30-91	Maj. Karl-Heinz Mai, GAF	GPE	
1-026	05-02-91	Mai	GPE	Fault instrumentation and detection (FID) during landing. Pilot did not turn on tape for landing.
1-027	05-03-91	Trombadore	GPE	CCDL message timeout.
1-028	05-31-91	Seeck	Plume line	
1-029	06-04-91	Knox	Line flutter at 6.2 and 9.7 thousand feet (kft)	Return to base (RTB) because of environmental control system (ECS) problem.
1-030	06-06-91	Dyson	Line flutter at 12.8 and 15.8 kft	FID during landing (speed brake, right WOW) left trailing edge inboard (LTEI) code during engine start.
1-031	06-07-91	Lang	Line and R1 mode	Alpha oscillation in R1.
2-004	06-11-91	Seeck	Subsystem and FQ checks	Actuators did not fade during engine start, and other problems.

Flight No.	Date	Pilot	Purpose	Comments
1-032	06-12-91	Dyson	Thrust vectoring (TV) calibration and FQ	
1-033	06-14-91	Knox	TV calibration	
1-034	06-18-91	Seeck	FQ and R1	Trailing-edge flap (TEF) failures during R1.
1-035	06-20-91	Dyson	Line flutter at 4.7 kft, 0.75 Mach (M)	Pitch stick looseness prior to flight.
1-036	06-21-91	Knox	Line flutter at 4.7 kft, 0.75 M	TEF failures during engine start, preflight bit (PFB) exit problem.
1-037	06-21-91	Dyson	Line flutter at 4.7 kft, 0.75 M	
2-005	06-25-91	Seeck	FQ and TV calibration	Same problems during engine start. Blew left tire on landing, rudder fail identifications (IDs).
2-006	07-10-91	Lang	FQ	Flight control system (FCS) reset button.
1-038	07-12-91	Knox	Line flutter 4.7 kft, 0.80 M	Beta failure during TEO symmetrical flutter sweep. Landed at Edwards in R2.
1-039	07-14-91	Dyson	Ferry flight	Edwards to Palmdale.
1-040	07-16-91	Seeck	Line flutter at 4.7 and 7.2 kft	
1-041	07-17-91	Lang	800 dynamic pressure (q) flutter at 7.2 and 10 kft	

Flight No.	Date	Pilot	Purpose	Comments
1-042	07-18-91	Knox	Line flutter at 10 kft	Main generator failed during windup turn (WUT). Landed at Edwards.
1-043	07-24-91	Dyson	TV calibration	Takeoff from Edwards. ECS buzz at 35 kft.
1-044	07-26-91	Seeck	Loads	
2-007	07-26-91	Lang	R-modes	Slight canard buzz in R-1.
1-045	07-30-91	Knox	Loads	
1-046	08-14-91	Dyson	Plume tracking	
1-047	08-14-91	Seeck	Plume tracking	
1-048	08-16-91	Lang	25° AOA	
1-049	08-16-91	Knox	25° AOA	
2-008	08-21-91	Dyson	FQ 30° AOA	Problem with clock. Recovered data for 12.5 Hertz (Hz) only.
2-009	08-23-91	Lang	Air data system calibration with tower flybys	
2-010	08-23-91	Knox	Flight aborted	Bad telemetry (TM).
1-050	08-26-91	Knox	30° AOA	Chute test aborted, no photo plane. Right WOW FID during landing.
1-051	08-27-91	Knox	Chute test	Chute test successful.
	08-28-91	Seeck	30° AOA, 40 kft	

Flight No.	Date	Pilot	Purpose	Comments
2-012	08-28-91	Dyson	ADC calibration	TV2 pressure too high, plume tracking canceled. Pacer points instead.
1-052	09-04-91	Lang	Centerline (CL) TV, 20 kft	TV closed-loop 1st time. Generator failed, reset after 2.5 min.; short in wiring.
2-013	09-05-91	Knox	Plume line, 11 kft and 20 kft	
2-014	09-06-91	Seeck	TV closed loop, 20 kft	TV closed loop 1st time on aircraft (A/C) 2. F-15 chase aircraft (Dyson) landed at China Lake.
2-015	09-11-91	Dyson	TV closed loop	F-8 chase aircraft (Lang) landed at Edwards. Antiskid problem during takeoff (T/O).
2-016	09-11-91	Lang	TV closed loop to 30°	30° FQ 1st time. R3 hi/lo switch FID. T-38 chase.
2-017	09-13-91	Seeck	TV closed loop to 30°	TV disabled (DIS) switch failure when TV engaged.
2-018	09-16-91	Knox	TV closed loop	
2-019	09-16-91	Dyson	TV closed loop	R1 request during right full stick roll three times.

Flight No.	Date	Pilot	Purpose	Comments
2-020	09-19-91	Seeck	FQ and parameter identification (PID) with flutter test box (FTB)	
2-021	09-19-91	Knox	FQ, PID, and TV calibration	Vane failures during TV calibration, vane commanded to +27° (+25.6° actual stop).
2-022	09-19-91	Dyson	FQ, FID	Right roll during landing.
2-023	09-24-91	Lang	FQ, 40 kft, TV on/off	
2-024	09-24-91	Seeck	PID, TV calibration	TV1 failure at 20 kft. OK at 30 and 40 kft. Right WOW switch failure during landing.
2-025	09-26-91	Knox	R3 FQ, tracking	
2-026	09-26-91	Dyson	R2 FQ	CCDL failure, reset during flight left LEF brake was set.
2-027	10-01-91	Lang	FQ, R2	R1 request during right full stick roll.
2-028	10-01-91	Seeck	PID, tracking	
2-029	10-04-91	Knox	Ferry from Palmdale	Static display at Edwards Air Force Base (EAFB).
2-030	10-08-91	Lang	Ferry	Return from EAFB, flight OK. TM room problem.

Flight No.	Date	Pilot	Purpose	Comments
1-053	10-18-91	Dyson	Loads	
1-054	10-18-91	Seeck	Loads	Left WOW during landing. Engine caution due to low oxygen (LO) pressure.
1-055	10-24-91	Knox	Loads	Rudder and canard solenoid built-in test (BIT) failed twice.
1-056	10-24-91	Lang	Loads	Left WOW during landing; no FTI data for landing.
1-057	10-28-91	Seeck	Loads, R1	Right WOW during landing. LO pressure four times, logic failure of the inertial navigation system (LFINS) once.
1-058	10-31-91	Knox	R1, FQ maneuvers	Canard solenoid failed during BIT.
1-059	10-31-91	Lang	Maneuvers	
2-031	11-11-91	Knox	FQ	WOW failed during landing.
2-032	11-11-91	Dyson	FQ, R3	Lateral acceleration (N_y) failures during WUT, leading edge flap (LEF) brake set, flight control computer 3 (FCC3) invalid. Left WOW. Bird strike.

Flight No.	Date	Pilot	Purpose	Comments
2-033	11-13-91	Lang	FQ	
2-034	11-15-91	Knox	Loads	
1-060	11-18-91	Dyson	Loads	T/O bird strike, engine caution during negative g's several times.
2-035	11-19-91	Lang	Loads	N_y failure during WUT to 30°.
2-036	11-19-91	Knox	Post-stall maneuverability (PST)	First PST flight. Command output failure at 40° AOA.
1-061	11-20-91	Cmdr. Al Groves, USN	GPE	Second GPE. Cmdr. Groves to join test pilot team.
1-062	11-20-91	Lang	GPE	
1-063	11-21-91	Groves	GPE	N_y failure after landing.
2-037	11-22-91	Seeck	PST	Porpoising at 45° AOA.
2-038	11-22-91	Dyson	PST	N_y during WUT. LEF brakes set. FCC3 invalid 160 msec during WUT.
1-064	11-25-91	Groves	GPE	
1-065	11-25-91	Knox	GPE	TV3 failure during "both" decelerations.
1-066	11-26-91	Seeck	Loads	Engine caution during negative g's.
1-067	12-06-91	Lang	TV effectiveness	

Flight No.	Date	Pilot	Purpose	Comments
2-039	12-11-91	Groves	GPE	
2-040	12-11-91	Dyson	PST	
2-041	12-13-91	Groves	GPE	Left WOW on landing.
1992				
1-068	01-20-92	Seeck	Ferry	To Edwards AFB. Fix-point overflow, software (SW) fix. Only time both X-31's flown together.
2-042	01-20-92	Knox	Ferry and PST	To Edwards AFB. TEF and N_y failures, aero buffet at 39° AOA. Only time both X-31's flown together.
2-043	04-23-92	Lang	System check-out (C/O), FQ, R1, R2, R3	First ITO flight (from Dryden). Antiskid not working.
2-044	05-07-92	Seeck	PST to 45°	FCC2 down during RTB, cannot reset.
2-045	06-04-92	Knox	FQ, PST	
2-046	06-04-92	Rogers Smith, NASA Dryden	Pilot checkout	Rogers Smith, NASA ITO Pilot
2-047	06-09-92	Lang	FQ, PST to 50°	
2-048	06-09-92	Seeck	FQ, PST to 50°	

Flight No.	Date	Pilot	Purpose	Comments
2-049	06-09-92	Lt. Col. Jim Wisneski, USAF	Pilot C/O	Lt. Col. Jim Wisneski, USAF ITO Pilot
2-050	06-11-92	Smith	2nd flight	
2-051	06-11-92	Wisneski	2nd flight	
2-052	06-11-92	Knox	FQ, PST to 50°	
2-053	06-16-92	Lang	FQ, rolled to inverted position, afterburner (AB)	
2-054	06-16-92	Seeck	FQ, AB, inverted	
2-055	06-16-92	Smith	FQ, AB, inverted	
1-069	07-02-92	Knox	PST, R-modes	First A/C's 1st ITO flight, from Dryden.
1-070	07-02-92	Wisneski	PST	
1-071	07-07-92	Seeck.	PST	
1-072	07-16-92	Groves	Deceleration, inverted	
1-073	07-16-92	Lang	PST	Hydraulic pressure failure during engine start.
1-074	07-16-92	Groves	Deceleration, inverted	
1-075	09-10-92	Knox	PST to 40°	
1-076	09-10-92	Smith	PST to 45°	
1-077	09-11-92	Wisneski	PST to 50°	
1-078	09-11-92	Groves	PST to 55°	Inertial navigation unit (INU) bus error. Av/air hot lite. Landed in R2 mode.

Flight No.	Date	Pilot	Purpose	Comments
1-079	09-16-92	Lang	PST to 60°	TV3 zero-detect failure after landing, beta oscillation at 60°.
1-080	09-16-92	Smith	PST to 62°	4 Hz oscillation in beta above 60°.
1-081	09-18-92	Groves	PST to 65° and 70°, 35 kft	TV3 zero-detect failure after landing.
1-082	09-18-92	Lang	PST to 65° and 70°, 35 kft	
1-083	09-18-92	Smith	PST to 55° and 70°, 35 kft	TV3 zero-detect failure after landing.
1-084	09-22-92	Seeck	70°, 35 kft, loads	
1-085	09-22-92	Knox	70°, 35 kft, loads	
1-086	09-22-92	Wisneski	70°, 35 kft, loads	Right WOW FID after touchdown.
2-056	10-09-92	Lang	70° AOA, 360° rolls, 35 kft	TV2 fail code twice during flight (trim resistor).
2-057	10-15-92	Smith	50° AOA, 360° rolls, 35 kft	TV2 fail code after engine start.
2-058	10-16-92	Seeck	70° AOA, 360° rolls, 35 kft	Input and output controller (IOC) power-up fail (servo amp test); asymmetry at 50° and 55°.
2-059	10-29-92	Knox	70° AOA, 35 kft	IOC frame overrun during power-up TV2 fail code five times during flight.

Flight No.	Date	Pilot	Purpose	Comments
2-060	10-29-92	Wisneski	70° AOA, 35 kft	First flight with grit on noseboom and radome.[1] TV2 fail code twice during flight.
2-061	11-03-92	Groves	50° AOA, 360° rolls, 35 kft	TV servo amp failed codes twice on ground, once in flight.
2-062	11-03-92	Lang	60° AOA, 360° rolls, 35 kft	Continued post-stall envelope expansion with grit strips.
2-063	11-03-92	Seeck	50° AOA, 360° rolls, 23 kft	Post-stall testing.
2-064	11-05-92	Knox	PST envelope expansion at 35 kft	Flight abort, FTI problem.
2-065	11-05-92	Wisneski	65° AOA, 35 kft	
2-066	11-06-92	Groves	65° AOA, bank-to-bank (B-B) rolls, 23 kft	
2-067	11-06-92	Seeck	70° AOA, B-B rolls, 23 kft	
2-068	11-06-92	Knox	70° AOA, 360° rolls, 23 kft	
2-069	11-06-92	Wisneski	70° AOA, 360° rolls, 23 kft	
2-070	11-10-92	Smith	70° AOA, 360° rolls, 23 kft	Grit on beta vane.
2-071	11-10-92	Seeck	70° AOA, 360° rolls, 23 kft	Photo session. Grit removed from beta vane.

Flight No.	Date	Pilot	Purpose	Comments
2-072	11-10-92	Knox	70° AOA, 360° rolls, 23 kft	
1-087	11-24-92	Lang	70° AOA, 360° rolls	Brake failed during landing.
2-073	11-30-92	Wisneski	2-g PST entry	Departure during PST entry.
1-088	12-01-92	Groves	Loads	
1-089	12-01-92	Smith	Loads	
1-090	12-01-92	Seeck	Loads	
1-091	12-08-92	Knox	Loads	
1-092	12-08-92	Seeck	Loads	
1-093	12-10-92	Lang	Loads	
1-094	12-15-92	Wisneski	Pitch pulls, 23 kft	
2-074	12-15-92	Smith	Pitch pulls, 30 kft	TV servo amp fail codes five times.
1-095	12-15-92	Knox	Wind-up turns (WUTs), 30 kft	
2-075	12-15-92	Seeck	WUTs, 30 kft	TV servo amp fail codes once.
1-096	15-92	Lang	WUTs, 30 kft	
2-076	12-17-92	Wisneski	WUTs, 20 kft	TV servo amp fail codes twice
2-077	12-17-92	Smith	WUTs, 20 kft	
1993				
1-097	01-12-93	Knox	20 kft turns, alter. Cards	First flight with forebody strakes and new LEF schedule, 90 percent cloud cover.
1-098	01-14-93	Lang	35 kft, PST to 40° AOA	
1-099	01-14-93	Smith	35 kft, PST to 50° AOA	

Flight No.	Date	Pilot	Purpose	Comments
1-100	01-14-93	Knox	35 kft, PST to 60° AOA	
2-078	01-19-93	Lang	35 kft, 40° AOA	Right WOW during landing.
2-079	01-19-93	Smith	35 kft, 50° AOA	IOC frame overrun during power-up.
2-080	01-19-93	Knox	35 kft, 60° AOA	TV servo amp fail codes eight times during RTB.
2-081	01-21-93	Groves	35 kft, 60° AOA	TM loss for few seconds during flight.
1-101	01-21-93	Lang	35 kft, PST to 60° AOA	
1-102	02-03-93	Wisneski	30 kft, PST to 70° AOA	
1-103	02-03-93	Smith	30 kft, PST to 70° AOA	
1-104	02-03-93	Knox	30 kft, PST to 70° AOA	
1-105	02-09-93	Lang	30 kft, PST to 70° AOA	
1-106	02-09-93	Wisneski	30 kft, PST, 0.4 M	Elevated entry.
1-107	02-11-93	Smith	30 kft, PST, 0.5 M	N_y TB failure during pull-up.
1-108	02-11-93	Knox	30 kft, PST, 0.5 M	
1-109	02-11-93	Lang	30 kft, PST, 0.5 M	
1-110	02-25-93	Groves	30 kft, PST, 0.5 M	1120 FID on 02-23-93. INU still aligning when entering PST.
1-111	02-25-93	Lang	30 kft, PST, 0.5 M	
1-112	02-25-93	Knox	30 kft, PST, 0.5 M	
1-113	02-25-93	Groves	30 kft, PST, 0.5 M	

Flight No.	Date	Pilot	Purpose	Comments
2-082	03-02-93	Wisneski	35 kft, 60° AOA	Left WOW during landing.
2-083	03-02-93	Smith	35 kft, 60° AOA	
2-084	03-02-93	Knox	35 kft, 60° AOA	
2-085	03-02-93	Lang	35 kft, 60° AOA	
1-114	03-17-93	Groves	30 kft, PST, 0.5 M	
1-115	03-17-93	Wisneski	30 kft, PST, 0.5 M	
1-116	03-23-93	Knox		
1-117	03-23-93	Lang		
1-118	03-23-93	Groves		
1-119	03-23-93	Groves		
2-086	03-30-93	Smith	Beta and roll stick checks	First flight with beta vane wedge to eliminate oscillations at 60–65° AOA.
2-087	03-30-93	Wisneski	23 kft, 50° AOA	
2-088	03-30-93	Knox	23 kft, 70° AOA	TV servo amp fail codes (2127) once prior to takeoff.
2-089	04-01-93	Knox	35 kft, 70° AOA, WUT	ECS problems.
2-090	04-02-93	Wisneski	30 kft, 70° AOA, WUT	ECS problems.
2-091	04-08-93	Lang	Tower flyby (Kiel probe)	1st flight with Kiel probe;[2] ECS problems.
2-092	04-15-93	Knox	35 kft, 40° and 50° AOA rolls	Extended nose strakes.
2-093	04-16-93	Smith	30 kft, 0.4 M, 45° split-S	
2-094	04-16-93	Wisneski	30 kft, 0.5 M, 60° split-S	2127 during RTB.

Flight No.	Date	Pilot	Purpose	Comments
2-095	04-21-93	Knox	30 kft, 70° diagonal pulls	Extended nose strake removed. Grit added from strake to canard.
2-096	04-21-93	Wisneski	30 kft, 0.4 M, 40° split-S	
2-097	04-22-93	Knox	30 kft, 0.5 M, 60° pulls	
2-098	04-22-93	Knox	30 kft, 0.5 M, 50° split-S	
2-099	04-23-93	Knox	30 kft, 0.5 M, 50° split S	
2-100	04-23-93	Knox	23 kft, 0.4 M, WUT	AOA failure, broken contracts.
2-101	04-29-93	Groves	20 kft, 0.4 M, 60° pulls	
2-102	04-29-93	Lang	20 kft, 0.4 M, 70° pull-downs	Milestone 4 test.
2-103	04-29-93	Smith	30 kft, 0.6 M, 70°	
2-104	05-05-93	Groves	20 kft, 70°, J-turn	Photo session with Lear Jet.
2-105	05-05-93	Groves	20 kft, 70°, J-turn	Photo session with Lear Jet.
2-106	05-13-93	Wisneski	70° AOA	Test for Kiel probe calibration.
2-107	05-13-93	Smith	Wake encounters	
2-108	05-13-93	Lang	20 kft, pitch captures 30° to 60°	
2-109	05-27-93	Knox	30 kft, 70° AOA	Software version 117 installed, retest of aircraft.
2-110	05-27-93	Wisneski	30 kft, 70° AOA	117 retest; right WOW during landing.

Flight No.	Date	Pilot	Purpose	Comments
2-111	05-27-93	Lang	30 kft, 70° AOA	117 retest.
2-112	06-01-93	Smith	Wake encounters	117 retest.
2-113	06-01-93	Wisneski	23 kft, split-S, scissors	117 retest, software commanded aircraft out of PST.
2-114	06-01-93	Lang	23 kft, J-turn	117 retest.
2-115	06-01-93	Smith	23 kft, 720° rolls	117 retest.
2-116	06-03-93	Wisneski	25 kft, low speed, J-turn	Low-speed expansion.
2-117	06-03-93	Lang	16 kft, J-turns	Low-speed expansion.
2-118	06-03-93	Smith	23 kft, low speed, J-turn	Low-speed expansion.
2-119	06-03-93	Wisneski	16 kft, low speed, J-turn	Low-speed expansion.
2-120	06-10-93	Groves	30 kft, 0.6 M	AOA Ch. 3 fail −84.71°. Broken wire, resoldered.
2-121	06-10-93	Lang	23 kft, 225 knot (kt) WUT, split-S	
2-122	06-10-93	Smith	Tactical	
2-123	06-10-93	Wisneski	Tactical	
1-120	06-29-93	Lang	30 kft, 0.8 M turns	RTB because of fuel pressure. Sensor. First use of head-up display (HUD) and over-the-shoulder videos.
1-121	06-29-93	Smith	30 kft, 0.5 M	Aileron (AIL) solenoid actuator (SA) failure during ground test.

Flight No.	Date	Pilot	Purpose	Comments
1-122	06-29-93	Lang	23 kft, 720° rolls	
1-123	06-29-93	Smith	30 kft, 0.6 M	Logical for reversionary mode 1 request (LR1RQ) abrupt pull-up.
1-124	07-08-93	Knox	30 kft, 0.6 M	RTB, transformer/ rectifier (T/R) caution lamp, and FTI power problem.
1-125	07-13-93	Knox	28 kft, 225 kt	
1-126	07-13-93	Smith	20 kft, 225 kt	
1-127	07-13-93	Knox	28 kft, 225 kt	
1-128	07-14-93	Smith	16 kft, 185 kt	
1-129	07-14-93	Groves	16 kft, 185 kt	
1-130	07-14-93	Knox	16 kft, 185 kt	
1-131	07-20-93	Maj. Quirin Kim, GAF	Pilot checkout	RTB because of noisy engine rotational measurement (N2S) signal at takeoff. Maj. Kim, ITO pilot, joins test pilot team.
1-132	07-23-93	Lang	15 kft, 185 kt	
1-133	07-27-93	Wisneski	15 kft, 185 kt	RTB because of high gen. case temperature.
1-134	07-27-93	Knox	Grit effect	Grit removed from radome.
1-135	07-29-93	Kim	Pilot checkout	Thrust-vectoring vanes (TVs) engaged during R3 because flight estimated thrust (FEST) was negative.

Flight No.	Date	Pilot	Purpose	Comments
1-136	08-04-93	Smith	15 kft, 225 kt	Overlay with lower limit on FEST because FEST was negative.
1-137	08-04-93	Lang	15 kft, 225 kt	INU trip.
1-138	08-04-93	Wisneski	15 kft, 225 kt	
1-139	08-04-93	Knox	15 kft, 225 kt	INU trip.
1-140	08-17-93	Lang	15 kft, 225 kt	
1-141	08-17-93	Wisneski	15 kft, 225 kt	
1-142	08-17-93	Knox	15 kft, 225 kt	
1-143	08-19-93	Knox	15 kft, 225 kt	
1-144	08-19-93	Kim	15 kft, 225 kt	
1-145	08-19-93	Lang	15 kft, 225 kt	
1-146	08-23-93	Wisneski	15 kft, 225 kt	
1-147	08-24-93	Knox	15 kft, 225 kt	
1-148	08-24-93	Groves		RTB for excessive engine mount vibration.
1-149	08-26-93	Groves	Tactical	
1-150	08-26-93	Smith	Tactical	
1-151	08-26-93	Kim	Tactical	
1-152	08-26-93	Lang	Tactical	
1-153	08-31-93	Wisneski	21 kft., 185 kt	Backup PST.
1-154	08-31-93	Smith	30 kft., 225 kt	
1-155	08-31-93	Kim		First basic fighter maneuver (BFM) tests.
1-156	08-31-93	Lang	21 kft., 225 kt	FIDs during power-up.
1-157	09-14-93	Knox	15 kft., 225 kt	
1-158	09-16-93	Groves	BFM	

Flight No.	Date	Pilot	Purpose	Comments
1-159	09-16-93	Wisneski	BFM	
1-160	09-16-93	Smith	BFM	
1-161	09-16-93	Lang	BFM	
1-162	09-20-93	Lang	BFM	Offensive.
1-163	09-20-93	Knox	BFM	High-speed line-abreast (HSLA).
1-164	09-21-93	Groves	BFM	HSLA, slow-speed line-abreast (SSLA), defensive.
1-165	09-21-93	Wisneski	BFM	HSLA, defensive.
1-166	09-28-93	Groves	BFM	Rear Adm. Mixson in F/A-18.
1-167	09-28-93	Smith	BFM	
1-168	09-28-93	Kim	BFM	
1-169	09-30-93	Lang	BFM	
1-170	09-30-93	Knox	BFM	
1-171	09-30-93	Wisneski	BFM	
1-172	09-30-93	Kim	BFM	
2-124	10-05-93	Lang	Software version 118 C/O	First flight with load 118.
2-125	10-05-93	Smith	118 C/O	
2-126	10-07-93	Knox	118 C/O	
2-127	10-07-93	Wisneski	118 C/O	
2-128	10-07-93	Lang	118 C/O	
2-129	10-07-93	Smith	118 C/O	
1-173	10-14-93	Kim	BFM	
2-130	10-28-93	Knox	Pull-ups to 70°, push-overs to 15°	
1-174	11-05-93	Kim	Close-in-combat (CIC)	FCC4 circuitbreaker (C/B) problem during pretaxi.
1-175	11-05-93	Groves	CIC	
1-176	11-05-93	Kim	CIC	
1-177	11-05-93	Groves	CIC	

Flight No.	Date	Pilot	Purpose	Comments
1-178	11-09-93	Kim	CIC	
1-179	11-09-93	Groves	CIC	
1-180	11-09-93	Kim	CIC	
1-181	11-09-93	Groves	CIC	Left WOW on touchdown.
1-182	11-19-93	Smith	Flutter, 0.9 and 0.95 M	Right leading edge (RLE) solenoid fail during PFB.
1-183	11-19-93	Knox	Flutter	Abort because of beta oscillation at 0.96 M. right WOW on touchdown.
1-184	11-24-93	Lang	Flutter, 1.05, 0.90, and 0.95 M	First supersonic flight. FID during power-up.
1-185	11-24-93	Wisneski	Flutter, 1.10 M	
1-186	11-29-93	Knox	Flutter, 1.15 M	
1-187	11-29-93	Lang	Flutter, 1.20 M	FID during power-up.
1-188	12-01-93	Wisneski	Flutter, 1.25 M	
1-189	12-02-93	Knox	Flutter, 1.25 M	
1-190	12-02-93	Lang	Flutter, 1.25 M	
1-191	12-07-93	Smith	CIC	
1-192	12-07-93	Wisneski	CIC	FID during power-up.
1-193	12-09-93	Smith	CIC	
1-194	12-09-93	Wisneski	CIC	Right WOW FID during landing.
1-195	12-10-93	Smith	CIC	
1-196	12-10-93	Wisneski	CIC	Generator overtemp during pretaxi for flight 1-197.
1-197	12-14-93	Smith	CIC	

Flight No.	Date	Pilot	Purpose	Comments
1-198	12-14-93	Wisneski	CIC	
1-199	12-14-93	Wisneski	CIC	
2-131	12-16-93	Smith	Various maneuvers	First helmet-mounted display (HMD) Viper helmet flight.
2-132	12-16-93	Kim	Various maneuvers, HMD	
2-133	12-20-93	Lang	Maneuvers, HMD	Forebody strake change. FID during engine start.
2-134	12-20-93	Wisneski	Maneuvers, HMD	FCC1 failed to power-up first time. Forebody strake change.
			1994	
2-135	01-06-94	Knox	Envelope expansion	Blunted nose.
2-136	01-06-94	Kim	CIC w/o PST	
2-137	01-06-94	Lang	Abrupt pulls	Yaw rate failed during taxi after landing.
2-138	01-06-94	Wisneski	CIC w/o PST	
2-139	01-11-94	Smith	CIC w/o PST	Main gear wheel damage and blowout after landing.
2-140	01-11-94	Wisneski	CIC w/o PST	Replaced both main gear wheels and tires.
2-141	01-11-94	Kim	CIC w/o PST	
2-142	01-12-94	Lang	CIC w/o PST	
2-143	01-12-94	Knox		FCC2 failed during climbout; RTB.

Flight No.	Date	Pilot	Purpose	Comments
2-144	01-20-94	Knox	Envelope expansion	Replace main gear tires prior to flight. Left WOW during landing.
2-145	01-20-94	Smith	Envelope expansion	
2-146	01-20-94	Lang	Envelope expansion	
2-147	01-20-94	Knox	Envelope expansion	
2-148	01-21-94	Smith	Envelope expansion	
2-149	01-25-94	Groves	1st dedicated HMD flight, CIC practice (CICP)	Completed required sorties for all X-31 pilots using HMD before performing PST CIC flights.
2-150	01-26-94	Lange	CIC	Air intake lip servo amp FID, successfully reset during flight.
2-151	01-26-94	Groves	CIC	
2-152	02-02-94	Lang	CIC	HMD did not function due to loose connector.
2-153	02-02-94	Groves	CIC 15 kft	Cloud cover.
2-154	02-08-94	Lang	CIC	Crosswinds marginal during landing.
2-155	02-10-94	Lang	CIC	TM time code problem.
2-156	02-10-94	Wisneski	CIC	Lakebed runways wet.
2-157	02-10-94	Lang	CIC	
1-200	02-22-94	Lang	Functional check flight (FCF), CIC	FID during power-up.
1-201	02-23-94	Hess	Familiarization	Air Force guest pilot Capt. Derek Hess, USAF

Flight No.	Date	Pilot	Purpose	Comments
1-202	02-24-94	Schmidt	Familiarization	Navy guest pilot L. Cmdr. Steve Schmidt, USN
1-203	02-24-94	Hess	Familiarization	
1-204	02-24-94	Schmidt	Familiarization	
1-205	02-24-94	Hess	Familiarization	
1-206	02-28-94	Schmidt	Familiarization	
1-207	03-01-94	Hess	CICP	High generator temp; RTB.
1-208	03-02-94	Hess	CIC	
1-209	03-03-94	Schmidt	CIC	
1-210	03-03-94	Schmidt	CIC	
1-211	03-03-94	Hess	CIC	
1-212	03-03-94	Schmidt	CIC	
1-213	03-30-94	Kim	CIC	
1-214	03-10-94	Smith	Quasi-tailless (QT)	0 percent QT Demo. Right LEF fail. PFB once.
1-215	03-10-94	Lang	Quasi-tailless	30 percent stable, 20 percent de-stable.
1-216	03-10-94	Smith	Quasi-tailless	40 percent stable, 20 percent de-stable.
2-158	03-15-94	Knox	Retest of X-31 with 119	Software load 119 installed before flight.
2-159	03-15-94	Kim	Photo flight	X-31, F/A-18 HARV, F-16 MATV.
2-160	03-15-94	Lang	Photo flight	F/A-18 chase and X-31.
1-217	03-17-94	Smith	Quasi-tailless	50, 60, and 70 percent stabilized.

Flight No.	Date	Pilot	Purpose	Comments
2-161	03-17-94	Knox	Envelope expansion	265 knot PST, 30 kft, split-S 45-70°. No HMD transmission to control room; C/B problem.
2-162	03-17-94	Kim	CIC	45° AOA limit to investigate variable AOA CIC maneuvers.
1-218	03-28-94	Lang	Envelope expansion	30 kft, 265 knot PST entry.
1-219	03-28-94	Groves	Envelope expansion, CIC	20 kft, military power PST entry.
2-163	03-29-94	Ed Schneider, NASA	Various maneuvers	Pilot familiarization. NASA guest pilot Edward T. "Ed" Schneider, NASA Dryden Flight Research Center (DFRC) pilot.
2-164	03-29-94	Groves	CIC, envelope expansion	Slow-speed line-abreast (SSLA) 45° AOA, military power PST entry. Intermittent HMD operation.
2-165	03-29-94	Schneider	Aerobatic maneuvers, CICP	HMD tracker not working.
1-220	03-31-94	Schneider	CICP	
1-221	03-31-94	Knox	Envelope expansion	265 knot and military power PST entry.
1-222	03-31-94	Schneider	CICP	
1-223	03-31-94	Kim	CICP	
2-166	04-06-94	Lang	Envelope expansion	265 knot PST entry, 15 kft.

Flight No.	Date	Pilot	Purpose	Comments
1-224	04-07-94	Knox	Envelope expansion	Military power entry, 15 kft, 185 and 225 knots. Right LEF failed twice during PFB.
1-225	04-12-94	Kim	CICP	Pt. Mugu F/A-18 adversary pilot.
1-226	04-12-94	Smith	CICP	Pt. Mugu F-14 adversary pilot.
1-227	04-12-94	Kim	CICP	Pt. Mugu F/A-18 adversary pilot.
1-228	04-12-94	Smith	CICP	Pt. Mugu F-14 adversary pilot.
1-229	04-13-94	Knox	CICP	Pt. Mugu F-14 adversary pilot. Failed right LEF deflection during PFB.
1-230	04-13-94	Kim	CICP	Pt. Mugu F-14 adversary pilot.
2-167	04-14-94	Groves	CICP	F-14 adversary.
2-168	04-14-94	Knox	CICP	F/A-18 adversary.
2-169	04-14-94	Groves	CICP	F-14 adversary.
2-170	04-14-94	Schmidt	CICP	F/A-18 adversary, 400th X-31 flight.
2-171	04-19-94	Lang	Demo practice maneuvers	Practice for Media Day.
1-231	04-21-94	Smith	Envelope expansion	265 knot PST entry, 20 kft, 30 kft, 15 kft.
1-232	04-21-94	Groves	Envelope expansion	265 knot PST entry, 20 kft, 30 kft, 15 kft. Failed left LEF PFB once.

Flight No.	Date	Pilot	Purpose	Comments
1-233	04-21-94	Lang	Envelope expansion	265 knot PST entry, 20 kft, 30 kft, 15 kft. Started engine during PFB, hydraulic depressurization.
1-234	05-10-94	Lang	CIC	119A retest and 265 knot PST entry CIC. Generator off during start.
1-235	05-10-94	Kim	CIC	Generator off during start.
1-236	05-10-94	Lang	CIC	Generator off during start.
1-237	05-10-94	Kim	CIC	Generator off during start.
2-172	05-18-94	Kim	Phasing maneuvers	RTB because of engine problem.
2-173	06-08-94	Kim	CICP sorties	Practice for visit of GAF chief of staff.
2-174	06-08-94	Knox	PID	PID points for Langley.
2-175	06-08-94	Lang	PID	PID points for Langley.
2-176	06-10-94	Kim	CICP	Demo for Lt. Gen. Hans-Jorg Kuebart (GAF chief of staff).
2-177	06-10-94	Knox	PID	PID points for Langley.
2-178	06-15-94	Lang	CICP	F/A-18 adversary.
2-179	06-15-94	Kim	CICP	F/A-18 adversary.
2-180	06-15-94	Smith	PID	PID points for Langley.
2-181	06-17-94	Lang	Standard evaluation maneuvers (STEMs)	Longitudinal gross acquisition maneuvers (LGAM).

Flight No.	Date	Pilot	Purpose	Comments
2-182	06-17-94	Knox	PID	PID points for Langley.
2-183	06-17-94	Lang	LGAM	Maneuvers to "acquire" the target F/A-18 aircraft.
2-184	06-17-94	Knox	STEMS	LGAM.
2-185	06-22-94	Smith	CICP, 45° AOA limit	SSLA and HSLA setups with F/A-18 adversary.
2-186	06-22-94	Kim	CIC	F/A-18 adversary.
2-187	06-22-94	Smith	CIC, 45° AOA limit	F/A-18 adversary.
2-188	06-22-94	Lang	CIC	F/A-18 adversary.
2-189	06-24-94	Kim	CIC	F/A-18 adversary.
2-190	06-24-94	Lang	CIC, unlimited AOA	F/A-18 adversary.
2-191	06-24-94	Kim	CIC	F/A-18 adversary.
2-192	06-29-94	Smith	CIC, unlimited AOA	F/A-18 adversary.
2-193	06-29-94	Lang	CIC, unlimited AOA	F/A-18 adversary.
2-194	06-29-94	Kim	CIC, unlimited AOA	F/A-18 adversary.
2-195	07-11-94	Smith	Virtual warfight	Practice for virtual war fight demo.
2-196	07-11-94	Lang	Virtual warfight	QT engaged. Fixed-point overflow FCS code necessitated RTB.
2-197	07-15-94	Smith	Virtual warfight practice	QT, simulated bomb drop, missile evasion.
2-198	07-15-94	Lang	Virtual warfight planned	Fixed-point overflow FCS code necessitated RTB.
1-238	08-02-94	Smith	Warfight demo	119C retest.

Flight No.	Date	Pilot	Purpose	Comments
1-239	08-02-94	Lang	STEMS	Gross acquisition.
1-240	08-04-94	Smith	STEMS	Fine tracking.
1-241	08-04-94	Lang	STEMS	Fine tracking.
1-242	08-09-94	Smith	CIC	30° off-boresight (OBS) missile.
1-243	08-09-94	Smith	CIC	30° OBS missile.
1-244	08-09-94	Lang	CIC	30° OBS missile.
1-245	08-09-94	Lang	CIC	Nose gear light on handle did not come on during landing. Four burnt-out bulbs.
1-246	08-18-94	Smith	STEMS	Fine tracking.
1-247	08-18-94	Lang	STEMS	Fine tracking. Trigger did not activate FTB, so STEMS was performed instead.
1-248	08-18-94	Smith	STEMS	Fine tracking.
2-199	08-25-94	Lang	FCF, CICP with HMD	Left WOW indication on during flight. Stuck WOW switch replaced after flight.
2-200	08-26-94	Lang	CICP with HMD	High off-boresight missile.
2-201	08-26-94	Kim	CICP with HMD	High off-boresight missile.
2-202	08-26-94	Kim	CICP with HMD	HMD failed and turned off.

Flight No.	Date	Pilot	Purpose	Comments
1-249	08-30-94	Knox	FTB PID	AIL servo amp failure during landing. FTB with Deutsche Forschungsanstalt für Luft und Raumfahrt (DLR) card.
1-250	08-30-94	Maj. C.J. Loria, USMC	Familiarization	USMC pilot "Gus" Loria's first flight. Loria replaces Cmdr. Al Groves, USN
1-251	08-30-94	Lang	FTB PID	FTB with DLR card.
1-252	08-30-94	Loria	Familiarization	
2-203	09-01-94	Knox	QT power approach	First QT subsonic flight.
2-204	09-01-94	Lang	QT power approach	
2-205	09-01-94	Smith	CIC with helmet	F/A-18 adversary.
1-253	09-06-94	Knox	FTB PID	FTB with DLR card. Caution/warning (CAUT/WRN) C/B popped during power approach (PA).
1-254	09-13-94	Lang	CICP	Against F-15 from Nellis.
1-255	09-13-94	Smith	CICP	Against F-16 from Nellis.
1-256	09-13-94	Kim	CICP	Against F-15 from Nellis.
2-206	09-13-94	Kim	CIC with 422 Test and Evaluation Squadron (TES)	Against F-16 from Nellis.
1-257	09-14-94	Lang	CIC	Against F-16 from Nellis.

Flight No.	Date	Pilot	Purpose	Comments
1-258	09-14-94	Smith	CIC	Against F-15 from Nellis.
1-259	09-14-94	Kim	CIC	Against F-16 from Nellis.
2-207	09-15-94	Smith	CIC with 422 TES	F-16 from Nellis.
2-208	09-15-94	Lang	CIC with 422 TES	F-15 from Nellis.
2-209	09-15-94	Kim	CIC with 422 TES	F-15 from Nellis.
2-210	09-15-94	Loria	CIC with 422 TES	F-15 from Nellis.
1-260	09-21-94	Lang	TV calibration	Low power calibration for QT.
2-211	09-21-94	Kim	CIC with HMD	Col. Tack Nix in 2nd F/A-18 chase airplane with Jim Smolka.
2-212	09-27-94	Knox		RTB because of ECS problem. Pressure relief valve replaced after flight.
2-213	09-27-94	Lang	PID and QT	ECS problem recurred but flight not curtailed.
1-261	10-06-94	Kim	STEMS	Fine tracking.
1-262	10-06-94	Lang	STEMS	Fine tracking.
1-263	10-13-94	Loria	STEMS	Fine tracking.
1-264	10-13-94	Smith	STEMS	Fine tracking.
1-265	10-13-94	Loria	STEMS	Fine tracking.
1-266	10-17-94	Kim	CIC	Demo for Lt. Gen. Gerhardt John, GMD.
1-267	10-17-94	Smith	STEMS	Fine tracking.

Flight No.	Date	Pilot	Purpose	Comments
1-268	10-18-94	Knox	STEMS	HSLA for Congressman Howard "Buck" McKeon.
2-214	10-27-94	Lang	ECS/FCS checkout	"Blue" fuel-control engine (GE F404-310) installed before flight.
2-215	10-27-94	Kim	STEMS	Lateral gross (target) acquisition tracking tasks.
2-216	10-27-94	Smith	STEMS	Longitudinal gross acquisition tasks.
2-217	10-27-94	Lang	STEMS	Helicopter gun attack evaluation, F/A-18 adversary.
2-218	11-01-94	Kim	CIC with HMD	
2-219	11-01-94	Knox	CIC with HMD	Off-boresight missile capability.
2-220	11-08-94	Loria	FCF, QT testing	QT PA.
2-221	11-08-94	Lang	QT in PA and cruise	
2-222	11-08-94	Knox	QT in PA and cruise	
2-223	11-17-94	Lang	QT, 8 kft., 170 & 220 knots indicated airspeed (KIAS)	TV plume boundary calibrations. Nose gear down-lock wire disconnected.
2-224	11-29-94	Loria	Practice approaches	Simulated carrier operations.
2-225	11-29-94	Smith	QT in PA and cruise	
2-226	11-29-94	Knox	Carrier suitability tasks	

Flight No.	Date	Pilot	Purpose	Comments
2-227	12-01-94	Smith	CIC with HMD	60° OBS-angle launchable missile.
2-228	12-01-94	Lang	QT, 8 kft	Cruise configuration.
2-229	12-06-94	Knox	QT, 8 kft	PA configuration, 170 and 220 KIAS.
2-230	12-06-94	Smith	QT, 220 KIAS	9.5–7.5 kft, right WOW during landing.
2-231	12-06-94	Lang	QT, 425 KIAS, 8 kft	QT and basic airplane (BA) also flown at 220 KIAS.
1-269	12-13-94	Knox	QT, 4 kft, 170 kt	500th flight, 1st flight with TV actuator modified for less damped bypass.
1-270	12-13-94	Smith	QT, 4 kft, 220 kt	
1-271	12-13-94	Lang	QT, 4 kft, 56° PLA	
1-272	12-13-94	Knox	Precision approach	Adaptable Target Lighting Array System (ATLAS).
1-273	12-15-94	Smith	QT, low altitude	No altitude restriction for TV and QT.
1-274	12-15-94	Loria	QT, low altitude	
1-275	12-15-94	Knox	QT, precision approach	
1-276	12-15-94	Loria	QT, precision approach	
1-277	12-20-94	Loria	QT, precision approach	
1-278	12-20-94	Knox	QT, precision approach	Technician bumped restore switch.

Flight No.	Date	Pilot	Purpose	Comments
1-279	12-20-94	Loria	QT, precision approach	
1-280	12-20-94	Smith	QT, cruise	F/A-18 chase low oil pressure, emergency land.
1-281	12-22-94	Lang	QT, cruise	Beta fail during QT roll 425 KCAS, 8 kft; landing in R-2.
1-282	12-22-94	Kim	Air-to-ground (A/G)	Replaced nose boom.
1-283	12-22-94	Lang	QT cruise	Speed brake close switch broken. Failed right LEF twice during PFB.
1995				
1-284	01-06-95	Smith	QT	
1-285	01-06-95	Lang	QT	
1-286	01-18-95	Lang	QT A/G	
1-287	01-18-95	Loria	QT A/G	
1-288	01-18-95	Kim	QT A/G	
1-289	01-18-95	Lang	PID	FTB with 120b software thresholds.
1-290	01-19-95	Loria	QT A/G	
1-291	01-19-95	Kim	QT A/G	
1-292	01-19-95	Lang	PID	X-31 crashed. Pilot ejected. LTEI failure prior to ejection.
2-232	04-13-95	Knox	PST	First flight after A/C #1 crash. Functional C/O.
2-233	04-13-95	Smith	PST	AB ignition problem.

Flight No.	Date	Pilot	Purpose	Comments
2-234	04-17-95	Knox	PST	Intermittent AB problem.
2-235	04-17-95	Kim	PST	Intermittent AB problem.
2-236	04-21-95	Kim	PST, 13 kft	Air data observer fail during pull to 4.5 g's from 350 KIAS.
2-237	04-22-95	Kim	PST, 13 kft and 5 kft AGL	
2-238	04-22-95	Smith	PST, 13 kft and 5 kft AGL	
2-239	04-22-95	Smith	PST, 13 kft and 5 kft AGL	
2-240	04-24-95	Knox	Airshow maneuvers at 5 kft AGL	
2-241	04-24-95	Kim	Airshow maneuvers at 5 kft AGL	
2-242	04-26-95	Knox	Airshow maneuvers at 2.5 kft AGL	
2-243	04-26-95	Smith	Airshow maneuvers at 1.5 kft AGL	First R3 landing.
2-244	04-26-95	Knox	Airshow maneuvers at 1 kft AGL	
2-245	04-28-95	Smith	Airshow maneuvers at .5 kft AGL	First AB takeoff
2-246	04-28-95	Kim	Airshow maneuvers at .5 kft AGL	
2-247	05-04-95	Knox	Airshow practice	First silent control room. 13° AOA landing.
2-248	05-04-95	Kim	Airshow practice	Silent control room.
2-249	05-04-95	Knox	Airshow practice	Silent control room. 13° AOA landing.

Flight No.	Date	Pilot	Purpose	Comments
2-250	05-05-95	Kim	Airshow practice	
2-251	05-05-95	Knox	Airshow practice	Drag chute not installed. Spin chute deactivated.
2-252	05-06-95	Kim	Airshow practice	Drag chute not installed.
2-253	05-08-95	Knox	Airshow practice	Drag chute not installed.
2-254	05-08-95	Kim	Airshow practice	Drag chute not installed.
2-255	05-10-95	Knox	Airshow practice	Nonfunctional drag chute installed.
2-256	05-10-95	Kim	Airshow practice	No chute installed.
2-257	05-10-95	Knox	Airshow practice	Max brake test at 100 KIAS.
2-258	05-12-95	Knox	Airshow practice	First drag chute deployment at 130 KIAS. No problems.
2-259	05-12-95	Knox	Airshow practice	Max antiskid braking at 125 KIAS.
2-260	05-12-95	Kim	Airshow practice	Normal landing.
2-261	05-12-95	Knox	Airshow practice	Drag chute deployment at 155 KIAS.
2-262	05-13-95	Knox	Airshow practice	Drag chute deployment at 170 KIAS. Release at 155 KIAS. Moderate braking.
2-263	05-13-95	Kim	Airshow practice	Drag chute arming failed. Moderate braking.
2-264	05-13-95	Knox	Airshow practice	Moderate braking.

Flight No.	Date	Pilot	Purpose	Comments
2-265	05-15-95	Kim	Airshow practice	Drag chute deployment jettison at 110 KIAS.
2-266	05-16-95	Knox	Airshow practice	Drag chute deployment.
2-267	05-16-95	Kim	Airshow practice	Last flight at Dryden before airshow. Loaded on C-5A on 05-20-95.
2-268	05-29-95	Knox	Aircraft (A/C) checkout and air show (A/S) practice	First flight at Manching, Germany. Problem with drag chute.
2-269	05-30-95	Kim	A/C checkout and A/S practice	At Manching. Bad weather prevented more flights.
2-270	05-31-95	Kim	A/C checkout and A/S practice	At Manching.
2-271	06-02-95	Knox	A/C checkout and A/S practice	At Manching.
2-272	06-02-95	Kim	A/C checkout and A/S practice	At Manching.
2-273	06-03-95	Knox		Ferry from Manching to Cologne. Stored heading INU for next flight.
2-274	06-03-95	Knox		Ferry from Cologne to Manching. Nose boom alpha failed after takeoff. R3 landing in Paris, France.
2-275	06-08-95	Knox	A/C checkout	First flight at Paris. Noseboom replaced.
2-276	06-08-95	Kim	A/C checkout and A/S practice.	

Flight No.	Date	Pilot	Purpose	Comments
2-277	06-08-95	Knox	A/C checkout and A/S practice	
2-278	06-09-95	Kim	High show practice	Both pilots now air show qualified.
2-279	06-10-95	Knox	High show demonstration	Drag chute failed.
2-280	06-12-95	Kim	Demonstration flight	Drag chute deployed successfully.
2-281	06-13-95	Knox	Low show demonstration	
2-282	06-14-95	Kim	High show demonstration	
2-283	06-15-95	Knox	High show demonstration	
2-284	06-16-95	Kim	High show demonstration	
2-285	06-17-95	Knox	Demonstration flight	
2-286	06-18-95	Kim	Demonstration flight	Last day of air show.
2-287	06-19-95	Kim	Ferry	Paris to Cologne. Drag chute deployment.
2-288	06-19-95	Kim	Ferry	Cologne to Manching. Last flight of aircraft in the EFM program.
2-289				There is no record of this flight being flown. Flight number omitted due to administrative error at start of VECTOR program.

Flight No.	Date	Pilot	Purpose	Comments
2001				
2-290	02-24-01	Cmdr. Vivian Ragusa, USN	FCF, 5K (PA) and 10K BASIC mode handling; normal drag chute deployment	First flight of the VECTOR program at NAS Patuxent River, MD. First flight of the reactivation phase (Phase 1). Flown using Operational Flight Controls Program (OFP) 122.
2-291	03-10-01	Cmdr. Rudy Knöpfel, GNR	FCF complete; 10K and 22K BASIC mode handling; R3 switchover	Cmdr. Rudy Knöpfel, German Naval Reserve, from WTD-61 joins test pilot team. Drag chute failure due to airborne mechanical decoupling.
2-292	03-20-01	Ragusa	20K straight and level (S&L) plume calibration; 10K R1, R2, and R3 mode handling	Drag chute failed to completely deploy (streamer).
2-293	03-20-01	Knöpfel	3.5K/17° AOA level acceleration, normal drag chute deployment	
2-294	03-27-01	Ragusa	22K BASIC mode handling; 20K S&L plume calibration; 9K R3 mode handling	Drag chute arming light failed during descent checks, no-chute landing.

Flight No.	Date	Pilot	Purpose	Comments
2-295	04-02-01	Knöpfel	10K S&L plume calibration; 20K level turn plume calibration; 9K R3 mode handling.	Normal drag chute deployment.
2-296	04-04-01	Ragusa	20K level turn plume calibration	Normal drag chute deployment.
2-297	04-04-01	Ragusa	10K level turn plume calibration; 5K S&L plume calibration.	Normal drag chute deployment.
2-298	04-05-01	Knöpfel	20K level turn plume calibration; 5K S&L plume calibration; 5K (PA) BASIC mode handling; 3.5K S&L stabilized points	Normal drag chute deployment.
2-299	04-06-01	Knöpfel	5K control law perf. (TV ON); 10K BASIC mode handling; sawtooth climbs	Normal drag chute deployment. Last flight of the VECTOR reactivation phase.
2002				
2-300	05-17-02	Knöpfel	20K/cruise configuration (CR); 23° AOA PID	First flight of extreme short takeoff and landings (ESTOL) Up And Away phase (Phase 2). Start of testing with OFP 123 A2.
2-301	05-23-02	Knöpfel	FCF continued; 5K (PA) airspeed/altitude checks; BASIC mode handling	

Flight No.	Date	Pilot	Purpose	Comments
2-302	06-08-02	Ragusa	FCF continued; 10K rig checks at 200 KCAS and 300 KCAS; 10K airspeed checks; 10K throttle transients; 10K integrated test block (ITB), 1G level deceleration to 30° AOA, 10K 3G WUT (2x R3 req.)	
2-303	06-18-02	Ragusa	FCF complete: 10K/24K delta specific excess power (P_s) and cabin press checks; 24K throttle transients; FQ verification: 10K ITB in R1, R2, R3.	
2-304	06-22-02	Knöpfel	5K/CR: 12° AOA and 15° AOA ITB; 9K/CR: 220 KCAS and 11° AOA ITB; 15K/PA/TV on: 235 KCAS, 15° AOA ITB and PID; SFO.	Landing from simulated flame out (SFO).
2-305	06-22-02	Ragusa	15K/PA: R2, R3 ITB at 235, 180 KCAS; 15° AOA and 18° AOA ITB and PID	

Flight No.	Date	Pilot	Purpose	Comments
2-306	06-25-02	Knöpfel	20K/CR/TV on: 20° AOA and 25° AOA throttle transients; 15K/PA/TV on: 21° AOA ITB and PID, 22° AOA ITB, 25° AOA throttle transient; 5K/PA: 235 KCAS and 13° AOA R1 ITB; 10K/CR/TV on: 25° AOA throttle transients; Integrity Beacon Landing System (IBLS) bubble pass	
2-307	06-25-02	Ragusa	25K/CR: 0.4 M, 0.5 M, and 0.63 M ITB; 39K/CR: 0.78 M ITB; 10K/PA: 18° AOA and 22° AOA Performance; IBLS bubble pass	
2-308	06-27-02	Knöpfel	6.5K/CR/TV on: 12° AOA and 18° AOA PID; 10K/PA: 24° AOA ITB; tower flybys.	Avionics air hot light, R3 requested; tower flybys for airspeed system calibration.
2-309	06-27-02	Ragusa	3.5K/PA: 18° AOA ITB; 4K/PA: 16° AOA and 18° AOA performance	
2-310	06-29-02	Knöpfel	20K/CR/TV on: 10°, 15°, 20°, 25° AOA ITB and PID	
2-311	08-08-02	Ragusa	30-day FCF	
2-312	08-27-02	Knöpfel	3.5K/PA: 20°, 22°, 24° AOA performance	

Flight No.	Date	Pilot	Purpose	Comments
2-313	09-04-02	Maj. J. Allee, USMC	4K/PA: 20° AOA performance, IBLS bubble pass	Maj. J. "Cody" Allee joins the VECTOR test pilot team.
2-314	09-04-02	Knöpfel	20K/CR: 30° AOA PID 20K/CR/TV on/PST on: 30α PID	
2-315	09-17-02	Allee	IBLS bubble passes	
2-316	09-17-02	Knöpfel	IBLS Bubble passes	
2-317	10-01-02	Allee	5K/CR: Phase checks, RTB (for roll rate gyro problem)	
2-318	10-02-02	Knöpfel	20K/CR/TV on/PST on: 30° AOA, PID; 35° ITB; 15K/PA/TV on: 24° AOA PID	
2-319	10-18-02	Allee	30K/CR: 0.5 M, 0.6 M, 0.7 M; FADS 35K/CR: 0.8 M, 0.7 M, 0.6 M, 0.5 M FADS; IBLS bubble passes	
2-320	10-18-02	Knöpfel	20K/CR/TV on/PST on: 35° AOA PID; 40° ITB, PID 45° AOA ITB	
2-321	10-22-02	Allee	20K/CR/TV on: 23° AOA PID, 25° AOA PID, 27° AOA ITB, PID	

Flight No.	Date	Pilot	Purpose	Comments
2-322	10-23-02	Knöpfel	IBLS bubble passes	
2-323	10-23-02	Allee	35K/CR: FADS 0.8 M, 0.7 M, 0.6 M; 20K/CR: 23° AOA PID; 20K/CR/TV on/PST on: 30° AOA PID, 35° AOA PID, 40° AOA ITB, PID	End of testing with OFP 123 A2
2-324	11-02-02	Knöpfel	123B4 FTF (partial complete)	Start of testing with OFP 123 B4
2-325	11-07-02	Allee	FCF complete: 10K 390 KCAS rig check/24K cabin press checks; 24K throttle transients	
2-326	11-07-02	Knöpfel	6.5K/CR/TV on: 12° AOA PID (force breakout checks)	
2-327	11-09-02	Allee	ESTOL Engage/ disengage checks: Virtual runway at 1.3 kft height above terrain (HAT)/CR/18° AOA target; Virtual runway at 1.3 kft HAT/CR/24° AOA target; Virtual runway at 1.3 kft HAT/PA/24° AOA target; Virtual runway at 1.3 kft HAT/PA/18° AOA target with AOB	

Flight No.	Date	Pilot	Purpose	Comments
2-328	11-09-02	Knöpfel	20K/CR/TV on/PST on: 50° AOA FQ, PID; 55° AOA FQ, PID	
2-329	11-18-02	Allee	6.5K/CR/TV on: 12° AOA PID (force breakout checks); ESTOL waveoff checks: Virtual runway at 1.3 kft HAT/PA/18° AOA target; Virtual runway at 1.3 kft HAT/PA/18° AOA target; Virtual runway at 1.3 kft HAT/PA/24° AOA target; Virtual runway at 1.3 kft HAT/PA/18° AOA target; ESTOL virtual runway at 1.3 kft HAT/PA/12° AOA target; ESTOL virtual runway at 1.3 kft HAT/ PA/12° AOA target	
2-330	11-19-02	Knöpfel	ESTOL virtual runway at 1.3 kft HAT/PA/16° AOA target; ESTOL virtual runway at 1.3 kft HAT/PA/18° AOA target; ESTOL virtual runway at 1.3 kft HAT/PA/20° AOA target; ESTOL virtual runway at 1.3 kft HAT/PA/24° AOA target; ESTOL virtual runway at 1.3 kft HAT/PA/18° AOA target	

Flight No.	Date	Pilot	Purpose	Comments
2-331	11-19-02	Lt. Gerald Hansen, USN	IBLS bubble passes	Lt. Hansen was a backup test pilot for the VECTOR program. While he flew as chase often, this was his only flight in the X-31.
2-332	11-20-02	Knöpfel	ESTOL virtual runway at 1.3 kft HAT/CR/14° AOA target; ESTOL virtual runway at 1.3 kft HAT/PA/18° AOA target; ESTOL virtual runway at 1.3 kft HAT/CR/18° AOA target; ESTOL virtual runway at 1.3 kft HAT/PA/24° AOA target; ESTOL virtual runway at 1.3 kft HAT/ CR/24° AOA target	
2-333	11-21-02	Allee	ESTOL virtual runway at 1.3 kft HAT/CR/28° AOA target; ESTOL virtual runway at 1.3 kft HAT/PA/18° AOA target	
2-334	11-23-02	Knöpfel	5K/CR: Flutter 0.45 M, 0.71 M; 11.5K/CR: Flutter 0.80 M (R3 request); ESTOL virtual runway at 1.3 kft HAT/PA/18° AOA target; ESTOL virtual runway at 1.3 kft HAT/PA/ 24° AOA target	

Flight No.	Date	Pilot	Purpose	Comments
2-335	12-09-02	Allee	FCF; 39K/CR: Flutter 0.88 M; 25K/CR: Flutter 0.88 M; 16.2K/CR: Flutter 0.88 M (not complete due to R3 request)	
2-336	12-12-02	Knöpfel	ESTOL waveoff performance: 24° AOA target, steep early; 20° AOA target, steep early; FADS, 180 KCAS, PST 30° AOA split-S entry (R1 request, so RTB)	
2-337	12-17-02	Allee	20K/CR/TV on/PST on: 55° AOA PID; 60° AOA FQ PID; FADS, 180 KCAS, PST 30° AOA split-S entry	
2-338	12-17-02	Knöpfel	20K/CR/TV on/PST on: 60° AOA PID, 65° AOA FQ PID, 70° AOA FQ PID; FADS, 180 KCAS, PST 50° AOA split-S entry	
2-339	12-18-02	Allee	IBLS bubble passes	
2-340	12-19-02	Knöpfel	IBLS bubble passes	

Flight No.	Date	Pilot	Purpose	Comments
2003				
2-341	01-13-03	Allee	FADS, 180 KCAS, PST 30°, 60°, and 70° AOA split-S entry (R1 request so RTB)	
2-342	01-14-03	Knöpfel	IBLS bubble passes	
2-343	01-15-03	Knöpfel	FADS, 240 KCAS, PST 50° AOA split-S entry (R1 request so RTB)	
2-344	01-16-03	Allee	FADS, 240 KCAS, PST 50° split-S entry (R1 request so RTB)	
2-345	02-06-03	Allee	FCF (minus 25K rig check); weather precluded FCF completion	
2-346	02-08-03	Knöpfel	Completed FCF and rig check; "bleed air hot caution," so RTB	
2-347	02-08-03	Allee	39K/CR: Flutter (stick/pedal raps) 0.92 M; canard "ringing," so RTB	
2-348	03-08-03	Allee	39K/CR: Flutter (stick/pedal raps) 1.05 M; FCC1 failure, so RTB	

Flight No.	Date	Pilot	Purpose	Comments
2-349	03-22-03	Knöpfel	FCF; 39K/CR Flutter: (stick/pedal raps) 1.10 M; 39K/CR Flutter: (stick/pedal raps) 1.18 M; 39K/CR FADS: Level deceleration 1.18 M to 0.80 M	
2-350	03-22-03	Knöpfel	39K/CR FADS: Acceleration 0.8 M to 1.06 M; 39K/CR FADS: Roller coaster at 1.06 M with sideslip; 39K/CR FADS: Roller coaster at 1.18 M with sideslip; 39K/CR FADS: Elevated-g deceleration 1.18 M to 0.80 M	
2-351	04-03-03	Allee	FCF (new software with re-installed bent airspeed probe); autothrottle PID disengage checks; R2 request on downwind prior to landing; R2 landing	First flight of ESTOL To The Ground phase (Phase 3). Start of testing with OFP 124-7.

Flight No.	Date	Pilot	Purpose	Comments
2-352	04-06-03	Knöpfel	FCF (straight boom installation); ESTOL engage/disengage checks; ESTOL approaches to waveoff at virtual HAT 900 ft engage	
2-353	04-06-03	Allee	ESTOL approaches to waveoff at virtual HAT 900 ft engage; ESTOL derotations from 12° to 18° target AOA at virtual HAT 900 ft engage	
2-354	04-12-03	Knöpfel	IBLS; ESTOL approaches to waveoff at actual HAT 600 ft engage	
2-355	04-13-03	Allee	IBLS; ESTOL approach to waveoff at actual HAT 600 ft engage	
2-356	04-14-03	Knöpfel	ESTOL derotations at virtual HAT 900 ft engage from 12° to 14° target AOA	
2-357	04-15-03	Allee	ESTOL derotations at virtual HAT 600 ft/900 ft engage from 12° to 18° target AOA	

Flight No.	Date	Pilot	Purpose	Comments
2-358	04-16-03	Knöpfel	ESTOL derotations at virtual HAT 600 ft engage from 12° to 18° target AOA, 0° decrab, 15° derotation; 13° to 14° target AOA, 7° decrab, 15° derotation	
2-359	04-16-03	Allee	ESTOL derotations at virtual HAT 600 ft engage from 14°, 16°, 18° target AOA, 7° decrab, 15° derotation; 18°, 20°, 22° target AOA, 0° decrab, 20° derotation	
2-360	04-19-03	Knöpfel	ESTOL To The Ground bubble passes only; unable to engage; RTB	
2-361	04-21-03	Allee	IBLS; ESTOL approach to waveoff at actual HAT 600 ft engage	
2-362	04-22-03	Knöpfel	ESTOL To The Ground, 12° AOA, 0° decrab	First flight of ESTOL to touchdown.
2-363	04-22-03	Allee	ESTOL To The Ground auto waveoffs; unable; RTB.	
2-364	04-23-03	Knöpfel	ESTOL To The Ground bubble passes; unable; RTB	·

Flight No.	Date	Pilot	Purpose	Comments
2-365	04-23-03	Allee	ESTOL To The Ground, 13° AOA, 0° decrab; 13° AOA, 7° decrab, 15° derotation; 14° AOA, 0° decrab; 14° AOA, 7° decrab, 15° derotation	
2-366	04-24-03	Knöpfel	ESTOL To The Ground, 16° AOA, 7° decrab	
2-367	04-24-03	Allee	ESTOL derotations at virtual HAT 600 ft engage from 16°, 18° target AOA, 7° decrab, 15° derotation; 18°, 20° target AOA, 7° decrab, 20o derotation; 24° target AOA, 7° decrab, 25° derotation	
2-368	04-25-03	Knöpfel	ESTOL To The Ground, 16° AOA, 7° decrab, 15° derotation; 18° AOA, 7° decrab, 15° derotation	
2-369	04-27-03	Allee	ESTOL derotations at virtual HAT 600 ft engage from 22°, 24° target AOA, 7° decrab, 20° derotation; 24° target AOA, 7° decrab, 25° derotation	
2-370	04-28-03	Knöpfel	ESTOL To The Ground bubble passes; unable to engage; RTB	

Flight No.	Date	Pilot	Purpose	Comments
2-371	04-28-03	Allee	ESTOL To The Ground, 18° AOA, 7° decrab, 20° derotation; 20° AOA, 7° decrab, 20° derotation; 22° AOA, 7° decrab, 20° derotation	
2-372	04-29-03	Allee	ESTOL To The Ground, 18° AOA, 7° decrab, 20° derotation; 24° AOA, 7° decrab, 20° derotation	Last flight of the VECTOR program. Last X-31 flight.

Sources: Data for the EFM flight logs were compiled by the X-31 EFM project office, supplemented by flight reports where available and by information collected by Peter Merlin, Betty Love, and J.D. Hunley from various sources, including project personnel. Data for the VECTOR flight logs were obtained from Harvey Schellenger of Boeing.

Endnotes

1. When the pilots started flying above 50° AOA, they encountered vortex-induced kicks from the side that they called "lurches." The international team added narrow ¼-inch-wide strips of grit to the aircraft's noseboom and radome to change the vortices flowing from them. The grit strips reduced the randomness of the lurches caused by the vortices, enabling the pilots to finish envelope expansion to the designed AOA limit of 70° α at 1 g of acceleration.

2. The Kiel pitot-static probe with a 10° downward cant was installed to solve the problem that, when pilots flew for extended periods above 30° AOA, the inertial navigation unit began calculating large but fictitious values of sideslip as a result of changes in wind direction and magnitude.

X-31 Dimensions, Weights, and Performance Specifications

General Characteristics

Crew: One

Powerplant: 1 x General Electric F404-GE-400 turbofan,

16,000 lb_f (71kN) (afterburning)

Dimensions, External

Wingspan: 23 ft 10 in (7.26 m)

Wing aspect ratio: 2.51:1

Foreplane (canard) span: 8 ft 8 in (2.64 m)

Length overall, including pitot probe: 48 ft 8½ in (14.85 m)

Length overall, excluding pitot probe: 43 ft 4 in (13.21 m)

Fuselage, excluding pitot probe: 40 ft 8 in (12.39 m)

Height overall: 14 ft 7 in (4.44 m)

Wheel track: 7 ft 6⅓ in (2.29 m)

Wheelbase: 11 ft 6⅓ in (3.51 m)

Areas

Wing area: 226.3 sq ft (21.02 m²)

Foreplane (canard), total: 23.60 sq ft (2.19 m²)

Ailerons, total: 13.88 sq ft (1.29 m²)

Trailing-edge flaps, total: 18.66 sq ft (1.73 m²)

Leading-edge flaps:

Inboard, total: 6.42 sq ft (0.60 m²)

Outboard, total: 8.28 sq ft (0.77 m²)

Fin, including dorsal fin: 28.87 sq ft (2.68 m²)

Rudder: 8.68 sq ft (0.81 m²)

Weights and Loadings

Weight empty, equipped: 11, 410 lb (5,175 kg)

Fuel Weight: 4,136 lb (1,876 kg)

Normal flying weight: 14,600 lb (6,622 kg)

Maximum takeoff weight: 15,935 lb (7,228 kg)

Wing loading at normal flying weight: 64.52 lb/sq ft (315.0 kg/m²)

Maximum wing loading: 70.42 lb/sq ft (343.8 kg/m²)

Power loading at normal flying weight: 0.91 lb/lb s.t (93 kg/kN)

Maximum power loading: 1.00 lb/lb s.t (102 kg/kN)

Performance (estimated, at maximum takeoff weight)

Never-exceed (V_{NE}) and maximum level speed:

Sea level to 28,000 ft MSL (8,535 m): 485 kts equivalent airspeed (898 km/h; 558 mph)

28,000 ft to 40,000 ft MSL (8,535 m to 12,200 m): Mach 1.3

Highest speed attained: Mach 1.28 at 38,000 ft MSL

Maximum rate of climb at sea level: 43,000 ft/min (13,106 m/min)

Maximum operating altitude: 40,000 ft MSL (12,200 m)

Takeoff run: 1,500 ft (457 m)

Takeoff over a 50 ft (15 m) obstacle: 2,700 ft (823 m)

Landing distance over a 50 ft (15 m) obstacle: 3,700 ft (1,128 m)

Landing run: 2,700 ft (823 m)

Design g limits: +9/–4

Sources:

Paul Jackson (ed.), *Jane's All The World's Aircraft 1996-97* (London: Jane's Information Group, 1996), pp. 228–229.

Dennis R. Jenkins, Tony Landis, and Jay Miller, *American X-Vehicles: An Inventory—X-1 to X-50—Centennial of Flight Edition*, Monographs in Aerospace History 31 (Washington, DC: NASA SP-2003-4531, June 2003), p. 39.

X-31 Chronology

Date	Purpose and Comments
1977	Work begins on post-stall maneuvering at MBB.
1983	Rockwell joins MBB in post-stall maneuvering studies.
Feb. 11, 1983	Rockwell's Mike Robinson and MBB's Wolfgang Herbst brief DARPA's Lt. Col. Jim Allburn, proposing SNAKE. DARPA approves funds for an initial study.
Nov. 1984	Phase I (feasibility study) begins; project now called EFM.
Dec. 1985	Results of Feasibility Study briefed to DARPA and BMV.
May 1986	U.S.-German MOA on EFM signed.
Sep. 1986	Phase II (vehicle Preliminary Design) begins.
Dec. 3–4, 1986	Concept Review—Baseline configuration defined.
Feb. 23 1987	Officially designated X-31A.
Dec. 1987	Preliminary Design completed.
Aug. 1988	Two prototypes funded.

Date	Purpose and Comments
Aug. 1988	Phase III (aircraft construction, assembly, and initial flight test—9 sorties) begins.
Mar. 1, 1990	Ship 1 (Bu. No. 164584) rolled out.
Oct. 11, 1990	First flight of Ship 1.
Jan. 19, 1991	First flight of Ship 2 (Bu. No. 164585).
Feb. 14, 1991	Start of Phase IV (flight testing). Ship 1 made first flight with thrust-vectoring paddles installed.
Apr. 24, 1991	Start of Government Preliminary Evaluation #1 (GPE I).
Sep.–Oct. 1991	Pinball I Twin-Dome Manned Air Combat Simulation.
Nov. 19, 1991	First "post-stall" flight.
Nov. 20, 1991	First Government Preliminary Evaluation #2 (GPE II) flight.
End of 1991	52° angle of attack reached, after a total of 108 flights.
Jan. 20, 1992	Both aircraft flown to Edwards AFB in formation—the only time the two X-31's were flown together.
Jan. 1992	International Test Organization formed, incorporating NASA and USAF.
Feb. 10, 1992	Testing moved to NASA Dryden Flight Research Facility.

Date	Purpose and Comments
Feb. 10, 1992	Both aircraft and test responsibility transferred to Dryden.
Apr. 23, 1992	First ITO flight.
Jun. 1992	Phase IV high-angle-of-attack tests started.
Sep. 10, 1992	First flight with aft strakes.
Sep. 18, 1992	Final target angle of attack 70° at 45° angle of bank.
Oct. 29, 1992	Ship 2 flown with "grit" strips added to control vortices that were causing "bumps."
Nov. 6, 1992	First-ever 360° rolls at 70° angle of attack.
Nov. 25, 1992	Unintended post-stall departure of Ship 2.
Jan. 12, 1993	First flight with forward strakes installed to control vortices.
Feb. 25, 1993	First "J" turn at 70° angle of attack.
Mar. 1993	Post-stall program completed.
Apr. 19–30, 1993	Pinball II Twin-Dome Manned Air Combat Simulation.
Apr. 29, 1993	First 180° heading-reversal "Herbst Maneuver" at 70° angle of attack achieved.

Date	Purpose and Comments
Jun. 10, 1993	Tactical utility trials at NASA Dryden commence with tactical maneuvering.
Aug. 31, 1993	First BFM flight.
Nov. 5, 1993	First CIC flight.
Nov. 24, 1993	First supersonic flight, achieving Mach 1.08 at 37,500 ft MSL.
Dec. 16, 1993	First flight with the GEC-Marconi Avionics Viper HMD.
Nov. 1993–Jan. 1994	During dogfights against an evenly matched NASA F/A-18, the X-31 showed high lethality in attack and good survival in defensive situations.
Jan.–Feb. 1994	Some close-in-combat dogfights flown against F/A-18 to validate "comparable" configuration of F/A-18.
Jan. 25, 1994	First dogfight missions flown with GEC-Marconi Avionics Viper visual- and audio-display helmet.
Feb. 23, 1994	First X-31 flight with a "guest" operational fighter pilot.
Feb.–Mar. 1994	Guest pilot evaluation flown with operational USAF and U.S. Navy fighter pilots flying the X-31 with minimal training sorties.

Date	Purpose and Comments
Mar. 17, 1994	Stability and maneuverability at Mach 1.2 demonstrated with fin and rudder used to destabilize the aircraft (simulating a tailless configuration) and only engine thrust-vectoring used for stability and directional control.
Apr. 12, 1994	First flight of the X-31 against a "guest adversary pilot."
Apr. 1994	Adversary evaluations flown against U.S. Navy VX-4 Squadron F-14 and clean F/A-18 aircraft.
Mar.–Jul. 1994	Close-in combat limited to 45° angle of attack to check the utility of going all the way to 70° angle of attack.
Sep. 1994	Adversary evaluations flown against USAF 422 Test and Evaluation Squadron F-15C and F-16C aircraft.
Aug. 2, 1994	First flight with a production-built F404 engine.
Aug. 4, 1994	Flight breaks the X-plane sortie record of 437, previously held by the X-29.
Nov.–Dec. 1994	Evaluation of post-stall maneuvering with a high angle of attack and high off-boresight-launch-capable missile.
Late 1994	Investigation of lateral/directional stability and control using thrust vectoring with a simulated tailless configuration throughout flight regime (including aircraft carrier approach and ground attack) in support of JAST program.
Jan. 1995	Fighting of a "virtual" enemy generated by onboard computers is demonstrated.

Date	Purpose and Comments
Jan. 19, 1995	Ship 1 (164584) lost following in-flight loss of control caused by pitot icing, with successful pilot ejection.
Early 1995	Flight test funding ends, with reporting period up to mid-1995.
Apr. 13, 1995	First flight (Ship 2) after crash of Ship 1; functional checkout of aircraft.
Apr. 13–28, 1995	Low-altitude envelope expansion in preparation for Paris Air Show.
May 4–16, 1995	Airshow practice for Paris Air Show at Edwards AFB.
May 20, 1995	X-31 loaded on USAF C-5A for flight to Manching, Germany.
May 29, 1995	First flight at Manching, Germany.
May 29– Jun. 2, 1995	Airshow practice at Manching.
Jun. 3, 1995	Ferry flight from Manching to Cologne to Paris.
Jun. 8, 1995	First flight at Paris; aircraft checkout.

Date	Purpose and Comments
Jun. 8–9, 1995	Airshow practice in Paris.
Jun. 10–18, 1995	Eight demonstration flights flown at Paris Air Show.
Jun. 19, 1995	Ferry flight from Paris to Cologne to Manching; last flight in the EFM program.
Jun. 24–25, 1995	X-31 flown from Manching to Edwards AFB on a USAF C-5A.
Jun. 28, 1995	X-31 Ship 2 placed in storage at Dryden.
Feb. 23, 1999	X-31 Ship 2 moved by flatbed truck to the Boeing facility at Palmdale, CA, to begin refurbishment for flight in the VECTOR program.
Mar. 2, 1998	Fit check of Swedish Saab JAS-39 Gripen fighter RM-12 engine (GE F404 engine derivative) in the X-31, and aircraft parts count begins at Dryden in preparation for the VECTOR program.
Apr. 11, 2000	X-31 transported from Palmdale to NAS Patuxent River by USAF C-5.
Feb. 20, 2001	Low- and high-speed taxi tests completed following extensive refurbishment at Patuxent River.
Feb. 24, 2001	First flight of VECTOR Phase 1 Flight Test (Reactivation Phase).
Apr. 6, 2001	Last flight of VECTOR Phase 1 Flight Test (Reactivation Phase).
Apr. 7, 2001	Start of aircraft modifications for ESTOL.
Mar. 27, 2002	Full systems checkout for ESTOL and low-speed taxi test, completing the ESTOL modification activity.

Date	Purpose and Comments
May 17, 2002	First flight of ESTOL Up And Away.
Mar. 22, 2003	Last flight of ESTOL Up And Away.
Apr. 3, 2003	First flight of ESTOL To The Ground.
Apr. 29, 2003	Last flight of ESTOL To The Ground at a 24° angle of attack approach; last flight of an X-31.

X-31 Pilots and Their Sorties

Pilot and Organization	Dates	Purpose	Sorties	Remarks
Ken Dyson **Rockwell**	10-11-90 thru 12-11-91	Contractor Test Pilot	27	Flew the first flight of Ship 1
Dietrich Seeck **DASA (MBB)**	11-6-90 thru 12-15-92	Contractor Test Pilot; ITO Pilot	38	Flew the first flight of Ship 2
Fred Knox **Rockwell**	11-15-90 thru 6-17-95	Contractor Test Pilot; ITO Pilot	128	Also flew in Paris Air Show
Karl-Heinz Lang **WTD-61**	3-15-91 thru 1-19-95	GPE 2 Test Pilot; ITO Pilot	117	Ejected safely from Ship 1 on 1-19-95
Maj. Bob Trombadore **USMC (NATC)**	4-24-91 thru 5-3-91	GPE 1 Test Pilot	2	
Maj. Karl-Heinz Mai **German Air Force (Luftwaffe)**	4-30-91 thru 5-2-91	GPE 1 Test Pilot	2	
Cmdr. Al Groves **USN (NATC)**	11-20-91 thru 4-21-94	GPE 2 Test Pilot; ITO Pilot	39	
Rogers Smith **NASA Dryden**	6-4-92 thru 4-28-95	ITO Pilot	80	
Lt. Col. Jim Wisneski **USAF (AFFTC)**	6-9-92 thru 2-10-94	ITO Pilot	44	

Pilot and Organization	Dates	Purpose	Sorties	Remarks
Maj. Quirin Kim Luftwaffe	7-20-93 thru 6-19-95	ITO Pilot	73	Also flew in Paris Air Show
Maj. Derek Hess USAF	2-23-94 thru 3-3-94	Guest Pilot	6	
Lt. Cmdr. Steve Schmidt USN	2-24-94 thru 3-3-94	Guest Pilot	7	
Ed Schneider NASA Dryden	3-29-94 thru 3-31-94	Guest Pilot	4	
Capt. Gus Loria USMC (NATC)	8-30-94 thru 1-19-95	ITO Pilot	13	
Cmdr. Vivian Ragusa USN (NATC)	2-24-01 thru 8-8-02	VECTOR Pilot	11	Flew the first VECTOR flight
Cmdr. Rudy Knöpfel German Naval Reserve	3-10-01 thru 4-28-03	VECTOR Pilot	41	
Maj. Cody Allee USMC (NATC)	9-4-02 thru 4-29-03	VECTOR Pilot	30	Flew the last X-31 flight on 4-29-03
Lt. Gerald Hansen USN (NATC)	11-19-02	VECTOR Pilot	1	

Acronyms and Abbreviations

2127	TV Servo Amp Fail Code
AA, A/A	Air-to-Air
AADS	Advanced Air Data System (see also FADS)
AAM	Air-to-Air Missile
a & b, a/b	Flight Control Overlays a and b
AB	Afterburner
A/C	Aircraft
ACA	Agile Combat Aircraft; Associate Contractor Agreement
ACC	Automatic Camber Control
ACD	Aerospace Change Directive
ACEVAL	Air Combat Evaluation
ACMI	Air Combat Maneuvering Instrumentation
ACT	Active Control Technologies
ACTIVE	Advanced Control Technology for Integrated Vehicles
ACX	Avion de Combat Experimental
ADC	Air Data Computer
ADFRF	Ames Dryden Flight Research Facility (see also DFRC)
Adm.	Admiral
ADS	Aircraft Dynamic Simulation
AEW	Airborne Early Warning
AFB	Air Force Base
AFCS	Aircraft Flight Control System (or Automatic Flight Control System)
AFFTC	Air Force Flight Test Center
AFRL	Air Force Research Laboratory
AFSC	Air Force Systems Command

AFSRB	Airworthiness and Flight Safety Review Board (NASA)
AFTI	Advanced Fighter Technology Integration
AFWAL	Air Force Wright Aeronautical Laboratory
A/G	Air-to-Ground
AGARD	Advisory Group for Aerospace Research and Development
AGL	Above Ground Level
AHRS	Attitude Heading Reference System
AIAA	American Institute of Aeronautics and Astronautics
AIL	Aileron
AIMVAL	Air Intercept Missile Evaluation
ALT	Altitude
amp	Amplifier
AOA, AoA	Angle of Attack (also expressed as α or Alpha)
AR	Analog Reversion (Flight Control System operating mode)
ARB	Air Reserve Base
ARPA	Advanced Research Projects Agency (see also DARPA)
A/S	Air Show
ASTOVL	Advanced Short Takeoff/Vertical Landing
ATF	Advanced Tactical Fighter
ATLAS	Adaptable Target Lighting Array System
AV	Aerospace Valley
Av	Avionics
AVEN	Axisymmetric Vectoring Exhaust Nozzle
BA, BASIC	Basic Airplane (no QT or TVV)
BAe	British Aerospace
B-B	Bank-to-Bank (rolls)
Beta, or β	Angle of Sideslip
BFM	Basic Fighter Maneuver
BIT	Built-In Test
BMV	Bundesministerium der Verteidigung (Federal Ministry of Defence, Germany)
BUR	Bottom-Up Review
BVR	Beyond Visual Range
BWB	Bundesamt für Wehrtechnik und Beschaffung (Federal Office of Defence Technology and Procurement, Germany)
CALF	Common Affordable Lightweight Fighter

Capt.	Captain
CASA	Construcciones Aeronauticas SA (Spanish aircraft company)
CAUT/WRN	Caution/Warning
C/B	Circuitbreaker
CCB	Configuration Control Board
CCDL	Cross-Channel Data Link
CCV	Control Configured Vehicle
CDR	Critical Design Review
CFD	Computational Fluid Dynamics
Ch	Channel
CHR	Cooper-Harper Rating Scale
CIC	Close-In Combat
CICP	Close-In-Combat Practice
CL	Centerline
Cmdr.	Commander
C/O	Check-Out
COD	Carrier On-Board Delivery
Col.	Colonel
CR	Cruise Configuration (normally "clean," with gear up)
CSCI	Computer Software Configuration Item
CTF	Combined Test Force
DARPA	Defense Advanced Research Projects Agency (see also ARPA)
DASA	Deutsche Aerospace AG
DDR&E	Department of Defense Research and Engineering
Decrab	Straighten flight path, removing drift correction and lining up with runway
DFBW	Digital Fly-By-Wire
DFCS	Digital Flight Control System
DFRF	NASA Dryden Flight Research Facility
DFRC	NASA Dryden Flight Research Center
DFS	Dual-Flug-Simulator
DGLR	Deutsche Gesellschaft für Luft- und Raumfahrt (German Society for Aeronautics and Astronautics)
DIS	Disabled
DLR	Deutsche Forschungsanstalt für Luft und Raumfahrt (German Center for Aviation and Space Flight)
DM	Deutsche Marks

DOD	Department of Defense
dof	Degrees of Freedom
EADS	European Aeronautic Defense and Space Company
EAFB	Edwards Air Force Base
EAP	Experimental Airplane Program
EASS	Emergency Air Start System
ECA	European Combat Aircraft
ECF	European Collaborative Fighter
ECM	Electronic Counter Measures
ECS	Environmental Control System
EFA	European Fighter Aircraft
EFM	Enhanced Fighter Maneuverability
EMI	Electromagnetic Interference
ES	Electronic Surveillance
ESTOL	Extremely Short Takeoff and Landing
EW	Electronic Warfare
FAA	Federal Aviation Administration
FADEC	Full-Authority Digital Engine Control
FADS	Flush Air Data System (see also AADS)
FBW	Fly-By-Wire
FCC	Flight Control Computer
FCF	Functional Check Flight
FCS	Flight Control System; Flight Control Software
FEST	Flight Estimated Thrust
FHILS	Flight-Hardware-in-the-Loop Simulation
FID	Fault Instrumentation and Detection
FL	Flight Level
FLOLS	Fresnel Lens Optical Landing System
FLT or Flt	Flight
FM	Frequency Modulation
FOD	Foreign Object Damage
FOV	Field of View
FQ	Flying Qualities
FQT	Flying Qualities Test
FRR	Flight Readiness Review
FSD	Full-Scale Development
FST	Full Scale Tunnel
FSW	Forward-Swept Wing
ft	Feet
FTB	Flutter Test Box
FTI	Flight Test Instrumentation

FY	Fiscal Year
G or g	Acceleration (1 g is equal to the force of gravity)
GAF	German Air Force (Luftwaffe)
GE	General Electric
GFE/P	Government Furnished Equipment/Property
GP	Guest Pilot
GPE	Government Performance Evaluation
GPO	Government Printing Office
GPS	Global Positioning System
HARV	High Alpha Research Vehicle
HAT	Height Above Terrain
HDD	Head-Down Display
HIKR	High Incidence Kinematic Roll
HiMAT	Highly Maneuverable Aircraft Technology
HL	High-Lift
HMD	Helmet Mounted Display
HQ	Handling Qualities
HQDT	Handling Qualities During Tracking
HSLA	High-Speed Line-Abreast
HST	High-Speed Tunnel
HTTB	High Technology Test Bed
HUD	Head-Up Display
HW	Hardware
Hz	Hertz
I-NIGHTS	Interim-Night Integrated and Head Tracking System
IABG	Industrieanlagen-Betriebsgesellschaft-GmbH (a German technology company)
IBLS	Integrity Beacon Landing System
ICAS	International Council of the Aeronautical Sciences
ICBM	Intercontinental Ballistic Missile
ID	Identification
INS	Inertial Navigation System
INU	Inertial Navigation Unit
IOC	Input and Output Controller
IPCS	Integrated Propulsion Control System
IRAAM	Infrared Air-to-Air Missile
ITB	Integrated Test Block (a series of test maneuvers done in sequence)
ITF	Integrated Test Facility
ITO	X-31 International Test Organization

JAST	Joint Advanced Strike Technology
JSF	Joint Strike Fighter
JTF	Joint Test Force
K2, p/δa	Roll Rate Gain
K-27	Lateral Stick Gain
KCAS	Knots Calibrated Airspeed
KEAS	Knots Equivalent Airspeed
kft	Thousands of Feet (measurement of altitude)
KIAS	Knots Indicated Airspeed
kN	Kilonewton
kt	Knots
LA	Los Angeles
LAAS	Local Area Augmentation System
LAT/DIR	Lateral/Directional
lb_f	Pound Force
L/D	Lift Over Drag Ratio
LEF	Leading Edge Flap
LFINS	Logic Failure of the Inertial Navigation System
LFTVS	Logic Failure of the Thrust Vectoring System
LGA	Longitudinal Gross Acquisition (of target)
LGAM	Longitudinal Gross Acquisition Maneuvers
LO	Low Oxygen
LQR	Linear Quadratic Regulator
LR1RQ	Logical for Reversionary Mode 1 Request
LRC	Langley Research Center
LSO	Landing Signal Officer
Lt.	Lieutenant, Left
LTEI	Left Trailing Edge Inboard
LTV	Ling-Temco-Vought
M	Mach number
MAC	Mean Aerodynamic Chord
Maj.	Major
MATV	Multi-Axis Thrust-Vectoring
MBB	Messerschmitt-Bölkow-Blohm (a German aerospace company)
MFE	Modified fighter escort
MIL	Military (maximum non-afterburning power setting)
MIL-SPEC	Military Specification
MLG	Main Landing Gear
MLS	Microwave Landing System

MOA	Memorandum of Agreement
MOU	Memorandum of Understanding
mph	Miles Per Hour
MRAD	Milliradian (a unit of angular measure)
MSL	Mean Sea Level (altitude as measured from sea level)
N_x	Longitudinal Acceleration in the X-axis
N_y	Lateral Acceleration in the Y-axis
N_z, n_z	Vertical Acceleration in Z-axis (commanded load factor)
N2S	Engine Rotational Measurement
NACA	National Advisory Committee for Aeronautics
NADC	Naval Air Development Center
NAS	Naval Air Station
NASA	National Aeronautics and Space Administration
NATC	Naval Air Test Center
NATO	North Atlantic Treaty Organization
NAVAIR	Naval Air Systems Command
NAVFAC	Naval Facilities Engineering Command
NAVSEA	Naval Sea Systems Command
NAVSUP	Naval Supply Systems Command
ND	Normal Digital (operating mode)
NKF	Neue Kampfflugzeug (New Warplane)
NORDO	No Radio
NTF	National Transonic Facility
OBS	Off-Boresight
OFP	Operational Flight Program
OIG	Office of the Inspector General
O&S	Operations and Support
OT&E	Operational Test and Evaluation
P_K	Probability of Kill
P_S	Probability of Survival, Specific Excess Power
PA	Power Approach (in gear-down aircraft configuration)
PC	Personal Computer
PCM	Pulse Code Modulation
PDR	Preliminary Design Review
PFB	Preflight Bit
PID	Parameter Identification
PIO	Pilot-Induced Oscillation
POPU	Push Over Pull Up (flight test maneuver)

PRV	Pressure Relief Valve
PST	Post-Stall Maneuverability; Pacific Standard Time
q	Dynamic Pressure
QT	Quasi-Tailless
R1, R2, R3	FCS Reversionary Modes: 1, INU; 2, AOA and sideslip; 3, air data
Radm.	Rear Admiral
RCFAM	Roll-Coupled Fuselage Aiming
R&D	Research and Development
RDT&E	Research Development Test and Evaluation
RIO	Radar Intercept Officer
RLE	Right Leading Edge
RM	Redundancy Management
ROE	Rules of Engagement
ROT	Rule of Thumb
ROTC	Reserve Officers' Training Corps
RPRV	Remotely Piloted Research Vehicle
Rt.	Right
RTADS	Real-Time All-Digital Simulation
RTB	Return to Base
RTO	Responsible Test Organization; NATO Research and Technology Organization
RTPS	Real Time Processing System (Control Room at NAS Patuxent River)
SA	Solenoid Actuator
SAS	Stability Augmentation System
SCW	Supercritical Wing
SETP	Society of Experimental Test Pilots
SFO	Simulated Flame Out
S&L	Straight and level
SNAKE	Super-Normal Attitude Kinetic Enhancement
SOW	Statement of Work
SPAWAR	Space and Naval Warfare Systems Command
SRB	Safety Review Board
SSLA	Slow-Speed Line-Abreast
SSWG	System Safety Working Group
STC	System Test Console
STEMS	Standard Test and Evaluation Maneuvers
STOL	Short Takeoff and Landing
STOVL	Short Takeoff and Vertical Landing
SW	Sensor Switch; Software

SYSCOMS	Systems Commands
TB	Tiebreaker
TEF	Trailing-Edge Flap
TEO	Trailing Edge Outboard
TES	Test and Evaluation Squadron
TIFS	Total In-Flight Simulator
TKF-90	Taktisches Kampfflugzeug 1990 (Tactical Combat Aircraft 90)
TM	Telemetry
T/O	Takeoff
T/R	Transformer/Rectifier
TTO	Tactical Technology Office (part of DARPA)
TUFT	Tactical Utility Flight Test
TV	Thrust Vectoring
TVV	Thrust-Vectoring Vane
T/W	Thrust to Weight
TW	Test Wing
UCAV	Unmanned Combat Air Vehicles
UHF	Ultrahigh Frequency
USAF	United States Air Force
USMC	United States Marine Corps
USN	United States Navy
VECTOR	Vectoring ESTOL Control Tailless Operation Research
VFC	Vortex Flow Control
VFW	Vereinigte Flugtechnische Werke (a German aerospace company)
VMAX or V_{max}	Maximum Velocity
VHF	Very High Frequency
V/STOL	Vertical/Short Takeoff and Landing
VST	Vertical Spin Tunnel
V&V	Verification and Validation
WAAS	Wide Area Augmentation System
WATR	Western Aeronautical Test Range
WOW	Weight On Wheels
WPAFB	Wright-Patterson Air Force Base
wrt	With Respect To
WSO	Weapons System Officer
w-t	Wind Tunnel
WTD	Wehrtechnische Dienststelle (Defence Technical Services, Germany)

WUT	Windup Turn
WVR	Within Visual Range
XST	Lockheed Have Blue Program (stealth airplane)

X-31 Lessons Learned: An Expanded View

The final reports discussed in Appendix 1 provide a great deal of information on lessons learned from the X-31 program. Lessons learned are also found in documents such as the *Ship 1 Mishap Report*, and in the various video and written reports that were created as a result of the accident. These lessons generally emerge from organizations associated with the X-31 program. Therefore, in this appendix they will be treated in that manner: as *lessons learned from X-31 organizations*. This appendix is an expansion of the information contained in Chapter 7 and Appendix 1, and it provides many lessons learned in *full text and detail* from the original sources. The author hopes that, since dissemination of many X-31 reports and technical papers has been minimal, this appendix will serve as a resource for managers, engineers, and test pilots on future programs.

Rockwell's Lessons

The Rockwell final report, *X-31 Enhanced Fighter Maneuverability Program Flight Test Final Report: Development of the X-31 Flight Test System* (Rockwell Report TFD-95-1563), contains several lessons learned. Some are embedded in sections such as "Flight Control System" and "Subsystems," and many are included in a large final section that will be discussed in a later portion of this appendix. In the "Flight Control Section," there is an explanation of the architecture of the X-31 flight control system, which contains a computer system that is basically a triplex system with a tiebreaker that was used after the second failure of a flight-critical function. The system has reversionary modes to handle failures of flight-critical sensors that are not quadruplex, such as the simplex INU or the duplex air data sensors. Rockwell's lesson learned relative to flight control architecture, quoted verbatim from the report, is,

The flight control laws, redundancy management and software design and maintenance would have been greatly simplified if all flight critical sensors and actuators were all quadruplex or all triplex. The need for reversionary control modes would have been eliminated and the software to handle different levels of redundancy would not have been necessary. And flight safety would have been enhanced. A lot of effort was expended to provide failsafe capabilities for the simplex INU and the duplex air data sensors.[1]

Flight control laws, an MBB (DASA) responsibility, are outlined in this Rockwell report. Rockwell's stated lesson learned gave great credit to the Germans:

DASA [MBB] did an excellent job in designing and developing the control laws as evidenced by the stunning results of the close-in-combat evaluations and the Paris airshow. This is the result of long-range planning, technical competence, and persistent pursuit of achieving a well-defined goal.[2]

Under "redundancy management (RM)," the report discusses flight control actuator RM, air data and INU RM, and engine sensor monitors, and it offers the following lesson learned:

The flight hardware-in-the-loop simulation (FHILS) has been critical in the development and evaluation of the redundancy management system. A thorough RM validation test matrix must be revised, reviewed and evaluated for each new software load to ensure that all flight safety concerns are addressed.[3]

Under "cockpit controls and displays," some of which were unique to the X-31 and developed for post-stall, quasi-tailless, and low-altitude flight, the importance of the early involvement of flight-test pilots is emphasized:

The flight test pilots must be involved in the definition of the cockpit control functions early in the design cycle and as the flight test program develops to ensure success.[4]

The "flight control computers" section emphasizes the development of ongoing versions of the flight software. It is noted that these software loads were developed with a relatively quick turnaround, allowing high sortie rates in the flight test. In explaining how this was achieved, the following lesson learned was offered:

The ability to achieve the high rate of X-31 flight tests at NASA Dryden is attributable to the co-location of the test engineers and the FHILS [flight-hardware-in-the-loop-simulation] simulation at the flight test site. Quick turnaround software overlays were defined, programmed in machine language, debugged and validated in the FHILS. Turnarounds as short as 3 days from the time of CCB [configuration control board] approval to flight test release were achieved with some overlays. In spite of the quick turnarounds, there have been no failures that affected flight safety because of a software overlay error.[5]

The section in this report on "subsystems" is rather extensive, and several lessons learned are gleaned from this section. These lessons are related to off-the-shelf flight-qualified equipment that, while imposing a weight penalty of 43 percent of the final weight, resulted in significant savings in program costs and schedule. Relative to the Government-furnished F/A-18 GE F404-GE-400 engine modified for single-engine use, the following lesson learned is provided without further explanation or rationale for the implementation of this modification:

> For thrust vectoring applications, special rigging of the lean-idle scheduling mode was required.[6]

The emergency air-start system was developed but not extensively flight-tested for the Northrup F-20. This system was powered by hydrazine, a very corrosive chemical that is hazardous to humans. The system had poor performance for the X-31 application due to excessive pressure buildup on the hydrazine-fuel-tank burst disks that caused fuel leaks, contamination of parts, and environmental alarms. These problems resulted in a redesign of the burst disks for a higher pressure and resulted in the following lesson learned:

> Before a system with set pressure tanks is used, it should be flight proven and parametrically evaluated for compatibility with the aircraft envelope and environment. Consideration should be given to other air start energy sources instead of hydrazine; the hazards and handling, shipping, and controlling of H-70 [hydrazine] are costly.[7]

Relative to the "electrical power generation and distribution system," there were problems with the Sundstrand generators that were initially chosen for the X-31 application. They were later changed to a Leland generator that proved to be reliable. This resulted in the following lesson learned:

The Sundstrand generators were not flight tested prior to X-31 use. This could have prevented many problems.[8]

The off-the-shelf cables that were used for communications between the flight control computers were too fragile for aircraft use, resulting in the following lesson learned:

Fibre-optic cables used for aircraft should be rated for rugged applications.[9]

Flying the X-31 in Europe involved significant electromagnetic interference (EMI) issues, and resolution of these issues required that the mission planners for Europe had to go back to the aircraft's EMI design to provide a baseline for determining clearances from high-power transmitters in Europe. EMI also proved to be problematic when the aircraft was flown at NAS Patuxent River in the VECTOR program. Rockwell stated that the resulting lesson learned, if it had been implemented at the time, would have saved the mission planners significant work:

When aircraft EMI levels are designed, entries/calculations should be included in the flight manual for separation required from high power transmitters (especially fly-by-wire aircraft).[10]

When the X-31 was designed, the fuel system was implemented as a simple single tank without baffles. This caused significant fuel sloshing at the very high angles of attack that the X-31 flew, which resulted in fuel-gaging inaccuracies and difficulty in computing accurately the center of gravity. The lesson learned was,

Design of fuel tanks for high alpha flight should consider adequate use of baffles to prevent slosh and/or means to use fuel flow information over the full engine operational envelope to derive fuel quantity.[11]

The environmental control system cabin pressure relief valve, which was from the F-5 aircraft, caused cabin pressurization "buzz" due to a part excessively wearing near the closed position. This resulted in the following lesson learned:

Selection and sizing of cabin pressure relief valve should be carefully matched to the aircraft cabin volume, bleed air input flow rate and cabin allowable leak rate to assure valve is not working at one end of its travel.[12]

The main landing gear wheels from the Cessna Citation III aircraft had fatigue cracks after 700 miles of use. In the VECTOR testing, these wheels would later prove unable to be operated over Navy arresting cables. During the EFM program, additional inspections at tire changes were used to assure safety. The following lesson learned resulted:

Wheel design should provide enough safety margin to allow usage over the expected life of the aircraft to prevent costly periodic inspections.[13]

When the spin chute was modified into a drag chute for operations in Europe, some flight testing of the system was done at Edwards but it was rushed due to the schedule pressure of getting the aircraft shipped to Europe. As a result, there were still failures of this system in Europe and fixes needed to be quickly found and implemented. Thus, the following lesson learned was identified:

More flights should have been made to assure reliability of design before committing the system to operational use. The number of flights available because of schedule constraints proved to be inadequate.[14]

The above are the only documented lessons learned that can be attributed to Rockwell and that resulted from the design, manufacture, and flight test of the X-31.

The Lessons Learned from the International Test Organization

Section 10 of the Rockwell report, *Development of the X-31 Flight Test System*, contains a very comprehensive and complete listing of lessons learned from the inception of the program to the return from the Paris Air Show. It is noted that these are not just Rockwell lessons learned but a compilation of inputs from all members of the ITO: government, contractor, U.S., and German. It is organized into the following subsections: Introduction, Engineering, Operations, Program Management, and Summary. The importance of these lessons learned is so significant that they are included here as a direct quote in their entirety.

Introduction

This section is a comprehensive review of the lessons learned during the X-31 program, from its inception through the return from the Paris Airshow 95. The section is divided into the subsections of Introduction, Engineering, Operations, Program Management and Summary. It is a compilation of inputs from all members of the X-31 ITO.

Engineering

FLIGHT CONTROL SYSTEM

The use of existing modern flight control law theory from the all-digital, fly-by-wire MBB F-104 and the incorporation of existing Honeywell all-digital fly-by-wire AOFS HTTB[15] [Emray Goossen, a X-31 flight control engineer of Honeywell, argues that "AOFS" is a typo and should be "AFCS (Aircraft Flight Control System)"] design experience was one of the two primary engineering initiatives (software & thrust vectoring) which enabled the successful achievement of the basic X-31 Enhanced Fighter Maneuverability (EFM) demonstrated goal.

The use of all-digital, fly-by-wire technology in prototype demonstrators is not new, however the use of the MBB modern flight control law theory as part of the technology to solve the post-stall, thrust vectoring control requirements is new and was a spectacular success!

The requirements for this innovation were successfully expanded to include quasi-tailless control at supersonic speeds, in the low-altitude power approach and ground attack modes and in low-altitude post stall maneuvering.

An integral and no less important part of the application were the reversionary modes incorporated in the software for failure control mitigation.

Any new prototype aircraft development or follow-on X-31 efforts should expand on and continue the use of this very successful technology.

THRUST VECTORING

The use of thrust vectoring control of the aircraft in pitch and roll/yaw at post-stall α [angle of attack] was the other of the two primary engineering initiatives contributing to the successful achievement of the basic X-31 EFM objectives.

When the concept of post-stall regime usage for fighter super maneuverability during close in combat was developed to the point of practical implementation, deflection of centerline engine thrust to achieve the required turning moments was the most viable option.

As a cost saving measure, thrust deflection was achieved in the X-31 design through the use of three vanes attached to the fuselage aft bulkhead. These vanes were developed by MBB and have dramatically exceeded the estimates of reliability and effectiveness. The cost saving vice an axi-symetrical [sic] nozzle were enormous at the time and made the program achievable.

Use of carbon-carbon composite material for thrust deflection vanes was successful, however, unknown environmental susceptibility had some impact on flight test operations.

The TV vane concept requires extensive in-flight calibration of plume boundary data and deflection effectiveness, if a large flight envelope and power setting spectrum are to be covered.

The use of thrust vectoring during X-31 quasi tailless testing also successfully demonstrated its effectiveness in aircraft control during subsonic and supersonic reduced tail and tailless scenarios.

Centerline engine thrust vectoring should be included in future supermaneuverable prototypes and in follow-on X-31 activities, particularly the installation of an axi-symmetrical nozzle for high α carrier approach and reduced tail/tailless flight test.

MODEL TESTS

An extremely cost effective but thorough series of aerodynamic tests were used to successfully develop the internal and external characteristics of the X-31.

The highly successful series of X-31 aerodynamic tests started at the beginning of program design development and continued throughout the program, until its completion.

The aerodynamic test facilities included the Swiss wind tunnel at Emden, the Langley 30x60 wind tunnel, the water pond and drop model. Included as part of the test series were the Rockwell low-speed and trisonic wind tunnels and the small-scale water tunnel. The NASA–Dryden Flight Research Center (DFRC) water tunnel was also used.

The aerodynamic characteristics designed into the X-31 as a result of this testing, allowed the aircraft to meet all initial program goals on schedule and at low cost, including the carefree maneuvering at high α needed for Close In Combat (CIC), supersonic flight to Mach 1.3 and the recent goals of supersonic and low altitude quasi tailless demonstration and low altitude post-stall maneuvering.

The series of tests used to develop and refine the highly successful X-31 aerodynamic characteristics should be used by the aerospace industry as a model for future prototype development and as a baseline for follow-on X-31 flight test.

PILOT VISUAL AIDS IN POST-STALL

The X-31 demonstrated that a helmet-mounted sight in conjunction with high-off-boresight capable missiles and high α close in combat capable aircraft would provide an overwhelming advantage to pilots of future super maneuverable combat aircraft. In addition, the possibility of pilot-aiding audio α & β [angle of attack and angle of sideslip] cues for situation awareness during high α flight, although not completely explored, certainly showed promise for future combat aircraft.

POST-STALL EFM

The X-31 demonstration of precision controlled thrust vectoring at high α to enhance close in combat was shown to be an insurmountable advantage against the world's best fighters and combat pilots. No other fighter or demonstrator can make this claim! Aerial combat in the future will almost certainly collapse into the within visual range arena. The victors of future combat engagements will be flying aircraft incorporating X-31 technology.

QUASI-TAILLESS FLIGHT DEMONSTRATIONS

The most dramatic lesson learned from the X-31 quasi tailless demonstrations were the near-term technological, cost and schedule benefits accrued from using a free-air, piloted simulator to validate wind tunnel and ground manned flight simulator results. This first of its kind in the world achievement was a clever way to safely validate the thrust vectored control of a tailless, unstable aircraft without removing the tail.

The use of this technology to fly supersonically and to demonstrate precision carrier approaches and air to ground maneuvers yielded invaluable data for future aircraft programs.

The barriers are down for the increased use of free-air piloted simulators in the near future!

FCS REDUNDANCY

Limited hardware redundancy in the flight control system is more expensive to the program, in the long term. The money saved on initial hardware cost is more than spent on software redundancy management as the program is executed. Primary, flight critical, sensors should not be derived from a single source; initial savings in hardware will turn into multiple costs later.

FCS "IRON BIRD"

Some limited "iron bird" capability is needed even for a research vehicle. Doing Flight Control System (FCS) integration on the aircraft itself delays final FCS development too long, could damage the aircraft and conflicts with other on-aircraft system test requirements. The program should have at least a representative test actuation system for each type of actuator on the aircraft. This would allow system integration and development on the FCS before the aircraft is ready to support the FCS. If some form of "iron bird" is not used, plan a few months in the schedule for on-aircraft FCS development.

Eliminating mockup and a dedicated iron-bird simulator achieved significant cost savings without the expenditure of design, construction, and maintenance funds for these facilities. No significant schedule savings were achieved by eliminating the iron bird because the same integration tasks still needed to be performed on the aircraft and system level integration could not start until the first aircraft had been completed and its electrical and hydraulic systems checked out. This resulted in the need for more efficient allocation of aircraft resources because other competing functions were also integrating various systems and subsystems on the aircraft. Also, more wear was accumulated on flight hardware due to the additional ground test time conducted on the aircraft.

An iron-bird simulator is not an absolute necessity in the flight control system integration process, but there are several trade-offs that must be considered.

The decision to include a dedicated iron bird strongly depends on the nature of the program in question - Small experimental programs can achieve cost savings, without the iron bird. Production programs can benefit from the iron bird by starting the overall systems integration prior to completion of the first aircraft.

DATA AND TELEMETRY

Use circularity polarized telemetry for an aircraft that is designed for maneuvers. This is both the aircraft and ground station.

ACTUATOR RM

Plan well for actuator redundancy management. Trying to monitor actuator servo loops with a bandwidth of 250 hz at 50 hz results in having to hand tailor failure thresholds. Little room is left between false alarms and unacceptable failure transients.

FCS TRANSPORT DELAYS

Measuring digital propagation delays in the FCS is difficult and the results have large effects on stability analysis. Measuring techniques and analysis procedures need to be defined at the beginning of FCS design so that everyone is working to the same model and requirements.

SIMULATION

The digital simulation allowed rapid testing of control law modifications. It also provided an easy to use tool for pre-flying the planned test cards without the requirement to bring up the full hardware simulation. The tool was much easier to use than a full up hardware simulation. The digital simulation was used with a full dome and flat screen. Though a flat screen was adequate, many of the post stall maneuvers required a dome (360° view) to perform the maneuver.

Flight hardware-in-the-loop simulation is an essential tool for development, verification, and validation of complex fly-by-wire flight control system software.

Flight Hardware in the Loop Simulation (FHILS) included the four flight control computers and flight software. This provided for verification and validation of the FCS hardware and software in a real time manned simulation. FHILS provided the primary development and testing tool for FCS redundancy management.

An automated software checkout capability such as that provided by the STC [System Test Console[16]] on the X-31 is critical to the successful and timely integration of a complex digital flight control system.

Flight-hardware-in-the-Loop-Simulation (FHILS) is a useful tool for software verification and validation, however, high fidelity sensor and actuator models are required.

High fidelity simulation (real-time and batch) is the most important tool for:
- Control law and redundancy management software development
- Non linear flying quality assessment
- Envelope expansion support

A fixed base simulator with a "flat plate" visual system is sufficient for FCS development, flying quality assessment and envelope expansion support.

A user-friendly simulation interface with flexible data recording capabilities with the possibility to introduce control law and model modifications, is essential for fast software development and flight test progress.

HELMET MOUNTED DISPLAY (HMD)

The tracker is a very important part of the HMD system and it was quickly discovered on the X-31 program that if tracker performance is poor the resulting action (for aircraft, planform stabilized symbology) is that the pilot finds the jitter and lag of the symbols (Flight Path Marker, Gun Piper) to be unusable and would de-clutter it. This forced the tracker to be used as a head position system that fed a head stabilized piper to enable missile cueing and lag jitter would be lost in the hysteresis of the symbology changes (Piper is dashed when out side [sic] of the defined missile cone). Desired tracker performance - zero lag and zero jitter.

The situational awareness symbology set was unnecessary in the environment at Edwards AFB where the sky is always blue and the ground is brown. However, the missile symbology was invaluable to the pilot during CIC. Pilot comfort factor with HMD symbology took at least 3 flights. Pilots were so use to looking at the HUD or Head down displays for information, that they forgot it is right in front of them even when looking to the left right or up down in the cockpit.

The value of symbology de-clutter function was validated by flight test. The center of the Field of View (FOV) was desired by the pilot for clarity of the aggressor in the pilots FOV. De-clutter options already programmed in the software became invaluable to the pilot to depopulate the center of the HMD FOV, and allow just the piper to be present, with air speed and ALT [altitude] displays.

It was found that if the helmet liner was not correctly positioned the pilot would not be centered in the HMD FOV and during maneuvers, the pilot would momentarily loose the HMD symbology. When fitted correctly, no problems were encountered.

It was found in the early days of the X-31 HMD program, that when the pilot was being secured in the cockpit by the support crew, that the HMD helmet cable was being pulled and tugged. This caused failure of the HMD due to broken wires in the quick disconnect. Briefing the support crew to not pull on the helmet cable corrected that failure.

Being able to reprogram the HMD system via a portable PC was invaluable in the symbology development for the program. Software was extracted from the GEC VAX[17] link via modem to the PC and then, using the 1553 data link[18] in the HMD, the system, was re-programmed.

The VIPER I HMD was so successful during the X-31 flight test that it has enabled the subcontractor GEC Marconi to progress with the VIPER II HMD to be flight tested on an AV-8B at China Lake NWC, as part of a JAST test program.

CONTROL LAWS

LQR [Linear Quadratic Regulator[19]] control law design with gain scheduling was successful.

Stability analysis via single loop cuts proved to be adequate to provide sufficient stability margins.

Proportional and integral feedback of stability axis roll rate and sideslip at high angle of attack helps to reduce steady-state errors due to model uncertainty.

Roll about the velocity vector and aircraft control via stick only (except for intended sideslip) at high α proved to be a very successful concept.

A roll mode time constant below 0.25 should be avoided (roll ratcheting).

A maximum roll rate of 290°/sec (initial design requirement) is too high.

AERODYNAMICS

High angle of attack aerodynamic asymmetries need to be considered early in the design (a blunt nose and nose strakes tend to reduce high-alpha asymmetries considerably).

Modifications to the aircraft effecting [sic] the aerodynamic characteristics need to be implemented in the simulation as early as possible to avoid misleading V&V results (pitching moment change due to modified aft fuselage shape).

Pitching moment story at high α - Two wind tunnels, similar models (both 19%, but with different afterbodies), different installation method (sting vs. strut), got different results (30x60 showed pitch-up wrt [with respect to] Emmen[20]). At the time, we weren't sure why (installation method/model afterbody/facility/etc.). Drop model predictions leaned toward the pitch-up result, but not as strongly as shown in 30x60 strut-mount test. Flight test results started to track the drop model prediction. Suspecting that the afterbody was the culprit indicated that a simple strake solution could be had (vs. the more time consuming and expensive alternatives such as canard resizing/relocation/etc.)[.] Results: Followed a very productive Path: (a) derived incremental nose-down requirements/guidelines (b) proposed candidate strake designs (incorporating real issues such as permissible locations for attaching "after-market" pieces, realistic load-restricted size limits, etc.); (c) narrowed the field down to a single candidate strake design that provided sufficient nose-down moment, yet uncertain for the strakes effects under dynamic conditions: (d) quickly validated pitching moment effectiveness and got a global evaluation of the strake's effect on dynamics (departure susceptibility/spin/etc,) using drop model.

Yaw asymmetry - very similar story in that: (i) what static w-t [wind tunnel] prediction to believe? (ii) aircraft shows phenomenon; (iii) using body of knowledge develop nose treatment (radius/strakes) and do initial evals in the wind-tunnel to thin the candidates; (iv) assess the chosen treatment "globally & quickly" with drop model.

Discovery of the HIKR [High Incidence Kinematic Roll[21]] mode-(i) Uncovered during drop model tests-this is precisely what the drop model technique excels in and was developed for (drop model testing is the only model technique that reliably predicts the flight behavior resulting from large amplitude or highly dynamic maneuvering-intentional or otherwise. It is the sole model-based means to explore departures, spin entries and the like). Also, remember the "pre-discovery" events during free-spinning tests, but too little confidence.(ii) Defined "parameters" using drop model such as entry methods, severity, recoverability, control law concepts to avoid HIKR, etc. (iii) using the drop model results as a guide, we were able to direct captive wind-tunnel studies to determine the underlying causes of HIKR. Recommend that we do comparisons between drop model HIKR and the last flight of ship 1.

SUBSYSTEMS AND COMPONENTS

In general the X-31 subsystems and components, most of which were off the shelf, performed as expected, with as expected maintenance. Note worthy exceptions are discussed in the following paragraphs:

Drag Chute Inadequacies - A newly designed drag chute was installed in place of the spin chute because of the short runways to be encountered in Europe. Deployment door complexity problems were corrected by replacement with a simple string/strap combination. Premature drag-chute separation, caused by a riser fraying on the runway due to a lower than required deployment angle, was corrected by riser beefup with stronger, larger diameter, material and replacement of the drag chute with a new unit after every deployment. It is recommended that future designs be refinements of existing successful drag chutes. Also, it is recommended that the existing drag chute and spin chute not be reinstalled for X-31 follow-on, unless absolutely required for safety of flight and the drag chute deployment angle is corrected to compensate for X-31 α at deployment.

Electric Generator-The original generator was a Sundstrand V-22 unit which was inadequate for X-31 requirements due to a liquid cooling mechanization failure which caused generator shut downs due to overheating. This problem was initially mitigated by control-room monitoring of a generator temperature sensor.

Final resolution was obtained by replacing the V-22 unit with a F-18 Eldec unit.

Ejection Seat - The X-31 Martin-Baker ejection seat contains a 17-foot diameter parachute, designed for F-18 combat operations. NASA Dryden is working to qualified [sic] a 24-foot parachute for use in the Martin-Baker ejection seats of their F-18 chase aircraft. It is recommended that this parachute be installed in the X-31 ejection seat for any follow-on flight test and that other and future programs verify that, where possible, high descent rate combat parachutes are not installed in the ejection seats of non-combat aircraft.

Environmental Control system (ECS) - The ECS provided excessive cabin air flow to the cockpit, resulting in high cockpit noise. Also the F-5 Cabin Pressure Relief Valve (PRV) had a failure mode which caused loud buzzing in the cockpit attributed to premature PRV valve stem wear from excessive usage near the closed position. This problem should be investigated thoroughly in future designs and mitigated for X-31 follow on.

Emergency Air Start System (EASS) - This F-20 system was not extensively flight tested and turned out to be incompatible with the X-31 pressure environment. Costly schedule delays were caused by leakage from the hydrazine propellant tank burst discs. The problem was resolved by increasing the disc burst pressure from 32 PSI to 50 PSI. Also, EASS spares were very inadequate. The system was removed from the aircraft prior to Paris Airshow 95. It is recommended that before use on future programs consideration be given to energy sources other than hydrazine. It is also recommended that this system not be reinstalled for follow on X-31 programs.

FCC Throughput - FCC throughput margin approached the point of concern, resulting in control room monitoring toward the end of envelope expansion. This was adequate for the recently completed program but does not afford the flexibility and increased throughput needed for projected modifications. For follow on X-31 activities, it is recommended that increased FCC throughput be seriously considered.

VALIDITY OF INTERNAL & EXTERNAL LOADS PREDICTIONS

Without Wind Tunnel Loads Data - The predicted loads derived without wind tunnel data that the X-31 was designed to meet were extremely accurate. In addition, the aircraft structural design was very conservative, and the aircraft was limited to 80% of design limit load, throughout the program. As a result, no loads issues were encountered. Vertical stabilizer buffet at 50 α which required beef up on the NASA HARV, was not a problem on the X-31. The new envelope expansion requirements imposed by subsonic and supersonic quasi-tailless flight test were marginally close to the 80% limit in a few cases easily mitigated by minor envelope restrictions with no impact on test objectives.

DESIGN FOR LOW COST

The use of off-the-shelf major components was a key driver in successfully meeting the X-31 program goal of demonstrating a "low-cost" prototype aircraft.

The X-31 design incorporated a significant amount of off-the-shelf major components. This was one of the key Drivers in successfully meeting the "low-cost" prototype program objective.

The use of off-the-shelf major components was imbedded in the design of the X-31 from its inception. Rockwell, Daimler Benz and the customer, NAVAIR, worked as a team in the successful procurement of these components from ongoing production and prototype programs.

These components included but were not limited to F-16 landing gear, Cessna Citation wheels, tires & brakes, F-18 windshield/canopy, instrument panel ejection seat & engine, XV-22 hydraulic/electric primary and secondary control surface actuators and C-130 High Technology Test Bed (HTTB) flight control computers.

Additional advantages to this policy included in-place repair and replacement sources, minimal airworthiness requirements and in-place maintenance procedures.

The savings of this design policy as opposed to design, develop and procurement from scratch would easily exceed the total cost of the X-31 program ($255M).

Operations

For a research flight test program it is essential that flight clearance be granted at the test location. The basic nature of the program requires change and remote clearance authority can significantly delay program progress.

Clear, specific program milestones and objectives are the key to test success and meeting schedule.

The benefits of an integrated team take time to realize. The first six months is inefficient due to duplicated efforts and the need for each team member to learn the culture of the various organizations and for the integrated team to evolve its own processes.

The X-31 aircraft was safely flown with flight control through-put up to 85% of maximum. With levels this high, need real time monitoring of through-put up and simulation to observe the effects of exceeding throughput limits.

Dual Dome Close In Combat (CIC) Simulation: Simulation allowed tactics development and provided a much more efficient test program. Effective use of post stall in CIC was much easier in the aircraft than in the simulator.

Flying a post stall aircraft was a natural extension of conventional flying. Pilots adapted rapidly and were capable of aggressive post stall maneuvers after only 2–3 flights in the aircraft.

In general the X-31 was easy to maintain. Noteworthy exceptions are discussed in the following paragraphs:

Control Surface Freeplay Measurement Setup - The original periodic inspection test using a static measurement technique was very time consuming. A significant reduction in the time required was made at NASA Dryden by implementation of a dynamic technique. It is recommended that use of the dynamic freeplay measurements technique be implemented on fly-by-wire aircraft programs where tight freeplay tolerances required.

Flight Control Computer (FCC) fiber-optic cable data links - Continual problems were encountered during the X-31 program keeping the FCC fiber optic data links clean and free from damage. Numerous cables and all of the FCC connectors were replaced due to cable fragility. It is recommended that robust and flightworthy fiber-optic cables be used in X-31 follow on and future aircraft designs.

Flight Test Instrumentation (FTI)/Flight Control System (FCS) - Some X-31 signals required for FCS operation are computed by the FTI system. This imposed undesirable support problems and in-flight risk. It is recommended that this mechanization be avoided in future designs.

Trailing Edge Flap Actuator Piston Wear-The use of trailing edge flap actuators with non solid pistons caused premature wear, control surface freeplay anomalies and time consuming delays. The pistons were replaced with a solid design which resolved the wear problem and allowed extension of the freeplay interval. The use of non solid piston actuators in fly-by-wire control surface actuators is not recommended.

EMI European Safety of Flight Clearance - To obtain safety of flight clearance for ferry flight in Europe, X-31 EMI fly-by-wire design data was used as a baseline to calculate and predict separation requirements to high powered transmitters. It is recommended that when aircraft EMI levels are designed, these separation requirements be included in the flight manual.

Fuel Tank Gaging Inadequacy-The X-31 fuel tank capacitance probe gaging system provides inaccurate fuel quantity readings to the pilot at high α. This problem, caused by fuel slosh, consumed valuable flight time to level off and get accurate readings. The situation was improved by displaying a reading in the control room derived from integrated flow meter data. It is recommended that the design of fuel tanks for high α flight consider adequate baffling or on-board derivation of the pilot fuel quantity indication from integrated flow-meter data.

Main Landing Gear (MLG) Wheel cracks-The X-31 MLG wheels are Cessna Citation units slightly modified to fit on an F-16 MLG. An X-31 wheel failed during taxi, late in the program. An investigation showed fatigue cracks on the wheel inner bead after approximately 700 miles of usage vice a quality life of 1,130 miles. The resolution was inspecting the wheels for cracks at each tire change and replacing the cracked wheels. Operationally, taxi maneuvering limits were imposed to reduce wheel side loads. It is recommended that this resolution be continued for X-31 follow on.

The Benefits of Built In Test (BIT)-BIT reduced X-31 preflight time considerably. Rapid turn around for multiple flight days would be impossible, without BIT. It is well worth the design and implementation cost, even on a low-cost demonstration aircraft.

Rapid Flutter Flight Data Analysis - During flutter envelope expansion to Mach 1.3 at NASA Dryden, the NASA automated wide-band data reduction/analysis facilities were used. This reduced continued expansion flight clearance turn-around time from one week to one day. It is recommended that facilities of this type be used on future programs, including X-31 follow on.

X-31 Flight Test Meetings and Procedures:

0800 Daily Status Meetings, ITO Bi-Weekly Program Reviews and Monthly ITO Council Meetings-These meetings were key to X-31 ITO communications and contributed to an extremely smooth running operation.

Mini-Technical Briefings, Technical Briefings, Flight Readiness Reviews (FRRs) and Airworthiness Flight Safety Review Boards (AFSRBs) - These presentations to NASA-Dryden management were used to obtain clearance to proceed with new activities, to provide updated program status, to obtain new software release approvals, to proceed with anomaly corrective action and to proceed in flight with the corrective action incorporated. The presentations are listed in the order of presentation complexity and the size of NASA management representation. We learned to have a well constructed and thorough presentation in every case and to dry run it to ourselves, prior to the presentation. We never failed to obtain the requested clearance at the meeting. The clearance process was a great improvement over that used prior to moving to NASA Dryden.

Flight crew Briefs, Flight Card Reviews, Weather Briefs and Flight Crew Debriefs-These are standard meetings developed by Rockwell and used with great success at NASA Dryden. They are similar to those used on other flight test programs. Their use should be continued for X-31 follow on.

Program Management

GENERAL

The use of customer/contactor negotiated and agreed to limitations on specifications, drawings and procedures and rigorous tailoring of the ones that were required was the cornerstone achievement in successfully meeting the X-31 program goal of demonstrating a "low-cost" prototype aircraft on schedule and within cost.

The X-31 program success can be directly attributed to the relaxation of the overwhelming quantity of rigid specification, drawing and procedure requirements normally imposed on the development of a demonstration aircraft.

The use of limited and tailored specifications, drawings and procedures greatly reduced the time and expense required to design the X-31. In addition, the follow-on activities of fabrication, assembly, checkout and flight operations were greatly enhanced by this policy.

The use of streamlined configuration management, manufacturing planning, checkout/ramp and flight test planning methods reduced their cost and time to complete through first flight below that of earlier and contemporary prototype aircraft. This program could not have been done without this policy. The economic and schedule benefits accrued to every aspect of the X-31 are incalculable.

This method of procurement is being adopted by a DoD initiative, not only for prototypes but also for production aircraft. The X-31 is a living example of its success.

THE MULTIPLE BENEFITS OF SUCCESSFUL
INTERNATIONAL TEAMING & CO-LOCATION

The X-31 is the only international x plane. The transfer of technical information between the German, British and American [This must have been an error since the British did not participate in the program.] members of the team was constant and without inhibition. This multicultural exchange provided a fresh approach to the solution of difficult technical problems, was a basis for lowering the interorganizational cultural barriers of each participating nation and resulted in a serendipitous increase in the value returned for each team member investment.

When the X-31s were moved from Palmdale to NASA Dryden Flight Research Center (DFRC), the organizational members of the team became the X-31 International Test Organization (ITO) and were collocated in Bldg. 4840. The aircraft, the manned flight simulator, pilots, the aircraft operations personnel, the flight test engineering and planning personnel and 90% of contractor and government design engineering needed to analyze, model and simulate flight data and then provide corrective action were all in Bldg. 4840.

NASA Dryden also provided outstanding on-site chase plane support, jet engine support, crew systems support and state of the art control room and in-flight optical tracking support.

Because safety of flight and configuration management responsibilities were transferred from NAVAIR to NASA DFRC, all of the segments of the ITO needed to approve continuation of flight were in residence. This collocation was a great boon to communications, team bonding and the achievement of program goals on schedule and under budget.

There has been an ongoing attempt by the aerospace community to take advantage of the collocated organization for flight test and evaluation. The location of design engineering at the test site is a key factor in the equation. The X-31 program is an extremely successful example of this philosophy.

PROGRAMMATIC

Significant lessons were passed along to the aerospace industry from the successful incorporation and flight demonstration of Aircraft 1 mishap mitigation measures.

A thorough post-mishap analysis and mitigation design effort was done in coordination with the mishap investigation team and ITO management. This was followed by the incorporation of approved software and hardware mishap mitigation measures. Simulation and in-flight validation were done where appropriate. The X-31 was returned to flight status four months from the mishap date, with NASA safety of flight approval.

The test pilot and flight test engineer are valuable members of the initial design team and should be part of the initial design effort.

Program reports should be written on an incremental basis with periods not exceeding one year. Writing a final report covering a period of many years after most program personnel and budgets are gone loses much of the data.

Build at least two research aircraft when doing a flight test program. The second aircraft allows comparison and understanding of unique aerodynamic characteristics, provides backup if one aircraft is lost and allows a more productive test program by flying one aircraft while the other is being modified or maintained.

Up to six pilots at a time were active on the X-31 program. The large number of pilots had both good and bad points.

Each organization was able to have an active pilot in the program which enhanced team interest. The pilots were able to provide direct inputs on aircraft performance to their parent organizations.

The varied backgrounds and experience of the pilots added significantly to the technical expertise of the team.

At times it was difficult to provide adequate flying for each pilot. In general a simple rotation was used. During the CIC phase, pilot teams were rotated.

Each pilot must make special efforts to stay current on the aircraft and test status.

The relatively simple systems and excellent flight characteristics of the X-31 were the main reason the large pilot team was successful. A more complex aircraft or flight test plan may work better with a smaller pilot team.

It is crucial that participants who will provide program and funding support be clearly defined in writing and that all managers of the organizations be amply briefed prior to initiation of the program. In particular, it is important to include requirements managers and their staffs to ensure continuing support when management heads move to other jobs or retire.

Substantial support in getting funding support and approval to proceed with a program can be obtained from important fleet potential users of the technology. Establishing advocates such as TOP GUN pilots and their commanders and obtaining their support in writing and by using them in person, in briefings [sic] lends credibility to the importance of the program.

In a program where numerous contract modifications and forms preparation are necessary to keep the program progressing smoothly, it is critical to establish a process, clearly defined and agreed to by the participants that is doable within an organization's structure without creating frequent stress and interference with other on-going programs.

Solicit suggestions from the individuals who will be responsible for the day-to-day actions and strongly encourage them to help develop the most efficient, least paperwork way of getting the job done. What is not often realized is that a unique method of operations for your program can be established which can provide a way to get things done quickly without the usual paperwork. Push management to support you in developing quick methods of doing things.

Paperwork management is crutial [sic] considering current regulations and policy emphasizing reducing requirements. Program technical support personnel generally still conform to old methods of conducting acquisition programs and frequently utilize specifications which could be reduced in content and still meet safety requirements for a technology program. It behooves a program manager to work closely with them to encourage limiting requirements and to "tailor" to specific requirements for the project.

An example (utilized by X-31) is the elimination of most reliability/maintainability requirements when the aircraft is designed for limited life and does not have to meet the carrier/sea environment. What is imminently sensible and logical may not prevail. Push your technical staff to consider other and better ways to get the job done.

Innovative engineering should be considered when initiating a unique technology program (which most are). Careful consideration should be given to novel methods to attain goals of reducing cost, expediting schedule and reducing inventories. Examples are: low-cost prototyping, using the actual aircraft or equipment as the test vehicle rather than an iron bird, utilization of components and substructures from other vehicles and designing the vehicle to be compatible with existing ground support vehicles (as should be the case with most acquisition programs).

However, special care must be taken to ensure that this process does not create unacceptable risk to the manufacturing process (e.g., using the aircraft as the load test vehicle could result in a failure which could prevent recovery of schedule if the failure were severe).

A large degree of success of a program lies with the clearly defined priorities that a program has, both in available manpower (critical in a matrix organization) and materials. Ensure you have in writing the highest priority you can get in these required assets. Further, ensure that the priorities allow you to realistically meet your schedule.

Unless cost factors are crucial or a contractor cannot obtain materials when needed, a program manager should attempt to require the contractor to provide all parts and materials. However, if the government is to provide all or some of the parts and materials, then establishing a high priority isn't enough. You must survey and place orders to ensure parts and materials are available when needed in the manufacturing/assembly process or serious delays and cost growth can ensue.

Program management of the engineering process is essential in a technology program where low cost and ambitious schedules are the norm. The process of engineering development requires a rigid, uniform review process to catch problems and redirect the effort. Weekly reviews of the process, broken down to subtopics such as engineering, manufacturing, assembly, logistics, testing, cost accounting etc. is an excellent way to monitor progress and prevent delays and overruns.

When several government agencies, including foreign government participation, are part of the program it is crucial to fully understand the philosophy of how each organization works. Does one organization require extensive analysis and simulation before releasing a design? Does one have a single individual who can make critical decisions before design and manufacture can proceed? Prior to initiation of the design process, an intensive review of each organization's methods of operation should be understood and agreements reached by managers on a clear operations plan integrating all participants.

The X-31 program expanded the thrust vector controlled 70° α post-stall envelope from 12,000 to 500 ft minimum altitude. No other aircraft has provided the aerospace community with precision high angle of attack control in this environment. This capability was dramatically demonstrated before the world at Paris Airshow 95. This was the technical highlight of the show and stimulated enthusiastic international interest in the benefits of X-31 EFM technology.

Summary

The X-31 Program, as in all experimental aerospace programs, had the primary objective of passing lessons learned to government and industry. This section of the final report summarizes the most significant lessons learned and provides a forum and solicitation for inquiries and additional analyses. There has been no attempt to emphasize the good and de-emphasize the bad. There were an overwhelming number of positive X-31 lessons, but we have included the negative as well and the corrective/mitigation actions already incorporated and /or recommended. The recipients of this report will recognize, through this section, the major contribution the X-31 Program has made to the future of supermaneuverable combat aircraft."[22]

MBB (DASA) Lessons

The DASA (MBB) Final Report does not list "lessons learned" per se, but it does have a considerable discussion on "conclusions" that will be discussed later in this appendix. It can be assumed that many MBB lessons learned are incorporated into the ITO lessons learned discussed previously. One comment that could be construed as a lesson learned is the statement, "The X-31 EFM Program set several records for flight test efficiency and productivity and serves as a benchmark for future international cooperation and achievement."[23] This reaffirms the usefulness of cooperative international programs in technology demonstration, and while much of the media spotlight is on international cooperation in astronautical endeavors such as the International Space Station, it is a lesson worth learning from the X-31 program that international aeronautical programs are very useful as well.

Dryden's Lessons

Since Dryden was a flight-test organization primarily responsible for safety of flight and flight clearance and not a management organization, it is natural to see that the lessons learned produced by Dryden deal with flight-test conduct and, in particular, the accident that resulted in the loss of Ship 1. This is not to say that there were no other "lessons learned" in the flight-test area; in fact, many are enumerated under ITO Lessons in the preceding sections. One lesson that is of particular note is worth repeating here:

> For a research flight test program it is essential that flight clearance be granted at the test location. The basic nature of the program requires change and remote clearance authority can significantly delay program progress.[24]

One of the major reasons for the move from Palmdale to Dryden at Edwards was the perceived length of time it took the management organization,

NAVAIR, in Washington, DC, to provide flight clearances to the flight test organization, Rockwell, at Palmdale during the early days of the program. Having flight clearance authority reside at Dryden was one of the reasons that the ITO, and ultimately the X-31 flight-test program, was so successful.

As a result of the accident, NASA Dryden produced a video entitled *X-31 Breaking the Chain, Lessons Learned.* In this video are a number of lessons learned that will be summarized below.

It was suggested that participants in an experimental aircraft test program "do their homework" by studying all mishaps of experimental aircraft in the last 20 years.

With respect to configuration control, it was noted that the inoperative pitot heat switch was not placarded, an action that may have alerted the pilot to its status has it been performed. Additionally, while notices of the change in pitot heat were sent out, there was no mechanism to ensure that the information had actually been received and read by the recipient.

Single point failures such as pitot heat were noted as early as 1989, 6 years before the accident, but complacency crept into the test team and this information was not revisited or reviewed in the later years of the program. As John Bosworth, NASA Dryden chief engineer, pointed out, there used to be a sign posted in the control room that read, "Prepare for the unexpected and expect to be unprepared."

Another point on the subject of complacency was noted: the flight that ended in the accident was the *last* scheduled data mission for Ship 1, it was the *last* data point on that mission, and it was the *last* mission of that day. People started relaxing thinking that they were done…but they were not done!

Communications were allowed to become suboptimal. There were sidebar communications in the control room that dealt with the lack of pitot heat on the Kiel probe, but the rest of the control room did not hear them. Due to problems with the retransmission of telemetered X-31 pilot radio transmissions, this was not available to the chase pilot. Excellent communication is vital to a successful flight-test program.

If something occurs that someone on the test team observes and does not understand, they should call a halt, perhaps only temporarily, to the test process until this issue is resolved. As Rogers Smith, the Dryden project pilot, stated, "stop the train" when things are not right.

Ken Szalai, the Dryden director at the time, observed that all flight testers should "learn from all accidents, even close calls!"[25] When a flight test team becomes "mature" and comfortable after years of testing a given airplane, they should look back and review all of their assumptions about the airplane and their procedures. Most important, *everyone* on the team should understand that they are a part of the "accident chain" and are responsible for safety of flight.

Preceding the production of the X-31 Lessons Learned video, Rogers Smith gave a presentation to the 1996 Society of Experimental Test Pilots Symposium entitled *X-31 Accident: Lessons to be Learned*. His summary slide has the following "Lessons to be Learned," which are the same or similar to what was later covered by the video but are of sufficient importance to be quoted directly from his slide:

> If you Do Not Understand or it Does Not Make Sense:
>
> 1) SPEAK UP!
> 2) STOP THE TESTS AND THINK!
> Communicate to all test players
> In the face of the Unexpected:
> Know the Quick System Path to Safety
> There is No Substitute for Good Flight Test Judgment
> Accidents Do Not Just Happen to "THEM"
> They Happen to "YOU"[26]

U.S. Navy Lessons

As with the MBB lessons learned, the Navy through NAVAIR did not specifically comment on lessons learned for the EFM program; however, one can assume that their lessons were incorporated in the ITO lessons discussed above. The Navy did write a three-volume final report on the X-31 VECTOR program, and this report is replete with lessons learned; each volume even has a section devoted to lessons learned.

Beginning with the first volume of the Navy VECTOR report, *X-31 VECTOR Final Report—Volume I—The Program*, there are several lessons learned that warrant inclusion in this appendix. The inclusion of foreign nationals—the Germans—in the program required a considerably more innovative and thorough access process for NAS Patuxent River than had been required at NASA Dryden on Edwards AFB. This resulted in the following lesson learned:

> Expect security issues to require a great deal more effort to work, especially when dealing with foreign nationals.[27]

Another security problem faced by the VECTOR team was the initial inadequacy of the NAS Patuxent River Visit Request system, which resulted in the following lesson learned:

Allow considerable dedicated time if trying to set up anything unusual security-wise.

Never assume the security 'system' will function properly to admit people onto the base, even when all entries of establishing the visit request and 'scheduling' the visitor have been accomplished.[28]

The VECTOR program fell victim to the "requirements creep" that is typical of many programs, in which new requirements are generated and made a part of the program after contract award. Also, delays in getting authorization to commence work and unforeseen maintenance and engineering issues caused the schedule to slip to the right. The resulting lesson learned is probably applicable to any complex technology program:

It took much longer and cost much more than even the experts could predict.[29]

The support of senior management for a program is always important. It is even more important when the type of program—science and technology—is not perceived to be a core mission (which was weapons system development, in the case of NAS Patuxent River) of the supporting organization. The following lesson learned resulted from this observation:

Upper level management's vision and direction to support is needed repeatedly when conducting a non-traditional program. Without high- level intervention, the program would have been buried as a low priority and would have failed. Lack of working level support can kill a program, even when funding is available.[30]

Funding limitations forced the VECTOR program to use part-time NAVAIR engineers to support their program. The conflict of priorities on these engineers' tasking dogged the program:

Relying on part-time USN engineering and suffering a severe lack of priority leads to schedule slides, lost productivity, lost flight test opportunities and "just in time" delivery at best.[31]

Remembering that many of the subsystems in the X-31 were composed of off-the-shelf parts that were supported by various Government supply agencies, and realizing that spares were limited and that the program often did not have the priority of other users in the field, a creative approach to supply support was required.

> Unique aircraft parts will always be a risk to an experimental aircraft program. Identify before it's needed the unique vendors and untraditional sources of parts that may be necessary. Be creative.[32]

Acceptance of risk, even in an experimental research aircraft program, is often difficult. This is especially true of organizations that do not routinely operate in the research aircraft arena. The following lesson should be useful to those planning such an endeavor.

> Risk mitigation will be the primary factor in setting requirements for scheduling, funding, and most importantly, design. Even when risk mitigation is fully addressed, those in oversight who maintain the highest risk aversion will still prevail, to the result that significantly greater effort will be required to address their concerns.[33]

Research aircraft are often built to the "intent" of Military Specifications but not to the letter of the MIL-SPECs. The flight-test team noted that the "requirements creep" of the aircraft build created problems. For instance, many aircraft wiring and installations were expected to have MIL-SPEC compliance, and nonprimary aircraft structure did not have a full strength analysis. This was intentional because the airplane was built as a research article; however, some Navy engineers did not have the same interpretation of what was required. These problems caused rework and resulted in cost growth and schedule slips. Some of these "requirements creep" issues were attributed to risk mitigation and risk aversion, as discussed above. This can impact the ease of getting a flight clearance when the aircraft is used by an organization or for a program that was not part of the original plan for the aircraft's use.

> Clearly define the ground rules for achieving a flight clearance and budget and plan accordingly.[34]

As requirements change for the program (which they almost always do), it is very important to communicate the new requirements to the contractors in a very timely manner.

> Delivering late requirements to contractors often results in cost overruns and schedule slides.[35]

The use of online tools was relatively new at the time of the VECTOR program; however, one of the VECTOR subcontractors made use of a secure website to give visibility of plans and technical documents to all on the program:

> The biggest external user of the website was a flight controls engineer reviewing the data for flight clearance purposes. He found that the data available on the website proved to be invaluable. Early in the program he was able to determine, at his own convenience and without the help of the subcontractors, that the processes defined by RJK Technologies [a flight control software subcontractor] were being followed consistently and in a way that produced sufficiently detailed documentation for software development. As an OFP [operational flight program] evolved, he could ensure that configuration control was maintained as design changes were incorporated in the OFP. Later, he was able to follow, and validate requirements traceability, from the software test descriptions to the functional requirements, online, to assess the acceptability of the open- loop software FQT [flying qualities test] plan. This online access also saved RJK employees from numerous coding-and test- interrupts to provide data or answer questions.[36]

Like the EFM program before, the VECTOR program realized that mutual trust between the multinational contractors and government agencies was essential to the success of the program.

> Your primary, pass/fail objective must include your partners [sic] pass/fail objective and you must prioritize it as high as your own. Loyalty to joint objectives must be maintained. All necessary actions from open communications, to coaching personal interaction skills, to providing a little more effort then you have to, are required to sustain the program.[37]

The flight software (SW) architecture was not known to a degree that allowed the VECTOR engineers to understand all the minor impacts of changes. Thus, any change required much testing or retesting to ensure flight safety. This could have been mitigated by a better understanding of the software architecture.

> Regression testing could have been tailored or focused more on the SW affected by each incremental build if it could have been demonstrated via SW "decoupling" scheme that specific retests were not required. Further more [sic], requirements tracking

would have been more precise, resulting in reduced effort during debugging or problem identification sessions.[38]

Because independent organizations were responsible for different simulation components of software and hardware (HW), the responsibility for simulation validation and configuration control were fractionalized, resulting in the following lesson:

> A great deal of time was lost initiating formal tests in the lab due to the delays in identifying and tasking the responsible parties for specific SW or HW configuration anomalies.[39]

The above lessons learned provide a compendium of information that can provide useful planning factors for conducting a flight-test program at a traditional military facility.

Unfortunately, the second of the VECTOR final reports, *X-31 VECTOR Final Report—Volume II—The Technologies*, was not available for review; therefore, its lessons learned are not included in this appendix.

The third volume, *X-31 VECTOR Final Report—Volume III—Flight Test*, is much more tailored to flight testing *specifically*, so the lessons learned are much more focused on this program area whereas previously discussed lessons were of a more programmatic nature. Several of the lessons learned are identical to those in *Volume I*, so they are not included. The unique lessons learned in *Volume III* are of sufficient interest to warrant discussion and inclusion.

Remembering that the X-31 was designed to be a "dry" airplane—no rain or adverse weather, and only a 10-knot crosswind limitation—operations of the airplane from a base like NAS Patuxent River had many more limitations than did X-31 operations from the dry desert environment of Edwards AFB. Therefore, the following lesson learned was observed:

> Weather played a major role, and was often times overly restrictive, resulting in a much less than expected sortie completion rate.[40]

Patuxent River, being a Navy facility, had arresting cables rigged on all of its runways. The X-31 wheels were not stressed for continual operation over arresting gear cables, resulting in the following lesson:

> The requirement to de-rigging arresting gear by removing the cable from the runway added a level of management not often considered in most other flight-testing programs at Naval Air Stations.[41]

The X-31 had a UHF antenna only on the bottom of the fuselage. There were no problems operating at Edwards, with its wide-open expanses. Operations at Patuxent River, however, became problematic due to the limited lines of sight provided by topography and foliage. Eventually, the UHF antenna was relocated to the top of the fuselage on the X-31, but a lesson remains for communication flexibility in flight-test aircraft.

> X-31A UHF Antenna Location (lower fuselage) not optimal for adequate communications during ground operations at Patuxent River.[42]

The X-31 was originally designed for operations on relatively long runways. Operations from shorter runways was somewhat mitigated by the modification of the spin chute installation to be a drag chute for operations in Europe, but the threat of hot brakes on landing was still present, and it resulted in pre-positioning a fire truck near the runway at Patuxent River.

> Requirement for pre-positioning fire trucks prior to launch added a level of management not often considered in most other flight-testing programs at Naval Air Stations.[43]

Simplicity in design, a hallmark of the X-31, resulted in a single fuel tank with limited fuel capacity and no air refueling capability. Fuel reserve requirements limited operations at Patuxent River, where alternate airfields were relatively distant. The fuel reserve requirements were the same on weekends as during the week even though the chances of simultaneously closing both runways at Patuxent River were remote on the weekends.

> Flight times rarely exceeded 45 minutes due to the 40% fuel reserve requirement. Flight-testing during weekend operations was no different, even though airfield traffic was much reduced if not non-existent and the risk greatly mitigated or mute [sic].[44]

Testers recommended a greater fuel capacity for experimental aircraft operating from Patuxent River and relaxed fuel reserve requirements for weekend operations.

Along with the previous lesson relative to potential hot brakes and the resultant fire truck requirement, there was a concern over marginal landing performance should a failure of the drag chute occur. Aerobraking after touchdown seemed to be a mitigating procedure.

Aero-braking should be standard procedure for all X-31A landings at NAS Patuxent River to allow for reasonable error margin in the event of a drag chute failure.[45]

Also, runway performance of the airplane caused concern over stopping distance during a rejected takeoff particularly from a takeoff in afterburner (AB). The recommendation was to conduct all takeoffs in military (MIL) power.

Conduct MIL power takeoff only, due to poor rejected takeoff performance during AB takeoffs.[46]

The test team discovered that it was very beneficial to conduct dry-run training flights in the simulator, with the simulator electronically linked to the control room, before commencing a test phase with a new aircraft configuration. These events were conducted with all test pilots and control room team members participating.

The RTPS [Real Time Processing System, i.e. the control room] / Simulator link was extremely beneficial to the test team in helping prepare for future phases.[47]

Test team engineers recommended using engineering test builds of software for initial integration and validation rather than waiting for formal operational flight programs. This resulted in the following lesson learned:

Finding software design or implementation flaws earlier in the process provides the best chances for a successful formal delivery without setbacks and costly schedule impact.[48]

Separation of the documentation of aircraft configuration and flight clearances was advocated. "Flight clearances should say where the aircraft can operate," and "Configuration description documents should say what the airplane looks like," according to Volume III.[49] This is an excellent lesson for future flight test teams.

Set agreed-to/approved policy to minimize occurrences of managing the aircraft configuration with the flight clearance.[50]

The test team noted that in several instances specific test requirements, such as fire truck placement and arresting gear derigging, were not always performed in a timely fashion. This resulted in the following lesson learned:

Due to numerous specific testing requirements (EMP secured, fire truck placement, arresting gear derigged, GPS jamming secured), it is extremely helpful to coordinate with all Patuxent River / NAVAIR divisions/branches on a daily basis to ensure efficient test conduct. While there is some central scheduling function performed at the Test Wing Atlantic level, it does not sufficiently include all the organizations involved in flight test.[51]

There were cases where the same mnemonic "name" was used for different types of data in different flight control software versions. This caused confusion and resulted in the following lesson learned:

Using the same mnemonic to identify more than one parameter of data is confusing and unnecessary. Data presentations real-time and post-flight are easier to verify and manage when unique names are used that don't vary over time.[52]

The importance for discipline engineers to attend meetings relative to their area of responsibility was emphasized by this lesson learned:

Unless the 4.3.2 [flight control] engineer keeps abreast of and is involved in the change and test process, flight schedule requirements will invariably slip to the right.[53]

Data link problems between pseudolites (GPS satellite surrogates on the ground) used for accurate navigation positioning of the X-31 and the aircraft were highlighted.

While data links are a well-understood issue in aircraft, it is still very difficult to maintain high-continuity connections. This was a major source of dropouts for IBLS [Integrity Beacon Landing System, the very high accuracy navigation system on the X-31 necessary for ESTOL landings to touchdown].[54]

Differences in the sensing of the static pressure of redundant sensors caused problems, primarily because they were located in different airflow regions on the aircraft. This air data redundancy was implemented to overcome the lack of redundancy that resulted in the Ship 1 accident! The team produced this lesson learned:

The main lesson learned is that when an air data system is used for redundancy management, both the primary and the secondary systems should be located in the same similar airflow region. In this case, the L-Probe [secondary pitot-static probe] could have been mounted on the flight test boom. For this program the other alternative could have been the calibration of the static source differences between the primary and the secondary static sources. This calibration could have been accomplished during the initial flights of the EFM configuration at Patuxent River.[55]

Another lesson on meeting attendance was noted. In this case, it was the importance of software team members attending the System Safety Working Group (SSWG) meetings. Information flow is again the lesson.

System team members should have participated in as many SSWG meetings as possible. Each software team member should have each participated in at least one SSWG meeting early in the VECTOR program.[56]

Flight control software testing was performed by three separate organizations. This was problematic in that a direct and verifiable trace of testing could not be performed. The following lesson learned resulted:

A single process, under one entity for requirements review and tracking, test script or procedure review and test results verification would have provided more confidence earlier on the CSCI's [computer software configuration item].[57]

As can be seen from some of the lessons above, the Navy was very proactive concerning the provision of redundancy in the aircraft systems (e.g., air data sensing). This was a notable improvement over the airplane configuration in the EFM program. One can, however, discern a distinct difference in the "culture" of operations at NAS Patuxent River from that of Dryden at Edwards AFB. If an airplane is designed and constructed for operation at a dry, open, and large facility such as Edwards and then moved to a location with a much different environment, problems are likely to occur. This is seen in the contrast of lessons learned in the EFM program and those written following the VECTOR program. These would have likely been seen if the original plan for EFM had been realized and the airplanes had moved to Patuxent River for the close-in-combat evaluation. Therefore, the environment for any possible testing location needs to be factored into the planning for test programs, even those involving research airplanes. Hopefully, this lesson was applied to the Boeing X-32 and Lockheed Martin X-35, which, while not pure "research airplanes," were test beds for new production airplanes that flew at Edwards and Patuxent River. The same issues that result from two differing test bases are present for the evolving Northrup Grumman X-47 aircraft.

Conclusions

In drawing conclusions about the X-31 programs, it is useful to go back to the original goals and evaluate what was accomplished against those goals. The first of the EFM goals was "*rapid demonstration of high-agility maneuvering concepts.*"[58] Certainly, the spectacular achievement of the X-31 during the close-in-combat evaluations and the breathtaking performance of the airplane at the Paris Air Show validated the achievement of this goal. Referring to the Paris Air Show, Rockwell stated, "The technical achievements of the program and the far reaching implications of the technology were clearly demonstrated to a vastly larger audience than ever before. The unprecedented success of the X-31 during the low altitude envelope clearance program and at the 1995 Paris Air Show will undoubtedly accelerate the use of integrated multi-axis thrust vectoring in both military and commercial aircraft of the future."[59]

DASA (MBB) offered the following comments: "The X-31 EFM Program has shown that flight at and beyond the stall boundary is technically feasible. The stall boundary, a critical barrier throughout aviation history, has disappeared."[60]

One could perhaps argue that the "rapid" aspect of the above goals' "rapid demonstration" was not achieved. After all, it took nearly 9 years from the start of Preliminary Design to the performance in the Paris Air Show. More funding continuity and the earlier use of "maneuver milestones," as advocated by Mike Francis after the program was transferred to Dryden, could conceivably have accelerated the program.

The goal to "investigate EFM benefits of the Enhanced Fighter Maneuverability technologies"[61] is highlighted by Rockwell's assessment of the success of the close-in-combat evaluation and is summarized by the statement, "Multi-axis thrust vectoring and the resultant post stall maneuvering capability provided a factor of 6 improvement in close in air combat effectiveness. Post stall tactics augment conventional air combat tactics and when used correctly provide the fighter pilot a significant advantage in air combat."[62]

DASA (MBB) similarly commented, "Thrust vector control and supporting EFM technologies provide tremendous airframe growth potential and should therefore be included in future fighter designs. These technologies should also be considered for mission-enhancement upgrades to current fighters."[63]

Unfortunately, the EFM program only investigated fighter combat in a 1-v-1 context. The Agile Warrior concept was an attempt to answer the questions of EFM technologies in a multibogie environment, but this was only funded as a study and never reached the flight-test stage. One only can conjecture what the results would have been if the X-31 were to fight multiple threats. Without flight tests of this environment, we have no real proof.

The goal to "develop design requirements and a database for future applications"[64] was perhaps partially fulfilled. There were a series of "final reports" produced for both the EFM program and the VECTOR program; however, one could argue that these documents are not easily accessible. There remain two of the Rockwell unclassified "final reports" and one volume of the VECTOR final report that were unavailable for the preparation of this book. So, without a doubt the data exists. Whether or not a future designer of a multiaxis thrust-vectoring fighter could easily access this wealth of information is somewhat in question.

The last of the EFM goals was to "validate a low-cost international prototyping concept."[65] The cost effectiveness of the program was illuminated in Chapter 5. It certainly can be claimed that this program, when compared to other similar programs, was very cost effective. While it was difficult for X-31 program managers to acquire enough funding to keep the program going, it can be argued that the program produced very significant results for minimum dollars spent. The international part of the program was very significant. While there are many parallels in the space program, X-31 was the first—and, to date, only—international aeronautical research airplane program. The success of the international aspect of this program has been stated often but most eloquently in a lesson learned from the ITO that was quoted previously:

> The transfer of technical information between the German, British and American [This must have been an error since the British did not participate in the program.] members of the team was constant and without inhibition. This multicultural exchange provided a fresh approach to the solution of difficult technical problems, was a basis for lowering the interorganizational cultural barriers of each participating nation and resulted in a serendipitous increase in the value returned for each team member investment.[66]

Similarly, the DASA final report states:

> The X-31 EFM Program set several records for flight test efficiency and productivity and serves as a benchmark for future international cooperation and achievement.[67]

The "quasi-tailless" (QT) experiments done toward the end of the X-31 EFM program were sponsored and funded by the Joint Advanced Strike Technology (JAST) program. This program was a lead-in to the X-32 and X-35 technology demonstrators, which ultimately led to the development of the Lockheed Martin F-35. The objectives of the quasi-tailless program were as follows:

- to investigate the level of directional stability reduction that can be handled with yaw/pitch thrust vectoring of a single-engine fighter under realistic flight scenarios;
- to assess the maturation of modern integrated flight control technologies for application on future single-engine strike fighters; and
- to look into simple methods for assessing thrust-vector-control power sizing.[68]

All three of these objectives were successfully attained. The best documentation of these results is from the *Rockwell Quasi-Tailless Final Report*, which states,

> The X-31 QT Experiment demonstrated that a carrier based, tailless strike aircraft is operationally feasible. Aggressive maneuvers, including offset carrier approach, pop-up ground attack, and slot formation were successfully executed in the QT mode. The experimental thrust vectoring system on the X-31 proves that thrust vectoring provides sufficient control power to perform maneuvers and coordination. Optimal design can be achieved when the TV [thrust-vectoring] system is properly blended with other aircraft effectors. The benefits of a tailless strike aircraft design can be realized without sacrificing mission capabilities.

> The X-31 experiment has demonstrated that flying a directionally unstable single engine attack fighter is viable. The X-31 is more directionally unstable than any existing US fighter for the same level of vertical tail reduction, making it a suitable testbed for the Quasi-Tailless experiment. Aerodynamically, it is feasible to reduce the vertical tail to a level of neutral directional stability....[69]

So, the viability of using thrust vectoring to control tailless strike fighter designs was proven.

Taking the X-31 to the Paris Air Show in 1995 was not a typical "test program," although the low-altitude post-stall envelope expansion did serve to complete the technical exploration of multiaxis thrust vectoring and to expand the low-altitude database for future aircraft design. The real reason for going to Paris was to "showcase United States' and German multi-axis thrust vectoring technology by demonstrating the post stall maneuver capability provided by thrust vectoring."[70] This objective was certainly accomplished in a spectacular fashion! As stated in the Rockwell report on this subject,

> The impact of demonstrating multi-axis thrust vectoring at the 1995 Paris Air Show was dramatic. The serious attention that the X-31 received from the world aviation community far surpassed the previous reach of the program. The technical achievements of the program and the far reaching implications of the technology was clearly demonstrated to a vastly larger audience than ever before. The unprecedented success of the X-31 during the low altitude envelope clearance program and at the 1995 Paris Air Show will undoubtedly accelerate the use of integrated multi-axis thrust vectoring in both military and commercial aircraft of the future.[71]

The VECTOR program initially had the following overall goals:
- Demonstrate two new capabilities to meet operational needs
  - ESTOL (Extremely Short Takeoff and Landing)
  - Tailless fighter/attack aircraft

Along with the overall goals were these technology goals:
- Develop enabling technologies
  - Advanced Air Data System (AADS)
  - AVEN (Axisymmetric Vectoring Exhaust Nozzle)
  - Integrated Flight/Propulsion Control
- Develop the capabilities and technologies to be ready for operational application[72]

The applications envisioned for these technologies were new fighter/attack aircraft designs such as Joint Strike Fighter (JSF), which became the F-35; unmanned combat air vehicles (UCAV); and future designs. Also envisioned were potential modifications to current fighter/attack aircraft as well as changes in their concept of operations. These aircraft applications included the Navy/Marine F/A-18, the Swedish JAS-39 Gripen, and the Eurofighter EF-2000 Typhoon. Further use on carrier-support aircraft and commercial transports was also imagined.[73] Thrust-vectoring experiments based on VECTOR were also thought to be capable of supporting the use of thrust vectoring to modify carrier operations and carrier basing modes and to impact new carrier concepts (such as smaller carriers with no catapults or arresting gear).

With the withdrawal of the Swedes and the Spanish from the VECTOR program due to lack of funding, the use of the AVEN nozzle went away. Also, the potential of actually removing all or part of the vertical tail was withdrawn due to lack of funding and safety concerns. The VECTOR program's purpose was modified to reflect these realities:

> VECTOR's purpose was to develop and demonstrate an Advanced Air Data System (AADS), Extremely Short Take-Off and Landing (ESTOL) and ESTOL supporting technologies, principally: integrated flight, engine and thrust vector control; automated landing system; and, pilot displays. In addition, VECTOR data developed during ESTOL engineering, development and demonstration was used to conduct engineering analyses of reduced vertical tail/reduced directional control with thrust vectoring.[74]

While the details of the performance of all of these technologies are not available, it is evident that the AADS; integrated flight, engine, and thrust-vector control; automated landing system; and pilot displays worked.[75] The X-31 did, during the VECTOR program, fly a completely automated approach at 24° angle of attack with an automatic derotation and touchdown—an impressive accomplishment. It is intriguing to think, given a little bit more money in the program, what could have been accomplished with approaches and landings at even greater angles of attack. One other VECTOR accomplishment that should not be overlooked is that they took an experimental research X-plane out of an unprotected storage environment and restored it to flyable condition to support a test program that was not even considered when the X-31 was designed, developed, and manufactured. This alone is a significant accomplishment—something never before done with an X-plane and not done since.

Endnotes

1. Rockwell International, *X-31 Enhanced Fighter Maneuverability Program Flight Test Final Report: Development of the X-31 Flight Test System*, Rockwell Report TFD-95-1563 (March 14, 1996), pp. 3-1.
2. Rockwell International, *Development of the X-31 Flight Test System*, p. 3-2.
3. Rockwell International, *Development of the X-31 Flight Test System*, p. 3-3.
4. Rockwell International, *Development of the X-31 Flight Test System*, p. 3-4.
5. Rockwell International, *Development of the X-31 Flight Test System*, p. 3-4.
6. Rockwell International, *Development of the X-31 Flight Test System*, p. 6-3.
7. Rockwell International, *Development of the X-31 Flight Test System*, p. 6-4.
8. Rockwell International, *Development of the X-31 Flight Test System*, p. 6-4.
9. Rockwell International, *Development of the X-31 Flight Test System*, p. 6-4.
10. Rockwell International, *Development of the X-31 Flight Test System*, p. 6-4.
11. Rockwell International, *Development of the X-31 Flight Test System*, p. 6-5.
12. Rockwell International, *Development of the X-31 Flight Test System*, p. 6-6.
13. Rockwell International, *Development of the X-31 Flight Test System*, p. 6-6.
14. Rockwell International, *Development of the X-31 Flight Test System*, p.6-10.
15. The High Technology Test Bed was an experimental C-130 aircraft funded by Lockheed Martin that was used to demonstrate innovative technologies, including modern flight control computers, for use in extremely short takeoff and landing missions.
16. The STC was a hardware rack, part of the simulation interface to the flight control computers.
17. VAX was an early computer manufactured by Digital Corporation that was used to compile the X-31 flight control software.
18. MIL-STD-1553 is a military standard published by the U.S. Department of Defense that defines the mechanical, electrical,

and functional characteristics of a serial data bus; it was originally designed for use with military avionics.

19. Linear Quadratic Regulator was an optimum control law method.
20. Emmen was a German wind tunnel.
21. HIKR is a departure/spin mode of the X-31 in which the aircraft rolls about its longitudinal axis, with the axis roughly horizontal.
22. Rockwell International, *Development of the X-31 Flight Test System*, section 10.
23. P. Huber, *X-31 Enhanced Fighter Maneuverability Final Report* (Daimler-Benz Aerospace: December 22, 1995), p. 32.
24. Rockwell International, *Development of the X-31 Flight Test System*, p. 10-9.
25. "X-31 Breaking the Chain, Lessons Learned," video discussion of X-31 Ship 1 accident (2005).
26. Rogers Smith, "X-31 Accident: Lessons to be Learned," *40th Symposium Proceedings* (Lancaster, CA: Society of Experimental Test Pilots, 1996).
27. U.S. Navy and NAVAIR, *X-31 VECTOR Final Report—Volume I— The Program*, p. 53.
28. U.S. Navy and NAVAIR, *The Program*, p. 54.
29. U.S. Navy and NAVAIR, *The Program*, p. 55.
30. U.S. Navy and NAVAIR, *The Program*, pp. 56-57.
31. U.S. Navy and NAVAIR, *The Program*, p. 58.
32. U.S. Navy and NAVAIR, *The Program*, p. 59.
33. U.S. Navy and NAVAIR, *The Program*, p. 60.
34. U.S. Navy and NAVAIR, *The Program*, p. 61.
35. U.S. Navy and NAVAIR, *The Program*, p. 62.
36. U.S. Navy and NAVAIR, *The Program*, p. 63.
37. U.S. Navy and NAVAIR, *The Program*, pp. 64-65.
38. U.S. Navy and NAVAIR, *The Program*, p. 66.
39. U.S. Navy and NAVAIR, *The Program*, p. 67.
40. U.S. Navy and NAVAIR, *X-31 VECTOR Final Report—Volume III—Flight Test* (NAS Patuxent River: NATC, October 16, 2003), p. 121.
41. U.S. Navy and NAVAIR, *Flight Test*, p. 122.
42. U.S. Navy and NAVAIR, *Flight Test*, p. 123.
43. U.S. Navy and NAVAIR, *Flight Test*, p. 124.
44. U.S. Navy and NAVAIR, *Flight Test*, p. 125.
45. U.S. Navy and NAVAIR, *Flight Test*, p. 126.
46. U.S. Navy and NAVAIR, *Flight Test*, p. 127.
47. U.S. Navy and NAVAIR, *Flight Test*, p. 128.

48. U.S. Navy and NAVAIR, *Flight Test*, p. 132.
49. U.S. Navy and NAVAIR, *Flight Test*, p. 134.
50. U.S. Navy and NAVAIR, *Flight Test*, p. 134.
51. U.S. Navy and NAVAIR, *Flight Test*, p. 135.
52. U.S. Navy and NAVAIR, *Flight Test*, p. 136.
53. U.S. Navy and NAVAIR, *Flight Test*, p. 137.
54. U.S. Navy and NAVAIR, *Flight Test*, p. 139.
55. U.S. Navy and NAVAIR, *Flight Test*, p. 141.
56. U.S. Navy and NAVAIR, *Flight Test*, p. 142.
57. U.S. Navy and NAVAIR, *Flight Test*, p. 144.
58. Rockwell International, *Development of the X-31 Flight Test System*, Slide 1.7.
59. Rockwell International, *X-31 Enhanced Fighter Maneuverability Program Flight Test Final Report: Program Summary*, Rockwell Report TFD-95-1564 (March 1996), p. 29.
60. Peter Huber, *X-31 Enhanced Fighter Maneuverability Final Report*, p. 32.
61. Rockwell International, *Development of the X-31 Flight Test System*, slide 1.7.
62. Rockwell International, *Program Summary*, p. 18.
63. P. Huber, *X-31 Enhanced Fighter Maneuverability Final Report*, p. 32.
64. Rockwell International, *Development of the X-31 Flight Test System*, slide 1.7.
65. Rockwell International, *Development of the X-31 Flight Test System*, slide 1.7.
66. Rockwell International, *Development of the X-31 Flight Test System*, p. 10-12.
67. P. Huber, *X-31 Enhanced Fighter Maneuverability Final Report*, p. 32.
68. Rockwell International, *X-31 Quasi-Tailless Flight Test Experiment Final Report*, Rockwell Report TFD-95-1261 (June 9, 1995), abstract.
69. Rockwell International, *X-31 Quasi-Tailless Flight Test Experiment*, p. 122.
70. Rockwell International, *X-31 Low Altitude Post Stall Envelope Clearance and Paris Air Show Report*, Rockwell Report TFD-95-1510 (March 8, 1996), p. 1.
71. Rockwell International, *X-31 Low Altitude Post Stall Envelope Clearance and Paris Air Show Report*, p. 13.
72. "VECTOR Program Briefing," presented at Dryden (n.d., c. 1998).
73. Current roles that are considered "carrier support" by the Navy include carrier on-board delivery (COD), electronic surveillance

(ES), electronic warfare (EW), airborne early warning (AEW), and possibly aerial refueling.

74. U.S. Navy and NAVAIR, *X-31 VECTOR Final Report—Volume I—The Program*, p. 7.

75. The report, *X-31 VECTOR Final Report—Volume II—The Technologies* (October 16, 2003), which discussed the success of the technology development in VECTOR, was not available.

Acknowledgments

Researching and writing a book is an incredibly involved and long process, one that requires a lot of help. This project started at Dryden Flight Research Center, located on the shore of Rogers Dry Lake at Edwards Air Force Base, CA. There, I was ably helped by Peter Merlin, the Dryden archivist; Karl Bender, the Dryden research librarian; and Freddy Lockarno, library technician. They all were extremely helpful in assisting me in digging out the piles of documents that formed the initial basis for this book. Peter and Karl are authors in their own right and offered much advice on the art of writing. Karl introduced me to Pat Stoliker and John Bosworth, who were Dryden engineers on the X-31 program. My interviews with them were a great help in gaining initial insight on the scope of the program, and they pointed me toward even more sources of information. While visiting Dryden, I interviewed Ken Dyson and Fred Knox, former Rockwell test pilots, as well as Rogers Smith, a former Dryden test pilot, and Jim Wisneski, an old friend, colleague, and former U.S. Air Force (USAF) test pilot. These gentlemen all flew the X-31 and thus were able to provide "pilot insight" into the program, airplane, and test organization. They also lent me much personal information on the X-31 program. Their help was extremely valuable. Jim's wife, Freida, who worked at the Air Force Flight Test Center History Office, furnished a crucial final report video on the X-31. Darrell Shipplet of the Air Force Flight Test Center Technical Research Library was a great help in finding significant material on the Air Force side of the program. Col. Dawn Dunlop, USAF, the former 412th Test Wing Commander, provided important information on some of the unique pilot rating scales used on the program.

At the Society of Experimental Test Pilots symposium in 2011, I met Ken Szalai, the Dryden director at the time of the X-31 and an ardent supporter of the program who was largely responsible for its success at Dryden. It was an honor to listen to his recollections of X-31 at the symposium banquet. Ken facilitated my subsequent contact with Mike Francis, one of the Defense Advanced Research Projects Agency's (DARPA) X-31 program managers. Mike Francis furnished vital insights into the Government program management side of the program. Ed Schneider, an old friend and former Dryden test pilot who flew against the X-31 in mock dogfights, told me what it was like to confront a "supermaneuverable" airplane in "combat."

Two others hugely contributed to my knowledge of this unique research program. Mike Robinson, a former Rockwell program manager on X-31, provided much information and insight into the X-31 program through e-mails and literally hours on the phone. Mike put me in touch with Harvey Schellenger, a former Rockwell chief engineer on the X-31, who provided historical Rockwell documents and photos and regaled me with many personal stories concerning the airplane's development and tests. I am truly indebted to these two people.

Navigating through the Navy system to obtain documents on the VECTOR program was a daunting task. Initially, Jennifer Young, a former Naval Air Systems Command program manager, spent many long phone calls giving me an excellent overview of the Vectoring ESTOL Control Operation Research (VECTOR) program. Lt. Cmdr. Sarah C. Higgins, U.S. Navy Office of Information–East, and Rob Koon of Naval Air Systems Command (NAVAIR) were invaluable in obtaining critical VECTOR program final reports.

Lt. Col. "Mo" Allee, U.S. Marine Corps (USMC), one of the VECTOR test pilots, gave an excellent paper on VECTOR at the spring 2011 Society of Experimental Test Pilots Flight Test Safety Workshop. At this forum, he expanded on his experiences with me in a very valuable exchange. Also, many hours were spent in e-mails and phone conversations with Gary Jennings, a former Boeing VECTOR program manager and classmate of mine in USAF Test Pilot School Class 74B. Special thanks are due to Lou Parks, a retired Rockwell systems engineer, for his very informative insights into bringing the X-31 out of storage to support VECTOR.

Security issues with certain Air Force documents were of concern. William Thomas and Scott Kuhnen of Headquarters Air Force Materiel Command at Wright-Patterson Air Force Base, OH, handled these issues superbly and in a most timely fashion. Media Fusion's extraordinarily dedicated personnel, particularly Cynthia Miller, Chris Yates, and Barbara Bullock, were extremely helpful in shepherding this book through the publishing process.

Lt. Gen. George K. Muellner, USAF (retired), the first Joint Advanced Strike Technology (JAST) program director (and subsequently Boeing vice president, American Institute of Aeronautics and Astronautics president, and Air Force Association president), provided valuable insights into the requirements decisions made within the JAST program and its relationship to the X-31.

A great editor is a necessity on a project like this, and I certainly had one: Dr. Richard P. Hallion, series editor for the NASA Aeronautics Directorate monograph studies and formerly the Historian of the United States Air Force, provided superb advice, mentoring, and encouragement. Dick is a longtime friend from days past teaching at the Air Force Test Pilot School in the early 1980s, and he helped shape my manuscript to its fullest potential.

And finally, I thank my wife Phyllis: mere words are not even remotely adequate to express what her support, encouragement, and love has meant to the success of this project.

Douglas A. Joyce
Stratham, NH
June 2013

Selected Bibliography

Contractor Reports

Huber, Peter. *X-31 Enhanced Fighter Maneuverability Final Report.* Daimler-Benz Aerospace (1995).

Rockwell International. *Final Report of Agile Warrior Concept Study.* Rockwell Report TFD-95-1101 (1995).

Rockwell International. *Flight Test Results of X-31 Helmet-Mounted Display and Audio Cueing Systems.* Rockwell Report TFD-95-1100 (1995).

Rockwell International. *X-31 EFM Tactical Utility Flight Test Evaluation Synopsis.* Rockwell Report TFD-95-1348 (1995).

Rockwell International. *X-31 EFM Tactical Utility Flight Test Final Report Appendix.* Rockwell Report TFD-1349 (1995, Classified SECRET).

Rockwell International. *X-31 Enhanced Fighter Maneuverability Program Flight Test Final Report: Program Summary.* Rockwell Report TFD-95-1564 (1996)

Rockwell International. *X-31 Enhanced Fighter Maneuverability Program Flight Test Final Report: Development of the X-31 Flight Test System.* Rockwell Report TFD-95-1563 (1996)

Rockwell International. *X-31 Low Altitude Post Stall Envelope Clearance and Paris Air Show Report.* Rockwell Report TFD-95-1510 (1996).

Rockwell International. *X-31 Quasi-Tailless Flight Test Experiment, Final Report.* Rockwell Report TFD-95-1261 (1995).

Rockwell International. *X-31 Structures Flight Test Report.* Rockwell Report TFD-95-1140-1, -2, -3, and -4 (1995).

National Aeronautics and Space Administration (NASA)

Banks, Daniel W., Gregory M. Gatlin, and John W. Paulson, Jr. *Low-speed longitudinal and lateral-directional aerodynamic characteristics of the X-31 configuration.* NASA-TM-4351 (1992).

Binkley, Robert L., and Dale Mackall. *System Overview of the NASA Dryden Integrated Test Facility.* NASA-TM-104250 (1992).

Bosworth, John T., and Patrick C. Stoliker. *The X-31A Quasi-tailless Flight Test Results.* NASA-TP-3624 (1996).

Bowers, A.H., G.K. Noffz, S.B. Grafton, M.L. Mason, and L.R. Peron. *Multiaxis Thrust Vectoring Using Axisymmetric Nozzles and Postexit Vanes on an F/A-18 Configuration Vehicle.* NASA-TM-101741 (1991).

Cobleigh, Brent R. *High-Angle-of-Attack Yawing Moment Asymmetry of the X-31 Aircraft from Flight Test.* NASA-CR-186030 (1994).

Cobleigh, Brent R., and Mark A. Croom. *Comparison of X-31 Flight and Ground-Based Yawing Moment Asymmetries at High Angles of Attack.* NASA-TM-2001-210393 (2001).

Cobleigh, Brent R., and John Delfrate. *Water Tunnel Flow Visualization Study of a 4.4 Percent Scale X-31 Forebody.* NASA-TM-104276 (1994).

Cooper, George E., and Robert P. Harper. *The Use of Pilot Rating in the Evaluation of Aircraft Handling Qualities.* NASA-TN-D-5153 (1969).

Fisher, David F., and Brent R. Cobleigh. *Controlling Forebody Asymmetries in Flight: Experience with Boundary Layer Transition Strips.* NASA-TM-4595 (1994).

Fisher, David F., and Brent R. Cobleigh. *Reynolds Number Effects at High Angles of Attack.* NASA-TP-1998-206553 (1998).

Gangloff, Richard P., and Edgar A. Starke, Jr. *NASA-UVA Light Aerospace Alloy and Structures Technology Program (LA2ST).* NASA-CR-204064 (1997).

Garza, Frederico R., and Eugene A. Morelli. *A Collection of Nonlinear Aircraft Simulations in MATLAB.* NASA-TM-2003-212145 (2003).

Kehoe, Michael W., and Lawrence C. Freudinger. *Aircraft Ground Vibration Testing at the NASA Dryden Flight Research Facility, 1993.* NASA-TM-104275 (1994).

Klein, Vladislav. *Program of Research in Flight Dynamics in the Joint Institute for Advancement of Flight Sciences [JIAFS] at NASA-Langley Research Center.* NASA-CR-203210 (1996).

Klein, Vladislav. *Program of Research in Flight Dynamics in the Joint Institute for Advancement of Flight Sciences [JIAFS] at NASA-Langley Research Center.* NASA-CR-204952 (1997).

Klein, Vladislav, D.R. McDaniel, G.P. Grenier, and L.V. Nguyen. *Program of Research in Flight Dynamics in the Joint Institute for Advancement of Flight Sciences [JIAFS] at NASA-Langley Research Center.* NTRS Accession Number 96N72218, ID 19960038238, NASA LRC (1996).

Klein, Vladislav, and Patrick C. Murphy. *Aerodynamic Parameters of High Performance Aircraft Estimated from Wind Tunnel and Flight Test Data.* NASA-TM-1997-207993 (1998).

Klein, Vladislav, and Keith D. Noderer. *Modeling of Aircraft Unsteady Aerodynamic Characteristics. Part 2: Parameters Estimated from Wind Tunnel Data.* NASA-TM-110161 (1995).

Klein, Vladislav, and Keith D. Noderer. *Modeling of Aircraft Unsteady Aerodynamic Characteristics. Part 3: Parameters Estimated from Flight Data.* NASA-TM-110259 (1995).

Larson, Richard R., and D. Edward Millard. *A Rule-Based System for Real-Time Analysis of Control Systems.* NASA-TM-104258 (1992).

McKinney, M.O., and H.M. Drake. *Flight Characteristics at Low Speed of Delta-Wing Models.* NACA RM L7R07 (1948).

Moul, M.T., and J.W. Paulson. *Dynamic Lateral Behavior of High-Performance Aircraft.* NACA RM L58E16 (1958).

Nguyen, L.T., and J.V. Foster. *Development of a Preliminary High-Angle-of-Attack Nose-Down Pitch Control Requirement for High Performance Aircraft.* NASA-TM-101684 (1990).

Norlin, Ken A. *Flight Simulation Software at NASA Dryden Flight Research Center.* NASA TM-104315 (1995).

Ryan, George W. *A Genetic Search Technique for Identification of Aircraft Departures.* NASA-CR-4688 (1995).

Shafter, M.F., R. Koehler, E.M. Wilson, and D.R. Levy. *Initial flight Test of a Ground Deployed System for Flying Qualities Assessment.* NASA TM-101700 (1989).

Smith, Mark S. *Analysis of Wind Tunnel Oscillatory Data of the X-31A Aircraft.* NASA-CR-1999-208725 (1999).

Stoliker, Patrick C. *A Discussion of the Last Flight of X-31A Aircraft #1.* NASA-DFRC-E-DAA-TN3495 (2011).

Stoliker, Patrick C., and John T. Bosworth. *Evaluation of High-Angle-of-Attack Handling Qualities for the X-31A Using Standard Evaluation Maneuvers.* NASA-TM-104322 (1996).

Stoliker, Patrick C., and John T. Bosworth. *Linearized Poststall Aerodynamic and Control Law Models of the X-31A Aircraft and Comparison with Flight Data.* NASA-TM-1997-206318 (1997).

U.S. National Aeronautics and Space Administration. *Fourth High Alpha Conference.* 2 volumes. NASA-CP-10143 (1994).

U.S. National Aeronautics and Space Administration. *NACA/NASA: X-1 through X-31.* NASA-TM-104304 (1994).

U.S. National Aeronautics and Space Administration. *NASA Aeronautics: Research and Technology Program Highlights.* NASA-NP-159 (1990).

U.S. National Aeronautics and Space Administration. *X-31 Resource Tape.* NASA-TM-104300 (1993).

U.S. National Aeronautics and Space Administration. *X-31 Tailless Testing.* NASA-TM-104306 (1994).

Villeta, Jose Rafael. *Lateral-Directional Static and Dynamic Stability Analysis at High Angles of Attack for the X-31 Configuration.* NASA-TM-111431 (1992).

Whiting, Matthew Robert. *Differential Canard Deflection for Generation of Yawing Moment on the X-31 With and Without the Vertical Tail.* NASA-TM-111357 (1996).

United States Navy, Naval Air Systems Command (NAVAIR)

U.S. Naval Air Systems Command. *X-31 VECTOR Final Report.* Volume I: *The Program* (NAS Patuxent River: NATC, 2003).

U.S. Naval Air Systems Command. *X-31 VECTOR Final Report.* Volume II: *The Technologies* (NAS Patuxent River: NATC, 2003).

U.S. Naval Air Systems Command. *X-31 VECTOR Final Report.* Volume III: *Flight Test* (NAS Patuxent River: NATC, 2003).

Advisory Group for Aerospace Research and Development (AGARD)

Beh, H., and G. Hofinger. "X-31A Control Law Design." In *Technologies for Highly Maneuverable Aircraft.* AGARD CP-548 (1994).

Herbst, W.B. "X-31 at First Flight." In *Flying Qualities.* AGARD CP-508 (1991).

American Institute of Aeronautics and Astronautics (AIAA)

Alcorn, C.W., M.A. Croom, and M.S. Francis. *The X-31 Experience: Aerodynamic Impediments to Post-Stall Agility.* AIAA-1995-362 (1995).

Canter, David E., and Allen W. Groves. *X-31 Post-Stall Envelope Expansion and Tactical Utility Testing.* AIAA-1994-2171 (1991).

Cobleigh, Brent R. *High-Angle-of-Attack Yawing Moment Asymmetry of the X-31 Aircraft from Flight Test*. AIAA-1994-1803 (1994).

Croom, Mark A., David J. Fratello, Raymond D. Whipple, Matthew J. O'Rourke, and Todd W. Trilling. *Dynamic Model Testing of the X-31 Configuration for High-Angle-of-Attack Flight Dynamics Research*. AIAA-1993-3674 (1993).

Grohs, Thomas, Balazs Fischer, Olaf Heinzinger, and Oliver Brieger. *X-31 VECTOR Control Law Design for ESTOL to the Ground*. AIAA-2003-5406 (2003).

Grohs, Thomas, Balazs Fischer, Olaf Heinzinger, and Oliver Brieger. *X-31 VECTOR-ESTOL to the Ground Flight Test Results and Lessons Learned*. AIAA-2004-5029 (2004).

Gutt, G., S. Fischer, J. Sheen, D. Lawrence, and S. White. *Precision Autoland Guidance of the X-31 Aircraft Using IBLS—The Integrity Beacon Landing System*. AIAA-2004-5027 (2004).

Huber, P. *Control Law Design for Tailless Configurations and In-Flight Simulation Using the X-31 Aircraft*. AIAA-95-3199 (1995).

Huber, P., S. Weiss, and H. Galleithner. *X-31A Initial Flying Qualities Results Using Equivalent Modeling Flight Test Evaluation Techniques*. AIAA-91-2891 (1991).

Jirásek, Adam, and Russell M. Cummings. *Application of Volterra Functions to X-31 Aircraft Model Motion*. AIAA-2009-3629 (2009).

Jirásek, Adam, and Russell M. Cummings. *Assessment of Sting Effect on X-31 Aircraft Model Using CFD*. AIAA-2010-1040 (2010).

Jirásek, Adam, and Russell M. Cummings. *Reduced Order Modeling of X-31 Wind Tunnel Model Aerodynamic Loads*. AIAA-2010-4693 (2010).

Joost Boelens, Okko. *CFD Analysis of the Flow Around the X-31 Aircraft at High Angle of Attack*. AIAA-2009-3628 (2009).

Klein, Vladislav, and Keith D. Noderer. *Aerodynamic Parameters of the X-31 Drop Model Estimated from Flight-Data at High Angles of Attack.* AIAA-1992-4357 (1992).

Knox, Fred D. *X-31 Flight Test Update.* AIAA-1992-1035 (1992).

Mackall, Dale, Kenneth Norlin, Dorothea Cohen, Gary Kellogg, Lawrence Schilling, and John Sheen. *Rapid Development of the X-31 Simulation to Support Flight-Testing.* AIAA-1992-4176 (1992).

Nangia, Raj. *X-31 Vector Aircraft, Low Speed Stability & Control, Comparisons of Wind Tunnel Data & Theory (Focus on Linear & Panel Codes).* AIAA-2009-3898 (2009).

Noderer, Keith D. *An Overview of the System Identification Procedure with Applications to the X-31 Drop Model.* AIAA-1993-10 (1993).

Powers, Sidney A., and Harvey G. Schellenger. *The X-31—High Performance at Low Cost.* AIAA-1989-2122 (1989).

Rein, N., G. Höler, A. Schütte, A. Bergmann, and T. Löser. *Ground-Based Simulation of Complex Maneuvers of a Delta-Wing Aircraft.* AIAA-2006-3149 (2006).

Rohlf, Detlef, Oliver Brieger, and Thomas Grohs. *X-31 VECTOR System Identification: Approach and Results.* AIAA-2004-4830 (2004).

Rohlf, Detlef. "Global Model Approach for X-31 VECTOR System Identification." In *Journal of Aircraft* 42, no. 1 (2005): 54–62.

Ross, Hannes, and Michael Robinson. *X-31: An Example of 20 Years of Successful International Cooperation.* AIAA-2003-2572 (2003).

Schütte, Andreas, Okko Joost Boelens, Thomas Loeser, and Martin Oehlke. *Prediction of the Flow Around the X-31 Aircraft Using Two Different CFD Methods.* AIAA-2010-4692 (2010).

Schütte, A., G. Einarsson, A. Raichle, B. Schöning, M. Orlt, J. Neumann, J. Arnold, W. Mönnich, and T. Forkert. *Numerical Simulation of Maneuvering Aircraft by Aerodynamic Flight Mechanics and Structural Mechanics Coupling.* AIAA-2007-1070 (2007).

Tamrat, Befecadu. *The X-31: A Post-Stall Technology (PST) Fighter Close-In-Combat Results Assessment, and a Look at New CIC Performance Evaluation Metrics.* AIAA-2004-5173 (2004).

Tomac, Maximilian, and Arthur Rizzi. *Creation of Aerodynamic Database for the X-31.* AIAA-2010-501 (2010).

Tomac, Maximilian, Arthur Rizzi, Raj Nangia, and Michael Nielsen Mendenhall. *Comparing and Benchmarking Engineering Methods on the Prediction of X-31 Aerodynamics.* AIAA-2010-4694 (2010).

Williams, D.L., R.C. Nelson, and David Fisher. *An Investigation of X-31 Roll Characteristics at High Angle-of-Attack Through Subscale Model Testing.* AIAA-1994-806 (1994).

Yeh, David T., Michael W. George, Willard C. Clever, Clement K. Tam, and Chung-Jin Woan. *Numerical Study of the X-31 High Angle-of-Attack Flow Characteristics.* AIAA-1991-1630 (1991).

Young, J. *X-31 VECTOR Program Summary.* AIAA-2004-5026 (2004).

Zammit, Steve, and Koos Zwaanenburg. *Real-Time Flight Simulation Support for the X-31 Aircraft Program.* AIAA-1989-3283 (1989).

Society of Experimental Test Pilots (SETP)

Allee, Lt. Col. Cody, USMC. "Save the Best for Last: The Last Flight of the X-31 VECTOR Program." In *SETP and Society of Flight Test Engineers (SFTE) Flight Test Safety Workshop* (Pensacola, FL, 2011).

Allee, Maj. J. Cody, USMC. "Automating Safety in Flight Test." In *2003 SETP Symposium Proceedings* (Lancaster, CA: Society of Experimental Test Pilots, 2003).

Flynn, Maj. Billie A., CAF, Edward T. Schneider, and Rogers E. Smith. "Thrust Vectoring: A New Dimension (F-18 HARV, X-31, F-16 MATV)." In *1994 SETP Symposium Proceedings* (Lancaster, CA: Society of Experimental Test Pilots, 1994).

Knox, Fred D., and Thomas C. Santangelo. "Taking an X-Airplane to the Paris Air Show." In *39th Symposium Proceedings* (Lancaster, CA: Society of Experimental Test Pilots, 1995).

Knox, Fred D. "X-31 Flight Test Update," In *1991 SETP Symposium Proceedings* (Lancaster, CA: Society of Experimental Test Pilots, 1991).

Knox, Fred, Cmdr. Al Groves, USN, Rogers Smith, and Lt. Col. Jim Wisneski, USAF. "X-31 Flight Test Update." In *1993 SETP Symposium Proceedings* (Lancaster, CA: Society of Experimental Test Pilots, 1993).

Loria, Capt. Christopher J., USMC, Lt. Mark Kelly, USN, and Ron Harney. "X-31 Quasi-tailless Evaluation." In *European SETP Symposium Proceedings* (Luzern, Switzerland, 1995).

Seeck, Dietrich, and Ken Dyson. "An Introduction to the X-31." In *1987 SETP Symposium Proceedings* (Lancaster, CA: Society of Experimental Test Pilots, 1987).

Smith, Rogers E. "X-31 Accident: Lessons to be Learned." In *40th Symposium Proceedings* (Lancaster, CA: Society of Experimental Test Pilots, 1996).

About the Author

Born in Rochester, NH, Douglas A. Joyce grew up in Barre, VT. He attended Purdue University, where he earned a B.S. and an M.S. in aeronautical and astronautical engineering. He was commissioned through the Air Force Reserve Officers' Training Corps (ROTC) program and obtained his M.S. at Purdue under the auspices of the Air Force Institute of Technology.

After graduation from USAF pilot training, he served two combat tours in Vietnam—the first tour in the McDonnell-Douglas F-4D Phantom II and the second in the General Dynamics F-111A "Aardvark." After returning from Southeast Asia, he attended USAF Test Pilot School at Edwards AFB. Upon graduation, he was assigned to flight-test duties at Eglin AFB. At Eglin, he participated in the testing of weapons-delivery systems on later models of both the F-4 and F-111. He also was the USAF Project Test Pilot on the prototype EF-111A "Sparkvark," an airborne electronic jamming version of the F-111A aircraft used with great success in Operation Desert Storm.

He served a tour at Headquarters Air Force Systems Command (now Air Force Air Materiel Command), where he worked on advanced fighter aircraft development plans in the early days prior to establishment of the Advanced Tactical Fighter (ATF) program that led to the Lockheed Martin F-22A Raptor stealth fighter. The next assignment found him reassigned to Edwards AFB as the director of academics at the USAF Test Pilot School, where he was responsible for teaching new generations of test pilots and prospective astronauts. He then moved on to become the deputy director of the F-16 Combined Test Force, where much of his work was testing the then-new General Dynamics (now Lockheed Martin) F-16C/D.

Following his assignment at Edwards, he served in the Philippines as the program manager for a new air-combat test and training range that was being built there, and then he moved into a leadership position in classified flight test before retiring from the Air Force with the rank of colonel.

Following his retirement from the service, he became director of flight operations and later professor of aviation and aeronautical engineering at Daniel Webster College, a small college in New Hampshire. He is an associate fellow of both the American Institute of Aeronautics and Astronautics and the Society of Experimental Test Pilots, and he presently lives on the New Hampshire seacoast with his wife, Phyllis, where he maintains and enthusiastically skippers his J/24 one-design racing sloop.

Index

Numbers in **bold** indicate pages with illustrations and figures

N

W

X

Y